FREE EXPRESSION, GLOBALISM AND THE NEW STRATEGIC COMMUNICATION

Vast changes in technologies and geopolitics have produced a wholesale shift in the way states and other powerful entities think about the production and retention of popular loyalties. Strategic communication has embraced these changes as stakes increase and the techniques of information management become more pervasive. These shifts in strategic communication impact free speech as major players, in a global context, rhetorically embrace a world of transparency, all the while increasing surveillance and modes of control, turning altered media technologies and traditional media doctrines to their advantage.

Building on examples drawn from the Arab Spring, the shaping of the Internet in China, Iran's perception of foreign broadcasting and Russia's media interventions, this book exposes the anxieties of loss of control, on the one hand, and the missed opportunities for greater freedom, on the other. "New" strategic communication arises from the vast torrents of information that cross borders and uproot old forms of regulation. Not only states but also corporations, nongovernmental organizations, religious institutions and others have become part of this new constellation of speakers and audiences.

Monroe E. Price is the author and editor of numerous publications, including *Media and Sovereignty: The Global Information Revolution and Its Challenge to State Power* (2002), *Owning the Olympics: Narratives of the New China* (2008, edited with Daniel Dayan), the *Routledge Handbook of Media Law* (2013, edited with Stefaan Verhulst and Libby Morgan), and *Objects of Remembrance: A Memoir of American Opportunities and Viennese Dreams* (2009). Professor Price directs the University of Pennsylvania's Center for Global Communication Studies at the Annenberg School for Communication, where he works with a wide transnational network of regulators, scholars and practitioners in Europe, Africa, Latin America and Asia, as well as in the United States. He also heads the Howard Squadron Program in Law, Media and Society at the Benjamin N. Cardozo School of Law in New York City, where he was dean, and he is now senior research associate at Oxford's Programme in Comparative Media Law and Policy.

Free Expression, Globalism and the New Strategic Communication

MONROE E. PRICE

Annenberg School for Communication, University of Pennsylvania

CAMBRIDGE
UNIVERSITY PRESS

CAMBRIDGE
UNIVERSITY PRESS

32 Avenue of the Americas, New York, NY 10013-2473, USA

Cambridge University Press is part of the University of Cambridge.

It furthers the University's mission by disseminating knowledge in the pursuit of education, learning and research at the highest international levels of excellence.

www.cambridge.org
Information on this title: www.cambridge.org/9781107420939

First published 2015

Printed in the United States of America

A catalog record for this publication is available from the British Library.

Library of Congress Cataloging in Publication Data
Price, Monroe E., 1938– author.
Free expression, globalism and the new strategic communication /
Monroe E. Price.
    pages   cm
ISBN 978-1-107-07251-0 (hardback)
1. Freedom of expression.   2. Telecommunication – Law and legislation.   3. Globalization.   4. Geopolitics.   I. Title.
K3253.P75   2014
302.2–dc23   2014021008

ISBN 978-1-107-07251-0 Hardback
ISBN 978-1-107-42093-9 Paperback

Cambridge University Press has no responsibility for the persistence or accuracy of URLs for external or third-party Internet Web sites referred to in this publication and does not guarantee that any content on such Web sites is, or will remain, accurate or appropriate.

Contents

Acknowledgments

Writing a book in an area changing as quickly as communication has been complex, especially when the project spanned many years, technological and political revolutions, and association with various great academic and policy-related settings. Elements hark back to the post-Soviet transitions in the 1990s, the Balkan conflicts later in the decade, and the aftermath of the Iraq War and the Arab Spring. It encompasses the introduction of satellites, of cable, of the Internet and social media.

My primary home for this project has been the Annenberg School for Communication at the University of Pennsylvania. There I was fortunate to have been appointed director of a new Center for Global Communication Studies with the support of the school's dean, Michael Delli Carpini. The Center provided an environment that encouraged wide-ranging exploration and hospitality to interdisciplinary views. My colleagues there furnished inspiration and guidance. Professor Elihu Katz was my constant mentor and friend. Joseph Turow, Guobin Yang and Barbie Zelizer, among many others, were available when advice and support were needed. A steady flow of visitors to Professor Zelizer's Scholars Program was an added enrichment of voices. At CGCS, I have been fortunate to have excellent staff, many of whom played critical roles in bringing the book to fruition. Libby Morgan, an acute, perceptive and dedicated editor, extended herself, even after leaving Annenberg, to ensure completion of this work. She demonstrated extraordinary editorial skills and gave of her deep well of wisdom.

Among past and present PhD students, I should single out Sun-Ha Hong, Lee McGuigan, Sandra Ristovska, Lokman Tsui and Christopher Finlay, who worked as principal research assistants. David Conrad, Lauren Kogen and Corrina Laughlin also contributed (Dr. Kogen, joined CGCS as a postdoctoral Fellow after her graduate studies). Such is the span of years that I have forgotten some who should be included, and I ask their forgiveness.

Christopher, now a faculty member at Loyola Marymount University in Los Angeles, collaborated, especially, on Olympics-related research. Amelia Arsenault, a Gerbner Fellow at the Annenberg School, and now a faculty member at Georgia State University, commenced a steady and productive collaboration – aspects of which are reflected in this book. Briar Smith, who now is the Associate Director of CGCS, started to work on elements of this book as a graduate student at Annenberg, and then became the director of CGCS's Iran Program. Other staff members who have been enormously helpful include Laura Schwartz-Henderson, Research Project Manager at the Center, Andrea Highbloom and Florentina Dragalescu. Sharon Black, Annenberg's poet-librarian, was her dedicated and useful self.

Some of the most important thanks relate to my ties, Zelig-like, to Oxford University and the Programme for Comparative Media Law and Policy at the Centre for Socio-legal Studies. Its current head, the extraordinary Dr. Nicole Stremlau, has been a constant inspiration, initiating ideas and demonstrating a deep critical and ethical approach to media development studies and a strenuous dedication to making scholarship useful and relevant. Much of the thinking that permeates this book comes from my colleagueship there with her but also with her partner Iginio Gagliardone. Susan Abbott, an invaluable collaborator, co-conspirator in many great efforts and friend throughout, worked with me for almost a decade building the network – in Oxford, Budapest (at Central European University) and Philadelphia – that nourished study of the questions treated here. Stefaan Verhulst, now at New York University, with whom I founded and codirected the Oxford Programme, remains a steady source of original and sweeping ideas, a standard for scholarship and, at the same time, a close friend. The Benjamin N. Cardozo School of Law at Yeshiva University, where I also happily hang my hat, is the home of the Howard Squadron Program on Law, Media and Society, which I have directed. My thanks for support to its dean, Matthew.

Professors Julia Sonnevend at the University of Michigan, Shawn Powers at Georgia State, Will Youmans at American University, and others are part of a next generation with whom it's been a pleasure to work. The always-generous Andrei Richter and Joan Barata Mir, both now at the Office of Security and Cooperation in Europe, read and commented on aspects of the manuscript as did Peter Molnar of CEu. James Deane, the perceptive director of policy and learning at BBC Media Action, provided the benefit of his great experience in reading the manuscript. Christian Sandvig has been a co-conspirator on more than a few projects that affected this text, not the least helping me in the wondrous days of the Stanhope Center for Communications Research in London. An important influence was Simon

Haselock, whose work I observed and admired when Albany Associates was still a twinkle in his eye. Much was to be gained from witnessing Haselock and Douglas Griffin and the rest of the company design a new kind of media and conflict-related enterprise. The Annenberg School for Communication and Journalism at the University of Southern California, particularly Nicholas Cull and Larry Gross, has been hospitable and invigoratingly helpful. Aspects of the text reflect longtime collaborations and conversations with Charlie Firestone and the Communications and Society Program of the Aspen Institute.

I have been fortunate to have had the opportunity to present versions of chapters in this book in a number of academic settings, all of which have been invaluable to the development of the text. Professor Andras Sajo, many years ago, invited me to give a paper at the Central European University for a conference on religion and communication, elements of which survive in Chapter 8. Stewart Hoover also invited me to present a version of this chapter at a conference in Nigeria and provided helpful comments. I am grateful to Daniel Dayan, with whom I edited *Owning the Olympics: Narratives of the New China*. Aspects of my contribution to that volume are in Chapter 10. Peter Molnar and Michael Herz made comments on what here is Chapter 11, parts of which appeared in their powerful volume, published by Cambridge University Press, *The Content and Context of Hate Speech: Rethinking Regulation and Responses*. I remain indebted to Gary Greenstein who, as a law student at the Yale Law School, was editor for my 1994 article in the *Yale Law Journal* and helped crystallize my thoughts concerning markets for loyalties, thoughts that persist in this book. Clark McCauley kindly read and commented on the chapter concerning asymmetries in media interventions and a version of it appeared in his journal, *Dynamics of Asymmetric Conflict*. Daniel McCarthy was a keen and constructive critic.

I'm grateful to the Rockefeller Foundation for sponsoring various visits and stays at the Bellagio Conference Center. Bits and pieces of the text arise from projects generously funded by USAID, the U.S. State Department, the Open Society Foundation, the Ford Foundation, the Markle Foundation, and the Annenberg Foundation. I learned much from my service on the Advisory Board of the Center for International Media Assistance, then headed by Marguerite Sullivan, and from the media development community in Washington, especially Internews.

Last, but far, far from least, my thanks to my family: Aimée who elegantly, persistently and lovingly set an unattainable standard with her great Puvis de Chavannes scholarship; my three sons, Joshua, Gabriel and Asher, each engaged in versions of publishing and persuasion; and our seven grandchildren.

1

Moving the Needle, Filling the Streets

Governments rise and fall, strengthen and weaken, in part because of their control of information flows. Militaries shift their attention increasingly to the impact of the media on their missions. Corporations prosper and blossom or are destroyed and wither depending on their mastery of the changed information technologies.[1] Civil society follows suit. New modes of affecting opinion, mobilizing populations and extending influence are developed, tested and measured for effectiveness. This race for new means for reaching populations – and the rise of new modes for assessing, influencing and regulating persuasion – becomes a massive exercise in what one might call "the new strategic communication," one that is persuasive and encompasses disruptive technologies for reception and pervasive technologies for surveillance. We have always had strategic communication. But the combination of new technologies, new tools of surveillance and new techniques for analysis of ever more available data raises the consequences and possibilities of strategic communication to new levels. And the structure, ubiquity and potency of strategic communication accentuate concerns about the relevance of existing norms and institutions, the existing underpinnings and foundations for thinking about freedom of expression.

In a world of totalizing capacities to collect and analyze data, old views of what constitutes "autonomy" or what constitutes privacy have a quaint, reality-denying, archaic quality. The president of Brazil, in an immediate reaction to disclosures that conversations among her government officials or national leaders in Latin America were monitored, called for a redesign of the Internet to prevent key messages from necessarily being transported through servers under U.S. jurisdiction. The recognition seemed palpable that an

[1] See Harold Innis's magisterial work, *Empire and Communications* (Toronto: University of Toronto Press, 1950).

observed society, whether observed by one's own government or a foreign one, will behave and speak differently from one that is unmonitored.

It is not just shifts in data collection and use that undergird or explain a new strategic communication environment. Cross-border efforts to persuade intensify. Two brothers in Boston wreaked havoc in 2013 using basic Internet-received knowledge to create homemade bombs. An immediate question was whether they were influenced by forces outside American borders; what was the role of an Imam in Yemen or of Salafist cells in Dagestan? Borders became significant markers for fathoming the depth of what occurred. And remedially, the issue was what mix of ideas, what pathways of education, what surveillance of speech would be necessary to prevent similar events from occurring in the future. There was nothing new in a distant group of dissidents reaching across boundaries to locate new recruits. Still, the wars of the twenty-first century seemed to be reshaping these efforts and certainly deploying new technologies in the process. The Boston Marathon bombing reinforced the high demand for intelligence information for preventative purposes in the post-9/11 world. Concern for general limits on government power were accompanied by a wish that benign governments would master information flows as a way of reducing risk. Events like these have intensified inquiry into patterns of discourse and efforts to understand how individuals and groups reach across swaths of physical and emotional terrain to dislocate violently the status quo.

The sense of disruption, of course, is not only about borders. Authorities fret about the gaps in their hold on quickly changing realities in processes of mobilization and disruption. In August 2011, British Prime Minister David Cameron momentarily called for consideration of special and sweeping powers in angry response to riots and looting in the streets of London. These involved new regulations to prevent the use of social media to encourage criminal behavior and endanger the social order. Cameron spoke of rules that would give government authority, in extreme circumstances, to shut down social networks locally or nationally.[2] Reactions to Cameron's remarks were harsh. What Cameron sought, critics around the world proclaimed, were just the kind of free-expression-threatening actions that were used that year by Mubarak,[3] Assad,[4] and

[2] See "London Riots 2011: David Cameron's Speech to Parliament," *International Business Times*, August 11, 2011.

[3] See, for instance, Joshua Hersh, "Egyptian Activists See Hypocrisy In BART Shutdown, London Riots," *The Huffington Post*, August 16, 2011.

[4] See, for instance, Marta Cooper, "Reaction to Cameron's Plans for Social Media Crackdown," *Free Speech Blog, Index on Censorship*, August 11, 2011.

their authoritarian ilk.[5] Questions were raised, as well, as to whether Britain, or any other state, could enforce any such law, underscoring the breadth of new challenges to state management of a demanding and complex information environment.[6]

The substantial changes in technologies, geopolitics and the flows of information necessitate a wholesale reevaluation of the way in which states might think about their powers and their role. States (and other powerful entities in society) might rhetorically embrace a world of transparency while simultaneously seeking, if they can, to master the new environment, turning new technologies to their advantage. States experiment with ways to "move the needle" of public opinion among targeted populations utilizing advanced tools of communication and integrate the consequences in their theories of speech and conduct. Understanding the transformed spheres of communication in the modern world also requires appreciation of the expanding application of international human rights norms. The heroic efforts, particularly in the post–World War II era, to create a coherent body of human rights and a set of institutions that would support these rights included, of course, international norms of free expression. It is a commonplace, and a comfortable one, that principles of free expression form the bedrock of Western society and, aspirationally, of the world at large. But challenges exist as to the meaning of these principles and how they are adapted in places that have very different cultures, very different organizations of the state and very different ideas of the individual in society. Indeed, describing them as "principles" seems to place them above the area of ordinary debate, yet they are both hard won and always and everywhere delicate. The very assertions that advocates of free expression take for granted – that is, the interpretation of norms, such as Article 19 of the International Covenant on Civil and Political Rights (ICCPR) – remain subject to extensive debate in courts and in legislatures.

Max Weber famously observed that a necessary condition of being a state is that it has a monopoly on the legitimate use of violence.[7] In the twenty-first

---

[5] See, for instance, Jillian C. York, "Democracies Learn from Mubarak's Example," *Al Jazeera*, August 18, 2011. See also Uri Friedman, "Twitter Braces for U.K. Censorship Following the Riots," *The Atlantic Wire*, August 11, 2011.

[6] See Omar El Akkad, "Britain's Musings of Social-Media Ban Fraught with Technical Difficulty," *Globe and Mail*, August 11, 2011.

[7] Max Weber, "Politics as a Vocation" (Munich: Duncker and Humboldt, 1919). This idea is also examined in Max Weber, *Economy and Society* (Berkeley: University of California Press, 1922). For a more recent exploration, see Hannes Wimmer, "The State's Monopoly on Legitimate Violence. Violence in History and in Contemporary World Society as Challenges to the State" (paper presented at Transformations of Statehood from a European Perspective, Austrian Academy of Sciences Vienna, January 23–25, 2003), http://homepage.univie.ac.at/johann.wimmer/Wimmer-AkadWiss.pdf.

century, the Weberian formula is in the process of being amended. The argument will be more frequently made that for a state to be a state, even a democratic state, it must have greater sway over the legitimate use of information. This is an idea so apparently inconsistent with existing notions of global press norms and human rights that I want to qualify it immediately. As with Weber's idea of the monopoly on the use of violence, the state's command over information can be delegated. As with the monopoly on the use of violence, it can be bargained away by treaty or agreement. Many states that deem themselves to be democratic have, over centuries, engaged in this process, bargaining their power over information or limiting it by law or constitution or treaty. But what is implicit in this argument is that a state will seek to recover elements of its monopoly over violence that it has delegated, bargained away or lost through other means. Perhaps the same is true with respect to speech and the state's recuperative impulse.[8]

States – for good and for ill – are the mode for organizing national defense and national security. They are structures that define, enshrine and protect the political system evolved within their borders. They are the imperfect backstop for language and culture. They referee national identity. States are the vessels for what may be a vanishing commodity: notions of citizenship and loyalty. I list these characteristics because all of them depend on systems of information and the flow of images – systems that have a profound impact on how a state functions and performs for its citizenry. Access to information and internal modes of freedom of expression to provide for accountability become crucial elements of conceptualizing the state and systems of information within it. These are merely part of an overall system that incorporates the architecture, uses and deployment of speech and expression.

Transnational strategic communication coupled with new technologies challenges these capacities, rendering problematic any neat summary of speech, regulation and the state. Let me refine my Weberian suggestion. The point is not that a state ought in principle to have management capability over information flows. Rather, it is that major elements of such management are inevitable – and their scope somewhat locally determined. Put differently, in the constitutionally circumscribed areas where a government justifiably (and consistent with carefully restrictive international norms) has a proper role to play, it should have the implied capability of doing so, including through

---

[8]   Harold Innis developed the related concept of a "monopoly of knowledge" to describe how institutions (e.g., the clergy, scribes, guilds, merchants, etc.) were able to secure power through control over or unique mastery of communication and information. See, especially, Harold Innis, *Empire and Communications* (Toronto: University of Toronto Press, 1950), and Harold Innis, *The Bias of Communication* (Toronto: University of Toronto Press, 1951).

managing technical challenges.[9] The new strategic communication capabilities often imply a search for an infrastructure of speech and society that shifts toward unencumbered speech but recognizes and honors an appropriate role for the state. This formula embraces responses to powerful states that abuse control of information and weaker states where the capacity to function needs buttressing.

ANXIETIES AND FREE EXPRESSION

How should those moved to think about expression in society consider the multiple impacts of the new environment on the rules of speech engagement? How can one freshly evaluate the stake that one state or society has in the media structure of another state or how the flow of information affects human rights and regional and global stability? What new institutions and new approaches will emerge from the current challenges? In struggling with these questions much of free expression jurisprudence will have to be reaffirmed so that its vital basic gifts are maintained. In some significant respects, that jurisprudence is pinned to a classic model of the diffusion of information in which deliberation and democratic processes establish a government that sets the rules (consistent with constitutional imperatives) about speech and its limits within the boundaries of its authority. International norms are an increasingly cited repository for foundational principles, but these norms, despite the huge efforts to ground them in practice, are themselves under scrutiny, the circumstances of their adoption put in question.

The ongoing processes of reexamination and reinforcement of free expression are the consequence of at least two major and disparate anxieties. Every day sees fear by those in power (governments, industry incumbents, long-established religions and others) that new technologies and new developments threaten their dominion. For these entities, particularly governments, the capacity to control information at critical moments becomes a defining element of stability and preservation of power. Disruption is basic to new communications capabilities, and disruption naturally leads to apprehension. And there is a sharply contrasting fear among civil society segments and others: deep anxiety about the future of freedom of expression itself – a haunting and often undeclared pessimism triggered by the feeling that these same potentially liberating technologies, the Internet and social media, have instead ushered in an era of surveillance and formal and informal government

---

[9] Austin Sarat, ed., *Sovereignty, Emergency, Legality* (New York: Cambridge University Press, 2010) explores some related questions.

control, with concomitant containment of individual autonomy.[10] These competing anxieties are backdrops for how states, civil society, corporations, religions and other organizations and groups seek to adjust and cope with a dramatically changing set of information-related realities.

Some states have migrated from exercising (often repressively) what seemed like a monopoly over information to being relatively weak in the face of sophisticated media organizations, corporations schooled in the arts of persuasion, a public empowered by information technology and, increasingly, media-savvy insurgent and rebel entities. Governments, rather than shaping their information environment, see themselves increasingly subject to the shaping processes of entities and forces (within and without the state's borders) over which they have little or no control.

These twinned and basic fears were on parade during the dramatic events of what is more nostalgically, ironically and quaintly called the Arab Spring. Events of 2011, 2012 and beyond in Egypt, Tunisia, Syria, Libya and Bahrain provided a new set of extraordinary examples for understanding the relationship of state power to free expression. Governments have been forced to engage with democratic protest or use brutal force to impair mobilization. States have been freshly confronted with the extraordinary strength of words and their combination into narrative – whether generated by social media, popular protests, neighboring polities, religious movements or reform and human rights organizations, domestic and transnational. One reality – and often a real shock across all states – is that at a critical moment the once overbearing state may turn out to be naked and powerless. States that prided themselves on their power to manage domestic narratives and influence international imaginings have found both talents in peril. In the era of WikiLeaks and the Internet, states have become ever more concerned about their ability to protect state secrets that in the past, even under the most restrictive notion of allowances, would have been protectable. In the United Kingdom, an exasperated member of parliament, commenting on social media's undermining of a superinjunction (a judicial order preventing newspapers from mentioning the name of a football player accused of peccadillos or even mentioning the existence of the order), said that Twitter made the "law look an ass."[11] An essay in *The Guardian* made a similar point:

---

[10]   See, for instance, Evgeny Morozov, *The Net Delusion: The Dark Side of Internet Freedom* (New York: PublicAffairs, 2011); Joseph Turow, *The Daily You: How the New Advertising Industry is Defining Your Identity and Your Worth* (New Haven, CT: Yale University Press, 2012).

[11]   Andrew Soar, "Ryan Giggs Named as Footballer at the Centre of Twitter Privacy Row," *culture and life*, May 23, 2011.

Twitter may have been credited with helping topple Arab dictatorships. [But] ... it is naive to assume that it, and other social media, are in essence benign, that their main political function since the Iranian protests of 2009 has been to aid revolutionaries in communication, although it is a point so often glibly made. What is accurate, then, is to see Twitter as an amoral, disruptive force.[12]

The architecture of speech in society is shifting and changing, then, and this intensifies anxieties of loss – loss of perceived past control – as processes of generating and diffusing information are moving into strikingly diverse paths simultaneously. I emphasize the double impact of these phenomena: the seemingly decentralized, disintermediated revolution in patterns of discourse called social media, and the consolidating relationship between information and power that can be called strategic communication. These two developments – each massive in scope – together place in doubt how societies, organized in states, come to think about images, words, power, borders and identity. These two tendencies – exemplified by increased use of social media and strengthened strategic communicators – seem oddly complementary in force and may converge. In its most typical instantiation, social media are deemed bottom up and strategic communication top down. But social media become invaded with power, and civil society becomes engaged in the power orientation of its more frequently strategic competitors. Together they can be cumulative in impact and challenge to the state. Social media – Facebook, Twitter, and the affordances of the Internet – create startling new networks of communication, expanding on person-to-person, person-to-group and group-to-person. The growth of strategic communication – heavily subsidized, usually transnational, engineered and often deceptive – can wreak havoc on traditional ideas of community realization and self-determination (for which speech is a significant element of making vital political decisions). As a result of the growth of social media and the expansion of powerful, cross-border engagements, the standard responses of states and their democratic adaptations are upended.

Speech rights have long been justified and ennobled as signals and aspirations of individualism, autonomy and informed self-determination; now, the tendencies are intensified for information and data flows to be captured by large-scale entities – corporations, states and others, a result contested by efforts to democratize access to knowledge and public rights to information. From a context in which speech, including speech of transnational origin, was

[12] Daniel Sabbagh, "Twitter's Wild West Brings Politicians into Line," *The Guardian*, May 23, 2011.

theorized as part of an ever-evolving mix for nurturing national identities, information flows are increasingly seen as overwhelming local cultures and undermining belief systems, thereby subverting traditional loyalties. From a context in which speech and its destabilizing capacity were often managed by all-powerful states, the borderless nature of speech flows now seems to present threats of random violence and conflict.

RETHINKING STRATEGIC COMMUNICATION

Each substantial technological and organizational breakthrough in information flows leads or should lead to revisiting and possible adjustment of the structure of free expression and the responsibility and privileges of the key actors, especially the state. In this book, I present a series of inquiries into global actors and the relationship between their information strategies and geopolitical impacts. The first half attempts to reframe the emerging world of information flows and reformulate the significant role of free expression concepts within it. In Chapter 2, I articulate specific definitions of "strategic communication" and "strategic communicators." The term "strategic communication," as it has developed, owes much to military vocabularies and uses, but the kind of interventionist approach that it entails spills over into the broader world of public relations, public diplomacy and intensive marketing. In Chapter 3, I turn to a specific strategic effort: organized advocacy of "narratives of legitimacy" as a way to provide moral and consensual bases for modes of governance. Governments seek to create temporary alliances or use other tools to produce or block such narratives with consequences that affect deployment of military assets, sanctions, preparation of shadow governments and mobilization of populations. Strategic deployment of narratives of legitimacy powerfully affects the success of large-scale multilateral approaches to conflict-ridden events, such as civil war in Syria or protests in Egypt and Libya. These narratives are often *performative*, designed to be effective in a way that ensures change, rather than merely to reflect it. Their target is a group of key actors rather than a mass audience.

An analytic turn is one indicator of what makes a communicator *strategic*. In Chapter 4, I introduce the concept of a "diagnostic" as a mode of analyzing information flows. The more the environment consists of strategic communicators, the more it will depend on increasingly scientific ways of understanding the context that various actors seek to change. In the "Long War against Terror," an entire industry emerged as an effort to describe how certain ideas filtered into societies and gained adherents. There were already important notions of evaluating the way media may intensify movement to reshape loyalties, enhance or diminish conflict or exacerbate or reduce deprivation of human rights and genocide. But this process is accelerating. No communications effort of scale and significance can be deemed strategic if it is not sensitive to the particular environment in which the information intervention takes place. No such communications effort can be strategic without an understanding of the increasingly elaborate techniques of competitors. The diagnostic approach outlined here arises from observations in the world of "media assistance" on the one hand and public diplomacy on the other, where fathoming the localized character of information flows is central to designing and implementing meaningful action. But all this is now supplemented by the transformation in gathering and analyzing "big data" to personalize, target and create new assemblages for persuasion.

The systemic efforts by which states attempt to produce and further strategic narratives, and the exploration of the different environments in which strategic communicators operate, emphasize the very different nature of the communicative strategies that all players now face on the ground level. In the last two decades, accentuating a long-existing condition, a number of *asymmetric* contexts of communication have emerged; these provide important clues into the rethinking of strategies of communication. Chapter 5 focuses on these contexts, in which innovation or unorthodox techniques and unethical uses of communications allow the weak or underestimated to threaten the strong and arrogant. These instances of asymmetry strike fear in governing authorities as "men in caves" purportedly do strategic battle with the historically triumphant keepers of Western public relations traditions. Asymmetric strategic players pit destabilizing communication efforts against more conventional approaches. The Internet may lend itself to asymmetric information techniques, both trans-border and local. Furthermore, the insufficiently examined area of shaping and funding circumvention techniques has elements of the asymmetrical. The process of designing, diffusing and encouraging the use of software that avoids state filtering and banning is an outcropping of potentially provocative intrusions on a state's own management of its narratives of legitimacy.

To emphasize the connection between structure and principle, I turn, in Chapter 6, to "strategic architectures" – large-scale efforts to fix or stabilize the relationship of states and other major players to information flows. These wholesale approaches include active rethinking of communications structures by powerful states so as to maintain control over their own narratives and affect relevant communications systems outside their borders. These are designs not only of government but of the corporate empires for whom communication is key and certainly for the media companies themselves. For those who seek to ensure a particular narrative – for example, of governmental legitimacy, religious authenticity or the advantages of consumerism – establishing an infrastructure they can control is significant. Globally and nationally, the efforts are many. In recent decades, debates over the means of designing broadcast systems, satellite systems, cable systems and, most recently, the Internet all involve these structural aspects of communications strategies. I use competing visions of Internet structures as an example of an exercise in strategic architectures of communication.

The second part of the book is composed of case studies. This includes inquiries into categories of strategic communicators, actors who work to expand influence and persuasion and manipulate or affect the rules of entry, and inquiries into the interaction among strategic communicators and system architecture (how any particular market is designed and structured). In Chapter 7, I use, as a case study, the perception by Iran (in the pre-Rouhani era) that its value system was being systematically attacked through information strategies of other states, particularly the United States. In this chapter, I explore circumstances in which external interventions are portrayed as "Soft War" as opposed to soft power. Media interventions that contribute – or are thought to contribute – to regime change are a trademark exercise of strategic communication, and their study allows the examination of important issues. This is a specific locus for understanding the key role of states as players in this strategic universe. Concern with information flows is a surrogate, in part, for concerns about general political attitudes in the market to be affected. Here, as advocate and seller in the marketplace, State A uses many tools – propaganda and public diplomacy, cultural outreach efforts and educational exchange, even force – to alter public attitudes in State B, State C and beyond. Chapter 7 also provides strong insight into competing ideas for Internet structure and how these ideas are framed for international discussion.

I do not include a chapter specifically on commercial entities, corporations and businesses as strategic communicators. They are vital players and pioneers, but much has been published about their history and continued role in defining transnational information flows.[13] They are often the leaders, for better or worse, in readdressing the relationship between sender and recipient, through the extended science of data gathering and analysis. Instead, I include case studies of two other categories of strategic actors: religions and NGOs. Chapter 8 looks at the realm of strategic communication concerning religious

---

[13] This has been the case for several decades. For two examples, see Armand Mattelart, *Multinational Corporations and the Control of Culture: The Ideological Apparatuses of Imperialism* (Brighton: Harvester Press, 1979), and Herbert Schiller, *Culture Inc: The Corporate Takeover of Public Expression* (Oxford: Oxford University Press, 1989).

entities. The chapter addresses how, often from outside a state's boundaries, such groups seek to shift the spiritual allegiances of a target population over time. Religions, as historic strategic communicators, use whatever new and old technologies are available. Religions compete with each other and with secular forces so the issues of "substitutability" emerge as well (who competes in what relevant market).

I turn to non-governmental organizations (NGOs) in Chapter 9. NGOs have become more significant players in the world of strategic communication as they seek to affect various publics. In tribute to the effectiveness of these creative entities, some governments (and not just those deemed repressive) dispute their roles in affecting a public sphere or competing to define rights and loyalties. These NGOs are in some ways creatures of modern opportunities. Many exist in a transnational space, but often have very specific localized targets and impacts. They may be less encumbered by local bureaucratic hurdles that impede thinking strategically about their objectives. Yet they are, despite their conveniently idealistic name, often supported by governments because they have this flexibility that may be denied to states themselves. I focus on NGOs involved in "democracy promotion," entities that seek to affect political reform and shape opinion and outcomes regarding media structures, including the structure of the Internet.

Chapter 10 is about an architectural feature of strategic communication that helps us understand competitive strategies. I discuss the concept of *platforms*, bases from which to proclaim and advance a brand, an idea, a film or a national identity. The objective is to show the struggle to seize such platforms as a zone for engagement in power. The platforms that are designed to project one narrative can be hijacked to produce quite a different one. I focus on the Beijing Olympics as a platform and the use of it by a variety of actors, each with its own strategic agenda. The platform (including the need for a platform, the effort to protect who gets to use the platform and the effectiveness of the platform) is fought over by many idea-related advocates. As the Internet becomes a site of immediate and viral platforms, with significant consequences for the debate of issues of public importance, the mode of creating, seizing and maintaining such platforms is important.

In Chapter 11, I look at the behavior of strategic communicators when faced with apertures created by new technologies and the complexities of an informal and uncertain governance structure. The case study is a challenging example – the world of delivery of channels through satellites – a mechanism for distribution that, in the past, has sidestepped sovereignty and sought to avoid content regulation. I have chosen this case study because of the significance of the story to the future of the Internet. It is a study that demonstrates the painful efforts to adjust or modify governmental inclinations to control new technologies where barriers to entry are low. But it is also an example of the persistence of states, determined to exercise control where needed, to experiment with regulatory alternatives. New modes of regulation become a defensive response to new styles of entry – as was the case with the expanded use of cable distribution of information in a previous decade.

INSTITUTIONAL FOUNDATIONS, THE MARKET FOR LOYALTIES AND FREE EXPRESSION

Looking at strategic communication through the lens of a "market for loyalties" will help in integrating all these ideas, in understanding how all the developments I have described, and the world as seen through the growth of the Internet and the strengthening of strategic communication and strategic architectures, affect issues concerning freedom of expression. In explicating these issues, I return to arguments I made in an earlier work, *Media and Sovereignty*. There I defined a market for loyalties as a context in which large-scale competitors for power use the regulation of communications to organize a cartel of imagery and identity among themselves. I wrote:

> The "sellers" in this market are all those for whom myths and dreams and history can somehow be converted into power and wealth – classically states, governments, interest groups, businesses, and others. The "buyers" are the citizens, subjects, nationals, consumers – recipients of the packages of information, propaganda, advertisements, drama, and news propounded by the media. The consumer "pays" for one set of identities or another in several ways that, together, we call "loyalty" or "citizenship." Payment, however, is not expressed in the ordinary coin of the realm: It includes not only compliance with tax obligations, but also obedience to laws, readiness to fight in the armed services, or even continued residence within the country. The buyer also pays with his or her own sense of identity.[14]

One can look at this idea of a market primarily within national boundaries, with government usually the entity that allows the cartel to operate and often part of the cartel itself. Indeed, the product of a stable market for loyalties could be a pragmatic version of "national identity." When the state and those in power are efficiently managing this market, the result may be what I have called a "bubble of identity," in which attention is paid, often censorial, to

---

[14]   Monroe E. Price, *Media and Sovereignty: The Global Information Revolution and Its Challenge to State Power* (Cambridge, MA: The MIT Press, 2002), 32. I also explore these issues in Monroe E. Price, *Television, the Public Sphere, and National Identity* (Oxford: Clarendon Press, 1995).

what is tolerated, encouraged and discouraged. It is this management of the market that yields what I call here narratives of legitimacy – the collection of ideas and narratives employed by a dominant group or coalition to maintain power. This market for loyalties approach has powerful explanatory force in a transnational form. Globalization involves, specifically, the desire by external strategic communicators to break or reinforce local cartels (depending on interest) and much of this book is devoted to showing how this happens. It is this process that creates opportunities for gain and anxieties for loss. In market after market, ideas of free expression developed with one set of "sellers" of allegiances in mind, only to see them replaced by others. And the replacements – those who succeed in breaking preexisting cartels – disturb and destabilize. What is significant is the scope and scale by which strategic communicators have succeeded in the process of cartel disruption and how home governments have responded.

For these reasons, the notion of the market for loyalties is a helpful prism for understanding what is "strategic" about strategic communication. Strategic communicators often understand that it has hardly ever been a single government alone that regulates or controls the nature of a market for loyalties within its boundaries. As strategic communicators increase, the market for loyalties within any state becomes the product of multiple interests – other states, transnational religious entities, NGOs and others. The idea of a market for loyalties, with competitors trying to enter or block others, also begins, in a new way, to reframe ideas of free expression. It is a roadmap for understanding strategic communication and strategic architectures for altering flows of information. Rules concerning the right to receive and impart information or otherwise enact free expression principles become instruments used by many, inside and outside the state, to help shape the market, in addition to serving as an overarching philosophy that should have a normative impact on the overall architecture of speech.

The market for loyalties analysis underscores how strategic communicators manifest the anxieties that come with increasing or decreasing power. The perception in the United States after 9/11 that it had inadequate knowledge or resources to affect the hearts and minds of Muslim youth led to a decade, at least, of efforts to alter patterns of communication, understand the impact of modes of communication and develop the relationship between communication and surveillance.[15] Top-level communicators enacted different approaches to free expression norms depending on their particular position or role at specific times in the War on Terror. Aggressive strategic communicators sought

---

[15] For a critique of U.S. diplomatic efforts to engage Islam internationally through use of social media, see Edward Comor and Hamilton Bean, "America's Engagement Delusion: Critiquing a Public Diplomacy Consensus," *International Communication Gazette* 74, no. 3 (2012).

to deploy free expression norms to break into markets; those with established positions, even dominance, often used their power in local, regional and national fora to guard their positions. These players were, of course, particularly susceptible to anxieties about the breakdowns in systems that have been relied on to maintain their defenses.

A next level of analysis involves methods of implementation, implementation for reinforcing or altering market shares in a domestic or target society that takes many forms. These include the use of law, the deployment of physical force, engagement in negotiations, adroit deployment of technology and creative use of subsidies. This kind of categorization can help demonstrate how societies are evolving by indicating which modes become more effective and which ones diminish. For example, one might track whether international norms (a form of law) have become more or less useful and in what contexts as a mode of affecting behavior and policing boundaries of persuasion. A related question would be the relationship of law to the use of force. Calling a means of implementation the exercise of law has different implications from characterizing the same or similar activities as an exercise of force. The order establishing the Iraqi Communications and Media Commission (inscribed by the U.S.-appointed Coalition Provisional Authority) has and had all the trappings of law.[16] But the law was the ukase of an unelected officer who was acting under the authority of the U.S. military, a belligerent occupier. Characterizing the order as law satisfied the authority, but it was a subjective labeling. The United States considers the projection of Radio Farda and the Voice of America into Iran as the furtherance of free speech, while efforts to block the channels by the Iranian government through jamming are considered (from the perspective of the sending society) closer to the use of force. Many of the steps now taken to affect the entry of signals into a society are areas for disputed characterization. These include monitoring, denying licenses, pressuring lessors of satellite transponders, seizing control of transmitters to prevent conflict-producing media and even bombing of offending broadcasting outlets. Establishing standards for these actions remains elusive.[17]

[16] Coalition Provisional Authority Order Number 65, "Iraqi Communications and Media Commission," CPA/ORD/20 March 2004/65. Order 65 mainly contains provisions that establish the Iraqi Communications and Media Commission. For an analysis of various rules affecting Iraqi media, including Order 65, see Monroe E. Price, Douglas Griffin and Ibrahim Al-Marashi, *Toward an Understanding of Media Policy and Media Systems in Iraq: A Foreword and Two Reports*, CGCS Occasional Paper Series, Number 1 – May 2007 (Philadelphia: Center for Global Communication Studies, Annenberg School for Communication, University of Pennsylvania).

[17] One locus for debate has been the pro-genocidal journalistic efforts in Rwanda, made subject to the jurisprudence of an international court, the International Criminal Tribunal for Rwanda. THE PROSECUTOR V. FERDINAND NAHIMANA JEAN-BOSCO BARAYAGWIZA

One modern response of states to these concerns about power is to try to replicate the old system and assure that, to the extent possible, information is funneled through regulable intermediaries. This is often part of what might be called the "architecture of the infrastructure" of information flows. There is a hierarchy of control. If information leaks around intermediaries, the next step will be to try to regulate the content providers. But they, too, are elusive in the Internet era. In authoritarian societies, the result is an increased emphasis on regulating the ultimate user, a crude return to punishment of the consumer, the citizen, the subject. It is not difficult to find explicit examples of this progression from structure to regulation to surveillance to punishment. Does the state or do other strategic players resort to force because of an inability to define and effectively apply law as a means of entering or defending a market? Does this process relate to the weakening of law as a tool of regulation (or the absence of law in fragile societies)? Violence against journalists could be an example of this shift. From WikiLeaks to Ai Weiwei, arrests become a more standard mode for controlling the narrative. When insecure and repressive leaders consider even arrests insufficient, direct violence becomes prevalent. What, in any circumstances – proclivities, racial attitudes, deep-seated hate, lack of training, lack of resources – leads to the choice of one mode of implementation rather than another? As the more acceptable of these elements become more costly or impossible to deploy in an intensifying competition among strategic competitors, the state attempts to restructure the communication environment and restore its instruments of influence.

Ultimately, these approaches raise the general question: How does one rethink and reclassify the structure of information flows in a time of strategic communication and intense expansion of social media? In other words, how do states respond? The question becomes of greater significance if, as many believe, the functioning of states is, in any important way, a reflection or consequence of the media system in which they operate. This is the kind of question that Hallin and Mancini ask in their great *Comparing Media Systems*.[18] Why do media systems look the way they do? Is North Korea only able to operate as it does because of its power to control patterns of distribution of information? Egypt's Mubarak may have fallen for many reasons, but Mubarak's inability to effectively control media was a contributing factor.

In these circumstances of regime or state survival (or anxiety about survival) in the face of changing information realities, historic definitions of and

HASSAN NGEZE, Case No. ICTR-99-52-T, International Criminal Tribunal for Rwanda, Trial Chamber I, December 3, 2003.

[18] Daniel C. Hallin and Paolo Mancini, *Comparing Media Systems: Three Models of Media and Politics* (Cambridge: Cambridge University Press, 2004).

justifications for media regulation or limitations on these forms come under intense pressure. It is a question of the entire strategic model – namely how states and other players will organize the architecture of information systems, how they will diagnose the context for targeting messages and how they will execute these strategies. This takes us back to the role of international norms and their implications for competing models of regulating expression. Speech regulation is an integral part of governance and national identity, but the scope of such regulation was meant to be limited by these international norms. After World War II and the introduction of the Universal Declaration of Human Rights (UHDR), the idea was substantially advanced (based on Enlightenment traditions) that the right to receive and impart information should exist regardless of frontiers. But Article 19 of the UHDR, and its later embodiments in the International Covenant on Civil and Political Rights and the European Convention on Human Rights, Article 10, have built in the notion of law-empowered limits. This notion of rights and limits is central, but the meaning of the phrase is hardly well mapped or tested, and the search for the appropriate interpretation of limitations continues. A world in which a state has and exercises greater sovereignty over the flow of information within its boundaries is different from a world in which a state is obliged to allow its citizens access to information from any source, domestic or foreign. It is these underpinnings, these institutional foundations for the relationship between information and society, that are increasingly in question. Changing conditions may alter how the various participants – including states, religions, corporations, NGOs and others – perceive the virtue of particular norms.

Consider that, for significant historical reasons, freedom of expression practices have most systematically been demarcated and organized through geographical and other boundaries of state. It is these boundaries and the governance they imply that have enabled and permitted specific and localized approaches within the narrowly permissible restrictions clause of Article 19. Where these regularized rules for expression and communication can no longer be enforced – for example, because of technological impositions – doctrinal confusion ensues. It is here that the reputed revolution in social media is particularly significant. When institutions of law find it difficult to address technological advances, states may resort to surveillance, violence and other direct techniques for reassertion of their power. And where states do not possess control over coercive, violent force either (where irregular clusters take force into their own hands), they reduce their status as functioning states. Such states cannot control their narratives of legitimacy.

This book, then, is an invitation to a dialogue or conversation that recognizes shifts in the underpinnings of free speech frameworks. By studying whether the bases of free expression are changing, it provides insight into possible remedial steps. By readdressing the response of states (and other strategic communicators) to shifts in information technologies, a better understanding of the dynamics of influence and persuasion is obtained. These two elements – a comprehension of rights and a description of institutional behavior – reflect anxieties that shape attitudes toward flows of information and the narratives of power.

Anxieties over information flows arise from collisions between existing patterns of regulation and radically changing patterns of dissemination and entry. Anxieties are intensified as ongoing events demonstrate the consequences of new modes of diffusion and control. Institutions change, indeed disappear, because of changes in information flows. Corporations have to change their strategies to survive. Systems of providing education transform. No wonder leaders quake; governments perceive such challenges as threats to their fundamental capacity to hold onto power. These anxieties lead to proposals to liberate and efforts to control, to advances in freedom of expression and defenses by those in power. Strategic communicators summoning such power as they have (and for many, it is considerable) use a variety of techniques to hold some competitors for control of narratives at bay and encourage others. How can one characterize the techniques of states to ban, channel, filter and otherwise control or affect the flow of information within their boundaries? How are those techniques changing over time? And how are such changes related to concepts of free expression?

The influence of strategic communicators is ubiquitous, as purveyors of allegiances seek to stake out zones of persuasiveness – to claim, as it were, real estate of potential loyalty. By examining this process, one might determine what new modes of thinking about communications in society are emerging – modes not always conveniently pigeonholed as authoritarian or promoting free expression, modes that take into account the great new dynamics of strategy and technology that each day intensify.

2

Strategic Communication and the Foundations
of Free Expression

Let me turn, then, to my use of the term "strategic communication" to define a class of activities that significantly marks the developing global information environment. The term is now so widely used and by so many that some idiosyncratic narrowing and explanation is necessary for it to have specific meaning here. Strategic communication exists in an environment in which it is hardly possible anymore merely to communicate. The term has come to imply, a bit too generally, forms and programs of communication that are undergirded with a specific vision, programs which are strategic insofar as they serve a larger set of goals. A more directed vector for the term is "targeted communication". – communication designed with a particular schema concerning who should be reached and in what way. In some fashion and in some realms, strategic communication has become a code word for communication strategies by defense and military establishments. Strategic communication, when civilian aspects of government are the communicators, implicates soft power. When the military or defense aspect of the state is concerned, specific objectives are involved, including protecting and advancing missions and complementing command and control. Vast realms of debate and discussion of strategic communication occur in connection with business; there, strategic communication may well mean only how to achieve a firm's (or state's or other entity's) objectives through astute use of modes of communication. This of course gives great leeway for defining what constitutes the "astute" relative to the circumstances and what justifies the intervention of great consulting firms. The consequence of this enlargement of category is that strategic communication is in danger of meaning and implying nothing more nor less than what an industry of autocrats and generals, prime ministers and company managers, scholars and consultants claim it to be.

In this book, I add to this definitional cacophony, seeking to rethink the term in the context of the general problems I put forward in Chapter 1. These problems include the capacity of the state to exercise authority in a world in which the large-scale strategic communication of others (including other states) becomes a defining factor in establishing a state's legitimacy. And these also include the stress that the continuing burst of trans-border information flows places on the logic of freedom of expression (a logic which, I argue for most contexts in this book, has its roots in in-state deliberation and individual empowerment). Strategic communicators often appropriate the language of free expression to justify the power that they exercise and to provide around them a circle of immunity from state regulation. Strategic communication, as I define it, is hardly inconsistent with a democratic society or necessarily destructive of constitutional and human rights. As strategic communication proliferates and even dominates, however, the role of various players, including the state, changes. As more and more expressions become classifiable as "strategic," it becomes more necessary that the rhetoric and root elements of free expression norms be re-addressed.

To understand where these challenges lie, I focus on communication that is relatively large-scale and often involves external or transnational players. This category of communication recalls propaganda study and encompasses the vast ideological conflicts of the twentieth century. It also embraces swaths of dramatic religious histories and advertising exhortations by which the world, or large parts of it, have become rampantly consumerist. Strategic communication, in this definition, is a set of speech practices undertaken to reinforce, subvert, undermine, overwhelm or replace a preexisting discourse on a subject significant to both the audience and the speaker. Often, these communicative efforts are designed to interfere with, preserve, adjust or destabilize a settled model of political decision-making. They might conceivably contribute to an idealized public sphere, but in many instances they overwhelm or distort it.

The campaigns of communication that interest me most for this book usually constitute a substantial and effective effort that is initiated from outside a target society and is designed to alter an existing consensus vital to the future shape of the target society. Strategic communication would include most efforts in the "battles for hearts and minds," a set of activities that intensified in the decade after 2001. Faced with such intense campaigns, target societies react in many ways. Some gain knowledge and wisdom and change organically. Others are powerless to assert themselves. Some are repressive and act inconsistently with international norms.

Examples of strategic communication proliferate. It includes Salafist plans to impose a fierce religious order within and across borders as, for example, efforts to install a caliphate in Iraq and the Levant. It includes collective efforts to increase the influence of moderate Islam and decrease the influence of those classed as "fundamentalists," efforts to spread the Word (of God) in Africa and efforts to promote democracy in the former Soviet Union. Observers may all have their own templates of benign or horrid strategic communication efforts. Strategic efforts can encourage conflict and instability by spreading ideas of hate or ethnic tension, or they may be designed to reduce conflict by establishing "peace broadcasting" or supporting particular groups of proponents of the status quo (or of more acceptable change). The canvas for strategic communication is a large one. State-supported stratagems include the mild activities the U.S. government exercises to achieve greater opportunities for evangelical groups and other religions to promote their views and exercise rights in otherwise hostile societies.[1] They also include efforts to amplify or lessen the importance of particular voices (increasing or decreasing, for example, public service broadcasting) as well as the now familiar approach to seek control of the media and deny media power to the enemy in conflict contexts.

Of course, there are problems with this categorization of strategic communication as directed campaigns, usually external, aimed at shifting or reinforcing a consensus on an issue significant to a society's identity. Each element of this definition is subject to healthy challenge. Campaigns that count as strategic may still be ineffective and inept, although designed to be otherwise. And while most of the communications campaigns contained in this book are initiated outside the target society, this is an ever-more artificial distinction. A widely accepted example of strategic communication would be a campaign to reduce the risk of AIDS by encouraging the use of condoms. But even where such a campaign begins in the West and is aimed at the developing world, the dynamic often shifts internally – indeed that may be part of the strategy – so it becomes more organic to the society of need. And the question of "intent" is significant; a set of broadcasts or channels may not have the goal of altering mores or changing consensus in a target society but have the effect of doing so nonetheless.

In this book, the point is not, or not primarily, to distinguish "good" or warranted strategic communication campaigns from those that are in the service of more evil purposes, although, of course, these distinctions between the benign and the destructive exist and are ultimately significant in the making of policy. Nor is this book primarily about what constitutes effective strategic communication, even though that is an ever-present consideration. It is about actions pursued in the belief, tested or not, that such actions will

---

[1]   For more on religions and strategic communication, see Chapter 8. Also see the International Religious Freedom Act of 1998, Public Law 105–292, October 27, 1998.

produce a desired impact. The main point here is to understand how an increased emphasis on strategic communication of the kind I have described affects the distribution of power and the articulation of rights. Judgments as to the appropriateness of response are often made in the target society or by the sender, sometimes invoking and sometimes ignoring international norms, human rights and other factors. In a more dynamic model, one in which, at times, technology is argued to be more determinative, it is the sum of judgments by many players that produce information flows and the responses to them. These are not decisions taken unilaterally, but among various competitors, who might include policy designers, those who seek to engage in direct assistance, or those who develop a counter communication strategy. And, as I have mentioned, there is the rising demand for universal standards for the assessment of strategic communication. Which of these approaches is more justified or accurate, more outdated, more naïve? These are questions that recur and reflect, in part, shifts in power and ideology.

STRATEGIC COMMUNICATION IN A FREE EXPRESSION CONTEXT

The relationship between strategic communication and free expression is central to this book. The act of engaging in strategic communication is often imagined – from the perspective of the passionate communicator – as privileged expression on a matter of public importance. Adverse reactions to strategic communication are often characterized by the strategic communicator as repressive or hostile. At the same time, elements of the receiving society may view the communication itself as threatening or harmful. External strategic communicators (as well as their domestic counterparts) overwhelm or only pay lip service to local speech regulatory structures in the target society, even when they meet international norms. After all, the point of the exercise is often to alter some of the local norms that such a structure incorporates. The strategic effort is designed to shift the existing weight of voices in a domestic sphere, sometimes merely by introducing new elements and adding voices, sometimes by actively intervening to alter the very institutions that govern expression. It is necessary to consider this interplay not just from the perspective of the strategic communicator, but from that of the target society, from that of the individual and, institutionally, from established or evolving international norms.

Rethinking how strategic communication and free expression interact – taking the assumptions apart and then remolding them – requires a starting point. Mine is the work of the late C. Edwin Baker. Baker demonstrated his devotion to opportunities for vigorous expression by rigorously questioning relatively standard arguments about the principles said to undergird them, testing how these concepts were being applied and checking to insure that the goals behind free expression were not being misrepresented and re-engineered in the modern world. It was his mission to strengthen our commitment to free expression by ensuring greater understanding of the foundation, role and implications of free expression concepts and therefore to strengthen our confidence in them. False invocations, twisted applications and deceptive claims about freedom of speech could destroy the integrity of the principle.

Take, for example, the ubiquitously invoked phrase, "the marketplace of ideas." However complex its origins, the marketplace metaphor has come to mean virtually unfettered belief in avoiding regulation. The answer to problematic speech, in this view, is almost always "more speech." Baker believed, of course, in "more speech," but he also saw fundamental problems with this standard formulation. Given the current information environment, he saw the necessity of challenging most inflections of John Milton's foundational idea, namely that in the marketplace of ideas, ultimately, "Let Truth and Falsehood Grapple. Who ever knew truth put to the worse in a free and open encounter?" Showing his strongly iconoclastic side, Baker asks, in *Human Liberty and Freedom of Speech*, "Why bet that truth will be the consistent or even the usual winner?"[2] For Baker, the wisdom of the bet meant a more detailed understanding of the market in which the bet took place. In the Miltonian universe, the "marketplace of ideas" may contain falsity, but falsity will be doomed and vanquished because of the radiant and persistent advantage of "Truth."[3] Milton could believe that truth would prevail because he had a deeply Christian view of truth and its relationship to divine revelation. Yet the patience of modern society is not so long and its beliefs not so deep; Baker was concerned with the nature of competition in the here and now of the ideas marketplace, in the context of the struggle as we know it.[4] In the social media universe, falsity may have a very long tail. And in a media system pervaded by strategic communicators, persuasion, not truth, is often the most prized quality. To write about the nature of a contemporary marketplace of ideas requires more of a specific understanding than a slogan can provide of how

[2] C. Edwin Baker, *Human Liberty and Freedom of Speech* (Oxford: Oxford University Press, 1989), 6.
[3] Milton, John. "Areopagitica: A speech of Mr. John Milton for the Liberty of Unlicenc'd Printing, to the Parlament of England (1644)." In *Milton's Selected Poetry and Prose*, edited by Jason P. Rosenblatt. New York: W. W. Norton & Company, 2011.
[4] Baker questions the validity of the assumptions that support "the classic marketplace of ideas." Baker, *Human Liberty*, 4, 12–17. These assumptions are that truth is "objective" and that "people are basically rational." Baker, *Human Liberty*, 6. These ideas are also pursued in Alan Haworth, *Free Speech* (London: Routledge, 1998).

ideas emerge, how they are sustained and what elements of a marketplace make it a fair one in which to compete.

Furthermore, as Baker put it, for elements of the "marketplace of ideas" structure to make sense, "truth must be 'objective' or 'discoverable.'"[5] "Truth is able to outshine falsity in debate or discussion only if truth is there to be seen." If the truth involved is subjective, however, "if it is chosen or created, an adequate theory must explain why and how the usually unequal advocacy of various viewpoints leads to the 'best choice.'"[6] Much of what leads to conflict and division might be resolvable by finding a "truth," if only it were the kind of truth that could be established by a blue ribbon commission dedicated to rooting out the facts. Rather, a great deal of what the modern world debates has to do with belief systems founded on religion, affiliation, class, history and alternate perceptions of the world. "Truth," moreover, is a path to legitimating power. For that reason alone, those in power seek to capture definitions of truth and keep them within their preserve.

Most significant for the general argument of this chapter, Baker contends:

> Incredible inequalities of opportunity to use the marketplace also undermine claims that the robust debate provides a "fair" or otherwise justifiable process for regulating the struggle between opposing groups. Reliance on the marketplace of ideas appears improperly biased in favor of presently dominant groups. These groups have greater access to the marketplace. In addition, these dominant groups can legally restrict opportunities for subordinate groups to develop patterns of conduct in which new ideas would appear plausible.[7]

Baker's perspective explains the unease that develops as the strong and wealthy deploy strategic communication with outsized influence and gain the ability to deprive subordinate groups of opportunities to compete. One response is that the increased deployment of social media provides a possible antidote to these power-based forms of such strategic communication. In this view, social media become a tool of subordinate groups to gain greater equality in the "marketplace of ideas." The history of communications policy, however, is not always favorable to this conception of the world. The transformation of supposedly democratizing media – radio and cable television are examples – to instruments of prevailing authority are too abundant to justify a complacent assumption about the long-term democratizing role of social media.

---

[5]   *Human Liberty*, 6. These questions are pursued, too, in Bernard Williams, *Truth and Truthfulness: An Essay in Genealogy* (Princeton, NJ: Princeton University Press, 2010).

[6]   *Human Liberty*, 6.

[7]   Ibid., 15, footnotes omitted.

I also emphasize Baker's questioning of modes of thinking of media, democracy and self-determination. The relationship between media and democracy is a major justification for many strategic communication efforts. Too often, the link between "democracy" and media is rendered in terms that simplify both alternative structures of the press and alternative conceptualizations of democracy. In an important essay,[8] Baker linked distinct bases for media and media structures to competing ideas of the appropriate definition of a democratic structure in a particular society. Each model of democracy requires a distinct companion model of the media. A media structure has an influence on the style of democratic governance that evolves around it, and the system of governance has an impact on the media system.

In *Media, Markets, and Democracy*, Baker asked:

> What type of free press does democracy need and why does democracy need it? Answers to these questions would allow the necessary follow-up questions. Are existing media [in . . . a particular country] adequate? Do they provide for the informational or communication needs of democracy? And if not, in what way do they fail, and what can be done? . . . Do inadequacies reflect, at least in part, deeper structural problems? And if governmental policy correctives are necessary to make matters better, what interventions would promote a more "democratic press" – that is, a press that properly serves a society committed to democracy?[9]

To approach these questions, Baker interrogates three theories of democracy: an "elitist" model, in which an informed set of influentials represents the public; a "liberal pluralist" ("interest-group conception") democracy, in which the democratic outcome of decision-making is the combined result of groups' and people's "preferences or desires"; and a "republican" theory of democracy that envisions an "open process of defining as well as advancing the public good" through participation by all in this process."[10] Baker added, as well, his own model: a "complex democracy" that combines elements of all three.[11] Holders of different views of what constitutes a well-functioning democracy have different objectives that the media should meet and different fears of what would occur in the absence of an effective press.

The point here is that advocacy of free expression often does not sufficiently take into account such substantial variegation in models of democratic

---

[8] C. Edwin Baker, "The Media that Citizens Need," *University of Pennsylvania Law Review* 147, no. 2 (1998).

[9] C. Edwin Baker, *Media, Markets, and Democracy* (Cambridge: Cambridge University Press, 2002), 125.

[10] Ibid., 126.

[11] Ibid., 125–127.

governance and that this can also be true of those engaged in strategic communication. The superimposition of patterns of communication from outside may change the balance among proponents of different styles. The correspondence of media systems and political systems underscores another complexity of the general free expression advocacy sphere: the design of press and media strategies for societies that feature few of the dominant variants of democratic practice, such as societies that are semi-authoritarian, conflict-ridden or without government authority. An analytic framework like Baker's that seeks to match media to political system works best in a background that is aspirationally democratic but fits uneasily with authoritarian or even some transitional societies. In the absence of a preferred theory of democratic practice that can be reinforced by a media system, the fallback is an idealized template.

A specific example of the problem of the complexity of matching strategic communication to democratic theory arises from the work of Robert Post (reflecting the scholarship of Owen Fiss). Post argues that a – and maybe *the* – premier purpose of free expression, certainly in the more specific and American sense of the First Amendment, "is to facilitate collective self-determination."[12]

> Collective self-determination is a social right theoretically distinct from and unconnected to individual rights of personal autonomy. Collective self-determination subsists in a rich public debate that fully informs voting citizens of available alternatives and options. A full and rich public debate requires that all voices be heard, most especially the voices that otherwise would be silenced or muffled.[13]

There are many interesting implications of this formulation as a way of evaluating strategic communication. As an example, included within the concept of collective self-determination, is the idea of defining the collective self: a realm that has boundaries of inclusion and exclusion. As states regulate discourse to further collective self-determination, there is some privilege to mark boundaries – to foster participation by protecting this sphere of expression from being overwhelmed or undercut by those not part of the collective self. The ideal of fostering collective self-determination, if so defined, can come into conflict with the universalized functioning of powerful external strategic communicators.

---

[12] Post is eager to mention, however, that an acknowledgment of this First Amendment purpose should not be made at the expense of its other purposes. Robert C. Post, "Equality and Autonomy in First Amendment Jurisprudence," *Michigan Law Review* 95 (1997): 1520 (citing Owen M. Fiss, *Liberalism Divided: Freedom of Speech and the Many Uses of State Power* (Boulder, CO: Westview Press, 1996)).

[13] Post, *Equality and Autonomy*, 1520.

The framework for freedom of expression I have drawn on here, from Baker and Post and Fiss, partakes of what is often called an "instrumentalist" theory of freedom of expression. These are theories tied to output or impact, in this case impact on democratic political development. I focus on these theories because many of the debates about strategic communication relate to these processes. A certain kind of strategic communication – what is called "democracy promotion" (discussed in Chapter 10) – feeds from these theories of freedom of expression. Yet other theories are highly relevant and could and should be considered in a fuller treatment of the subject. These great theories, shaped by Thomas Emerson, Ronald Dworkin, Robert Nozick, Thomas Scanlon and others are chiefly deontological: freedom of expression is adopted, celebrated and followed not because of its impact on democratic development or other attractive consequences that ensue, but because of principle, moral determinant or sense of what it means to be human. In an instrumentalist world, strategic communication might trump freedom of expression principles if the ultimate objective can be achieved; in a frame of principle (often captured by international norm), it is the mandated ideal that is decisive.[14]

Free expression norms, in this wider scope, cannot be reserved only for societies in which collective self-determination means an idealized set of democratic institutions or their approximation. Indeed, the furtherance of international norms of free expression, such as Article 19, is particularly significant in societies where the capacity for self-determination is extremely limited in terms of formal (and actual) democratic practices.

ASSUMPTIONS OF FREEDOM OF EXPRESSION

These critical and questioning views give rise to a more general line of inquiry. Norms of free expression – and support for such norms – are built on certain assumptions about the society or societies in which robust speech practices are more easily adopted. An example is the assumption I have already discussed: proclaiming that vigorous debate will eventually lead to truth. I have mentioned how this relates to the Miltonian assumption of divine assistance in finding a "Revealed Truth." The marketplace of ideas metaphor may still be vital, but some aspect of the core meaning of Milton's observation has been altered by changes in the context of language. Identifying these assumptions is a difficult and controversial task. It is

---

[14]   For a discussion of instrumentalist versus deontological approaches, see Frederick Schauer, "Who Decides?" in Judith Lichtenberg, ed., *Democracy and the Mass Media: A Collection of Essays* (Cambridge: Cambridge University Press, 1990).

important, however, to try, in part because resulting institutional practices (those that depend on fundamental assumptions) may otherwise hollow out and become vulnerable. Advocates of freedom of expression must be careful in their arguments, avoiding building blocks that are weakened remnants of a previous world. Practices change and with them, to some extent, the assumptions behind the principles. In one period, for example, epistolary practice served as the undergirding of discourse.[15] Coffeehouse cultures have famously played a role in forging a public sphere (and Starbucks may be a curious instrument of the practice's restoration).[16] Large-scale changes in strategic communication offer a window into the current transformations that affect the public sphere. Important shifts take place between self-generated or civil-society generated contributions and the directed, overt and disciplined imposition of information flows from highly organized strategic communicators. Each shift will have consequences; it may lead to the reassertion of state power, in some cases, or the weakening of such power in others. In some circumstances, the state may properly be called on to act as a meaningful referee, regulator, even partial sponsor of the public debate. In a crowded, global and highly competitive context, the state may seek a more public role in which it seeks to assert its own voice.

The point is that the extraordinary phenomenon we call "free expression" is not only a set of principles and practices but also a set of institutions. These institutions include the mechanisms that exist in a society for the production and diffusion of information – the infrastructure of information flows – as well as the processes by which people process information as they function as citizens or as members of a community. These institutions incorporate the rules and norms of governments and other actors who affect the interplay between principles and actions. Most important, they encompass the patterns for information flow and the massive change over time in the types of information that range across boundaries. Change any one element of an existing equation and all other elements are affected as well. Of course, principles must endure while the phenomena in which those principles live may change. That, after all, is what makes for overarching principles. But even if principles are constant, how they can be achieved – indeed, whether they can even be optimally applied – differs when the mechanisms of daily life are materially altered.

These institutions of free expression have always and are always altering, and it is difficult to tell in advance what implications even basic changes might

---

[15] Michele Dillon, Introduction to Sociological Theory: Theorist, Concepts and their Applicability to the Twenty-First Century, second edition (Chichester, West Sussex: Wiley-Blackwell, 2013).
[16] Ibid.

have.[17] The institutions changed with the development of institutionalized mail services and again with the telegraph; they changed with the industrialization of society and also with the coming of the railroad. Satellites altered patterns of communication profoundly. It is possible to argue that the current rounds of change – including the Internet and the growth of social media – are so much more transformational that they affect the assumptions of freedom of expression in ways that are qualitatively different from anything that has occurred before. A more modest claim is that whenever such transformational changes take place, it is important to reexamine the fit between free expression principles and their underpinnings.

What, then, are some examples of fundamental assumptions or practices that undergird a system of free expression? These assumptions are basic; they are what might be called the plumbing of information flows or the infrastructure of communication. Democratic societies may have, indeed should have, an expectation about the availability of information, the opportunity to express views and the receptivity of government and other players to the exercise of free expression. These societies gain legitimacy (often in their own self-assessment) because of the self-respect and respect of others for the practice of free expression. Such societies engage in critical analysis, ideally, to determine whether the values they proclaim are being realized. Free expression and its exercise presuppose some value in the aggregated output of information and debate. And that presupposition may turn on a consensus (validly earned or not) that what is produced has the capacity to provide informed contributions to a public sphere.

Current apprehension concerning the future of the press relates to this question of legitimacy. The set of institutions called "newspapers," which have been instrumental in producing and diffusing news and information, has changed constantly over the last two centuries. Now there is a sense of mild panic as to the future of that particular industrial practice, which has played so significant a role and has been the underpinning for thinking about watchdogs, furthering deliberation and contributing to creativity.[18] It is not inappropriate to evaluate how weaknesses in those institutions alter prescriptions for free expression. Some argue that newspapers (in some form or another) are so key to the legitimacy of free expression that there should be

---

[17] Carolyn A. Lyn and David J. Atkin, *Communication Technology and Social Change: Theory and Implications* (Mahwah, NJ: Lawrence Erlbaum Associates, 2007). See, too, Carolyn Marvin, *When Old Technologies Were New* (New York: Oxford University Press, 1988).

[18] Leonard Downie, Jr. and Michael Schudson, "The Reconstruction of American Journalism," *Columbia Journalism Review*, October 19, 2009.

greater efforts to subsidize them.[19] Others argue that an emerged, post-print newspaper world would not necessarily be less free, with new channels for distribution abundant, convenient, tailored and useful.[20] What is certain, however, is that a complex system of existing thinking about free expression, and the rules and mechanisms established to administer it, is dependent on the institutions that deliver on the promise, or fail to do so.

The decline of newspapers (or the rise of substitutes, like social media and blogging) is one example of changes in the free expression equation, but there are many others. Free speech principles breathe best in the absence of substantial external or internal threats or perceptions of such threats. As national security concerns intensify, the equation of freedom of expression is propotionally affected. Invocation of terms like "information war,"[21] cybersecurity[22] and cyberattack define a context in which speech-related dangers must be increasingly monitored and confronted. Another example involves the way freedom of speech principles are connected with political processes. A description of free speech that includes, at its heart, an electoral process, for example, may be twisted out of shape if the process becomes corrupt or the major contributors to political speech in the public space are entities from outside the polity. Confidence in free speech may depend on some perception, widespread in society, that it is a broad privilege to speak that is being protected (and perhaps exercised) and that the space for speech is not monopolized or controlled by special interests or exclusionary interests. In this view, the rise of social media should heighten the idea of breadth of privilege and greater equity and equality in shaping the public communicative space, while the growth of focused, powerful groups as speakers moves in the other direction.

Free speech, in its ideal conception and exercise, may contemplate a minimum level of civility and acceptance of difference of views. Not that speech should avoid harshness, but rather, at some level, speech privileges might include consideration of competing views and some form of social resolution. Peter Molnar has spoken of the too-seldom willingness of a strong majority power to subordinate its voice, somewhat, to allow other groups in society effectively to make their voices heard. If harmonic compromise disappears as a run-up to division, secession or violence the potential for the assumption of pluralistic representation where there is a too-dominating

---

[19] On the role and benefits of subsidy, see Baker, *Media, Markets, and Democracy*.

[20] See Yochai Benkler, *The Wealth of Networks: How Social Production Transforms Markets and Freedom* (New Haven, CT: Yale University Press, 2007).

[21] "Secretary Clinton: U.S. is losing the information war," *FREEMEDIAONLINE*, May 4, 2011.

[22] For example, the Comprehensive National Cybersecurity Initiative. See Kim Zetter, "U.S. Declassifies Part of Secret Cybersecurity Plan," *Wired*, March 2, 2010.

super-majority, weakens. Often, apprehension that there is rising hate speech in a society is an example of worry about this element of the institutional equation of free speech institutions. Identifying and recognizing a category of hate speech virtually implies that such expression should not and must not be given voice. It is a suggestion of a limitation on pluralism – a boundary of what should be expressed in this cauldron of self-determination. Yet those who advocate laws restricting or punishing "hate speech" often do so on the basis that there must be some basic level of human dignity in regular discourse, and the legal framework should embrace that. Jeremy Waldron's book *The Harm in Hate Speech* argues that "public order . . . includes the peaceful order of civil society and the dignitary order of ordinary people interacting with one another in ordinary ways. . . . Above all, it conveys a principle of inclusion and a rejection of the calumnies that tend to isolate and exclude vulnerable religious minorities."[23]

Free speech depends very much on the rule of law. In the language of this chapter, the existence of a legal system that can fairly recognize and enforce limits is one of the key aspects of an institutional foundation for free expression. "Free expression," in the evolved tradition, depends on the idea that judges can hold the government accountable if it oversteps its bounds and likewise – perhaps equally important – that judges can sanction individuals or groups who violate constitutional rules that set sanctioned boundaries (in accordance with Article 19). To the extent that the rule of law weakens, and to the extent that appropriately bargained-for or legislatively agreed upon limitations cannot be enforced, the right itself may be at risk.

There are other factors. Societal tolerance for free speech principles may depend on what I have called a balance between open and closed terrains of speech.[24] A society requires a theater of public representation of ideas, public speeches, posters, sermons, dance, art and music. It also requires space for individuals and groups to communicate privately, beyond the surveillance of the state and other powerful forces in the society. Increasingly, with the revelation of widespread government surveillance, the assumption of the existence of an adequate closed or private terrain of speech is undermined. One can imagine a society in which the balance is not quite right, in which the open terrain of speech is barren and devoid of meaning and private discourse is hushed and paranoiac, or one in which private discourse abounds but is not

---

[23] Jeremy Waldron, *The Harm in Hate Speech* (Cambridge, MA: Harvard University Press, 2012), 232.

[24] Monroe E. Price, "Free Expression and Digital Dreams: The Open and Closed Terrain of Speech," *Critical Inquiry* 22 (Autumn 1995). See also Monroe E. Price, *Television, the Public Sphere, and National Identity* (Oxford: Oxford University Press, 1995).

allowed to blossom into the public realm. How to gauge health on such a scale has hardly been defined, but one of the unarticulated assumptions of free speech may be that the balance is a "proper" one. As an example somewhat outside the usual scope of free expression, take the issue of the burka and facial disclosure. A general societal norm of exposed faces comes into conflict with changing cultural practices as more and more women follow religious mandates, France being an important case study. The norm – an institutional foundation for a mode of personal expression – becomes subject to re-examination.[25]

Ultimately, as a world in which strategic communication – as I have defined it – gains strength, particular free expression issues arise. Systematic and external efforts to address and alter a basic tenet of a target society may afford particular privileges and responsibilities to the governments involved. Societal assumptions about the ideal functioning of free expression may include some idea of proportionality: the ratio between what might be called human scale communication and strategic communication. Habermas sought a public sphere relatively free of the overwhelmingly corrupting element of power-related, statist, corporate and commercial and propagandistic speech. Yet we live in a world where bombardment by those engaged in strategic communication is practically the norm. One can think of societies that are virtually defenseless against strategic communication. These may be communities where there is little in the way of effective, nationally developed (whether "independent" or not) radio or television, where there is an insufficient local tradition to support the institutions of governance, or where a lesser-used language may become an orphan. Almost all states deemed "failing" or "fragile" fall within this category.

Several decades ago, it was fashionable to talk of "cultural imperialism," at least in some quarters. The world was seen as one in which the United States wielded its hegemony of information and in which an American culture industry dominated music and film and therefore shaped attitudes globally.[26] Much of that feeling persists, but flows now seem more multipolar, and more regional nodes of power exist to regulate these flows and provide counter flows. One could see in all of this a modification of who controls the levers of strategic communication – the rise of powerful satellite channels with

---

[25] For instance, see Steven G. Gey, "Free Will, Religious Liberty, and a Partial Defense of the French Approach to Religious Expression in Public Schools," 42 *HOUS. L. REV* (2005–2006). Also see Steven Erlanger, "Parliament Moves France Closer to a Ban on Facial Veils," *New York Times*, July 13, 2010.

[26] For instance, see Herbert Schiller, *Communication and Cultural Domination* (New York: International Arts and Sciences Press, 1976).

Middle East parentage, the formation of a European Union that seeks to manage imagery to some extent and the shift in ownership of the largest entertainment companies to provide more plural geographic sources of control. But this would not be the whole story. The relationship of power to imagery persists and intensifies. For some, it is a fundamental assumption of systems of free expression that powerful, sometimes corrupt, often state-sponsored strategic communicators are or should be offset by conditions of diversity, by independent media, or by public service media. But these are aspirations that are often unrealized. It is in this context that institutional aspects of free expression norms totter. Consider a target society in a transitional phase, confronted with a series of forces of strategic communication seeking to reshape or "rehabilitate" it – convert its citizens to a different religion, alter their consuming habits or place them under the sphere of influence of one neighboring or foreign state rather than another. The search might be for a formulation of principle or law that allows that state, assuming it has the capacity, to construct a response consistent with free expression norms.

The existence of the state system is itself a major aspect of the structure of free expression. Historically, the state has been the instrument for organizing a national definition of rights and responsibilities for speech practices. That idea, that working assumption, is in perpetual tension with ideas of globalization and technologies that make borders porous. Saskia Sassen has been original and perceptive in dissecting the changing framework of the nation-state in the dynamic of globalization and its impact on rights, and it is useful to apply parts of her analysis to the specific rights we denominate as the right to receive and impart information.[27] How is our set of rights embedded in the structure of the nation-state and therefore altered by changed global circumstances?

FREE EXPRESSION IN A WORLD OF SOCIAL MEDIA

One would think, and happily so, that the new social media and their transforming ilk present no or little negative challenge to the institutions of free expression, but rather provide yet another opportunity for realization of individual autonomy and the other goals of the doctrine. I have suggested that the rapid diffusion capacity of social media clearly transforms the information ecology. The rise of social networks leads to a rethinking of the power of the individual in receiving information, deliberating and mobilizing. Social

---

[27] Saskia Sassen, *Territory, Authority, Rights: From Medieval to Global Assemblages* (Princeton, NJ: Princeton University Press, 2008).

networks change the balance between open and closed terrains of speech. They threaten existing intermediaries and create new ones. They are a challenge for governments, democratic or not. They alter the status quo. And social networks themselves may yet yield another newly empowered, all-seeing, all-knowing oligopoly of private entities, with new names and the potentially deceptive appeal of positive change. It would not be the first time that pioneers of progress in communications technology become the new wielders of old authority, with a transfer of power, not a radical reduction in power, as the consequence. Social networks themselves are seeking to define their relationship to the existing status quo of institutions of free expression. Facebook and YouTube become the operative gateways for this new tribe and determine what controls to impose. Do they enact and replicate, enforcing old standards, or do they produce a new world? Do they act wholly independently of government or increasingly at governmental behest? The protestors of the Arab Spring, seen as owing much of their momentary success to social media, offered a significant though still confusing tutorial in these questions.

In 2011, Alec Ross, then the guru of social media in the State Department, reflected on ways in which the Internet and other "connection technologies" affected processes of change and the effectiveness of free expression in Egypt and Tunisia.[28] He counted four distinct impacts. First, these processes "accelerated" mobilization, allowing "movements that normally would have taken years to build" to come together "in the course of weeks and months." Second, these new media processes "enriched the information environment," bringing more people into it and conveniently giving them a treasure trove of information. Third, these processes "made weak ties strong," unifying for the moment "the 57-year-old member of the Muslim Brotherhood with the 27-year-old digital hipster who is educated at the Sorbonne." Fourth, the new technology processes "distributed leadership." In prior "revolutions," a single hero emerged: "Lech Walesa in Poland[,] Vaclav Havel in the Czech Republic[,] or Nelson Mandela in South Africa." It was Ross's judgment that social media would lead to different forms of political organization.

The Boston Marathon bomb incident of 2013 illustrated some of these points, although from a different vantage. The availability of the Internet and social media contributed to the environment in which the Tsarnaev brothers functioned. *Inspire*, the largely online publication of al Qaeda in the Arabian Peninsula, appeared to be a vehicle for the brothers' instruction in bomb-making and in their own mobilization (obviously in combination

---

[28] Alec Ross, interview by Golnaz Esfandiari, "U.S. Innovation Adviser: 'Internet Freedom Is Not A Regime-Change Agenda,'" *Radio Free Europe/Radio Liberty*, July 2011.

with many other factors). The new media accelerated and sharpened their activities, providing Ross's "treasure trove of information," although not for the positive democratic purposes that are often cited for the Internet. The instance once again highlighted the fears and concerns about the Internet as a site for insidious recruitment and training and it raised new demands for surveillance and control. Ultimately it had features relating to the definition of strategic communication – namely the reaching across borders by purposive communicative action to reach a vulnerable target audience (here the Chechen brothers). As David Remnick put it in the *New Yorker*, "The digital era allows no asylum from extremism, let alone from the toxic combination of high-minded zealotry and the curdled disappointments of young men."[29]

Deployment of social media and related changes have already disrupted preexisting institutional assumptions of freedom of expression through the more sophisticated surveillance that has accompanied it. Notions of privacy are profoundly affected by the information-gathering and user identification aspects of social media. The relationship between privacy and free expression is both complex and significant. Notions of anonymity – often essential to fundamental aspects of free expression – are marginalized in the operation of the social media-era Internet. It becomes invaluable to investigators to recreate lives and relationships, sifting through thousands of posts and tweets, tracing how individual attitudes, representations and capacities change over time. Manipulators of "big data" rely on social media-generated data to recreate a network of communication and influence. We are only beginning to fathom the impact on privacy – and consequently on freedom of expression. Disclosures in mid-2013 about the deep and wide program of the U.S. National Security Agency and its counterparts have placed a new frame and context about the tensions (always present) over the use of the new media. Organizations like the Global Network Initiative, with significant company representation, seek to identify principles that should guide an understanding of what privacy sacrifices are taking place and what policy modifications should occur as privacy concerns interact with freedom of expression principles.

FREE EXPRESSION AND INTERMEDIARIES

A related significant impact on ideas of free expression exists because of the apparent change in the role of intermediaries. In the pre-social media world,

[29] David Remnick, "The Culprits," *The New Yorker*, April 29, 2013.

much of media was filtered through intermediaries – newspapers, television networks, even state related entities. Freedom of expression existed in this highly intermediated world, where the often unstated assumption was that these intermediaries would function (or would be obliged to function) as guardians of the public interest. These were "gatekeepers." There were many valid objections to intermediaries as false guardians, over-filtering, themselves not democratically responsible. But it is possible to think of intermediaries as an important institutional aspect of the structure of free expression. One of the major sources of liberation, but also of current unease, lies in the rapid disappearance of familiar intermediaries – particularly those entities that can be subjected to government control and influence. Much of the debate over the responsibility and role of Facebook and Google to filter or take down material (about hate speech, violence against women and material deemed by governments insulting and destabilizing) relates to the question of the penchant for intermediaries. Governments and other strategic communicators seek to shift the discourse from providing safe harbors for the new intermediaries to making ISPs or platforms more responsible, enlarging their roles as mediating gatekeepers or, through processes of surveillance, aiding the government. Intermediaries can also be the enforcers of territorial distinctions.

FREE EXPRESSION AND THE WEAKENING OF LAW

A next step in understanding the foundations for a system of free expression is the concept of legality – and with it the extent to which that concept is fraying as an available element of the system. It is common in the literature of rights and rights enforcement to mention the function of the rule of law. What is usually meant by legality is the need for the government in a society to act in accordance with law – to have clearly stated and transparent law and to create a culture in which proper legal norms are actually followed. The rule of law, in this sense, is significant for free expression as an encouragement of states not to violate constitutional and international norms, not to have vagueness as a mode of obscuring the boundaries of free speech and not to have secret ways in which speech is confined and confounded, notwithstanding appropriate public legal norms.

What is less understood is the *necessity* of law, including its limitations on individual action as well as its enabling of expansive opportunities. Without a legal system that functions, rights may themselves be in danger. In "Why the State?" and other writings, Owen M. Fiss argued against an overemphasis on individual autonomy as the basis for freedom of expression on the ground that such an emphasis leads to the domination of debate by those who control the

economic and political power structures of society.[30] Law and public intervention, in this view, are used to further public discourse. Examples Fiss provides
are hate speech prohibitions and restrictions on Holocaust denial, as well as
positive steps like enactment of a "fairness doctrine" and the sustaining nature of
public service broadcasting. Law – in this sense as a set of boundaries or
exceptions – is a necessary element of robust freedom of expression. It is often
argued that free expression in the United States is an "absolute" and the more
it achieves that status, the more it is to be applauded. But "free expression" as a
set of practices in most places is a collection of capabilities and limits – of
encouragements and boundaries – and law is wheeled into place as a way of
defining and enforcing these limits, few as they may be, whether they are
limitations of time, place and manner, or content, or other modes of achieving
what a particular society, consistent with international norms, considers an
appropriate balance.[31]

A system of free expression may have as an assumption that government
will effectively be able to implement limitations when it is constitutionally
authorized or directed to do so. For the government to be told it *cannot* – for
technological or other reasons – may have unanticipated consequences. Some
governments, undoubtedly as a justification, will think there must be some
switch they should be able to pull in some circumstances. Shutting down the
Internet as occurred in Egypt is a drastic and illuminating signal of the
dramatic problems that arise; reactions have also included blocking cell
phone service in some areas for some time and other intermediate, more
frequently invoked techniques, such as more pressure on ISPs to retain records
and cooperate with government, more attention to post-violation use of criminal or other sanctions, or more surveillance.

Again, this goes to the question of institutional foundations of the concept of
freedom of expression. If a foundation of a scheme of freedom of expression
is that its legitimate boundaries can be observed and enforced, then weakening
that foundation may require some form of corresponding adjustment in
the conception of the right. When Article 19 was adopted internationally in
the 1950s, there appeared to be bargaining on what would be listed as limitations and in what way.[32] The *travaux preparatoires* of Article 19, paragraph 3,
indicate the existence of debates particularly over controversial language such

---

[30] Owen M. Fiss, "Why the State?" *Harvard Law Review* 100 (1987). See also Fiss, *Liberalism
     Divided*.
[31] In *Liberalism Divided*, Fiss argues for interpreting the First Amendment to accommodate
     contemporary social change.
[32] Research Memorandum "The Adoption of Article 19, Paragraph 3 of the International Covenant
     on Civil and Political Rights" by Robyn Mohr, prepared for the author (July 4, 2011) (on file with
     author).

as "duties and responsibilities" and "public order." One of the notable ideas that guided the legislation-making process was "strik[ing] a balance between the rights of the individual and the requirements of society and the State."[33] The ultimate profile of the right contains both the entitlements and the limitations. One can see limitations as an intrinsic part of the general acceptance of the formulation of the right.

The effectiveness of a law often deals with the technology of its enforcement. A duly enacted law might be so clumsy in its administration or enforcement, so oppressive, that it ought to be nullified. Or it could be assumed that government has the responsibility for engineering its relevant world to make enforcement more feasible and fairer. Mandatory withholding and bank reporting regulations, for example, help ensure that there is greater compliance with income tax law requirements. Modern camera systems are designed to "catch" violators of traffic regulations although there are, increasingly, constitutional limits to their use. Companies build "click" software into their programs to gain records of consent by consumers because of various legal requirements (say with respect to privacy). The general acceptance of principles of free expression in many, if not most, societies is based on a set of assumptions, one of which is that government has the authority *and* the power to police, subject to constitutional limits, their boundaries (including obscenity and child pornography – categories that are so solidly in this framework that some courts do not call them "speech"). This hardly means that the state always does police this border or that enforcement should be uniform and complete. But that is different from arguing that it does not have the capacity to do so. Shaking this foundational assumption of free expression theology could shake support for the principle itself.

This argument applies to language in Article 19 that sweeps in the right to receive and impart information *regardless of frontiers*. That language could mean that a government cannot restrict language and images from outside its boundaries on grounds broader than those it uses to restrict language within. But such a reading is inconsistent with many current state practices that seek to prefer domestic producers (often on economic grounds). A more radical reading of Article 19 would be that a state should have a more stringent test for regulating speech that originates outside its borders than for the home-grown variety. Of course, any restriction, under the international norms, must meet the conditions and standards of Article 19 (3). And there is another consideration. What if, as a condition of modern technology, sources of information

---

[33] "Draft International Covenants on Human Rights, Report of the Third Committee," *United Nations General Assembly*, Sixteenth session, Agenda item 35, December 11, 1961.

from outside a state's boundaries cannot be subjected to the restrictions applied to those within? The result could be (and perhaps already is) a kind of Gresham's Law of Information,[34] in which uncensored or unmonitored programming drives monitored, intermediated and law-complying programming out of circulation.

FREE EXPRESSION IN A WORLD OF NATIONAL SECURITY

Another institutional foundation for a system of freedom of expression is a certain level of confidence in the security of the national polity. It may well be that the level of fear or paranoia is a better predictor of the extent of living, breathing freedom of expression than is the language of constitution or law. During wartime, societies steeped in a tradition of free expression engage in deep compromises, although they may also strive to maintain as much capacity for unencumbered discourse as is possible. National experiences in the World Wars and the conflicts of the twenty-first century demonstrate how a society can, at the same time, both clamp down and consciously search for ways to make expression freer and more constitutive of a democratic society. In such an environment, persuasion, peer pressure and the government's penchant to manage information all contribute to mediating between spaces of freer speech and spaces of greater control.[35]

Some boundary of preoccupation with national security is a condition of freedom of expression jurisprudence, at least in common experience. National "emergencies" have been one of the most frequent reasons for suspending privileges of free expression or modifying them beyond recognition. India, Egypt, Georgia and other states have all had short or long "emergencies" in which speech regulation has been an integral and often a seriously unpleasant ingredient. The declaration of a global war on terror has been the occasion for systematic review and revision of the underpinnings of free expression – surveillance, data storage, data retention and reexamination, declaring certain kinds of speech efforts as, themselves, acts of terrorists and therefore unprotected. Heightened national security fears intensify self-censorship. Legislation that would normally be implausible gains currency during periods of fear. The systemic question here is whether there is a shift from the norm of a democratic state to a norm of a security state or some novel melding of the two. Again, the point is to determine whether the ordinary rhetoric of free expression – the

---

[34] Gresham's Law states that "bad money drives good money out of circulation."
[35] Geoffrey R. Stone, *Perilous Times: Free Speech in Wartime from the Sedition Act of 1798 to the War on Terrorism* (New York: W.W. Norton, 2004).

models that are put forth, the limitations deemed suitable – is changing because of these geopolitical transformations.

Tied to these questions of security is how technology causes a shift in the plurality of citizenship. Not only the Internet and social media but satellite as well facilitate the retention of old loyalties and have an effect on the making of new ones. Social media occupy some of the enforcement space; Facebook establishes rules about what can be seen and what is filtered. States beseech Google to block or allow information. Altered conditions change the real world constitution of rights, including the right to freedom of expression. Here, especially, the machinery of human rights is increasingly impressive with the capacity to appeal outside territorial bounds for a declaration that international norms and laws apply. These are all elements, for Saskia Sassen, of the reconstitution of the nation-state: "Insofar as citizenship is at least partly and variably shaped by the conditions within which it is embedded, conditions that have changed in specific and general ways, we may well be seeing a corresponding set of changes in the institution itself."[36]

CONCLUSION

A world of pervasive social media use and intensive penetration of strategic communication presents circumstances sufficient to call for a rethinking and reinforcing of fundamental speech rights. In a way, such a reconceptualization is ongoing, as states, corporations and other large-scale speakers, together with civil society, seek to understand whether and how processes of change take place and with what consequences. As one hypothesis, for example, consider whether speech flows are regulated more through infrastructure design than through the machinery of rights. If this is the case, practice could be as much affected by architectures of the Internet (discussed in Chapter 6), pricing mechanisms for data, the health and capacity of the printed press or the regulation of satellite transponders and cable systems as it is by free speech rules. The locus of control of information moves steadily to monopolies or oligopolies on the traditional media side or, in a newer world of social media, to self-generated and unmediated producers of information. Both modes fit with difficulty in elements of the old paradigm of speech and society in which mediators or gateways were recognizable and largely accountable. The porousness of borders means that regulation, in its historic sense, is less and less effective. Such a reconceptualization must also consider the relationship between the ineffectiveness of regulation or the weakening of law and the rise

[36] Sassen, *Territory, Authority, Rights*, 280.

of violence, a possible consequence, unintended, to reduced legitimacy for state institutions.

My point here is that when we are looking at the institutional bases for free expression, there are large-scale, meaningful, often neglected factors that should be considered. These elements – aspects of the institutional foundations for free expression – include the way in which states think about their strategic narratives and how these narratives are affected by internal and external modes of expression; the balance or distribution among strategic communicators within and without a society; our changing understanding of the meaning of self-determination and its relationship to information and deliberation; the shape and nature of information infrastructures and their design and, in particular, the rise of social media; our sense of the reliability of "law" or of law as a guarantor of free expression; and, finally, the shifting perceptions of the society's immunity to external or internal threat, invasion and catastrophe. Assumptions about each of these elements undergird the way we think about free expression. And assumptions about each of these elements are, as I have tried to show, in the process of re-examination. There is a great unnoticed shift: The post–World War II mode of articulating freedom of expression was built on the hope for a system of individual rights, but the process of communication is often one of organized direction and the assertion of exogenous power over discourse.

In the next chapter, I turn to what I describe as strategic narratives – narratives developed across borders to fix expectations and, at times, to manage interventions. How societies themselves engage in this process tests legal rules. States engage with free expression principles in expansive ways to curtail or support a particular narrative. Public investments in the narratives of school books are examples, as are the subsidization of patriotic events, the shaping or proclaiming of a particular set of stories, the endorsement and protection of a national flag (or other emblems). Attitudes toward determining what a state can or cannot do rest, almost tautologically, on how strategic narratives are fostered.

This is a time of opportunity but also a time of great angst. A simpler moment is longed for, a moment when national security measures did not seem so pervasive, when the model of a nation-state capable of fostering free information within its own deliberative community was an adequate explanation and stage for thinking about these questions, when security in information flows at home and a desire for universal rights created an appetite for the right to receive and impart information "regardless of frontiers." As these great remembered moments are rendered more complex, more mythical, frustrations mount and alternative methods for coping with the idea of rights creep in from the periphery.

3

Narratives of Legitimacy

A state is, in part, a collection of stories connected to power. Remembered traditions, obligations and laws – all stories in themselves – shape internal and external perceptions of a state and the range of its efficacy. But the collection of stories that define the state transforms over time with important consequences. Within the bandwidth of circumstances we might call reality, it is important to understand who manufactures such stories and what levers of control are deployed in their diffusion. Viable states fight to manage and limit the process of narrative transformation both at home and abroad. A sense of loss of state power intensifies when significant aspects of self-characterization fall out of national control, when, for example, a state or its leadership change in the global imagination from moral hero to delegitimated villain, from keeper of ideals to perpetrator of evil, from agent of desirable stability to vessel for potential protest and disorder, from representative of financial reliability to economic profligate. Because narratives are part of the mythic architecture of the state, how they are produced, and with what consequences, becomes an important part of understanding state power, regime stability and the interactions between local and global processes and structures. The narratives – and their shaping – are products of the global and local speech and press environments in which the state is made legible. Those strategic communicators designing and shaping the narratives are "ideational entrepreneurs" who form or enrich "epistemic communities"[1] that sustain and legitimate alternative futures.[2] Other states and major groups (NGOs, rival political

---

[1] These communities are constituted as "a network of professionals with recognized expertise and competence in a particular domain and an authoritative claim to policy relevant knowledge within that domain or issue-area." Peter Haas, "Introduction: Epistemic Communities and International Policy Coordination," *International Organization* 46, no. 1 (1992): 3.

[2] Vivien A. Schmidt, "Discursive Institutionalism: the Explanatory Power of Ideas and Discourse," *Annual Review of Political Science* 11 (2008). An interesting collection of essays relating to ideational entrepreneurship is Andreas Gofas and Colin Hay, eds.,*The Role of*

entities, etc.) have a stake, often quite a desperate one, in how these narratives are framed, and the effort to affect such narratives both draws on and challenges ideas of free expression. The daily dramas, bold adventures and frequent tragedies of expression take place against the background of intense, large-scale maneuvering.

In this chapter, I focus on the interaction among strategic communicators to create or modify what I call "narratives of legitimacy" and render them as effective as possible. Narratives of legitimacy include the highest-level justifications for states and regimes, narratives of divine right, narratives of electoral or democratic affirmation, narratives of conquest, narratives of historical entitlement. These narratives can seem solid and eternal, yet history shows they are fragile and ephemeral, that they can vanish in a day. They are the product of myth (birthright, for example, or manifest destiny), past achievement (e.g. conquest) and international accord and external, if shaky, consensus. Shifts can come from economic pressure, from internal or external ideological challenges, from changes in the state's own telling of its story, both at home and globally, from the increasing role of other major players in accepting, fashioning, or rejecting such narratives, from dissent or even from improbable moments of mass conversion. States without any convincing narrative of legitimacy are, often, described as "failed" or "failing" states. A narrative of legitimacy that gains regional and international approval has not only symbolic value but can reduce costs for the state – for example, costs of defense or avoidance of sanctions.

The narratives here described are dynamic and contested. The narrative of legitimacy is hardly ever the exclusive domain of the state to which it pertains, although part of the romance of such narratives is to argue otherwise. Narratives of legitimacy, and their alternatives, are nourished by competing groups – for example, supporters of a regime and its opponents (both domestic and foreign). Regimes strive to maintain or deepen their narratives of legitimacy against global efforts to redefine them in many ways. Increasingly, the theater of performance is global, not national, and, as a result, the ordinary tools of crafting narratives, including censorship, are less effective. Deployment of these narratives and the struggle to affect them are often the ragged products of classic diplomatic efforts. They are normally attempts at the highest government levels to arrange an understanding of scenarios, moving forward. Simultaneously, however, other players – the "street," the "society," the "crowd" – fight to intervene in the process of narrative production and management, creating additional challenges for governments. A new dynamic arises as

Ideas in Political Analysis: A Portrait of Contemporary Debates (London and New York: Routledge, 2009).

the increasing use of social media and technology, more broadly, augments and supplements efforts by local and world leaders to fashion and influence key narratives.

Each period in modern times has seen its own struggles to validate narratives of legitimacy forged in a prevailing political consensus or historical events. In the 1990s, the redefinition of the post-Soviet states required assertion and protection of new formulations based on free market capitalism and parliamentary democracy. The dissolution of Yugoslavia led to extraordinary conflicts and international intervention to help define and defend certain narratives of legitimacy concerning ethnicity, self-government and the limits of regional integration. Shifting narratives filled the Balkans, feeding raptures of renewed nationalisms, and at war's end the Dayton Accords contained within them a strategic narrative for the region in which a series of states would seemingly glide toward European Union membership or association. The Oslo Accords contained a narrative for Israel and Palestine: the contested narrative of a two-state solution built on UN resolutions. In Africa, the processes of narrative legitimation and delegitimation permeate the post-colonial period. Secessionist entities like Somaliland exist and function without international recognition yet have a strong internal narrative of functionality. In Sudan, civil war gave way to plebiscite and the nervous creation of South Sudan as the narrative of separatism gained legitimacy as a political solution. The Arab Spring was a concatenation of narratives bidding for legitimacy and acceptance.[3] Each of these episodes had the potential for success, each for failure. Each was dependent on parties to agree to its terms. But each involved a complex search, often frustrated, for an overriding dramatic element – a transcendent vision designed to overcome otherwise incontrovertible obstacles.

Narratives are interlaced with power. States scramble to find techniques, pursue international negotiation and gain economic and diplomatic clout to maintain conditions of legitimacy. A successful narrative produces "loyalty," a quality Albert O. Hirschman identifies as one which raises the price of "exit"

---

[3] Indeed, even in the choice of umbrella term – Awakening or Spring – there is an implied turn to the narrative. The Arab Spring terminology (already strained and somewhat fixed in a disappearing past) is evocative of 1968's Prague Spring and, by extension, of the dissolution of the Soviet bloc after 1989. See Ben Zimmer, "The 'Arab Spring' has Sprung," *Word Routes*, May 20, 2011. The Arab Spring idea, he pointed out, has a built-in irony because of the tragic end of the Prague forebear. The term bears within it the prospect of failure. Awakening also suggests a narrative that has more of a mass impact, the slumbering multitudes coming to an awareness of their future. Spring is an externally determined event, cyclical, almost divine. Awakening could be self-generated.

or non-participation by citizens and subjects in the functions of the state.[4] A successful narrative (internally or externally) may lubricate, underwrite and mask power. States suppress dissent, produce propaganda, nourish histories (false and true) and use the levers of policy, of sanction and reward, all in the service of such narratives. While a narrative of legitimacy may momentarily mesmerize, it is not always sufficient to hold sway over time. Thus, fateful episodes of post-Soviet transitions, of the Arab Spring, of the European economic crises and reinventions of African states, frequently solid in their apparent hold, dissolve into mockeries of themselves in the face of challenges. An enduring and successful narrative can hold a coalition together, maintain investment confidence, foster a resolution to a divisive conflict and encourage collective dedication to a politically viable outcome. Narratives, of course, can be destructive as well as rehabilitating; they can be used to move a society toward a more democratic practice, but they can also be used to destructive authoritarian and totalitarian ends.

NARRATIVES AND STRATEGY

This process of creating and sustaining basic justificatory mythologies can be understood through the expanding literature on strategic narratives. "Strategic narrative" is a term that has been resuscitated and burnished in the last several years as a more specific and narrower element of strategic communication. Narratives are "frameworks constructed to allow people to make sense of the world, policies, events, and interactions."[5] Strategic narratives have been defined as stories forged by a state to achieve "desirable end-states" and "to influence states' perception of their interests and how the world works and should work."[6] Niels Röling and Marleen Maarleveld take a longer view of the function of narratives. They rely on Giddens' notion of "double hermeneutics" to clarify how stories, images, theories, slogans and axioms are woven together, become widely shared and dominate behavior.[7]

Single hermeneutics refers to the act of making sense of objects and events. For example, Copernicus, the 16th Century Polish astronomer, established

---

[4]   Albert O. Hirschman, *Exit, Voice, and Loyalty: Responses to Decline in Firms, Organizations, and States* (Cambridge, MA: Harvard University Press, 1970).

[5]   Laura Roselle, "Strategic Narratives of War: Fear of Entrapment and Abandonment During Protracted Conflict" (APSA 2010 Annual Meeting Paper), 6.

[6]   Andreas Antoniades, Ben O'Loughlin, and Alister Miskimmon, "Great Power Politics and Strategic Narratives," *Center for Global Political Economy*, Working Paper No. 7, March 2010.

[7]   Anthony Giddens, *Social Theory and Modern Sociology* (Cambridge: Polity Press, 1987).

that the earth is not the center of the universe. Instead, the earth is a rather insignificant planet turning around the sun. Double hermeneutics refers to the fact that sense making by some can affect the sense making and behavior of others. In other words, whether people believe the earth turns around the sun or vice versa does not affect the behavior of these celestial bodies. But the way people make sense of the world can certainly affect the sense making of others.[8]

As Röling and Maarleveld put it: "Widely shared narratives are constructed that influence individual sense making by highlighting and legitimating some options and making invisible others. ... Strategic narratives shape social relations by determining our expectations about other people's behavior. Social relations produce structure and structure produces social relations."[9] As a result, "social science can be as powerful as natural science because it can equally affect people's sense making. It is not the power of its predictions that give social – or any – science its influence, but the extent to which its perspectives or narratives take hold of people's imagination and enthusiasm, and especially the extent to which that sense making begins to justify policies and shape enduring practices, institutional design and the use of natural resources and ecological services."[10] In this sense, "narrative" must be separated from merely observing the world and recording what is observed. Narrative is interpretive, not merely or even necessarily objective. This potential gap between narrative as myth and narrative as representation of the world is the basis for its strategic significance.[11]

Laura Roselle captures an important logic in what makes narratives strategic. She cites Lawrence Freedman, a forerunner of strategic narrative theory, who has argued that narratives are "compelling story lines which can explain events

---

[8] Niels Röling and Marleen Maarleveld, "Facing Strategic Narratives: An Argument for Interactive Effectiveness," *Agriculture and Human Values* 16 (1999): 296.

[9] Ibid., 297.

[10] Ibid.

[11] Another way of addressing these questions emerges from the work of Harold Innis. James Carey wrote: "Innis argued that changes in communication technology affected culture by altering the structure of interests (the things thought about) by changing the character of symbols (the things thought with), and by changing the nature of community (the arena in which thought developed)." James Carey, "Space, Time, and Communications: A Tribute to Harold Innis," in *Communication as Culture: Essays on Media and Society*, Revised edition (New York: Routledge, 2009), 122. Edward A. Comor presents a similar analysis of "conceptual systems," discussing how technologies mediate the ways people experience, perceive, and imagine reality along dimensions of space and time. Edward A. Comor, *Consumption and the Globalization Project: International Hegemony and the Annihilation of Time* (New York: Palgrave Macmillan, 2008).

convincingly and from which inferences can be drawn."[12] But Roselle seeks to distinguish narratives from stories. She cites Douglas, who argues that "what makes such efforts 'narratives' instead of plain 'stories,' domestic 'spin,' or 'propaganda' is the fact that they are less retrospective explanations than they are forward-looking conceptual frameworks for explaining and interpreting events yet to come."[13] What makes a story a strategic narrative in international relations is the implicit inclusion of a "tacit set of rules," as Antoniades, Miskimmon and O'Loughlin put it, "for how foreign policy actors are to perform in certain speech situations and articulate responses to policy challenges and problems."[14]

Archetti enlarges the lens of strategic narratives from state actors to non-state actors: "Narratives are central to the practice of international relations. Governments use narratives strategically to achieve desired objectives: defining their countries' identities, explaining their role in the world, identifying allies and enemies, establishing the nature of the relationships among them; contextualizing historical events, as well as policy decisions."[15] But, as she points out, "the context in which contemporary international relations take place . . . is not characterized by the interaction among states only. Access to global communications has empowered . . . states, NGOs, corporate actors, transnational actors, even private citizens, [all of whom] have acquired a voice."[16] The possibility of communicating instantaneously with global audiences across distances at almost no cost gives non-state actors both the visibility and the power, to different extents, to influence the conduct of international politics. Indeed, "these actors might not have substantial financial, material or military resources, yet through the persuasive power of strategic narratives can mobilize audiences across national borders."[17] Thus we see the stage is set for the increasing

---

[12] Lawrence Freedman, *The Transformation of Strategic Affairs* (London: IISS, 2006), 22; quoted in Roselle, "Strategic Narratives," 6.

[13] Frank (Scott) Douglas, "The Year After Zarqawi: Strategic Narratives, Peripheral Operations, & Central Visions in the 'Long War,'" (Paper presented at ISA 2008 Annual Convention, San Francisco, 2008), 4; quoted in Roselle, "Strategic Narratives," 7.

[14] Antoniades et al., "Great Power Politics," 4.

[15] Cristina Archetti, "Terrorism, Communication, and the War of Ideas: Al-Qaida's Strategic Narrative as a Brand" (Paper presented at the International Communication Association (ICA) annual convention, Singapore, June 22–26, 2010).

[16] Jana Valencic, "The Individual and International Relations," in *The Image, the State and International Relations*, ed. Alan Chong and Jana Valencic (London: London School of Economics and Political Science, 2001), quoted in Archetti, "Terrorism, Communication, and the War of Ideas" 2.

[17] Archetti, "Terrorism, Communication, and the War of Ideas," 2.

proliferation of strategic narratives, as social media users and NGOs empowered by such tools seek to utilize their power.

In this chapter, I focus on strategic narratives as a subset of narratives of legitimacy, mildly modifying the definitions within the family of possibilities. Consistent with this book's emphasis on strategies of communication, I focus on narratives that have a certain kind of strategic pedigree. They are usually the consequence of an external international agreement, either formal or tacit. The agreement (and the process of attempting an agreement) contemplates actions that enact a transformative drama of governance. The international parties seek to assure that the story predicted by the narrative will take place, and threaten consequences if it does not. These narratives reflect, in some manner, major recent transnational struggles to invent or construct approaches that will help resolve a conflict or crisis in which the ongoing reinvention of the polity is an important and vital part of an emerging reality. These narratives seek to introduce discipline for different actors playing key roles. They frequently revise the conditions and assumptions for legitimacy. Some succeed; some fail; some appear to flourish, then flounder. They require, of course, some degree of cooperation from internal warring parties as well as the government itself. My approach to this understanding of strategic narratives is formulated against the backdrop of the Arab Spring and other contemporary and critical transnational episodes that touch on governmental legitimacy. All seek to fashion scenarios, cease-fires, truces and negotiated agreements that would alter existing political arrangements and create a new platform for governance.

Narratives are strategic in that they perform the functions that scripts play in conventional theater, namely to bind actors to roles or to set an approximate trajectory, to hold the actors (with wild differences based on authorial or directorial perquisites) to more or less expected ways of behaving. Strategic narratives, in this sense, are exceptional. They purport to pull leading participants into their sweep, not only those who are the easily managed *dramatis personae* but also those, often involuntarily bound, who can affect whether the script will be successful in its performance. Narratives that are strategic are anthems to the future of the state. They must be related to history – often distorting or reinventing it but doing so to chart future paths. Strategic narratives may (and often do) incorporate a brokered solution between parties. They embrace a resolution within a larger mythology designed to suppress internal divisions, at least momentarily, and create at least the illusion of forward motion. The practicalities of compromise are significant. These strategic narratives often promise dramatic consequences to satisfy the international community that one more crisis is at least temporarily thwarted.

Strategic Narratives in the Arab Spring

Two events early in the Arab Spring illustrated the interplay between strategic narratives and legitimacy and set the tone for what would come afterward. In retrospect, these early examples were somewhat misleading. By February and March 2011, an informal consensus had emerged in Western capitals: Hosni Mubarak would have to resign, as would Colonel Muammar Gaddafi. Narratives developed to compel both results. Yet both Mubarak and Gaddafi sought to resist rather than accept that scene-shifting account. Each incumbent held the illusion that he could propound an alternate vision and hold on to the previous arrangement of power. In each case, circumstances demonstrated the consequences of resisting the emerging story. By holding on to so much of a former, now discredited narrative, the leader aggravated a hostile reaction. In Egypt's case, the resulting ouster was swift and relatively bloodless (misleadingly so) from the outset while, in Libya's case, the rejection was more protracted.

When Mubarak, then still Egypt's long-reigning authoritarian president, spoke, on what turned out to be his last public speech in his official capacity (on February 10, 2011),[18] he varied from the international narrative for change. Then-U.S. Secretary of State Hillary Clinton had already proclaimed an anticipated result in Egypt and appointed a special representative to convey the United States' determination; the U.S. military leadership (in concert, undoubtedly, with European counterparts) had also pronounced a prospective outcome to the Egyptian command. As such, it was widely anticipated that Mubarak would make generous obeisance to the protestors at Tahrir Square, recognize the importance of the rising civil society, speak respectfully of processes of fundamental change and gracefully announce a purposive set of measures to precede his shuffling off the political stage.[19] The regime's very narrative of legitimacy, it was believed, would change, showing positive evolution. Instead, Mubarak gave a somewhat angry, defensive speech in which he emphasized the ways he would continue to control the levers of power rather than summarily disappear. The reaction among the Egyptian military, the protestors in the street and the international policy world in

[18]   "Transcript: Hosni Mubarak TV Address to Egypt," *CBS News*, February 10, 2011.
[19]   See, for example, Anthony Shadid and David D. Kirkpatrick, "Mubarak Refuses to Step Down, Stoking Revolt's Fury and Resolve," *New York Times*, February 11, 2011.

Europe and the United States was virtually unanimous. Mubarak had blundered badly; he had violated expectations in some fundamental way. Within twenty-four hours, he resigned.

In Libya, the initial efforts were equally dramatic. When protests spread to Libya, the processes for intervention, the parties to intervention and the justification for intervention were each highly disputed. It was necessary to find a strategy, including an evolved narrative of legitimacy, to form an umbrella for joint action and to define or maintain the limits of collaboration. The strategy had to negotiate a carefully defined goal (protecting civilians from their own government, reducing the number of civilian deaths and, more controversially, removing Gaddafi from power); suggest a viable technique (no-fly zone versus other forms of combat intervention); and provide a motivating drama that would build consensus (increasingly a mix of stories of torture, rape, delusion, irresponsible wealth, over-maintenance of power and lack of democratic institutions). Consistent with my earlier definitions, the narrative needed to be credible but it did not need fully to represent the complexities of the events on the ground. And it did not need to dictate day-to-day conduct, just the general roles of the actors.

Consider the actions of Gaddafi's son, Saif al-Islam, in February 2011 and compare them to those of Mubarak. Like Mubarak, Saif was set to deliver a defining speech. In the days and indeed moments before the speech, the default narrative he was expected to follow was transition – and transition into Saif's own hands. The son had been trained for this moment of reform at the London School of Economics, where he received a PhD and was for years projected as the person groomed to guide Libya to a more democratic, civil society-based future. He may have meant to articulate that narrative, but, as part of a ceremony of recalcitrance, he fully and devastatingly failed. "We will keep fighting until the last man standing, even to the last woman standing," Saif said. "We will not leave Libya to the Italians or to the Turks. . . . Our spirits are high." Speaking of the rebels, he said, "They now want to transform Libya into a group of [Islamic] emirates – small states – and even [cause] separatism. They have a plot. Unfortunately, our brother Arabs [allowed] their media, their stations and the inflammatory coverage."[20] The consequences of not "following the script" played themselves out.

By April 2011, the fate of Libya's vivid and contentious ruler was sealed. U.S. President Barack Obama, UK Prime Minister David Cameron and French President Nicolas Sarkozy wrote a joint letter for global public consumption (addressed to *The Times of London*, the *International Herald*

---

[20] "Gaddafi Son: 'We Will Eradicate Them All,'" *Guardian*, February 21, 2011.

Tribune and *Le Figaro*). The letter was a significant example of forming and promulgating a strategic narrative – and doing so not through a formal organization or classic agreement. The letter stated that for "a transition to succeed, Colonel Gaddafi must go, and go for good. At that point, the United Nations and its members should help the Libyan people as they rebuild where Gaddafi has destroyed – to repair homes and hospitals, to restore basic utilities, and to assist Libyans as they develop the institutions to underpin a prosperous and open society. This vision for the future of Libya has the support of a broad coalition of countries, including many from the Arab world."[21] The three leaders had announced that a narrative of legitimacy that included Colonel Gaddafi in a position of leadership was unsustainable.

The international narratives in Egypt and Libya had expectations built into them, expectations of what the leaders would do and, before that, what they would say. For those proclaiming such narratives, some kind of sense (at least temporary sense), had been made of the world, and mechanisms were put in place to enforce them. These strategic narratives were not quite "law" or contracts, though they were designed to regulate behavior. It was expected that even actors not fully party to the narrative's construction would see the light and, if at all possible, conform. Yet, as with all strategic narratives, they may not have had the necessary acquiescence of all key players.

Later events demonstrate all too sharply the tenuous hold of strategic narratives. Mubarak's exit led to periods of alternating euphoria and despair. The end of the Gaddafi regime led to its own extraordinary instabilities. The point here is to look at the consequences of shifts in narratives of legitimacy. A delegitimated regime has an altered status in the international community. The consequences might be sanctions, more difficult access to zones of discourse, weakening influence in international bodies or all-out regime change imposed from outside. Delegitimation has important internal consequences. For domestic citizens, the promise of protest, the values of adherence to the rule of law, the level of general obedience and loyalty and the willingness to fight are all affected by rejection of elements of a previously consensual narrative of legitimacy and a shift to a new one. When Mubarak faced the microphones and gave "the speech," he was defying – perhaps consciously – a rising narrative of social change and what would become a tumultuous transfer of power.

---

[21] Barack Obama, David Cameron and Nicolas Sarkozy, "Libya's Pathway to Peace," *New York Times*, April 14, 2011.

A TAXONOMY OF LEGITIMACY NARRATIVES

Looking at recent embodiments of narratives of legitimacy, the following model may clarify the argument. Narratives of legitimacy are "strategic" in the sense I have suggested if:

- The new narrative has gained consensus among key international actors (consensus-based narrative), or:
- In lieu of consensus among such actors, the narrative is deemed binding because of the power held by the maker or collaborative makers of the narrative (power-based narrative), or:
- In lieu of such external power, the narrative has such strength in an "aesthetic of interpretation" that it becomes an (or the) accepted version of what should occur (charismatic narrative).

Each configuration has its examples, and most instances are partly representative of all three. Take the first – an agreed-upon approach among key international actors that accompanies or precedes an action. This does not mean, necessarily, a reenactment of a Yalta-like event with powers formally meeting and coming to a complex understanding. It may be an agreement that is formed by a series of diffuse policy statements, slowly emerging over time, explicitly or by nods and winks. Such a narrative is designed to build further consensus among domestic or international publics. The narrative might reveal an accurate portrayal of why a decision to act was taken or of what is planned or proposed as a course of action coherent with the past, but a narrative, to be strategic, need not and often is not fully accurate in its depiction or understanding of reality. Because the strategic function of the narrative is to achieve and build consensus, transparency and credibility are often critical, but it is primarily for that (excellent) reason of furthering support that accuracy and truth-telling are factors. It is a matter of prudence and efficacy rather than principle. "Accuracy" and "credibility" are measured in terms of impact on the stakeholders in the particular strategic debate. What is significant – and hard to achieve – is for key actors to agree upon the narrative and bind those over whom they have influence.

In the second case, power, not consensus, legitimates. Power creates the illusion of consensus, but it is often precisely this power to create that illusion that undergirds the strategic narrative in the first instance. Understanding power is central to understanding why the narrative takes on its particular guise. Strategic narratives based on power were characteristic of the Cold War period, when, for example, Warsaw Pact countries followed a Soviet lead. Today, "superpowers" are still a reality; narratives invented in Washington – one might think of Iraq or the "War on Terror" more generally – are subscribed to elsewhere. But there are ever-fresh sources for narratives as singular powers develop within regions. The uniting of force with sweeping narrative was a characteristic of the extensive initiative in 2014 of the Islamic State of Iraq and the Levant (commonly referred to as ISIS). One might quibble, arguing that where it is power that does the work, the nature of the strategic narrative is less important. But we have seen narrative's efficacy in consensus building, which in turn maintains the legitimacy of power.

The third case may be closest to what might be called a "pure" strategic narrative, in which it is the compelling nature of the narrative itself that marshals support and agreement among key players and key publics. This could be strategic narrative by epiphany or strategic narrative by the most artful understanding of the needs of contending participants. It might be strategic narratives that are based on religious fervor, in which the emotional ingredients for consensus-building are already present amongst significant participants. Globally diffused ideologies like "democratization" sometimes take over and assume the form of such a "pure" narrative, where the idea of a common desire for more democratic practices is thought to work its own mobilizing magic. After Tunisia, a default narrative arose – a narrative of liberation – that seemed to affect the complex environment of ordinary compromise and political arrangement. The restoration of an Islamic caliph-ate is another charismatic form of conferring legitimacy. Such pure narratives permeate networks and gain strong adherents. These narratives persist, often, in the face of shifting attitudes of political actors and may have greater endurance in the face of the use of force.

One can begin to ask, as a guide to future events, for each of the states involved in and out of the Arab Spring, questions like these: a) Were there settled narratives that came to meet one of the three models?; b) can one describe in what stage of social and political dislocation the strategic narrative was involved?; c) what are the benchmarks for determining whether the strategic narrative in some articulable way "succeeded" or "failed" in its ability to foster change?; and d) was the absence of an effective strategic narrative a telling factor in an arc of continuing conflict? A narrative can, and often does, fail at its strategic purpose. The narrative can carry emotion, build consensus and still falter, as I have indicated earlier in this chapter. Failure, with accom-panying Schadenfreude, is frequent enough that it too must be analyzed. Key actors may, for one reason or another, depart from an explicit or implicit agreement and erode the consensus at critical moments. Governments fall out with their peers and partners and change the nature of their commitments. Disclosures, new information or changing facts on the ground may make the narrative untenable. Some narratives, to continue to have strategic value, may be dependent on representations of the real world that no longer have credibility (one can think, for example, of the loss of legitimacy suffered by the United States upon the revelation that no WMDs were present in Iraq). The publics that narratives were designed to influence may turn out to be particularly resistant. The potential for such disintegration of the strategic narrative was always present in Egypt and in rebel Libya. In Egypt, the international narrative of peaceful transition was and continues to be threatened, if not overwhelmed, by the enduring power of the military, by political errors of the Muslim Brotherhood, by violence against civilians and by the lingering ambitions and sense of entitlement of the old guard. In Libya, to the extent the international community's narrative was built on the premise that there were rebels capable of gaining control, the regaining of ground by loyalists, persistence of a stalemate, errors by NATO forces, and disarray in rebel ranks all posed momentary and recurring problems for the strategic narrative. The narrative may persist in public discourse, but it is drained of its disciplining force.

The process of delegitimation, like that of affirmatively building a new narrative, could have a complementary analysis. Delegitimation of the old (Mubarak in Egypt, Assad in Syria, Gaddafi in Libya, Saleh in Yemen, al-Malaki in Iraq) has elements of consensus and of rewriting or reconceptualizing history and is a critical part of informing a new narrative. Delegitimating may be a prerequisite element of most new narratives, a necessary aspect of creating an alternative. Delegitimating can occur even where the strategy for promoting a replacing narrative falls short. Establishment of a new consensus for government requires a narrative related to but different from one that deposes a leader. And relegitimation, or partial narrative redemption, also occurs. Previous tyrants can become negotiating parties and members of an "axis of evil" may suddenly reemerge as constructive partners in international relations. This, too, occurred to some extent in accounts of Egypt, Syria and Iran.

There is one important caveat in presenting this taxonomy: It can too easily underplay the revolutionary dynamics, the protests, the internal mobilizations, the effective interrelationships between crowds and global audiences. The proper emphasis on the role of the elite over the masses and the role of the "international community" over the politics within each state is hard to assess. Internal protest, in Egypt especially, was almost always a catalyst for the West to pay attention, an attitude characterized, early in the Arab Spring, as a desire to be on "the right side" of history.

The development of strategic narratives concerning Ukraine in 2014 and, as well, in the sudden march of ISIS, add texture to the making of a taxonomy.

Ukraine presented a more standard instance of conflicting approaches: building consensus, shaping international opinion, relating the external forces to those within the state. As events unraveled, there were explicit and implicit agreements, often winks and nods, between the key outside entities, Russia, the United States and the European Union. Dueling strategic narratives of Ukraine may have been written in part by Ukrainians, through elections, through acquiescence, through the expression of secessionist or loyalist tendencies. Yet the main parameters were set by those outside the state's boundaries: Vladamir Putin, Angela Merkel, Barack Obama and others.

One characteristic of these events was new attention to how media aspects of the narrative could be structured. In Ukraine, for example, much notice was given to the alacrity with which Russian-originated and Russian-language programming could be turned to fulfilling a Russian-oriented outcome (including the seizure of Crimea, the rise in secessionist tendencies in the East and the general pressure for a more federalist constitution). Ukraine presented a typical case of regulation of local media pressed into action to reinforce strategic narratives, with Russian channels propagating Russia's view and Ukraine's government seeking to regulate flow. Globally, Russia had in place, in key markets, RT (the former Russia Today), with its subtly built constituency based on persistent critical programming questioning basic U.S. and Western positions, its careful development of an accessible video archive and its aggressive tone. It was a tool that reflected substantial advance investment. RT became a useful tool, for example, in the United States, during a United States-Russia split over UN votes regarding Syria in 2013, and now it became a useful forum for highlighting or fostering contradictions and flaws in the U.S. narrative concerning Ukraine.

When the quickly spreading energy of ISIS sprang forth in mid-2014, it became immediately clear that not only was there a surprising use and success of force, but there was a strong narrative, a differentiated approach to legitimacy and, with that, an accompanying propaganda strategy (with an emphasis on social media). Out of the woodwork came observers in Washington and London and elsewhere who had tracked ISIS's tweeting campaign and the heretofore ignored sophistication of its use of YouTube and Facebook. In the tremor of a moment, borders and boundaries that had been set in 1916 through the Sykes-Picot Agreement were put in question. The foundations of legitimacy were further delegitimated. The narrative of a reestablished caliphate, under substantial Sunni control, became the temporary organizing factor. And as was true in Ukraine (where a changed narrative for Crimea sent shock waves through Latvia, Lithuania and elsewhere) the assertion of new prominence for a particular narrative had predictable knock-on effects.

ISIS's dissolution of old approaches created new opportunities for a reimagined Kurdistan, and a reimagined Kurdistan required a reimagined Iraq. Narratives proliferated and collided with one another.

The Kiev government sought to regulate Russia's influence within Ukraine: one of its initial efforts was to limit cable systems, by prohibiting their carriage of certain Russian-source channels delivered via satellite. A communiqué of the Representative on Freedom of the Media of the Organization of Security and Cooperation in Europe (OSCE) observed that Ukrainian officials "concern[ed] about the influence of Russian television on information security...effectively suspend[ed] or ban[ned] all or some programmes produced in Russia." The communiqué also noted that "de facto authorities in Crimea several weeks ago abruptly and brutally switched off almost all Ukrainian television channels and replaced them with channels originating from the Russian Federation." The Representative, Dunja Mijatovic, recognized that there were circumstances in which restrictions might be appropriate if the right standards and procedures were followed, but "arbitrary attempts to restrict media pluralism must be opposed. At all times, and especially in difficult times, blocking is not the answer; more debate is." As to what might be called central instruments of narrative production, the Representative said, "I see a danger to media pluralism in the very existence of state-owned and state-controlled media as they can be easily used to promulgate state propaganda," which the Representative labeled as "the evil all international media-freedom agreements aspire against." Somewhat boldly and against the course of events, the Representative called on "all participating States to stop the information war, stop the manipulation with media and ...ensure journalists' safety."[22]

Study of these events – in Ukraine and the Middle East – reinforce and enrich the taxonomy of narrative development that differentiates among consensus, power and charisma. Who initiates and creates a consensus and how is related to the overarching accounts of legitimacy that combine with the raw implications of power. As part of strategic narratives, alternate histories become profoundly significant with new priorities assigned to ancient facts. Great reservoirs of emotion and suppressed relationships contribute to new formulations of entitlement. Buried narratives reemerge and have continued to have significantly guiding impact. Ukraine and the Middle East were contrasts as well in the laboratory of conflict resolution narratives. Narratives had quickly to be invented that allowed for Iran to perform a role as ally of Iraq and the United States (and the West). Narratives had to be burnished that

---

[22] "Communique by OSCE Representative on Freedom of the Media on Blocking Television Channels," *osce.org*, March 27, 2014, http://www.osce.org/node/116888

had the potential for re-legitimating Assad. As mentioned, dexterous minds would have the task of considering how a plural Iraq could be reinvented; how to recognize the emerging fact of an even more autonomous Kurdistan; how that contributed to a more autonomous Sunni hegemony that crossed Syria and Iraq; and how that all related to Lebanon and eventually Israel and the two-state solution.

NARRATIVES OF LEGITIMACY AND SOCIAL MEDIA

Consideration of strategic narratives and their impact began in an era of more conventional media, when leaders had greater capacity (or at least considered that they did) to control messages and their diffusion, that is, to shape opinion about a narrative. Even before the Arab Spring, Hoskins, Awan and O'Loughlin had asked whether the rise of digital innovations would mean significant changes in the structure and function of strategic narratives.[23] The Arab Spring reinforced the idea that top-level development of narratives and strategic modes of embedding them are supplemented and altered as new technologies become more widespread; and a broader public and an unstructured, crowd-related set of interests may become more decisive in calculating what narrative of legitimacy should survive. The "CNN effect" was the name given to an earlier systematic challenge to a system of managing the production and distribution of strategic narratives. Steven Livingston, among others, documented ways in which traditional diplomatic interchanges were modified by the capacity of new networks to disrupt old practices.[24]

The Internet, social media, cellphones and satellites all now seem insistently to affect how narratives, especially international strategic narratives, evolve and what constitutes their life cycle. Previously dominant narratives are more vulnerable because of the potential volatility of extraordinarily passionate entrants who use new technologies to alter the rhythm of accepted approaches.[25] In Chapter 5, I focus on the implications of asymmetry in information wars. Social media underscore the instabilities of asymmetry.

---

[23] Andrew Hoskins, Akil Awan and Ben O'Loughlin, *Radicalisation and Media: Connectivity and Terrorism in the New Media Ecology* (London: Taylor and Francis, 2011).

[24] Steven Livingston, *Clarifying the CNN Effect: An Examination of Media Effects According to Type of Military Intervention*. Research Paper R-18 (Cambridge: Joan Shorenstein Center on the Press, Politics and Public Policy, John F. Kennedy School of Government, Harvard University, 1997). Also see Lauren Kogen and Monroe E. Price, "Deflecting the CNN Effect: Public Opinion Polling and Livingstonian Outcomes," *Media, War & Conflict* 4 (2011).

[25] It also allows for the spreading of "memes" of protest. For instance, see the essay by a British protest/radical theory group: "Egypt, Bahrain, London, Spain? Tahrir as Meme," *Deterritorial Support Grouppppp*, May 21, 2011.

Because of social media, the received wisdom is subject to more immediate challenge. Deviations from accuracy – real or imagined – are confronted by crowd-sourced material and citizen journalists, but control over stories and their diffusion is diminished as well. Because of social media, secret or discreet agreements to strategic narratives are more likely to be uncovered and publicized. New and competing narratives – ones that represent a more compelling myth, a more impressive group of key players or a different concatenation of power – can be produced and rendered viral instantly. The half-life of a reigning narrative may become shorter and shorter. An international narrative that is out of sync with facts on the ground is always susceptible to challenge. But the increased penetration and use of social media makes this lack of synchronicity particularly salient.

In understanding the process of interaction between social media and strategic narratives, one could posit several subcategories: one in which the local, socially-mediated reality is congruent with the strategic narrative being propounded internationally (Tahrir Square) or one in which the local reality is strongly inconsistent with its reigning international counterpart (occasional reflections on the reality of Libyan rebel forces). One can differentiate circumstances where those propounding the narrative take substantial control of how it is propagated. Social media shifts power, speeds mobilization, decentralizes leadership, unifies across class – or at least has this potential. From the perspective of security, this combination of strategic communication from abroad and social media within can be particularly toxic. Another related variable is whether the social media platforms are highly controlled.

There is also social media's relationship with other forms of mass communication, which still have undoubted influence. Sami Ben Gharbia, the observer and participant in the Tunisian revolution, put forward a loop or progression analysis.[26] He observed a three-part model that "treats social media as part of a . . . complex ecosystem," involving Facebook as a publishing platform, multiple curation platforms (Nawaat, Global Voices, Twitter, Posterous), and eventually broadcast platforms (Al Jazeera and France24 among others). Sites like Nawaat identified content posted on Facebook, tagged and categorized it and made it accessible to other media organizations, particularly Al Jazeera. Then the loop or interaction began. "Once content made it onto Al Jazeera, it began filtering back into Tunisia, letting Tunisians who weren't looking for content online understand what was unfolding." Al Jazeera thus "became an extension of the internet, publishing user-generated

---

[26] See the commentary on Ben Gharbia's arguments in Ethan Zuckerman, "Civic Disobedience and the Arab Spring," . . . *My Heart's in Accra*, May 6, 2011.

content and using it to educate Tunisian citizens about what was going on in their own country, and eventually the whole region." This process created an information cascade that was instrumental in hastening or deepening the revolution. Ben Gharbia's analysis can lead to a more complex understanding of the dynamics of the situation, in which social media interacted with old forms of media and politics to synthesize new ones rather than simply usurping what went before. In Bahrain, where social media use is high, the blogosphere reflected the intense division of perspectives on how to characterize events – a division that was partly spontaneous, and accounts of that division then seeped into the mainstream international media.[27] In the early days of the Syrian protests, when there were efforts to seal what was occurring from foreign reporting, it was social media risk-takers who provided rare insight into the events, with substantial influence on what perceptions appeared at the transnational level.[28]

Social media illustrate how actors attended to at least two audiences as they sought to embed a narrative. The world was fixated on the celebration of the emerging narrative in Tahrir Square or in the protests in Syria or Bahrain or Yemen. But for strategic narratives of international importance, there is also a home audience of the major powers where populations are called on to support, finance and enforce the playing out of a world view. A narrative for Libya and Egypt that was determined in international capitals had to resonate with the political desires of the populations of the UK, the United States or France as well as in Tahrir or Tripoli. Political leaders had to persuade their constituents and shape an account that brought them gently into the frame. What seemed to be emerging in Iraq and Syria in 2014 was the search for a strategic narrative that would control the advance of insurgent entities like ISIS itself shaped a narrative that, combined with force, had dramatic reach and extraordinary effect. And its use of social media became a subject for significant diagnostic analysis.

THE COMPLEXITY OF RELIANCE ON STRATEGIC NARRATIVES

There are many hazards in the invocation of "strategic narratives" in the account of international policy decisions, even in the narrower framework of the episodes I have discussed. There is a fragility. Where they exist, strategic narratives are contingent, contingent on alliances, on continued force, on the

---

[27] See, for example, Mona Kareem, "Bahrain: Liliane Khalil, Another Blog Hoax or Propaganda?" *Global Voices*, August 5, 2011.

[28] Hugh Macleod and Correspondent, "Syria's Young Cyber Activists Keep Protests in View," *Guardian*, April 15, 2011.

fickle quality of beliefs. It is difficult to evaluate what disciplining power can be attributed to the narrative itself as compared to the power structures that underlie it. And it is difficult to pinpoint how precisely strategic narratives affect public opinion or are affected by it, both in the target society and at home. The important role of militaries in deciding the outcome of most of the events in the Arab Spring and beyond is indicative of the potential for confusion – the interaction between the word and the bullet is not always easy to classify. It will certainly be difficult to assign each struggle over narrative to the categories I have suggested (consensus-based, power-based or charismatic), how to evaluate the success or failure of a strategic narrative, and whether, more existentially, a strategic narrative (one that guides) turns into a viable narrative of legitimacy. Each instance provides an example, at least at the time of writing, of the turmoil in understanding the competition for narratives, the surprises in who produces those that are effective and that seize and hold the mantle of legitimacy. In the early days of the Syrian conflict, seemingly then a revolt or civil war, the United States could not establish a persuasive and effective strategic narrative alone; no strategic narrative would bind Assad so long as Russia and China were not part of its formation either in ratifying it or not opposing it. At times, as "legitimacy" seeped from the Assad regime, splintering of the country seemed more and more likely. Then, the interventions of Hezbollah, the rise of the Islamic State (ISIS) and the consequent involvement of Iran led to the rush for new and dramatically altered accounts. As groups sought to seize power in different sections of Syria and Iraq, the possibility of a radically different narrative laid the basis for a substantially different strategic consensus.

Illustrations beyond the Arab Spring and its sequelae are, as I have tried to show, legion and show these hazards as well. Take the strategic narrative that accompanied the decision to go to war in Iraq in 2003 that had the presence in Iraq of weapons of mass destruction as a key element.[29] The narrative was strategic because it bound sufficient international players for key moments in time. It was effective because the key players actually performed, the role for the time needed for the narrative purpose to be achieved. It had elements of all three categories I have described above: agreement, exercise of power and a sufficiently compelling story to adequately enlist and carry public opinion. That the narrative was not based on actual facts ironically illustrates the significance of the story independent of reality. The years of seeking a "solution" to the Middle East peace process constitute efforts at developing a

[29] Amelia Arsenault and Manuel Castells, "Conquering the Minds, Conquering Iraq: The Social Production of Misinformation in the United States – A Case Study," *Information, Communication & Society* 9, no. 3 (2006).

strategic narrative but also illustrate the limits of such efforts. The Oslo Accords, the Camp David Agreements and any number of "roadmaps" all were preceded by or reflect narratives that might or might not animate formally and explicitly binding documents. Here, the strategic narratives included "land for peace" and movement toward a two-state solution. They provided a grand picture in which the actors would enact certain set roles on a determined trajectory. Examining these efforts against the models, however, it is evident that the strategic narrative was fragile, as key parties withdrew or took actions inconsistent with it. Time and again, as the power basis for the agreement collapsed, the narrative proved not sufficiently compelling to keep all parties at the table. Iran is a related and distinctive case. The election of Hassan Rouhani as president of Iran suggested that a dramatically new narrative might be possible and that a strategic approach that could bind significant parties to take constructive action was possible as well.

In later chapters, I examine other aspects of the struggle over narratives. A state may seek to discriminate between efforts to influence the strategic narratives that arise from within the community and efforts to influence from outside. The preoccupation of pre-Rouhani Iran, discussed in Chapter 7, that it has been subject to a Soft War is an example, although one from an already highly constrained speech environment. Authoritarian states (for example, North Korea and, at least until recently, Myanmar) have sought to entirely close their information space in order to shut down entities perceived as providing alternate narratives of their legitimacy.

Whether it is the clash of civilizations, the loss of "values," or the need to protect jobs or economies, competition for national narratives of legitimacy – for good and for ill – will persist. Traditional formulae for managing what I call the "bubble of identity" for a particular state, the outcome of a regulated market for loyalties, have become frayed as states become more anxious about these narratives and how they affect power. States are preoccupied both with what they can do to establish and enforce a narrative for themselves and with developing strategic narratives that control other actors.[30] Even this basic principle frays as borders are weakened and non-state actors become more salient. A foundational aspect of a society with a robust free expression tradition is that the state's hold on its identity as a community is subtly within its shaping grasp. Yet in a world with a global flow of images, states and other

---

[30] Entman uses the term mediated public diplomacy to characterize the use of mass communications and the internet "to increase support of a country's specific foreign policies among audiences beyond the country's borders." Robert M. Entman, "Theorizing mediated public Diplomacy: The U.S. Case," *International Journal of Press/Politics* 13, no.2, (2008): 88.

major actors see all narratives of identity and legitimacy as a product of mutual interactions, more tenuous and more constantly in play.

Strategic narratives are not just the product of vast changes in the global information environment; they can be, but are not necessarily, the products of the transnational efforts of one state to alter the media space of another. They are not dependent on, though they may be affected by, the rise of social media in a particular context. A strategic narrative can be destabilizing as well as stabilizing, reshaping as well as unifying. The construction of the narrative can and does become a matter of great state interest. Control of information by elites has had overwhelming significance in shaping these narratives. Yet, the crowds in Tahrir Square in Egypt, and those in Yemen and Syria, surely had a say in the strategic narrative that would arise from multilateral negotiations. They became a Fifth Estate – asserting their own authority and seeking to become at least an equal in terms of bargaining over the way the future would be defined. If narratives have this power, then the continuing process of producing them becomes a matter of deep transnational concern and a subject for intense scrutiny.

4

Strategies of the Diagnostic

One characteristic – or, perhaps, illusion – of the new strategic communication is its homage to analytics. The capacity to think through the contours of a local context and the possible impact of various ways to deploy the media have been deepened in recent years. There has been a revolution in the ability to collect and analyze vast amounts of data points, often arising from collecting information on millions of social media interactions and applications of such technologies as mobile phones. In this chapter, however, I focus on modes of understanding based on more traditional qualitative techniques, interviews, focus groups and informal surveys, often ethnographic in temperament. All of these together can be captured in a concept that might be called a diagnostic of information ecologies.[1] This approach seeks to overcome predispositions, assumptions, even ideologies – all of which may limit analysis and curb appreciation of empirical observations. A diagnostic seeks to trace how particular ideas leak into a society and, over time or suddenly, change public opinion and local and regional loyalties. As Nicole Stremlau, who has helped shape the concept, puts it in her definition:

> A diagnostic refers to a particular set of questions that seek to shift discussion from normative precepts about communication and governance to local understanding and practices of communication and governance. At its core, a diagnostic offers a framework for analysing voice and expression in a society, and how it is actually regulated, negotiated and influenced, rather than suggesting how it *should* be regulated according to normative ideals. In essence, this is a bottom-up, or grassroots, analysis that focuses on indigenous structures, and the interactions or fusions with more 'official' government

---

[1] See Nicole Stremlau, "Towards a Diagnostic Approach to Media in Fragile States: Examples from the Somali Territories," *Media, War and Conflict* 6, no. 3 (2013) and Nicole Stremlau, "Hostages of Peace: The Politics of Radio Liberalization in Somaliland," *Journal of Eastern African Studies* 7, no. 2 (2013).

structures. The basic focus is how people on the ground actually experience and participate in this complicated relationship between communication and governance.[2]

Use of this approach is especially important in fragile societies. It is in such contexts that the ordinary capacity of the state to gain and maintain authority over information that flows within its borders is attenuated; in these states, the very absence of power implies a theater of speech outside the framework of Western ideas of generation and regulation of discourse. Here the prevailing theories of the "marketplace of ideas" and flows of information "regardless of frontiers" are most vulnerable and, in some sense, devoid of their traditional meanings. These are states that are in the process of defining themselves or being redefined. They are often the targets of the communications strategies that are featured outline throughout this book. Of particular relevance are those diagnostic efforts related to media assistance, media development or media intervention – for example, assessing the potential impact of the introduction of independently owned commercial radio or community broadcasting outlets on democratization efforts in a society, or research by international broadcasters to understand the structure of media and the flow of information in a target society.

These states are often laboratories for the unusual combination of intense use of traditional modes of communication (person-to-person, hierarchical tribe or group-based modes), intense use of social media (especially with diasporas) and the heavy influence of strategic communicators (external efforts of information coupled with power). It is precisely in these societies that the impact of external voices and the eruption of new technologies (mobile, social media) can be pivotal for a state's future. This chapter focuses on approaches to analyzing information flows in these more fragile societies, which function on premises not often reflected in the long-standing repertoires of marketing. But the concept of a diagnostic applies to all communications and media interventions.

A diagnostic, in these circumstances, often begins with an understanding of the local or vernacular politics, arrangements that are beyond the central state and, in much of Africa, the Middle East and parts of Asia, present complicated issues of state-building and stability. Diagnostics of such societies have often relied, although decreasingly so, on accepted templates, measures based on factors, some more objective, such as the number of radio and television stations, some more difficult to fashion, such as hallmarks of "independence" or freedom from government regulation. Templates may overlook

[2] Stremlau, "Towards a Diagnostic Approach to Media," 280.

the significance of varying forms of governance and theories of speech and society.[3] These analyses should be rooted in political, socioeconomic and specifically media-related examination of a country rather than the advancement of a particular model of media development. Critiques that media development approaches are overly normative, ideological and have too standardized an approach have had some effect, as has the maturing of the sector and the increased sophistication of funders. At least as a goal, research into diagnostic and evaluative techniques should be designed to ensure that entities are responding to a cognizable reality and that interventions are research-driven, and to the extent possible, evidence-based.

Existing communications mechanisms within the society are often informal, and the structure of connections among individuals and within communities may be virtually unknown to many outside it. Conflict – violence and war – render communication subject to unexpected linkages or to dangers hardly anticipated by the sender. Histories and memories may cast arcs of meaning that have enduring implications and throw unwitting messages into disarray. This itself renders a diagnostic complex. In addition, strategic communicators have informational objectives that are difficult to articulate and raise complicated questions of quantification and evaluation. Assessing whether a strategic communication even reached its target audience and how it was received can often remain a mystery to the communicators.

The diagnostic provides a framework of analysis that helps present the operation, impact and influence of communication networks within a society.[4] The term "diagnostic" purposefully invokes a medical model. As Basurto and Ostrom put it, a diagnostic approach should be a way of avoiding two traps: "(1) deriving and recommending 'panaceas' or (2) asserting 'my case is unique.'"[5] By self-consciously building diagnostic theory, an analyst can help unpack and understand the complex interrelationship among multiple factors, looking for commonalities and differences across studies. At the same time, the diagnostic is a means of questioning accepted bromides – principles or "solutions" that are thought to be applicable in all contexts. It is also a way of overcoming the concern that it might be impossible to understand all of the cumulative and incidental factors that affect the consequence of an additional informational input.

---

[3] James Putzel and Joost van der Zwan, *Why Templates for Media Development Do Not Work in Crisis States: Defining and Understanding Media Development Strategies in Post-War and Crisis States* (London: LSE Research Online, 2006).

[4] Karl W. Deutsch, *The Nerves of Government: Models of Political Communication and Control* (London: Free Press of Glencoe, 1963).

[5] Xavier Basurto and Elinor Ostrom, "Beyond the Tragedy of the Commons," *Economia delle fonti di energia e dell'ambiente* 52, no. 1 (2009).

The diagnostic can help decision-makers understand the position of a state athwart the flows of information within its borders and its relationship to outside forces. It is, of course, theoretically available to all competitors in a market for allegiances in the effort to shape identities and to contribute to strategic narratives. Diagnostics usually are created at the direction of one strategic communicator; those who write them should, however, be sufficiently independent that meeting the desires or expectations of the commissioner does not control the analysis. Most attention has been paid to the diagnostic efforts of the great commercial players – the for-profit broadcasting networks, corporate social media entities, producers of brands and the consumerist revolution[6] – or those seeking to understand how electorates behave in modern democracies. These entities are masters of the diagnostic. They have had the incentive, the skills and the resources to dissect particular markets and make recommendations for sellers of products and candidates who seek to launch within them. They are the pioneers of marketing; they have extended their expertise as new technologies proliferate and more and more of the world's population falls within a modern communications network. This is not to say that these analysts are always successful or are sufficiently sensitive to market factors, but they have created a science of understanding.

The emphasis here is on giving more attention to this art form in more fragile political and social contexts: fragmented, strained, economically pressed and stability-deprived states that present fundamental questions of governance and quality of life. If one of the major needs is to understand the mode by which information affects loyalty, citizenship, identity, culture, language and aspects of economic development, then a state's information ecology is a key determinant of state strength. In particular, the information ecology in a fragile state offers an index of the competing entities, internal and external, for defining the future of the area. Ultimately significant – and often missing in analysis – is determining the relationship of the fragile state and its media to larger institutions of control. What are the implications of the particular institutional setting of the country that is subject to the diagnostic? Are there supervening powers, like the Office of the High Representative in Bosnia-Herzegovina, an active set of international NGOs or vigorous efforts among one or competing religious entities? What is the status of those seeking to radically change the political system as compared to those seeking change

---

[6] These kinds of "diagnostics" would include analytics that produce targeted advertising and audience research more broadly in the commercial sector. Joseph Turow, *Breaking Up America: Advertisers and the New Media World* (Chicago: University of Chicago Press, 1997).

in leadership? The condition of these supranational institutions in a given society must impact a diagnostic approach.

The U.S. military has tried to integrate the approaches of the commercial sector in its field analyses, as demonstrated by a somewhat exuberant RAND Corporation Report for the Joint Armed Forces Command. Conveniently, the report is called "*Enlisting Madison Avenue: The Marketing Approach to Earning Popular Support in Theaters of Operation*."[7] The report sought to apply lessons from business marketing for "improving U.S. military efforts to shape . . . audience attitudes and behaviors." It argued that "U.S. forces should continue anticipatory . . . activities that influence the attitudes and behaviors of indigenous populations in areas in which the United States is not presently involved (training indigenous security forces, engaging in civil affairs activities, cultivating relationships with indigenous influencers, collecting cultural intelligence and providing humanitarian assistance)."[8] Ultimately, the report lists lessons that apply marketing principles to "shaping," shaping being the quasi-euphemism for altering attitudes and creating a better environment for future U.S. action. Shaping is also "U.S. military parlance for battlefield operations designed to constrain adversary force options or increase friendly force options."[9]

These lessons include:

- "*Know the target audience through segmentation and targeting*. The U.S. military should adopt the business strategy of segmentation and targeting, wherein the military partitions the indigenous population into groups based on the individuals' levels of anticipated support for coalition presence and operations."

- "*Develop meaningful and salient end states*. Positioning is a business tool used to create product identities that are meaningful and salient in the consumer marketplace. The essence of positioning is the promise a brand makes regarding what consumers will achieve by using the brand. Positioning may hold value for U.S. efforts to craft end states for indigenous audiences."

- "*Understand key branding concepts*. While the term *brand* often refers to a product name (e.g., Lexus is a brand name), it is more importantly construed as a collection of perceptions in the minds of consumers (e.g., Lexus may mean different things to different people: expensive,

---

[7] Todd Helmus, Christopher Paul and Russell W. Glenn, *Enlisting Madison Avenue: The Marketing Approach to Earning Popular Support in Theaters of Operation* (Santa Monica, CA: RAND, 2007).

[8] Ibid., xix.

[9] Ibid., xiii.

luxury, Japanese, and so on). Every interaction influences user perceptions of a product or service."

- *"Synchronize the U.S. operational portfolio.* The business practice of strategically synchronizing brand actions so that they convey a single and clear message to target audiences affords another valuable lesson. If the U.S. military opts for a new brand identity, it should seek to synchronize all its actions and messages around that identity. All actions in a theater of operations should be designed to serve shaping needs."
- *"Achieve civilian satisfaction: Manage and meet expectations.* Customer satisfaction refers to the level of fulfillment consumers experience after using a product or service. Civilians who live in areas where U.S. and coalition forces are conducting stability operations have a choice to make in terms of which side they support (or refuse to support). The degree to which they are satisfied with the various aspects of force presence will be a critical determinant in their decisionmaking."
- *"Listen to the voice of the civilian: Make informed decisions.* The most successful business endeavors are those that are premised on meeting customer needs and desires. Products that are thought to be superior from a business standpoint but fail to meet customer needs court failure."
- *"Apply discipline and focus to communication campaigns.* Social marketing is the application of well-grounded commercial marketing techniques to influence noncommercial behavioral change in a target audience. Social marketing campaigns have previously sought to motivate audiences to quit smoking, reduce littering, give blood, and recycle paper. Social marketing practices provide a well-grounded template for U.S. military efforts to motivate specific behaviors."[10]

This set of questions is more of an introduction – a setting of a tone of inquiry. The quality of methodology and the level of commitment, among other things, determine what kind of diagnostic is being undertaken. Here, the objective is gaining popular support in theaters of operation.

Entities committed to shaping political understandings and international attitudes abroad are obvious actors in media interventions that have diagnostic requirements but are not always diagnostic-based. International broadcasters such as Deutsche Welle (in Germany), the BBC World Service (in the UK), the Broadcasting Board of Governors (in the United States) and a host of their fellows seek to develop their own critical capacity to comprehend target markets, designing extensive research efforts to do so. Different political cultures determine how "scientific" these diagnostics can be. One well-known example

[10] Ibid., 171–175.

that illustrates the span of possibilities was the effort by the U.S. Broadcasting Board of Governors (BBG) after 2001 to determine how to use radio to reach post-adolescent Arab youth in the cities of the Middle East. The stated objective was to impart to this target audience a greater appreciation for the values and purposes of the United States. The phrase that became famous was asking what intervention "moved the needle." In this effort, the BBG engaged in media mapping to gain an understanding of the political economy of radio stations that existed in important areas and to gain an understanding of their reach among the target group. Through audience research and public opinion polling, the BBG attempted to understand how effective their policy was in operation and, if possible, whether the program not only reached the audience, but also affected the audience positively in terms of shifting attitudes.

In this given challenge, the Broadcasting Board of Governors radically shifted its approach to reaching the desired demographic. In 2002, the BBG introduced Radio Sawa, with a format very different from that in Voice of America's existing repertoire. The emphasis moved from news and information to music and, unusually, a mix of music from the West and the Middle East, with the first five minutes of each half hour, at the outset, reserved for news and information. Interestingly, the decision was largely a result of individual Board expertise gained in assessing U.S. urban commercial media markets rather than purely a product of conditions in Cairo. It was, in a sense, a transposed analytic, taking experiences from operating in Detroit or New York or Los Angeles and applying them in the Middle East. Turning to highly commercialized and monetized urban markets as a lens through which to perceive delivery of a service resulted in shifts in understanding the culture of reception, tracking how the target audience received information generally.

The best strategic communicators strain to perfect their diagnostic techniques, moving toward more interdisciplinary and scientific, data-driven inquiries. Some entities, like BBC Media Action – an outgrowth of the old BBC World Service Trust – rearticulate their methodology as a complement to the traditional focus on building or nourishing plural media "institutions" with an emphasis on "the needs of audiences," with that encompassing term here designed by them to reflect attention to achievement of the UN's Millennium Development Goals.[11] By finding specific objectives in this way – that is,

---

[11]   See, for example, the blog post by James Deane, BBC Media Action's director of policy and Learning, "What would a post-2015 development goal on free media mean?" *BBC Media Action blog*, June 5, 2013. For an example of how an association of media development sees these issues of definition, see Global Forum for Media Development, "2013–2015 Work Plan: Strengthening Independent Media Through the Global Forum for Media Development."

toward specific markers – there is an important impact on both the shaping of a diagnostic and a later evaluation of performance.

One could frame a diagnostic in terms of the "market for loyalties" analysis I outlined in Chapter 1. What is the existing structure of such a market in the zone marked for impact? Who are the players seeking to maintain the status quo and who are trying to change it? What are the technologies of entry? What apertures are creatively available to change the pattern of allegiances? How can a diagnostic help break the barrier of oft-formulaic answers to complex research questions? Is hunch and intuition a necessary additive to research? And, of course, the ever-more important question: what is the relationship of social media use to the habits of broadcast reception and other patterns of information consumption?

In this chapter, I take two case studies and look at them for the potential of a diagnostic analysis. These are insights into struggles – struggles to define a methodology and an approach. Each has limitations, set by context, by contract, by funding, by reservoir of skill. The first is a pioneering examination of information ecologies in Somaliland by Nicole Stremlau and Iginio Gagliardone, specifically designed to articulate, apply and explore the idea of a diagnostic and demonstrate its capacity and limitations. The second involves a systematic study of radio and television broadcasting in Afghanistan.

AN INFORMATION ECOLOGY FOR SOMALILAND: A PIONEERING APPROACH

In 2010, Stremlau and Gagliardone directed and published, under the auspices of Oxford University's Programme in Comparative Media Law and Policy, the "Somaliland Communication Flows Research Report."[12] This document was designed as a way of rethinking the role of media and communications systems in the wake of violent conflict and subsequent efforts at peacebuilding. The report focused on Somaliland, the relatively stable secessionist state that was formerly – and is still formally – part of Somalia. The report struggled with a methodology for engaging in a study of information ecologies in fragile societies. It is an illustration of the strategic step of understanding context, particularly structural context, as a precedent for action.[13]

---

[12] "Somaliland Communication Flows Research Report," PCMLP and Stanhope Centre. Report to the UK's Foreign and Commonwealth Office (FCO). On file with the author.

[13] Much of the text of this section is adapted from the Somaliland report, buttressed by conversations with its authors.

Describing an "Information Diagnostic"

Their "information diagnostic" sought to understand why media, broadly defined, developed as they did and to understand their current role. A new research approach was needed, the authors contended, to supplement the dominant approaches to studying media interventions; in particular, a new approach should explicitly address the role of ideologies behind the interventions. These media interventions cover the range of steps taken by media development agencies: funding broadcast outlets, providing journalist training, engaging in strategic messaging. But in most discussions, these interventions have been "viewed through a normative lens where only general questions about the politics, legal and economic environment are asked."[14] And the goal was often loaded, for example, querying "why the media may be falling short of the role it plays in many western democracies – as a watchdog and check on the government – or to the question of how free or unfree the media is."[15] Stremlau and Gagliardone sought an analysis that, rather than "focusing on how to advance media freedoms, or how to manage the voices that counteract freedom," would "pay attention to how the local media functions, including whether journalists, "free" or not, write against what is perceived to be the patriotic grain, build trust between particular actors, serve as a forum for elite negotiation, mediate competing ideas of justice, and strengthen or weaken other group approaches to violence and conflict resolution."[16] They deemed their diagnostic as testing how broadcasting efforts (in Somaliland, for example) relate to "competing versions of history . . . political and ethnic identities . . . [and function as] effective mediators."[17] Instead of focusing on measurement against a universal template, their emphasis was on how a media intervention contributes to governance, how it impacts divisions in society, what relation it has to longer-term trends in the state's structure.

Understanding efforts to shape opinions and influence the public would mean enlarging the definition of "media" far beyond press and broadcasting. In Stremlau and Gagliardone's view, understanding what constitutes the communications system as a whole (and radio or broadcasting within it) is a necessary aspect of a diagnostic. For example, in relevant societies, song, sermon, poetry and other mechanisms are too often ignored in analyzing the modes through which attitudes toward conflict and reconciliation are forged. In the authors' reading of Somaliland's unusual media structure, poets loom

---

[14] "Somaliland Communication Flows Research Report," 6.
[15] Ibid.
[16] Ibid.
[17] Ibid., 7.

large because of the respect they command, the journalistic function they perform and the dispute resolution role that they play. Western studies typically focus on NGOs and the donor community's efforts in shaping and pushing for the building of a more ideal civil society, but with insufficient attention to the prisms through which such efforts are driven. A more complete diagnostic looks at the areas of strength in the interpersonal, at the relationship of leading voices to very local conversations, at ancient forms of persuasion. It not only looks forward to new technologies, but also backward to old, lingering technologies, examining how the culture has shifted from one major approach of communication to another. Different demographics or regions within a society may experience these shifts to varying degrees, if at all.

The diaspora is often politically significant in fragile states, where the media ecology is often deeply impacted by these distant yet powerful voices and structures, and the diagnostic must note how messages produced by them penetrate the local conversation. It is important to understand not only how each media outlet operates, which groups or parties it represents and how it singularly influences specific publics, but also how it serves as a vehicle for the dissemination of messages originating from a variety of sources and acts as a node in a wider media network. Figures in the Somaliland diaspora frequently operate as gatekeepers of information, receiving news directly from Somaliland, often by phone, and sharing it in their close network of family and friends. Similarly, it is common for eminent diaspora members to have direct access to newspapers and to be able to have their views published at home in Somaliland when they seek actively to contribute to the political debate.

A diagnostic, particularly of a fragile society, must be insightful about the deep and enduring complexities of local history, the factors that lead to fragility or that undermine stability. In the case of Somaliland, the extraordinary historic event was its secession from Somalia after a civil war and its difficult and tenuous hold on an independent future. The report argues that Somaliland has "a culture of freedom of expression" deeply rooted in Somaliland's political history and practice. A country essentially of nomads with an egalitarian, pastoralist, decentralized approach to politics, Stremlau and Gagliardone suggest, provides a foundation for a society generally opposed to authority. Their diagnostic emphasizes how in Somaliland this underlying political and communicative culture created a somewhat atypical media system. For example, "news is often conveyed through poems that are memorized and transmitted orally. . . . Somali did not have an official written alphabet until 1972 and poems were the most important means of communication – both social and political. The free flow of information, uncensored but truthful, is particularly prized."[18] One final complicating factor in Somaliland is that the international community, through the United Nations, has supported a transitional federal government of Somalia – sometimes with the implicit assumption that all the parts of Somalia be included in a federated whole, including Somaliland. That major potential structural intervention would have significant implications, of course, for media organization and sense of purpose.

Questioning what is almost a universal element of the Western template for progress toward a free media, one of the report's key areas for inquiry was whether the existence of media pluralism, achieved through multiple radio outlets, would be suitable for Somaliland. Stremlau and Gagliardone sought to determine the extent to which the population favored multiple radio outlets with a wider span of voices and more segmented reflection of opinion. The study's findings suggested a belief that carelessly competing radio services could further divide society. In interviews, respondents regularly referred to how radios have been used in South Somalia. "Stations there have operated as mouthpieces of competing warlords, clans, and religious factions."[19] As a consequence, there was noticeable resistance toward a more diverse media environment. One interviewee stated:

> You hardly see a radio which is operating impartially, but it is each and every radio station or newsletter ... based on individual and clan interests, which is really contributing to the current problems in south Somalia, so really the Somalia media is in such a chaotic manner, no editing, no ethical journalists.[20]

Another respondent noted:

> I'm worried [about what] might happen in Somaliland because ... you have young journalists who are morally, ethically ... still [lacking many things]. Even the facilities they are using, they don't have someone [that regularly pays them]. They get their priorities from who pays them. Also clans influence them. That we cannot underestimate. We have to understand the present situation because you say America has got freedom of expression, Europe has got it, Asia. ... Okay fine but we are not at the same level economically, politically, socially, militarily. I mean you name it. Don't compare the two countries.[21]

[18] Ibid., 89.
[19] Ibid., 87.
[20] Ibid.
[21] Ibid.

Some respondents expressed concern that the government already had limited control of state functions and that private radios might challenge the little power they had.

> I support that there should be one single radio station in the country because radio is good for state control. If the radio comes to be controlled by individuals there may be contradictions . . . that can create a lack of stability and make harm to the nation.
>
> I would like to see one radio station in Somaliland because all of the people they would have to listen to this one radio station. . . . If they listen to one radio, they take one idea about events and the news of the country.[22]
>
> In Somaliland, the press, the media contributes to reconciliation and state and nation building. But in Somalia all these are missing because they are only talking about individual interests. So if I want to listen to some radios in Mogadishu, where you get millions of radio stations, they are only talking about individual interests, so there is a lack of peacebuilding, lack of control.[23]

Similarly, a system of numerous stations might deepen clan loyalty and exacerbate dangers to the political and economic systems. As one person noted, there has been a:

> problem of tribal media in Somalia. Every tribe will have a station . . . every clan and then they talk to every clan and maybe this will cause problems in the stability of the country. That's why Somaliland is refusing to have more radio stations.[24]

Two other respondents stated:

> I think my idea is that there should be one [broadcaster] since the people are not mature enough to have their own radio. We are still clan based so because of this one clan makes a radio, the other will have to do the same. . . . So I say one is enough and enough.
>
> Because you know we are clans so if the government opens a private radio station every clan will get its own so that would be a problem. So I think the best choice is to have a single radio station in the country. I mean too many cooks spoil the soup.[25]

The Stremlau-Gagliardone report concluded with recommendations for potential action after a public consultation and education campaign. One recommendation addressed the importance of public discourse concerning

[22] Ibid., 87–88.
[23] Ibid., 88.
[24] Ibid., 86.
[25] Ibid.

religious extremism. The authors argued that the advantages of radio challenging religious extremism were likely to be greater than the threat of extremists
capturing the airwaves. The government, the authors found, would be in a
stronger position if it could gradually and incrementally regulate radios.
Expansion should take place in an envelope of understanding of the internal
dynamics in Somaliland, rather than in reference to an abstract framework.

AFGHANISTAN AND THE ALTAI REPORTS

An elaborate contrast to the Somaliland evaluation is found in studies of
media and strategic communication in Afghanistan. In 2001, the United
States government committed itself to establishing a strong central government in Kabul as a way out of conflict, toward stability and protection from
"extremist" influences that could ultimately be threatening to the United
States. Since that time, primarily through USAID, it has supported a "free
and independent" media sector as a potential pillar of an Afghan society that
reflects these values and interests. In terms of the thesis of this book, it could
be said that the United States had, as a strategic goal, the reinforcement of a
media system that would provide the Afghan government with greater ownership of and influence over its own information space. This would be done,
however, in a manner consistent with U.S. traditions of media development
and U.S. free expression values. The ultimate diagnostic (or evaluative) questions could be quite complex: would furthering the kind of media system that
emphasized free and independent media, in the applied U.S. definition,
actually achieve the goal of greater influence for the central government
over the information space, and would doing so create greater support from
the people of Afghanistan for the government?

To have a better understanding of what had occurred, in part because of its
sizable investments in developing the media sector, Internews, a prime NGO
entity charged by USAID with fulfilling the general project, commissioned
Altai Consulting, starting in 2004, to conduct a comprehensive media evaluation of the republic. Altai would examine the impact of the Afghan media on
opinions and behaviors three years into the country's reconstruction.[26] The
evaluation found, among other things, that Afghans were "intensive media
users" who trusted the media, especially as a source of education and public
information. These were largely usage conclusions about patterns of listening,
and primarily focused on industry standards such as coverage, demographics

---

[26] Altai Consulting, *Afghan Media – Three Years After*, March 2005, http://www.altaiconsulting.
com/docs/media/2005/II-2.Internews_Assessment.pdf.

and trust. The report was not generally or even necessarily about the state-building and political implications of media. In its exploration of media usage, the study did not explore whether media usage and particular embodiments empowered individuals or whether the empowerment of individuals would lead to greater support for an Afghan center, and the question of how Afghans gain information or form public attitudes was only touched on indirectly. As a result, the findings were helpful, but not central, in understanding how competitors for control in the Afghan media space, including the Taliban, neighboring countries, Iran and Pakistan, and many other influences, worked. And as to the specific role of the U.S. media assistance strategy, it would be difficult to disaggregate, in a complex media scene, the contribution of USAID-assisted media or even the strategy of establishing "free and independent media."

Because of rapid changes from 2005 to 2010 and because of the gaps in the original study, USAID sought a subsequent report, more intensely incorporating the approach of a diagnostic, a report that was completed and published in 2010.[27] The commissioning document asked to "assess the current state of the Afghan media," with a central focus on "drivers of opinions and behavior" in the country, and what pockets of opportunity for investment this environment presented.[28] This language demonstrates how the 2010 report was designed to provide international donors and implementers with sufficient information to make decisions in the media assistance field in the future.

The structure of the second study had characteristics that enhanced the report's useful diagnostic aspects. The overall Synthesis Report was based upon and built on a cluster of local district reports, which sought more intimate knowledge about patterns of gathering information by various Afghan audiences – for example, some district reports studied areas where there was little or no radio service. Much more work was done on the informal ways in which information was obtained, comparing, for instance, Taliban modes of distributing information with those of a modern, Western-designed media system. District studies also contrasted reactions among Afghans who had been refugees abroad with those who stayed, or commented on responses

---

[27] Altai Consulting, *Afghan Media in 2010: Synthesis Report*, October 13, 2010.

[28] Ibid., 8. A large-scale research project was planned and conducted from March to August 2010. "This research included a deep probe into the media sector and the public's behaviors and expectations." The report stated that the methodology used to achieve this included a combination of: literature review; direct observations; key informant interviews with the most relevant actors involved in the media sector; 6,648 close-ended interviews in more than 900 towns and villages of 106 districts, covering all thirty-four provinces of the country; an audience survey on more than 1,500 individuals run daily for a week; about 200 qualitative, open-ended interviews; and ten community case studies.

to Taliban influences. There was an effort to encompass "military radios" in the overall analysis, looking in part at the diverse ways USAID and the Defense Department used such assets to affect Afghan media space. "Media mapping," a baseline of what media functioned in Afghanistan, was the most attainable objective, but it was only a threshold for approaching the questions that were significant to the international donors and others for whom the study was designed.

The 2010 study should be read against a general USAID and Internews effort to create the "free and independent media sector" that is the foundation of much U.S. media assistance. That goal had implications for structuring a media intervention and evaluating its results; "free and independent" often emphasizes private ownership and commercial or similar funding. It would prove difficult to sufficiently establish that one system of media assistance was more effective than another, that the elaborate and creative network established by Internews would be more likely to achieve the ultimate political goals (in terms of buttressing a more responsive and stable government, for example) than some alternative system. The analysis would also be interpreted against a background of conflicting views of what a media system should look like and its role, in Afghanistan, in defining and crafting a relationship between listeners and the central government. A shorter-term goal, not necessarily so explicitly stated, focused on counteracting insurgent communications in order to win the hearts and minds of the Afghan people.

Conclusions in the report underscored the variety of purposes and goals USAID and Internews had for the system of communication. The report flagged the importance of the question of media and nation-building:

> There is a widespread feeling among Afghans that the media do not put enough emphasis on achievements and progress. .... There is high demand for the media to help Afghans rebuild a set of common values, foster national unity and build an Afghan identity that currently does not exist. .... One of the highest expectations voiced by the public across the country was that media should promote a sense of national unity, rather than trying to further divide people of different political, ethnic or religious groups.[29]

In exploring what media are effective in achieving such a goal, the Altai report cited the possibility of using the public broadcaster, Radio Television Afghanistan (RTA), to have a greater role in the nation-building process: "Programs focusing on positive achievements, showing the results of the nation-building effort, testimonials of conflict resolution and well-administered justice, examples of successful (and not corrupt) business ventures and clever

---

[29] Ibid., 162 and 174–175.

promotion of Afghan history, culture and identity can contribute to fostering a sense of national unity."[30]

Could and did such a study analyze "drivers of opinions and behavior in Afghan society and the expectations of Afghans in terms of information"?[31] Did it adequately report on "drivers of influence on key social issues"?[32] These were difficult goals to achieve. So too was the objective of providing insight into Afghans' expectations "in relation to the current direction that the country is taking."[33] Altai deployed quotations, gleaned from its interviews, to dramatically illustrate its conclusions on public opinion questions. For example, as to reconstruction and achievements, covered under nation-building, the report found a widespread feeling among Afghans that the media did not put enough emphasis on achievements and progress, including better accountability of the different actors involved in reconstruction:

> If we watch the news for 30 minutes, it's 20 minutes of killing and suffering and the other 10 minutes is about meetings that have occurred between ministers and politicians. There is no news on development, or economics, the value of our commodities, the value of our currency, things like that. For example, does anybody know anything about our progress this year? How many students went to university this year? How many graduated from high school? I don't know. (Male, Kandahar city)

> We would also like to know more about how NGOs spend the money and if projects are good quality or not, and how much budget of the PRT was allocated to Jalalabad and how it was spent, because we heard there were millions of dollars but the quality was very low. (Male civil servant, Jalalabad)[34]

An interview process was only part of the methodology for understanding nation-building in the Afghan setting. But a comprehensive study of the relation of media to nation-building was far outside the reach of the Altai remit. Such a study would have required a much deeper exploration of historical divisions, more local knowledge and techniques that are not yet mastered. It would have required a greater sense of the nation that might be built and the obstacles that exist in terms of identity, leadership, political divisions and alliances. Media would definitely have a role to play, but assessing how that would be accomplished and with what structure would

---

[30] Ibid., 175.
[31] Ibid, 9.
[32] Ibid.
[33] Ibid.
[34] Ibid., 162.

be difficult to accomplish within the USAID-Internews-Altai mandate. Such an analysis would also be victim to changing U.S. roles in Afghanistan as well as the United States and Afghanistan's complex relationships to a mercurial Pakistan. More sweeping alternative modes of implementing an intervention would have to be considered.

As to culture, unity and identity building, the Altai report was on somewhat firmer footing. It concluded that the return of 5 million Afghans from faraway and neighboring countries, including Iran, meant there was a high demand for the media to help Afghans "rebuild a set of common values, foster national unity and build an Afghan identity that currently does not exist."[35] The report usefully brought in perspectives that might challenge standard approaches to media policy, including a better understanding of the role of a diaspora in the information mix. But the report necessarily sparked significant questions: How does one shape a "common set of values" in the environment of Afghanistan, and who should do this? What role can media play? And if media do have an important role, is the existing strategy of founding and establishing stations a useful way of accomplishing that objective?

The district study of Jibrail, demonstrating the importance of localized studies, includes discussions with elders in Herat that emphasize this point of need for reaffirming cultural identity. There is the suggestion of strategic implications:

> In terms of media, the inhabitants feel quite strongly that there is a lack of variety on Afghan TV. The community feels that the majority of channels broadcast only news and political shows, or entertainment, but little or nothing in the way of education, culture, children's shows or sports. Among parents, school teachers and *shura* members, there is a great deal of discussion about *culture building*, and many see this as one of the roles the media should play. It was expressed that the government should invest in cultural shows and also in the general promotion of Afghan culture via the media; some even felt that a *mullah* should present such a show on TV. One *shura* member, also the principal of a private school, stated that, "The influence from Iran is a good thing because it encourages education, but we need to build our own culture so that our youth don't attach to foreign cultures." Culture building is seen as the primary means for the creation of national Afghan unity that could supersede any tribal/ethnic loyalties, something that is clearly very important to the Hazara community, and also as a response to extreme attachments to religious identity. The same man stated that, "The Taliban has done so much in the way of propaganda that people are now prepared to die for them because they believe that they will go to heaven

---

[35]   Ibid.

for it. The Afghan police and army need to invest in culture building and advertising so that people feel just as passionately about defending their country."[36]

The district study concluded that these communities, having spent a large portion of their lives in Iran, "feel a large cultural void in their lives on their return to Afghanistan, because of the relative vacuum that exists in this regard. On many occasions, it seemed that people's strong sense of Islamic identity stemmed from the fact that they had no cultural identity,"[37] and that cultural void made people cling to Islam more. The report quoted respondents as indicating that for many, "being Afghan had become synonymous with being Muslim,"[38] often because of a lack of alternatives more than as a result of belief. Yet, if developing a common cultural identity were a need, and even if one could identify "common values," the report did not easily indicate which techniques manifested the best ways to inculcate them or whether the existing approach to programming would contribute to this outcome.

Important elements of the Altai report dealt with prospects for the general future of media in Afghanistan – private and public, satellite and terrestrial. The conclusions were mixed. Growth in the sector would gradually slow down as USAID and similar efforts declined. "More media will be created at a relatively fast pace in the near future, but this is going to be increasingly marginal: mostly some minor players for niche media and probably a handful of relatively large investors. It is likely that the most successful outlets will start to focus on increasing their user base, through extension of their coverage area."[39] Entertainment programming would increase as a way to obtain the largest user base as sustainability in a market context would become more of a factor. Quality stations with small markets would have more difficulty. While entry would be relatively easy, the larger private players would tend to thrive. Intriguingly, the report pointed to a risk for the media field: "the growing weight of 'gang media,' that is, media with a strong political or ethnic agenda."[40] Altai also saw a risk for the political landscape in general, in terms of "transforming the media into a platform for political campaigns more than for debate, one for voicing resentment and partisan opposition rather than diversity and one focusing on clienteles rather than the nation at large." Such an outcome would likely "artificially foster tensions that are not

---

[36] Ibid., 161.
[37] Ibid.
[38] Ibid.
[39] Ibid., 166.
[40] Ibid., 167.

yet particularly strong in the country, such as the opposition between Shias and Sunnis."[41]

The report lauded the existence of "an increasingly vibrant" media sector, but cautioned that Afghanistan is also a country where "the government will shut down a private television channel, for example, charging it with inciting sectarian tensions and threatening national unity (as was the case with Emroz TV on July 27, 2010): pressure, self-censorship and insecurity are part of the daily lives of media actors."[42] The report cited the fact that government advisers had "underlined the need for a more balanced Afghan Media Law," and left open the possibility that a new law should be "one which reflects the mixed system of Islam, tradition and secularism and that is not a copy of Western laws."[43]

An illustration of the utility of the Altai report as an analytic tool is its characterization as to what RTA might ultimately become: "a national broad-caster which is fully independent from the Minister of Information and Culture yet remains under the control of the government (a model that the government seems more supportive of); or a public broadcaster governed by an independent commission, more similar to a European model of broad-casting, as in the case of the BBC (a model more supported by the interna-tional community)."[44] From a diagnostic perspective, the questions might go beyond which model is adopted to examine how the local context influences the process; how, in the local or national imagination, these issues should be approached, as opposed to merely fitting existing models to very different situations Even the idea that there is a "European model" of public broad-casting hardly bears continuing weight, given the various dramatically chang-ing roles these famous public service broadcasters now play. By framing the issue as a choice between "government" and "public" – the approach that is often taken in media development contexts – one may be playing into a mode of choice that is neither adequate nor informative.

The Altai report was designed to help inform USAID about the effectiveness of its funding priorities, within a limited range of evaluative criteria. It is always difficult to know whether such an evaluative document influences its specific audience. Put differently, one challenge is whether the strategic communica-tor can effectively use information from a diagnostic to alter its patterns of intervention. Is the information received in a time and manner that makes it potentially influential? And, in this case, how much leeway does Internews or

---

[41] Ibid.
[42] Ibid., 22.
[43] Ibid., 25.
[44] Ibid., 26.

even USAID have, internally, to alter their media development strategy in Afghanistan? The client was not the Afghan government, and the question was not how that government could better develop a strategic narrative that would lead to long-term stability and a resolution of current conflict. There was no adequate consensus on what that process should be in Afghanistan. The actors who would become central had not yet been fully identified and brought into a process of formulating a narrative that would be future-oriented, that would command consensus, that would, because of the narrative itself, carry along competing players toward a more unified whole. Competing narratives, from various sources (Taliban, NGOs, Iran, the government, the United States and the UN), would seek to capture the day. A diagnostic, to be valuable, can indicate how these competing narratives might interact, might lead to dominance for one, might find a negotiated *modus vivendi* or other resolution for their combination. These areas for influence may be too much for a media intervention study to bear.

Altai noted that Afghan media were "still being actively shaped."[45] The question might be framed as being actively shaped *for whom* and *for what purposes?* Does the basis for shaping change over time, as for example when the United States and others are winding down and leaving? One could also ask what the relationship is between the structure of information supply and the distribution of power among competing groups (national, international, insurgent) in particular sub-target audiences. Ultimately, the question is how competing or alternate communications systems affect the ability of the state (or others) in Afghanistan to govern in variously structured communities. How does the structure of information contribute to or detract from the shaping of a national identity and the strengthening of a central government? And what relationship can be identified between information structures and the diffusion of relevant ideas in communities differentiated by the presence or absence of the state or quasi-state actors?

CONCLUSION

These examples – one from Afghanistan, one from Somaliland – differ in terms of the light they shed on a diagnostic, particularly for fragile or crisis states in a modern information environment. What they have in common is a desire to match operations to impact. They are both sensitive to complex differences in local histories, local technological capabilities and the meaning of the "local" in a context of extensive influences from neighboring states, from

---

[45] Ibid., 165.

foreign powers and from various forces within. The Somaliland document in particular considers what media arrangement can bolster a weak state. These are instances in which the state has relatively few resources, there is no strong strategic narrative, there are major competitors seeking to alter and shape the targeted community, and new media technologies, such as mobile telephony, seem to make the state's task even more complex. The Altai report demonstrates the value of localized, micro studies in better understanding the intricacies of an information ecology. It demonstrates the difference between "media mapping" and seeking to describe the interplay among many media influences. It opens the way for comparing "independent" media as a mode of contributing to a goal of nation-building, with other systems of media investment. And it takes into account vast demographic changes, like the return of Afghans from Iran, for the shaping of a media strategy.

In conflict and near-conflict zones, a diagnostic will have to take into account the relationship between military and civilian interventions in media systems. The military is thought to be (and often is) a competitor in system design, with different goals, a different sense of immediacy and a more authoritarian manner of implementation. A diagnostic can assess a fragile government's capacity to effectively face and adapt to technological change and its impact: A fragile state cannot have much if any sway over the largest-scale decisions, but, for example, it might make key decisions on the introduction of mobile phone services, the availability of satellite signals or the location of Internet cafes. A diagnostic can determine where, if any, there are "choke points" or opportunities to filter, open, control or regulate information that relate to the way information enters the society. Another area central to any diagnostic is not taking for granted what mode of diffusion of information most shapes public opinion. In the diagnostic of the media sphere in Somaliland, Stremlau and Gagliardone determined that poetry had an effect on public opinion comparable to that of the printed press. The function of radio, essential in societies with lower literacy, is often underestimated; the impact of community radios and temporary or mobile radios is insufficiently assessed. Particularly in societies with pervasive systems of control, alternate systems (like *samizdat*) emerge. And, finally, a diagnostic can assess whether lessons learned from prior experiences are actually absorbed across bureaucratic divides.

In the past several years, the appetite for monitoring and evaluation of media interventions has increased in an effort to create a reliable, evidence-based approach to media assistance and to demonstrate program impact to funders and the public more broadly. Given the complexity of media development programs (including the multifaceted role that media play in contributing to the broader goals of democracy and governance), it is improbable that this level of science can be achieved. But a richer, more nuanced approach will occur as strategic communicators become more sophisticated. The use of "big data," for example, will enrich the diagnostic toolbox.

Ultimately, there is the central and somewhat obvious point that, for interventions to be wisely strategic, the particular roles that media play in a target context should be carefully understood. As the Somaliland diagnostic recognized:

> Media may place greater stress on fragile states both in terms of being a component of war as well as exacerbating and escalating tensions. In contrast, media can also be a tool that increases a government's capacity and capability to respond effectively to sectarian or other violence from outside the government, improving and extending its reach beyond capital cities as well as managing and mediating expectations about the state-building process.[46]

All this underscores the question of perspective; for whom is the diagnostic undertaken? In the case of the Altai reports, the client was presumably USAID and Internews. There is no exact "client" in the Somaliland study, but one can read it as being written in part from the perspective of the needs of a Somaliland government. The study asks the questions that the government should ask, in terms of the media ecology in which it has to operate. The communications structure implied by the Somaliland study would have an important role in managing the expectations of citizens and would reflect the very local sense of what media are vital for this purpose.

One goal of the process might be to understand the local context sufficiently so that the state, or those who are part of the nation-building process, may choose the best available instruments for promoting national objectives and do so comfortably in compliance with international norms. Unless these mechanisms are properly placed in context and so understood, efforts toward stability, peacekeeping or conflict prevention, whether government-led or external, are at risk of failing. It is through a diagnostic that the potential effectiveness and strategy for information interventions can best be determined, evaluated or enhanced. But the ideal is not always the goal of a diagnostic; it is important to understand that it is a tool for any strategic communicator – for those seeking to destabilize as well as to buttress, for those seeking to change and shift a society's direction regardless of the vector.

This chapter, then, is based on a simple claim about strategic communication: An understanding of context is a precondition for intelligent action. This seems so obvious that it would ordinarily not need further discussion, but it is

[46] "Somaliland Communication Flows Research Report," 1.

astonishing how often the communicative task occurs without sensitivity to the complexity of reception and diffusion. The collision of external factors, political pressures on the decision-maker and the tyranny of embedded assumptions conspire against a systematic approach. These and other barriers prevent strategic communicators from being adequately analytical. In the field of media assistance, for example, the tendency is to commit to a particular outcome without sufficient differentiation of the context in which that outcome is to be produced. Those who seek, for excellent reasons, to provide broadcast stations or train journalists, for example, may have settled habits of thinking that limit inquiry into what it means to be a journalist in a given environment or whether new technologies or other elements (such as the existence of conflict or a polarized press) alter the journalistic role. Domestic political concerns in the sending nation often skew a pattern of information intervention.[47]

In the case of strategic communication, simple claims can have complicated consequences. Time constraints, the inevitable impulse to rely on intuition, bureaucratic requirements, ideological predilections, inevitable shortcomings in local knowledge – all these and more stand in the way of a full analytic diagnostic. Yet a diagnostic approach is a vital part of an evidence-based strategy and a necessary corrective to pressures and hunches. The task is to design a diagnostic that is timely, efficient, constructive and capable of being absorbed by a decision-making process.

---

[47] "Information intervention" is a handy term for the collection of strategic communication efforts that compete with those of a target state. Indeed, the idea of a "diagnostic," although not traditionally given this name, could be the preparatory evaluative effort of the information intervener into the media structure of the target society.

5

Asymmetries and Strategic Communication

On April 24, 2011, in the early days of the Syrian civil conflict, the *New York Times* reported a curious imbalance. In the absence of systematic access by reporters to the scene, one or two dozen diasporic "geeks" were a principal source for capturing and shaping the way the narrative of the Syrian protests was being received in Western capitals. These amateurs were, at the time, outperforming the entire Syrian government in the process of informing the world of the nature of the emerging conflict and the Syrian leadership's response. As the *Times* reported, the small number of activists "coordinated across almost every time zone and managed to smuggle hundreds of satellite and mobile phones, modems, laptops and cameras into Syria. There, compatriots elude surveillance with e-mailed software and upload videos on dial-up connections."[1] The intense efforts presented a sharp contrast with global coverage of civil disobedience and protest in Syria in 1982. Then, noted the *Times*, Syria's government managed to hide "its massacre of at least 10,000 people in Hama in a brutal crackdown of an Islamist revolt. But [now], the world could witness, in almost real time, the chants of anger and cries for the fallen as security forces fired on the funerals for Friday's dead." President Bashar Assad's government was left staggered by the coverage, forced to face the reality that it "has almost entirely ceded the narrative of the revolt to its opponents at home and abroad." For Joshua Landis, a professor of Middle East studies at the University of Oklahoma, this led to an interesting, not necessarily exaggerated, conclusion: "These activists have completely flipped the balance of power on the regime, and that's all due to social media."[2]

By the fall of 2013, this shift in information power had been redressed by the authorities. And when negotiations began over chemical weapons, the

---

[1]   Anthony Shadid, "Exiles Shape World's Image of Syria Revolt," *New York Times*, April 23, 2011.
[2]   Ibid.

principal parties, including Assad himself, continued to reassert control over the narrative. What Assad (and other states with interests in the conflict) faced at the outset, however, was an increasingly typical state of affairs: a perceived reversal of an existing distribution of power in the information sphere. From a context in which the state had overarching control over how words and images were diffused, states now sometimes found themselves stutteringly impotent. These changes altered the state's self-image of authority and, moreover, the image of its authority among its peers. Governments and those seeking to reform them scrambled to understand the dynamic. In this chapter, I explore whether many of the reactions to the impact of these new media uses can be captured within the framework of "asymmetry."[3]

Asymmetry in the sense I use it here has its source and origin in the concept of "asymmetrical warfare," a concept that has its own vagaries. One definition from the force-related context calls asymmetrical those conflicts in which one opponent can take actions that are not available to its foe.[4] This is an asymmetry in the quiver of techniques, where the unavailability may stem from legal, ethical or pragmatic reasons: historic differences in access to information, differences in access to and control of the means of distribution, or differences in the capacity to create and produce messages. In contemporary usage, warfare asymmetry often describes circumstances in which a conventionally powerful state is faced with a ragtag set of protestors or adversaries who are, at the outset, hardly worth dignifying as enemies. A final definition of warfare asymmetry is functional; it describes techniques that an adversary exercises to "undermine an opponent's strengths while exploiting his weaknesses using methods that differ significantly from the opponent's usual mode of operations."[5]

In recent decades, we have associated asymmetrical warfare with acts of terrorism, tactics like hostage taking, the use of biological weapons and the use of torture. Asymmetric warfare is contrasted with a conventional "ideal," one where sides are evenly matched, use similar kinds of techniques, and where, over centuries, rules (whether fully respected or not) have developed regarding the limits on what one side can do to the other. To put it simply, asymmetry in warfare occurs when parties to conflict are mismatched – when one combatant is far stronger in terms of firepower and wealth than the other, or when the

[3]   For issues of coverage and their consequences, see "Media Coverage in Asymmetric Conflict," a special issue of *Dynamics of Asymmetric Conflict*, eds. Ifat Maoz and Menahem Blondheim (2010).

[4]   Roger W. Barnett, *Asymmetrical Warfare: Today's Challenge to U.S. Military Power* (Washington, DC: Brassey's Inc., 2003).

[5]   Franklin B. Miles, *Asymmetric Warfare: An Historical Perspective* (Carlisle, PA: U.S. Army War College, 1999), 2–3.

strategies of one combatant are radically different from the strategies of the other and from the norm.

What does the concept of asymmetric warfare have to offer us, if anything, in terms of strategic insight into current modes of information conflict?[6] Like asymmetry in war, asymmetry in the battle for hearts and minds involves undermining an enemy's strengths and exploiting its weaknesses. Gains are achieved through the pioneering use of techniques not available to the other side because it has not discovered them, has not mastered them or is otherwise disdainful of their adoption. Asymmetry in communications techniques often involves significant disruption of the status quo, initiated by entities that are often scorned as disempowered.[7] Underestimation is a characteristic byproduct of asymmetry. The lack of conventional equality masks the resourcefulness of desperation. In terms of the market for loyalties analysis explored in Chapter 1, the successful surmounting of asymmetrical weaknesses occurs when a group, excluded from the cartel of entrants eligible to shape national identity, breaks through and uses the breakthrough to substantially change the distribution of allegiances in a target audience.

The challenge of understanding and appreciating asymmetries in the battles for hearts and minds is highlighted by a now somewhat forgotten 2006 speech given by Donald Rumsfeld, then Secretary of Defense, to the Council on Foreign Relations in New York. The talk, titled "New Realities in a Media Age," was a candid discussion by a person of immense power who was perplexed by what seemed to be the sudden and unexpected diminution of that power.[8] The plaintive premise of the talk was that "Our enemies have skillfully adapted to fighting wars in today's media age, but for the most part we, our country, our government, have not adapted." For Rumsfeld, this asymmetry of adaptation meant that "violent extremists" had gained an edge in "manipulating the opinion elites of the world." In addition, "They plan and design their headline-grabbing attacks using every means of communication to intimidate and break the collective will of free people." These individuals were not bound, Rumsfeld argued, by the standards of legality and ethics that bound the United States. Rumsfeld recognized that this was not just a question

---

6   For insight into the general concept, see FM 3–24, U.S. Army/Marine Corps Counterinsurgency Manual. A thorough explanation is contained in Clark McCauley and Sophia Moskalenko, "Recent U.S. Thinking About Terrorism and Counterterrorism: Babysteps Towards a Dynamic View of Asymmetric Conflict," *Terrorism and Violence* 22 (2010).

7   Annabelle Sreberny-Mohammadi and Ali Mohammadi, *Small Media, Big Revolution: Communication, Culture, and the Iranian Revolution* (Minneapolis: University of Minnesota Press, 1994).

8   "New Realities in the Media Age: A Conversation with Donald Rumsfeld," *Council on Foreign Relations*, February 17, 2006.

of tactics or purpose – it was also one, in part, of superior practical application. "They're able to act quickly. They have relatively few people. They have modest resources compared to the vast and expensive bureaucracies of Western governments." In spite of these qualities, or perhaps because of them, these groups had, in Rumsfeld's view, prevailed in the media sphere. Rumsfeld summarized this asymmetry with a metaphor that demonstrates the irony and tragedy of power – the turn from strength to weakness, from dominance to something closer to cluelessness: "Our federal government is really only beginning to adapt our operations to the 21st century. For the most part, the U.S. government still functions as a five and dime store in an eBay world." But Rumsfeld saw only part of the problem; the asymmetry was not only because the U.S. government had not modernized. It also had not seen the potential for asymmetrical, terrifying and sometimes pre-modern modes of shifting allegiances and turning weaknesses into strengths.

Much has changed since Rumsfeld's speech, and many governments have sought, not always successfully, to avoid the shock of surprise that leads to crises in communications. The Obama State Department, especially under Hillary Clinton, persistently devoted itself to changing the culture of the institution to remedy the deficit that Rumsfeld pinpointed. Whiz kids surrounding Secretary Clinton became transfixed with the task of transformation – with, for example, the creation of what they called a doctrine of "21st Century Statecraft" meant partly to obviate elements of adverse information asymmetry.[9] Technical updating – becoming more fluent in social media, for example – offers a relatively easy area for catching up. Far more difficult are those circumstances where the asymmetric advantage of a foe comes from its more sophisticated understanding of customs engrained in the cultures of the societies where allegiances are being shifted. An insurgent opponent might have better knowledge of family and educational structure in a contested zone or greater familiarity with language. Significant are examples of asymmetry where ethical or other reasons lead to the inability of one party to use effective approaches practiced by the other (suicide bombings or beheadings are examples at the margin).

These asymmetries provide a window into the complexities of strategic communication. The tricks of asymmetries reveal new approaches to shaping the information sphere and call forth a counter-strategy in which those used to

9   See "21st Century Statecraft," U.S. *Department of State*; Daniel W. Drezner, "Does Obama Have a Grand Strategy? Why We Need Doctrines in Uncertain Times," *Foreign Affairs*, July/ August 2011. The ambiguous results of this ongoing effort have been captured by critics. For instance, see Evgeny Morozov, "The 20th Century Roots of 21st Century Statecraft," *Net.Effect Foreign Policy*, September 7, 2010.

conventional modes of responding learn to adapt or fail. The subversive techniques used in asymmetric contexts have different names at different times: the *samizdat* of the Soviet Union or the graffiti of the urban streets, the language of filtering and blocking circumvention (about which I write later in this chapter), innovative forms of text messaging or novel uses of Facebook or Twitter. The locus of these asymmetric modes can be found in the streets or in the mosque, on the computer or in the comic book.

In analyzing asymmetric contexts, rather than ask who has the most weaponry, one could ask which agents have the most sophisticated sense of using the information tools they have, including marketing or use of social media. Often, asymmetry in formal, visible organization is taken as asymmetry in potential impact. Rumsfeld, in his talk, suggested asymmetries in moral expectations, with the "weaker," non-state actor willing to use communicative techniques that implicate lower ethical standards.[10] There also may be an "asymmetry of patience"; citizens of a Western democracy may tire of persisting in a conflict while the asymmetrical opponent can maintain its slow and dogged approach. Writing about asymmetrical warfare, Uroš Svete has argued that the "essential point of asymmetry thus lies in pursuing ... [approaches] that are contrary to realistic ideas of the balance of power in the quantitative/conventional sense."[11] What I suggest — in a way that is related to the theme of this book — is that strategists of communication recognize a historical jujitsu, reversing the power context so that the weak appear to become strong, and the strong become weak.[12] The counter-strategist recognizes the vulnerabilities that may lead to this kind of reversal of fortune. Protestors and their supporters internalize the existence of new means to break a wall of access; the state and existing authority seek new ways to compensate for the weakness of old defenses.

The chemistry of innovation — the invention, adaptation, deployment and effective use of intrusive information techniques that affect multiple allegiances and mobilize change — is still elusive. The nature of the asymmetry between, for example, an authoritarian government and an evolving protest group, between a superpower and Al Qaeda, or between the Taliban, NATO and the Afghan government, may be quite different. In the following section,

---

[10] "New Realities in the Media Age."

[11] Uroš Svete, "Asymmetrical Warfare and Modern Digital Media: An Old Concept Changed by New Technology?" in *The Moral Dimension of Asymmetrical Warfare: Counter-terrorism, Democratic Values and Military Ethics*, eds. Th. A. van Baarda and D. E. M. Verweij (Leiden: Martinus Nijhoff, 2009).

[12] See chapter 11 of Clark McCauley and Sophia Moskalenko, *Friction: How Radicalization Happens to Them and Us* (Oxford: Oxford University Press, 2011).

I outline a schema for information asymmetry that provides insight into how to understand these variations, and explore various cases and their implications.

A SCHEMA FOR INFORMATION ASYMMETRY

In constructing a schema for information asymmetry, let us return to the model of the market for loyalties in Chapter 1. Participants who have controlled their national market and who try to maintain their dominance are presumptively powerful players. It is their very power and connection to the state that allows the cartel to succeed and seem, for the moment, impermeable. But these dominant players are almost always faced with the danger of unanticipated openings by new entrants seeking to establish a footing, mere shadows on the horizon that suddenly loom as potential or real threats.[13] Increasingly, splinter groups – those who are otherwise barred from the communications landscape – turn to new and viral forms of strategic communication as they seek to break monopolies or cartels. Much of what occurs in terms of censorship, control, violation of human rights and, increasingly, the use of violence, constitutes a blunderbuss of responses of the powerful in this paradigm-shifting asymmetric world.

Historically, the state's control over the technologies of distribution has been central to giving an existing group of "sellers" in the market for allegiances the capacity to regulate entry (in league with the state). When that control disappears (or until it is reestablished), excluded entrants hurtle in, disrupt existing market shares and undo the oligopoly over access to users. Radio stations that broadcast, unlicensed, from the sea (so-called pirate ships) caused turmoil in the radio sphere of the 1960s. In the 1990s, the brashly competitive introduction of satellite technology over existing transponders broke the illusion of total control over the information space, but even then, for the most part, weak players were not able to take advantage of the apertures because of inexperience, prohibitive costs and gateway barriers. In the 2000s onward, the disruption has come, in large part, from the Internet and social media.

Many modern debates concerning free expression principles deal with ways of reacting to the disruptions and asymmetries these technological changes have created. Asymmetry is significant, for example, if the characteristics of "weakness" result in one player being more innovative and responsive than

---

[13] "Inventions in communication compel realignments in the monopoly or the oligopoly of knowledge;" furthermore, and more relevant, often those inventions most likely to challenge power had their birth in "technological change which has taken place in marginal regions which have escaped the influence of a monopoly of knowledge." Harold Innis, *The Bias of Communication* (Toronto: University of Toronto Press, 1951), 4.

another in a way that is destructive of existing institutions. The important variable is how these opportunities are seized and by whom. In *The Cultural Industries*, David Hesmondhalgh distinguished (in a very different context) between large commercial, corporate bureaucracies and small network organizations.[14] Bigger bureaucracies with all their resources and hierarchical structures find it hard to move quickly enough to address changes in the market, while smaller, more nimble, decentralized network organizations are often more successful, especially in early adoption of trends. A similar phenomenon is at work in the political context. Of course, large entities may use their scale and control to stifle innovation; and some large entities (companies and countries) have sought nevertheless to maintain an innovative edge.

Asymmetry and the Weak-Strong Dichotomy

Asymmetry in a strategic communication context generally features a narrative dimension; stories shift and are transformed by the specific asymmetric relation of a particular context. As an example, if one wanted to consider a model for information asymmetry in Egypt, on the eve of Tahrir Square and the moment of high hopes for the Egyptian "revolution," one could think – highly simplified – of two sets of players, the "Putatively Powerful" and the "Putatively Weak." I use the term "putative" here because the designation of powerful and weak is even less enduring than we often think and can sometimes be more a matter of appearances than actual capacity. The incumbent government may deem itself (or be deemed by others) as categorically powerful even if in a particular setting or at particular time it is weak and outmaneuvered. The putatively weak, often agents of subversion from the perspective of the established states, consciously look to the margins as modes for entering the market. If they gain a foothold, the response of the powerful can be one of sharp self-realization. If the Emperor has no clothes, he is only provisionally the Emperor. He or she has hidden vulnerabilities. In Mubarak's Egypt, there were, superficially, clothes aplenty. The state controlled the broadcasters, most of the newspapers, the police and the military. The incipient protestors controlled nothing except, apparently, word of mouth, cell phones and instruments of social networking.

The model for asymmetry, then, should capture situations in which a weak player has the potential to upend the status quo and in which, as a consequence, a seemingly powerful state is seeking to even temporarily, limit access

---

[14] David Hesmondhalgh, *The Cultural Industries* (London: SAGE, 2007).

to the tools of persuasion that have the potential to disrupt. But asymmetry can also exist where powerful global agents, with funds and expertise, tend to overwhelm the governmental efforts of weak or failing states. As a simplified way of schematizing, it is possible to posit four primary situations in which asymmetric methods are used, and their associated strategic implications:

1. A "weak" player is struggling to enter a marketplace in which entry is strongly regulated:
   a. The weak player enlists a strong ally (such as one providing financial support or support in the production or diffusion of messages);
   b. The weak player employs a technique that bypasses existing barriers;
   c. The weak player has a message that uniquely resonates.
2. A "strong" external player is seeking to alter the information market-place in a state with few tools of resistance or a tradition of abstaining from regulating flows (reverse asymmetry):
   a. The strong player seeks alliances or partnerships with agents or actors within the target state;
   b. The strong player employs a technique that bypasses existing barriers;
   c. The strong player has a message that uniquely resonates.
3. A strong state uses asymmetric techniques against another strong state.
4. Weak entrants are dealing with a weak or failing state and characteristics of asymmetry hold both for the entrant and the status quo.

Strategy in Asymmetrical Contexts

States' and other players' responses to the new information asymmetries vary across categories. Adaptation to information asymmetry can mean adoption of the new or adaptation of the old. In response to the often stunning and surprising communications innovations by asymmetric opponents, governments – as we witness – fluctuate between repression and creative response. They extend the ordinary processes of control to modes and technologies by which the marginal or innovatively subversive express themselves. But that is often not enough. Harshness may be the initial impulse, but it is often ineffective in staunching the effects of the innovation. Counter-strategies evolve to emulate the creativity of the subordinated or, architecturally, to deny them the new or unanticipated podium that has been constructed.

All sides in an asymmetric context have similar categories of target audiences – usually populations in the zone of conflict (Afghanistan or the Egypt of the Arab Spring) and a global audience as well. Furthermore, as I discussed earlier, the entity engaged in the strategic communication may have a home market (the domestic audiences of the coalitions of the willing, the donor audiences of the NGOs and so on).[15] In all of these, there are allegiances to shift. Each audience requires a different strategy, and asymmetries have different implications for each audience and each strategy. There is a difference between the use of media, even asymmetrically, to persuade generally – to reach a large audience to change opinion – and its use to "recruit" a dedicated core of workers or supporters or those who engage in acts of terror, such as suicide bombers. And counter-strategies differ depending on cross-national support for asymmetric efforts. The ability of the "weak" – the creative exploiters of information asymmetries – may depend on help from others (the international press, international actors) with whom their message resonates more strongly, rather than exclusively in the streets they seek to influence. Recall that in 2009 it was an American official who successfully urged Twitter not to disable its service in Iran for scheduled maintenance in order, it was said, to allow protestors to use the service to build its constituency in the face of government technology denial.[16]

Strategies of innovation and response depend on understanding patterns of information flow. A first look at the Arab Spring cases suggests that the reverberation from street protest to international or regional press to Al Jazeera beaming back into Egypt was a formula that wreaked havoc with existing patterns of state control over information. And – certainly this was the case in Egypt – the major global attention created a second relevant audience, one that was meaningful not only within the state but also internationally. In the international market, elements of asymmetry were almost reversed. "Heroic" representatives of such nominally weaker entities – local protestors – could gain and hold access to huge media markets far more readily than could official spokespersons for aging leaders and increasingly unpopular agendas. Looking across the sweep of instances – from Tunisia to Libya – one could see how the once weak and asymmetrically positioned overcame or exploited that status, what markets (domestic elite, domestic popular, international officialdom, international public opinion) they appealed to and what combination of external coverage and internal growth could be held accountable for change.

Weak players have certain tropes, tropes that resonate, as I have suggested in my schema, that they advance to gain sensational and immediate entry to an

---

[15] Consider Putnam's well-known two-level game theory, in which strategic communicators look to both "home" and "target" markets even as they engage with the asymmetry *within* the target market. Robert D. Putnam, "Diplomacy and Domestic Politics: The Logic of Two-Level Games," *International Organization* 42, no. 3 (1988).

[16] Damien McElroy, "Twitter Maintained Service During Iranian Elections after US State Dept Request," *The Telegraph*, June 16, 2009.

audience's attention. Terrorist acts have this quality. One response is to determine ways to neutralize such tropes. During the worst days in Iraq and Afghanistan, the Bush administration sought to deny its enemy, the comparatively "weak" proponents of powerful images such as the Taliban and Al Qaeda, such external amplification. This was attempted, for example, by seeking (sometimes in vain) the assent of broadcasters not to diffuse photographs of dismembered heads or flag-draped coffins of returning American military.

In the annals of strategic communication, then, the most notable cases will be the ones in which seemingly disadvantaged asymmetric entrants become strong and influential (if not dominant), moving from exclusion or subordinate status to being effective participants in key markets for loyalties. It is this success that becomes the study text for innovative asymmetries and for consequent countermeasures. This is the drama of the isolated, distant Ayatollah, distributing audiocassettes in the Shah's Iran and overwhelming the advantages of state control and the sophistications of modern public relations.[17] Shudderingly threatening to some but romantic to others is the idea of the excluded becoming the prevailing figure, almost as if being an outsider becomes a talisman for entry. Some combination of exclusion, striking of a sympathetic cord and a capacity to play the instruments of communication leads to an unexpected triumph. In the aftermath, the world searches for hidden signs that elements of asymmetry were a façade – that those who appeared weak were heavily financed, that there were powerful players in league with the seemingly powerless. Conspiracy theories, not always unfounded, crop up to shift the characterization of the enterprise from one of weak to strong, for example, to one of strong to stronger.

The sympathy is often with the weaker player – the hunger striker, the initial protestors, the proto-Gandhis of the world. But there is a curious question about the very semantics of the asymmetric. Take the ubiquitous David and Goliath metaphor, so firmly in our mind – the mythically unstoppable, powerful figure attacked by a nonentity armed with a seemingly inconsequential weapon. In retrospect, that is an illusion. The match is asymmetric if the two are fighting in different worlds with different rules, different technologies, even different strategic capacities. But as time passes and circumstances shift, balances may change, and the clash is no longer so asymmetric. Innovators use asymmetries in the commercial field to bring down media giants; the frequency and bases for that become the stuff of military and political analysis. The lesson has been established and the lesson should be learned, whether

---

[17] Sreberny-Mohammadi and Mohammadi, *Small Media, Big Revolution.*

David triumphs because of skill or fortune (or divine blessing). Information asymmetries are thus time-bound, though the learning curve and repair phase could be long. Finally, asymmetry fatigue may set in, as the insistent message of a proponent, too steadfastly portraying its David-like status, loses credibility. For these reasons, asymmetries are inherently unstable.

One can think of contexts that appear to fit many of the categories outlined earlier.[18] The Arab Spring, generally, was a sandbox of experiments in asymmetric communication. One immediate question is whether any asymmetric innovator long relies exclusively on its own capacity or, rather, must rely on allies. For example, the anti-Mubarak Tahrir Square protestors, at the beginning, fit within the category of the weak against the strong. But it was not the technique of protest and grassroots mobilization alone that led to the success of the protestors and their emergence as effective asymmetric actors. It is hard to determine what gave rise to the international support for Tahrir Square or to assess the exact balance of forces that led to change, but it is clear that that additional support was crucial. In terms of control of information flows, protestors faced a substantial fortress – the government of Egypt – yet proved extraordinarily successful in an international market for the validation of ideas and the obtaining of support. Face time on channels in the United States and Europe could and did influence coverage in Cairo. Looking across the canvas of protests in the Arab Spring, one can try to determine what characteristics and techniques led to certain groups being more effective than others at gaining support (either in domestic or international markets). For example, in Egypt, the Tahrir protestors went out of their way to underscore the near absence of their formal and informal organization; and throughout, most protest entities suggested a lack of strong affiliation with religious movements – a matter of slight irony given the victory of the Muslim Brotherhood in later elections.[19]

---

[18] My focus in this book is on trans-border contexts, in which the entity trying to penetrate the market is outside its boundaries, but that condition is not essential for understanding (and questioning) this taxonomy.

[19] Gandhi's Satyagraha is also relevant as an embodiment of turning weakness into strength, of using unorthodox techniques effectively to alter large-scale popular allegiances. Take an account of Gandhi's participation in the famous Dandi March, a protest against a salt policy of the colonial power. He saw the march not only as a non-violent weapon of struggle against injustice but "also as a medium of dialogue and communication with the people along the route of the march." The march became a series of events, of moments to alter consciousness. See Madhu Dandavate, "Gandhi's Dialogue with the Nation," *The Hindu Online*, April 6, 2005.

The effectiveness of Gandhi's philosophy and methodology – in a context where disadvantageous weakness was turned to strength – altered the textbook of strategic communication. This was the trajectory of the civil rights revolution in the United States and decades beyond in the color revolutions in Ukraine, Lebanon and Georgia. What for Gandhi had been innovation, experimentation and, to some extent, spontaneous endorsement of a particular philosophy

As to the second major category I have described, we can easily identify strong global players intervening in markets for loyalties where there is little organized defense against entry. "Occupations," wherein the strong player asserts direct government control, are a useful example (although the histories of resistance movements underscore the fragility of the occupier's strength). Post–World War II Germany and Japan were extreme, and extremely interesting, examples of seizing the information space. Iraq, post-invasion, became an episodically weak state with a strong international entity having the (squandered) opportunity to enter and manage its information space. My discussion of the International Religious Freedom Act in Chapter 8 describes an area where the United States (a strong state) takes credit for – or is charged with coming to the assistance of – disfavored entities (some weak and some with substantial domestic support) in states that would otherwise resist giving greater greater voice to them. Through this action, the external state helps gain a foothold for these disfavored religions in third markets, although it may also injure them through the burden of association with a foreign entity.

The most important example of a "strong" state seeking to alter views in another strong state is China and the United States. There is a great deal of feinting and experimenting, as when the United States seeks to pipe Radio Free Asia into China or to diffuse circumvention techniques (discussed later in this chapter). One could ask whether strategies aimed at Cuba are effective, as when the United States, through Radio and TV Marti, has sought to alter allegiances there: Is Cuba "weak" and the United States "strong" in the relevant information space?[20] Chapter 7 deals with efforts to use asymmetric techniques to affect loyalties in Iran and could be seen as an example of two strong states interacting.

The fourth category, weak communicators functioning in weak environments, may be the most unstable aspect of the schema. For decades, the conditions for this analysis seemed to be in place in Somalia, i.e. there were few formal "controls" and a variety of players had free access. Non-state actors, such as Al Shabaab, materially shaped the conditions for entry. The internationally sanctioned temporary government struggled to govern and manage information flows. Elements of this case were discussed in Chapter 4. Strength emerges in these environments from surprising candidates, insurgent groups with communications talents, diasporic groups that invest in media, religious

became more programmed, financed, virtually industrialized at the end of the twentieth century and the beginning of the twenty-first. Nonviolence, demonstration, crowd accretion, developing support – all this began to have a playbook, a circle of philanthropy and NGO support (and certainly in many cases support from states).

[20] Shanthi Kalathil and Taylor Boas, "Internet and State Control in Authoritarian Regimes: China, Cuba, and the Counterrevolution," *Carnegie Endowment Paper* no. 21, July 2001.

entities and NGOs with communication strategies. Regular and irregular military units seek to place their own stamp on the informational context. In this fourth category, the category of compounded weakness, "strategies" are short-term if they exist at all.

CASE STUDIES OF ASYMMETRY

Circumvention in Iran and China

"Circumvention" is a relatively recent – but increasingly important – technical episode in the processes of asymmetric information strategy. Circumvention primarily involves informal efforts to help putatively weak players, including individuals, civil society groups and other advocates, subvert barriers to access to meaningful information that would help them gain their objectives (including, at times, mobilizing to affect the leadership of the country in question). The issue becomes particularly relevant in societies where access to information is highly restricted. Repressive regimes use filtering and blocking devices systematically to impair the communicative capacity of individuals living under their control. They are denying individuals the right to receive and impart information, often information that is vital. Elements of civil society work to find ways to break through the censor's hold – to defeat the technological modes used for repression and open the society up through asymmetric techniques such as blogging, hacking and circumvention.[21] For example, in both Iran and China, specific groups, often marginal, have long sought innovative ways of self-strengthening by gaining access to information of their choosing.

On a global level, however, circumvention has geopolitical implications as it becomes one technique to adjust an external market for loyalties. Just as filtering is a method of suppressing certain sellers in the market for allegiances, the use of circumvention technologies liberates those sellers to be more effective, by empowering the demand side to gain access to the material. The presumption is that problems of collective action – the capacity of individuals to gain an understanding that they could be part of an effective whole – would be eased through knowledge of the thoughts and views of others. Under this pragmatic view, those on the outside – civil society groups, Western governments – have sought to strengthen internal players by subsidizing techniques to circumvent. Documenting U.S. investments in the proliferation of tools for circumventing filters or preserving anonymity, ongoing

---

[21] An extensive discussion of the technical and policy aspects of circumvention appears in a series of reports published by the Berkman Center for Internet and Society at Harvard University. See a listing at "Circumvention Publications," *Berkman Center for Internet & Society*.

since at least 2001, Daniel McCarthy notes that these efforts are not sanitized of strategic effect: "They represent an attempt to reinstitute the free flow of information on the Internet, enabling access where it has been denied. In the process, of course, they also work to cement the cultural values expressed by the Internet via these material practices."[22]

Circumvention has historically employed a variety of technologies and methods – smuggling hidden books, facilitating the passage of secret manuscripts of *samizdat*, the protection of house churches. In recent years the process has primarily involved the manipulation of Internet accessibility and the avoidance of blocking mechanisms using various software tools. The asymmetry here is between the machinery of government and the norm-threatening innovation of smaller individuals and groups. Tinkering and computer science form the basis for foiling government techniques to control the flow of information. Large-scale strategic players (primarily the United States) have seen opportunities to intervene by assisting the group of weak players by subsidizing innovation and by furthering production and refinement of software (providing, as it were, David with his slingshot).[23] Without a context in which information is sought and its diffusion enabled, circumvention does not become an instrument to reshape asymmetries. But in China and Iran, that context of diffusion to alter power is definitely present. For instance, since the Voice of America website may be blocked or filtered, the U.S. Congress has funded efforts by the Broadcasting Board of Governors (which oversees all U.S. government-sponsored international broadcasting) to provide circumvention technology that has the potential to remove the block.

Self-adjustment to local conditions by the participants in asymmetric information contexts partially explains the circumvention battles. Individuals and groups innovate in breaking barriers to the gaining of information. Interesting complexities of strategy emerge as external states – particularly the United States – position themselves in this effort to shift allegiances. While the strategic goal of each individual player is readily justifiable, the question is how to account for the assistance provided by external governments to groups and individuals in target societies. The problem is illustrated in the long-time and convoluted relationships between the United States and China and the United States and Iran. When the Global Internet Freedom Consortium (affiliated with China's banned Falun Gong group), among others, sought to

---

[22] Daniel R. McCarthy, "Open Networks and the Open Door: American Foreign Policy and the Narration of the Internet," *Foreign Policy Analysis* 7, no. 1 (2011): 102. See pages 101–105 for more on U.S. involvement in exporting circumvention tools.

[23] Malcom Gladwell, *David and Goliath: Underdogs, Misfits, and the Art of Battling Giants* (New York: Little Brown, 2013).

lobby Congress for $30 million of circumvention funding, a U.S. national interest argument, readily found, had to be implied or expressed over the distinct goals of the advocating organizations.[24]

Elements of this cross-national approach call for closer examination. Those seeking funding for circumvention tools on the Chinese mainland found it advantageous to broaden their claim from an assault on speech controls in China to a large category of regimes (North Korea and Laos in addition to Iran and, until recently, Myanmar). In this respect, the post-election events of 2009 in Iran offered a substantial and dramatic opportunity. The Global Internet Freedom Consortium and others worked to develop and make available in Iran software to allow individuals and groups to circumvent Iranian government efforts to block websites.[25] The Iran event was to the testing of new information technologies what the Spanish Civil War was to experimentation with new military techniques. Within a short period after the elections, the United States Senate passed a bill authorizing the circumvention funds. The bill was renamed the VOICE Act, an acronym for Victims of Iranian Censorship, a marker that demonstrated the significance of Iran as a rallying site for building consensus. The bill became law.[26]

How did the United States frame this intervention? In contrast to Rumsfeld's quandary of lagging in the area of media innovation, here the United States was more aggressively forwarding, in Ithiel de Sola Pool's famous phrase, "technologies of freedom," in the drama of seeking to shift allegiances.[27] Some version of the following was consistently argued: the United States stands for unencumbered speech and efforts, particularly in repressive societies, to eliminate barriers to opposition to a regime – and circumvention is a way to do so. More complex and gingerly articulated were less neutral objectives. For the most aggressive proponents, circumvention was one element of furthering the cause of regime change (an alternative to the use of force) in specified areas, such as China and Iran. Circumvention thus became part of a general Internet freedom agenda as well as a more specific agenda with respect to select countries.

---

[24] The figure – sometimes as large as $50 million – has been in circulation at least in the 2007–2012 period, with U.S. strategic interests articulated in explicit and implicit forms. See, for instance: "Groups Ask US for Funds to Break China 'Firewall,'" *AFP*, February 23, 2010; Jackson Diehl, "Time to Reboot Our Push for Global Internet Freedom," *Washington Post*, October 25, 2010; Nicole Gaouette and Brendan Greeley, "U.S. Funds Help Democracy Activists Evade Internet Crackdowns," *Bloomberg*, April 20, 2011.

[25] "Use of Censorship Circumvention Services Soars in Iran – GIF Resumes Anti-censorship Services to Iran Due to Election Crisis," *Global Internet Freedom Consortium*, June 17, 2009.

[26] "Senate Adopts Victims of Iranian Censorship (VOICE) Act," *mccain.senate.gov*, July 24, 2009.

[27] Ithiel de Sola Pool, *Technologies of Freedom* (Cambridge, MA: Harvard University Press, 1983).

There was distant resonance between the circumvention debate and discussions of corporate sales of surveillance and monitoring software to authoritarian regimes. The flip side of the circumvention technological arms race involves the empowerment of such regimes with technologies that facilitate control – sometimes reinforcing and sometimes foiling the exporting state's perceived interests. In the VOICE Act, Congress "condemn[ed] companies which have knowingly impeded the ability of the Iranian people to access and share information and exercise freedom of speech, freedom of expression, and freedom of assembly through electronic media." The act further directed appropriate officials to "examine claims that non-Iranian companies . . . have provided hardware, software, or other forms of assistance to the Government of Iran" that furthered efforts to "filter online political content, disrupt cell phone and Internet communications; and monitor the online activities of Iranian citizens" (Section 1247).[28]

Afghanistan and Asymmetric Creativity

Many aspects of the Afghan War cast light on information asymmetry and strategies of communication, illustrating aspects of the schema I sketched earlier. In some respects, the United States was a strong player entering a weak marketplace. The Afghan War illustrates the shaping of new techniques and their cross-adoption between the off-kilter and the dominant, the "occupier" and the guerrilla, the innovator and the adapter. In a war in which the hearts and minds of the Afghan people were a major battleground, strategies related to information asymmetries were central. I discussed aspects of the U.S. efforts in Chapter 4, but more in terms of the evaluative than the asymmetric.

As between the Afghan government and the Taliban, one could ask which was the strong and which the weak player, who controlled cartels of information and in what areas of the country. The United States (through USAID, the State Department and the military), as well as some other states involved in the International Security Assistance Force (ISAF), invested heavily in media distribution systems with the hope of building up loyalty to the Afghan government and, to the extent necessary, acceptance of the temporary presence of U.S. and other international troops. For example, in early August of 2009, the Obama administration announced a new unit within the State Department

---

[28] "VOICE Act," *United States Congress*. There are ironies in this condemnation of techniques given that they may be used by democracies as well; see Evgeny Morozov, "Political Repression 2.0," *New York Times*, September 1, 2011.

for countering militant propaganda in Afghanistan and Pakistan.[29] The approach would be neither mimetic (copying the methods of the insurgents) nor primarily repressive (using force or similar measures to shut down the effective asymmetric player). The State Department would act not simply with the usual repertoire of a dominant player but with one adjusted to insurgent techniques. One approach was to create an infrastructure for facilitating government messaging. A large budget was invested to develop local FM radio stations to counter what was labeled as "illegal militant broadcasting."[30]

The U.S. approach was a response to initiatives of the Taliban, although a systematic study of the communication approach of the Taliban was hardly at hand. An example of the Taliban's asymmetric (often improvisational) approach was documented by Human Rights Watch; its study of the circulation of intimidating "night letters" included useful examples:

1. "Islamic Emirate of Afghanistan: This is to warn all the teachers and those employees who work with Companies to stop working with them. We have warned you earlier and this time we give you a three days ultimatum to stop working. If you do not stop, you are to blame yourself."

2. "Muslim Brothers: Understand that the person who helps launch an attack with infidels is no longer a member of Muslim community. Therefore, punishment of those who cooperate with infidels is the same as the [punishment of] infidels themselves. You should not cooperate in any way – neither with words, nor with money nor with your efforts. Watch out not to exchange your honor and courage for power and dollar."

3. "By the Name of the Great God: Respected Afghans – Leave the culture and traditions of the Christians and Jews. Do not send your girls to school, otherwise, the mujahedin of the Islamic Emirates will conduct their robust military operations in the daylight."[31]

Cell phones presented another useful example of asymmetric strategy and response in Afghanistan. Insurgents apparently threatened commercial cell phone providers with attack if they did not switch off service early each night. According to the *New York Times*, the goal was to prevent villagers from calling

[29] Thom Shanker, "U.S. Plans a Mission Against Taliban's Propaganda," *New York Times*, August 15, 2009.

[30] Ibid.

[31] A selection of Taliban night letters targeting teachers and schools is available at "Lessons in Terror: Attacks on Education in Afghanistan," *Human Rights Watch*, July 2006. Also see Tim Foxley, "Countering Taliban Information Operations in Afghanistan," *Prism* 1, no. 4 (2010).

security forces if they saw militants on the move or planting roadside bombs; the lack of cell phone service at night would also impair the police and non-governmental development agencies. The counter-strategy for the U.S. military was to establish additional security for cell phone towers by offering local communities money, electricity or free service to guard the towers and erecting additional cell phone towers on allied military bases. The argument was that these efforts "amplify the voices of Afghans speaking to Afghans, and Pakistanis speaking to Pakistanis, rather than have 'Made in the U.S.A.' stamped on the programming."[32]

These and other "irregular" information efforts from the Taliban and others were met by counter-strategies from NATO forces, including "psychological operations" or PSYOP.[33] These responses were central to the ideas of counter-insurgency as developed by General David Petraeus even before he became commander of the U.S. Forces-Afghanistan and the International Security Assistance Force in Afghanistan.[34] For example, a propaganda unit would seek ways to denigrate the enemy in the eyes of the target audience. Ashley Bommer, an information advisor to the late Ambassador Richard Holbrooke, was quoted by the *New York Times* as saying, "Given the archaic values of Al Qaeda and the Taliban, we must devise policies that expose the true nature of the militants. And we must shift the paradigm so that the debate is not between the United States and the militants, but between the people and the militants."[35] A report on the Taliban's communication activities suggested a number of short-term approaches for the international community and Afghan and ISAF forces to counter Taliban propaganda. Among other things, the report suggested the following:

1. More detailed analysis of Taliban communiqués should be made, including their draft constitution. . . .
2. The Taliban is by no means a cohesive, unified force. Splits and divisions within and around the Taliban leadership should be highlighted.

---

[32] Shanker, "U.S. Plans a Mission."
[33] The U.S. recently retired the term PSYOP in favor of MISO ("Military Information Support Operations"), defining it as "Planned operations to convey selected information and indicators to foreign audiences to influence their emotions, motives, objective reasoning, and ultimately the behavior of foreign government's organizations, groups, and individuals in a manner favorable to the originator's objectives." See Joint Chiefs of Staff, "Joint Publication 1–02: Department of Defense Dictionary of Military and Associated Terms," 2013, http://www.dtic. mil/doctrine/new_pubs/jp1_02.pdf.
[34] Thomas Rid and Thomas Keaney, *Understanding Counterinsurgency: Doctrine, Operations, and Challenges* (Abingdon: Routledge, 2010).
[35] Shanker, "U.S. Plans a Mission."

3. There should be regular media reminders of just what the Taliban did during their regime and therefore what could be expected if they did return to power.

4. Efforts should be made to draw the Taliban out to discuss wider issues, such as accountability to the population, politics, reconstruction and development. The debate should be publicized and their absence of plans for the country should be highlighted.

5. Compel the Taliban to explain their tactics (suicide bombing, attacks on civilians and schools, attitudes to poppy cultivation) in order to expose the contradictions in their arguments.

6. The Afghan Government must be more visible and more regularly present in problematic regions. Greater efforts should be made to talk frankly and openly with tribal elders and villagers to understand their problems and concerns and demonstrate commitment to addressing them. This must be an Afghan-driven initiative rather than that of external actors.

7. In order to help "manage expectations," better explanations should be given to the Afghan populace, both from the international civilian development agencies and the Afghan Government, about reconstruction plans in general and progress in them. Making promises without the ability to deliver must be avoided. This should be combined with reminders of the real difficulties for the international community, the practical limitations to its work and the fact that only the Afghan population can ultimately make this work.

8. Key Pakistani and Arab media that carry Taliban interviews and messages should be engaged with positively and pro-actively to ensure that Afghan Government and ISAF messages are also represented, preferably before the Taliban get their story out.[36]

A final example of creative innovation and asymmetrical responses involves the mild innovation called "Radio in a Box" (RIAB), as used in Afghanistan.[37] As the Army and Marines became more involved in counterinsurgency activities in Afghanistan, and, in particular, after they were assigned to work with Afghan troops, a way was needed to communicate with the communities that the joint efforts had under nominal control. As one staff sergeant put it, perhaps in too telescoped a fashion: "What is the best way to get

---

[36] Tim Foxley, "The Taliban's Propaganda Activities: How Well is the Afghan Insurgency Communicating and What Is It Saying?" *SIPRI Project Paper*, 2007, 18–19. A later report by Foxley suggested that his earlier recommendations and conclusions stood: Foxley, "Countering Taliban Information Operations."

[37] Spencer Case, "Army Reservist Fights Information War in Afghanistan," *Army.mil*, October 20, 2010.

[the Afghan people] to see our side of the story? If they're attacking, how do we get them to stop attacking? If they're rioting, how do we get them [to stop rioting]? In short, [it's about] behavior modification."[38] Another objective was to develop ties between communities under supervision and the central government. For these purposes, RIAB became popular. It was a small, mobile FM radio system that could be easily deployed throughout a region with the intent of delivering public information and news ultimately connecting citizens to the Islamic Republic of Afghanistan. The radio station could also report the activity and whereabouts of insurgents in a given area to the citizens and also known hot spots where IEDs were a potential threat.

A young Marine lieutenant, Samuel Jacobson, in charge of an RIAB, wrote as follows in 2010 to provide insight into the role RIABs were intended to play, how the system was used and with what impact:

> How would I evaluate Radio in a Box? It's very useful for the Afghan unit; it allows the Afghan commander [the captain whom I most directly mentor] to communicate his thoughts directly to the people in a way that he can't through small shuras (meetings) with the elders and patrolling from one village to another. In fact, sometimes he becomes over-reliant on the RIAB, neglecting more traditional forms of media – like talking to a person face-to-face. We were going to have a lunch for some local tribal elders and he wanted to invite them by playing a message on the radio. This week as space filler we've been playing some canned medical broadcasts that are sent down to us. How to prevent malaria, etc. Very important stuff, but it always seems a bit out of touch with the most immediate concerns.
>
> As for the relative impact of various media interventions, RIAB wins. Not necessarily for any inherent quality, but because of lack of access to other media. The vast majority can't read or write; and even if they could, we don't have enough copies of the Afghan National Army newspaper to disseminate. And the newspaper comes in a one-size-fits-all standardized format, with no room for our additions or subtractions. And there's no cell phone service [just some satellite calling centers in the bazaar]. And there is zero access to internet, or knowledge of how to use it.[39]

---

[38] Ibid.

[39] Samuel Jacobson, email message to author, 2010, Concerning this Military Response in Context of asymmetries. For a more extended treatment of this Radio in a Box experiment, see Monroe E. Price and Sam Jacobson, "'Radio in a Box': Psyops, Afghanistan and the Aesthetics of the Low-Tech," *USC Center on Public Diplomacy at the Annenberg School*, June 23, 2011; Sam Jacobson, "*Radio-in-a-Box*: Afghanistan's New Warrior DJs," Parts 1 and 2, *Huffington Post*, July 2011.

This is a micro insight into innovation in an environment of asymmetry and response. The account informally confronts basic questions about competing media influences and their absence.

COMMUNICATION STRATEGY AND ASYMMETRY: CONSEQUENCES

Strategies of contemporary wars have been revolutionized by thinking about asymmetric conflict.[40] Indeed, asymmetric warfare studies created a new and dynamic taxonomy for military approaches. The asymmetries in battles for hearts and minds can and have led to similar transformations. Struggling to maintain primacy in contexts of information asymmetry is an ongoing effort for all competing actors. Certainly, the dissidents of the world (those initiating protests and seeking visibility for them and those moved by the events of Tahrir Square or Tunisia) and many others of similar ilk use these events as a text from which to learn for the future. Those in authority do so as well – those who see an advantage in supporting one side or another, enhancing surrogates in some complex multi-party, long-term effort to strengthen or weaken allegiances. The main condition for understanding asymmetry in information exchanges is that circumstances change as participants learn and adjust to previously exposed weaknesses. Circumvention, for example, is often characterized as a technology arms race. Governments filter; "liberation technologists" break the barriers; governments respond and seek to close the gap; dissidents and their supporters respond.

Perhaps this is the primary lesson in understanding information asymmetries: Authorities adjust or they are doomed (or certainly disadvantaged). Similarly, if the "protestors" or destabilizers cannot adjust to change, cannot learn sufficiently from prior processes of dynamic adjustment or cannot forge alliances with strong players who enable them, they too are rendered less successful. What works in terms of use of media to mobilize an internal target audience one day may not work the next. Some basic constants, however, may be identified. Reflection on efforts in Egypt, Afghanistan, Libya and elsewhere suggests it is important to stay "on message," especially when a message that seems to strike a significant note has been discovered. So a lesson may be that the content may be iterated, but the mode for delivering it may alter as previous modes for diffusion are impeded.

From the perspective of the state, gaps in technological development are particularly difficult to surmount. Bureaucracies – particularly sclerotic

---

[40] See Th. A. Van Baarda and D. E. M. Verweij, eds., The *Moral Dimension of Asymmetrical Warfare* (Leiden: Martinus Nijhoff, 2009).

bureaucracies in authoritarian regimes or bureaucracies that have been nepotistic, as opposed to meritocratic – attempt to buy external expertise at high cost and have a delayed capacity to respond to the use of new technologies and social media. What this has meant is that there is a new race to learn what was not learned before, to overcome the deficiencies Rumsfeld noted, to eliminate the weakness of social media tone-deafness. It is important to remember the key mantra of asymmetry: Exploit your opponent's weaknesses, and avoid their strengths. The implication is to anticipate weaknesses and convert them in advance to strengths. This was a central tenet of the Petraeus counter-insurgency strategies in Iraq and Afghanistan.

I have suggested that asymmetry also occurs if one side considers itself empowered to use techniques that are denied to the other, whether this denial is for ethical or legal reasons. As a way of evening out the playing field, "adjustments" in these legal and ethical barriers may occur. Consider the United States and its rolling, shifting effort to compete in the market of effective techniques that asymmetry has produced. Principles – even constitutional principles – that limit surveillance, hamper eavesdropping or restrain coercion are modified so that the capacity to interrupt or monitor flows of information is increased. Governments overcome reluctances to subsidize messages, or to co-opt journalists, if they consider that techniques useful to them, or undertaken by their foes, must be enlisted. One important example of this process is the drone-based killing of Anwar Al-Awlaki and Samir Khan, both American citizens who were deeply engaged in effective messaging on behalf of Al Qaeda in the Arabian Peninsula (AQAP) as well as in certain acts of terrorism. Khan occupied a unique position as editor of the online terrorist magazine, *Inspire*, said to be a vital recruiting tool for AQAP as well an effective way of advancing its beliefs in English; it was *Inspire* that was said, later, to be the source of information for Dzhokar and Tamarlen Tsarnaev, the Chechen-American brothers suspected in the Boston Marathon bombing. Although the information-related justifications may not have been at the forefront, they were a possible element of the decision. The implication is this: Where barriers exist because of domestic limitations, seemingly hamstringing transnational efforts, those barriers will be under pressure, and will sometimes be torn down.

Similarly, all societies, and particularly democratic ones, are at an asymmetrical disadvantage if their capacity to fashion an effective transnational information campaign is hampered by domestic politics and that of their opponents is less restrained. As an example, American international broadcasting investments such as the Voice of America and Radio Marti could reflect foreign relations needs and necessities but also pressures created by internal domestic politics. Resources for international broadcasting may be aimed at Cuba for reasons of local political pressure rather than otherwise assessed national preferences, and effective diaspora groups can hijack the process for their parochial needs.

Maintaining control over an internal information space is also the basis for renewed national interest in versions of the "on-off switch" for advanced information technologies. Again, the mantra for avoiding the disasters to the state of destabilizing asymmetry is finding, in advance, points of vulnerability: the openings through which an information cartel can be broken, the space that might allow a mobilizing, perhaps electrifying, message to get through. For the stability-seeking state, the search is to identify the possibility of such a weakness and plan effectively against its exploitation. While furtherance of asymmetry may mean encouraging circumvention of local filtering, as I described it earlier, the stifling of circumvention and heightened surveillance is the response of the targeted state.

A curious and important asymmetry – relevant to strategic communication – involves the different capacity of the government and dissenters to control whether individuals in society can sense the changing political mood of the community. It is one thing for individual citizens to wish a change in government. It is another if these same individuals are aware that their views are widely or pervasively held – an awareness that could eventually accelerate efforts for change. By controlling information, the state has traditionally been in a position to reinforce a view of what the public generally believes, even if that is inconsistent with rampant private beliefs. In this sense, Elihu Katz has linked asymmetric strategies to concepts of "pluralistic ignorance" and the "spiral of silence."[41] Pluralistic ignorance is a term introduced by Floyd H. Allport in 1931 that describes "a situation where a majority of group members privately reject a norm, but assume (incorrectly) that most others accept it."[42] The spiral of silence, a concept developed by Elizabeth Noelle-Neuman, asserts that a person is less likely to voice an opinion on a topic if he or she feels in the minority and is therefore in fear of reprisal or isolation from the society for expressing sharp dissent. Situations of asymmetric communication usually involve efforts by the state to maintain pluralistic ignorance and spirals of silence and by agents of change to reduce or end them. The mood in Tunisia, Egypt and Libya altered when masses – who in the past had been held in check by government efforts to present an image of consensus through

[41] Elihu Katz, "Publicity and Pluralistic Ignorance: Notes on 'The Spiral of Silence,'" in *Public Opinion and Social Change*, eds. H. Baier, H. M. Kepplinger and D. A. Reumann (Weisbade: Westdeutscher Verlag, 1981).

[42] Daniel Katz and Floyd H. Allport, *Student Attitudes* (Syracuse, NY: Craftsman, 1931), 152.

state-controlled broadcasting, restrictions on public gatherings and other efforts – realized that their attitudes were widely and passionately embraced.

Understanding these asymmetries may also be key to comprehending significant elements of a government's right to intervene under international norms. It is an extension, although an honorable one, of the principles of free expression to support cross-border intervention to empower those whose information production and distribution resources are restricted. In terms of Article 19 of the International Covenant on Civil and Political Rights, one could justify intervention by defining the right to impart information as a lifeline to those with highly constrained knowledge about the impact of their own protests against a repressive government.

At the same time, Article 19 reserves power for the state, under Paragraph 3, to limit the right to receive and impart information "for the protection of national security or of public order" (so long as the limitations are "provided by law" and are "necessary" in a democratic society and the response is proportionate).[43] The ordinary problem, however, is that many contexts of information asymmetry that might be construed by the authorities as threatening the public order are inchoate. The issue is delicate; how does one characterize instances where the potential threat seems small but is like a storm in the distance? That may be a classic instance of asymmetry.

Finally, an emerging area of information asymmetry – increasingly related to governance and the power of the state – is cyberwarfare and cyberterrorism. This is not always furtherance of information asymmetry of the kind discussed in this chapter (asymmetry in access to markets of allegiances). It is the use of technical (if immoral and illegal) approaches to hampering the capacity of states to function by attacking their infrastructure. Destructive hacking may be the action of individuals demonstrating their prowess, or it may be in the service of other states, their militaries or organized groups. Cyberwarfare raises the ethical questions often present in asymmetric conflict, including the very permissibility of the tool. It emphasizes the innovative and, as such, has the quality of rapidly changing circumstances of strength and weakness.[44]

What is emerging is a context of new technological and institutional arrangements in which responses to asymmetries yield ever greater unpredictability.

---

[43] UN General Assembly, *International Covenant on Civil and Political Rights*, United Nations, December 16, 1966.

[44] For indications of U.S. concerns about cyberwarfare vis-à-vis asymmetric war and communication, see Richard A. Clarke and Robert Knake, *Cyber War: The Next Threat to National Security and What to Do About It* (New York: HarperCollins, 2010); Martin C. Libicki, *Cyberdeterrence and Cyberwar* (Santa Monica: RAND, 2009). The first was written by a former special advisor to the president on cybersecurity; the second was commissioned by the U.S. Air Force.

Asymmetries have always existed. But new media technologies, coupled with aggressive use of them by increasingly sophisticated players (those invoking the power of the protesting streets to the hackers of Anonymous and WikiLeaks), upend traditional arrangements and traditional doctrines. An increase in information asymmetry leads to weakened confidence in existing institutions and accommodations. In this environment, understanding the dynamics of strategic communication and fashioning strategies of response becomes more and more urgent.

6

Strategies of System Architecture

In this chapter, I shift to a broader strategic lens. Most examples I have discussed so far have been about how various entities (states, religions, etc.) manipulate markets for loyalties to further a specific strategic goal. These efforts can be to give voice to a specific group, to mobilize the young and disaffected, for example, or to energize a certain minority, such as the Kurds in Turkey; they can also be strategies of exclusion (for example, establishing rules that deprive groups deemed "terrorist" from platforms of communication or suppressing certain images of women). These kinds of efforts are the bread and butter of strategic communication. But they should not deflect attention from a more comprehensive way of thinking about many communication transformations, what I call "strategic architectures of media and information systems."

I start with a fairly reasonable proposition. Governments, commercial entities and other powerful organizations, all concerned with the potential triumph of seen and unseen competitors for control of information, seek to design communication infrastructures to optimize achievement of their own strategic goals. In pursuing these ambitions, strategic communicators go beyond relying on law or cartel alone to control or regulate patterns of delivery. These influential actors embrace large-scale comprehensive strategies with national or global pretensions, seeking to reassure (at least from the perspective of the strategic communicator) that goals will be met. These strategies mean thinking architecturally about the process as a whole, focusing on the overall structure. They often call for a vision of a future communication system and a comprehensive plan for achieving that vision.

The history of system design in media has an expansive sweep. Hardly a modern phenomenon, the nourishing of an architecture of information management within a state or empire's own domain could be seen as a root characteristic of governance. This remains true regardless of technology.

Innovations may have within them the capacity to be "technologies of freedom," and that was the aspiration of such scholars of system architecture as Ithiel de Sola Pool. But information breakthroughs become modified or redesigned in the interest of major participants. I argue that governments of various stripes, and certainly transnational corporations striving for global influence or maximizing profit, have long exercised architectural ambitions. They wish to be able to deploy the resulting system, both domestic and international, in furtherance of their social, economic and political goals. Vast rearrangements of infrastructure are engendered to reflect technological feasibilities and geopolitical realities. Strategic moments occur over decades, as, for example, with the establishment of the newspaper industry, the introduction of radio, the shift to television, to color television, to cable, to satellite, and now to mobile and the Internet.[1] They may characterize the operation of business tycoons like Rupert Murdoch, who early on saw the opportunities and limits for satellite distribution in Europe and long persisted in hopeful modes of thinking about large-scale entry in China. Generally, there is very little public notice or awareness of the implications of these transformations. The major consequences of these changes for thinking about elements of free expression are usually submerged in the torrent of seemingly uncoordinated decisions. Some transformations seem merely to have occurred, without intent, planning or any articulation of social consequences. In other cases, one can sense change in slow motion: transformations come wrapped in specific banners – cybersecurity, copyright reform, protection of children, nationalism – all of which are modes for rethinking portions or aspects of information flows.

It is true that pathways of communication are initiated, in large part, through millions of small human interactions. They follow personal byways, just as roads sometimes grew out of the meandering customs of ancient residents in a region. But pathways of communication are increasingly the result of large-scale public and private interventions, aspects of design at a national or global level, sometimes based on economic advantage and sometimes based on the hard-wired zest for dominance.[2] Governments are hardly the only innovators of these ambitious designs; software engineers, garage tinkerers, dreamers of all stripes engage in the fantasies of new possibilities. These interventions repurpose previous systems, deploy innovative techniques, take advantage of economies of scale and use political or economic power to impose a favored outcome.

[1]   See, for example, Joseph D. Straubhaar, *World Television: From Global to Local* (Los Angeles: SAGE, 2007).
[2]   Laura DeNardis, "Hidden Levers of Internet Control: An Infrastructure-Based Theory of Internet Governance," *Information, Communication & Society* 15, no. 5 (2012).

The transitions that followed the fall of the Soviet Union, and those that are now taking place in the wake of the disruptions and destructions of the Arab Spring, are examples of strategic moments when new architectures are forged. Transition-produced systems look the way they do as a result of a competition among parties interested in the future of the media market and, at times, the future of the country. Purveyors of technology must convince officials (often the officials of donor countries, not officials at home) that their tools can capture the dreams of those who commission them. Officials bring politics, ideology and corruption to systemic options. And there comes to be a kind of world view of the normal (for example, that broad access to the Internet is a necessity, that there must be spectrum allocated for community broadcasting, or that "free and independent" licensing of radio or television stations should be the foundation of an acceptable media system). System design represents the combination of competitive strategic efforts as shifts occur from the parochial to the general, and vice versa. An entity, such as a company, an NGO, or a governmental agency, starts with an ambitious goal – for example, protecting asserted intellectual property rights. But to achieve the solution at scale, the task may mean extraordinary architectural shifts, guaranteed, for example, through legislation that has a wholesale impact on the way in which information flows[3] or through international assistance programs designed to have a large-scale, system-wide impact.

In parts of the former Soviet Union, particularly Central Asia, ample state ownership and management of the press systems, the historic norm, persists as a characteristic strategic approach, although often through oligarchic partnership. The complexity of wholesale control was certainly the architecturally distinguishing feature of the Soviet system, portrayed in terms of its purposive structure.[4] Yet such architectural control has been a feature of even those states with longer traditions of democracy. It is easy to forget that the BBC had a virtual monopoly over broadcasting in the UK until the 1950s. The long dominance of the BBC in the UK was tribute to a sense that the broadcasting system played a key role in the national consciousness.[5] Similarly, consider how, over decades, Canada puzzled how to maintain influence over Canadian identity with the United States looming as an

---

[3]   In France, in the United States and elsewhere, legislation sought to reshape Internet protocols to provide greater sanctions against individuals who illegally downloaded protected files. See U.S. Congress, "S.968 – PIPA," 2011; Peter Yu, "The Graduated Response," *Florida Law Review* 62, no. 5 (2010).

[4]   See Brian McNair, *Glasnost, Perestroika and the Soviet Media* (New York: Routledge, 1991).

[5]   Asa Briggs, *The BBC: The First Fifty Years* (Oxford: Oxford University Press, 1986).

avalanche of identity next door.[6] The CRTC – Canada's regulatory agency – was charged with the responsibility of designing a system that was consistent with international norms but enlarged the prospect of sustaining a Canadian national identity. Affirmatively encouraging Canadian content was key, but underlying this were efforts at system design, including encouragement of Canadian content producers, Canadian ownership of transmission facilities and Canadian control of access to satellite transponders. Scrutiny of Canada's broadcasting policy, and its capacity to achieve publicly stated goals, continues.[7] In France – and by extension throughout the Francophone world – state influence on broadcasting to enhance state identity was taken for granted, and its influence persists. Much has been written about Singapore and Malaysia's efforts to build information and media systems that would sustain strong and modern economies while simultaneously managing – often harshly – unwanted speech and debate. Singapore created a system of almost universal multichannel high-capacity cable that could deliver droves of information but still reflect governmental preferences and priorities and filter unwanted material. Malaysia created a similar system through the deliberate design of a monopoly satellite entity. These communications systems were often in private hands with close ties to government, and cooperation between state and private power was relatively unproblematic.[8]

Another contemporary example of media architectures of scale was the Venezuela of the late Hugo Chavez, which sought – through actual force and the force of governmental domination – to transform its national information space as well as affect cultural and political landscapes throughout Latin America.[9] Chavez's decision to change the informational structure from one that was predominantly private had both a charismatic and an institutional, infrastructural side.[10] Like Fidel Castro, Chavez personalized control of the airwaves through persistent and overwhelming presence as representative of the state. He occupied the airwaves. He weakened the

---

[6] See Richard Collins, *Culture, Communication, & National Identity: The Case of Canadian Television* (Toronto: University of Toronto Press, 1990); Marc Raboy, *Missed Opportunities: The Story of Canada's Broadcasting Policy* (Montreal: McGill Queens University Press, 1990).

[7] For instance, see Robert Armstrong, *Broadcasting Policy in Canada* (Toronto: University of Toronto Press, 2010); Michael Dewing, "Canadian Broadcasting Policy" (Background Paper 2011–39-E, Ottawa: Library of Parliament, 2012).

[8] William Atkins, *The Politics of Southeast Asia's New Media* (London: Routledge, 2002); Cherian George, *Freedom from the Press: Journalism and State Power in Singapore* (Singapore: NUS Press, 2012).

[9] See Craig Hayden, *The Rhetoric of Soft Power: Public Diplomacy in Global Contexts* (Lanham: Lexington Books, 2012); Jairo Lugo-Ocando, ed., *The Media in Latin America* (Berkshire: Open University Press, 2008).

[10] For instance, see "Caught in the Crossfire," *Human Rights Watch*, May 31, 2003.

opposition, rendering it difficult and sometimes impossible for oppositional media to continue broadcasting. Licenses of opponents were not renewed. Significant for the idea of system architecture, Chavez sought to extend his policy throughout Latin America with the founding of the satellite service, TeleSUR. In Chavez's Bolivarian strategy and vision, it was not just Venezuela that was relevant to the revolutionary conversion, nor only the media that were involved. In terms of the scope of persuasion, the process was more pervasive, including control of systems of public education and expansion of government as speaker. A satellite service like TeleSUR would, hypothetically, become a building block in a controversial hemispheric strategy.

One of my favorite examples of system design involves state and society in the Netherlands. For more than half of the twentieth century, the Netherlands sought to deepen an architectural system for society in its many aspects that could reflect a special Dutch pluralism, implementing a complex *Verzuiling* (pillarization) in institutional structures. Society was organized in "pillars" (often religious pillars) and this organization suffused all significant elements of life – education, politics, where people lived. This general organization of society was mirrored in the radio and, later, television broadcasting systems. Just as in schools, in sports and in newspapers and clubs, major groups (Catholics, Protestants, etc.) had their own separate channels or portions of channels and frequencies. A charming village – Hilversum – existed where each "pillar" had its own house for production and management. This strategic design of broadcasting governed who had access, how material was produced, and who, almost naturally, controlled the boundaries of what was acceptable. For reasons of technological change and European law, only remnants of this Dutch system remain; what is important here was the fact that such a total system could exist and function for a significant period.[11]

One could argue that new variations on communications technology – that is, the Internet – allow a wildly distinctive variant on pillarization, though perhaps personalization is a better term. This variant involves reorganizing modes of control through analytics, the amassing and dissection of data achieved through systems of management.[12] This is the current large-scale systematic transformation, one chronicled by, among others, Professor Joseph

[11]   The Dutch *Mediawet* (Media Act) was finally replaced by the *Mediawet 2008* (Media Act 2008), signaling this final shift. Also see Willem F. Korthals Altes, "European Law: A Case Study of Changes in National Broadcasting," *Cardozo Arts & Entertainment Law Journal* 11, no. 2 (1993).

[12]   Viktor Mayer-Schonberger and Kenneth Cukier, *Big Data: A Revolution That Will Transform How We Live, Work, and Think* (Boston: Houghton Mifflin Harcourt, 2013).

Turow.[13] A successful use of analytics depends on a new architecture of the media system. Related are the observations of Professor Siva Vaidhyanathan who writes, in *The Googlization of Everything*, about the extraordinary, though not always successful, strategy that Google has undertaken in terms of rethinking publishing, copyright and the diffusion of information.[14] Even when Google has ended up with less than it desired, it has done so in the context of thinking strategically and contemplating an almost totalizing solution for the reorganization of the production of and access to information, how to reinvent the mode by which people gain access to the world's storehouse of ideas. Professor Susan Crawford has written, similarly, about the strategies of Comcast, the U.S. communications giant, as it extends power from one market to another, both geographically and technologically – a strategy for which, as is often the case, the reconceptualization of media in society is tied to mastery of marketing data.[15]

MEDIA DEVELOPMENT AND THE CASE OF MYANMAR

Media development – soft interventions by external governments and NGOs to shape a media system – is an important example of strategic architecture. I want to raise the case of Myanmar (also and previously known as Burma) to illustrate how an expanding number of well-intentioned development actors can lack coherence in implementation. Media development is usually a purposeful set of interventions, sponsored by foundations or national and international government agencies, to change a media system to further political, social or economic goals. Media development has become a generating sector for strategic architectural experiments.

In 2011, Myanmar's military-dominated government began the process of commanding change, change of a sort that would yield a society much more in accord with international norms. The question might be what would strategic actors do, in an environment where structural advances had been repressed, to affect media structures with democratic consolidation as a goal? How does the emerging state establish its own internal architectural capacity? With which global powers and transnational corporations does it associate? What role do global civil society organizations play in this process?

---

[13] Joseph Turow, *The Daily You: How the New Advertising Industry Is Defining Your Identity and Your Worth* (New Haven, CT: Yale University Press, 2012).

[14] Siva Vaidhyanathan, *The Googlization of Everything: (And Why We Should Worry)* (Berkeley: University of California Press, 2011).

[15] Susan Crawford, *Captive Audience: The Telecom Industry and Monopoly Power in the New Gilded Age* (New Haven, CT: Yale University Press, 2013).

The story of Myanmar and media development is still taking shape. Some anecdotes may, at an early stage, provide insight. In 2013 and after, there were gatherings under the aegis of the Minister of Information to identify the range of actors available from the West who could be helpful in the process of system design and implementation. An organization called International Media Support (IMS), funded largely by Scandinavian governments, was tasked, together with the Center for Law and Democracy, with providing technical assistance in drafting media laws and policies, strengthening media associations, capacity-building for early and mid-career journalists and enhancing the internal peace process through training in conflict-sensitive reporting. All this was in the service of building an infrastructure of improved journalism, on the assumption that it would bolster democratic tendencies in Myanmar. Canal France International, in partnership with a private Burmese broadcast entity, would provide video journalism training. BBC Media Action would conduct a six-month journalism course online in Burmese facilitated by local mentors. Deutsche Welle (DW) was involved in the "training of trainers" in TV journalism. The United Nations Development Program (UNDP) sought to strengthen the capacity of local media institutions in support of local development and civic awareness at the district and state/regional levels. The United Kingdom Embassy became involved in capacity-building of local journalists, covering subjects such as media ethics. The American-based Open Society Institute was more "strategic," a donor rather than an implementer. It, together with USAID, the Department for International Development, the Swedish International Development Cooperation Agency and others, determined how to allocate funds to support the various actors and determine priorities, the goal being media assistance to strengthen democracy in Myanmar. UNESCO planned a broad portfolio: (a) media legislation (print, broadcast, public service media, cinema, telecommunications); (b) capacity-building for journalists and government public relations officers; (c) promotion of press freedom; (d) support for media development in the context of democratic reforms and peacebuilding initiatives in cooperation with the European Union; (e) strengthening of the Department of Journalism of the National Management College. The U.S. State Department financed the travel of lawyers specifically to review a new broadcast law, a draft press law and other pieces of industry-defining legislation.

I have listed all these organizations involved in Myanmar – and there were more – to indicate the range of international interests in an evolving media system, interests that wheeled into action to yield change in existing arrangements. Media assistance, of the kind that was bursting out, assumed a structure that would allow independent voices, encourage a public service broadcaster, fit with a system that reflected new technological opportunities. It was the benevolent face of strategic communication. Embedded in a series of assumptions, the objectives and means of achieving them seem hardly disputable. Media assistance, in this developed Western vocabulary, is committed to greater pluralism, less censorship, more training and better journalism. The actions are so much a part of the system of accepted patterns of media development that adjustment to Myanmar realities is hard to recognize, although it is an inevitable part of the process of adjustment. It will take years to see whether these initiatives respond adequately to problems that arise out of the legacy of the military regime: the decades in which the strategic communication policy of the government was to wall the population from outside information sources.

Issues of strategic intervention and design face a particular reality: Myanmar was in the process of being reborn in a world of highly competitive strategic communicators. Satellite dishes would begin to sprout like flowers in the spring. Mobile phone sales would escalate phenomenally. Modes for reaching individuals and publics would proliferate. New modes exist for the human and capital infrastructure to rehabilitate, not necessarily dependent on traditional media development institutions. Journalism practices would continue to suffer from the long period of being, in large part, a professional wasteland, but innovative publishers and driven young entrants would forge new patterns for entry. Capacities for production were at a low level. Different national media development styles brought and would continue to bring varied cultures of assistance to the table. The history and traditions of British entities, U.S. organizations and Scandinavian players varied, as did their ties to the region. In addition, different entities faced a spectrum of questions from their home constituencies: Were they there for the long or short term? What constituted specific anticipated outputs? What would be the relationship of media interventions to a set of democratic principles?

In the case of Myanmar, the international actors I have mentioned were all committed to democratic consolidation. But as processes of organizing change develop, differentiated goals and contextual factors will affect investment. China's influence could expand. Other factors might overwhelm media policy and design. Myanmar will be a new market for goods and a source of labor. Outbreaks of violence showed that there will be pressing interests in conflict resolution as violence occurs between the Buddhist majority and the Muslim (and specifically Rohingya) minority. How information will inflame or moderate those circumstances will be important. Higher on the strategy chain, as budgets and actions are defended or justified in parliaments, in defense establishments, in governments, additional national interests may take precedence over media development and shift priorities.

Evolved approaches to "free and independent" media systems often serve as a default mode for the architectural shaping of a media system. If applied in an automatic, template-like fashion, however, external pre-fabricated designs can deter consideration of complex issues of institution-building. In the case of Myanmar, for example, traditional approaches to democratizing media development might or might not buttress the hold of the military, allowing it to retain interests in private stations. Regulatory agencies can be established and broadcast licenses issued, but those close to ancient power may be the major beneficiaries. Strategic architectures also have to address particularities of ethnic conflict and Myanmar's religious background. Opening the market widely almost always leads to commercialization, with ownership structures that further oligarchic power, producing content that weakens values of local history and culture. Such are the hazards and risks of modernization. Implementing models of media development require adjustment where the goals are, among others, to achieve higher literacy rates, a more informed citizenry and a more accountable government. Opportunities to leapfrog, through a focus on broadband and Internet development, might be embraced or slighted in favor of developing more limited, more traditional media outlets including community broadcasting.

ARCHETYPES OF ARCHITECTURAL STRATEGIES

How are these large-scale architectural approaches, successful or not, born? Ideology and information strategy of the most ambitious scale is everywhere present: in the shaping of the broadcasting industry in the twentieth century, in the turning of cable television from a humble operation of hardware store owners to a multi-billion dollar business, in the installation of a system of satellites and their transponders and in the engineering of the Internet. Visions are not all business-driven or ideological. Some spring from the mind of a single person of imagination, some from science fiction, some from backyard tinkerers. Visions often become quickly organized and corporatized. National defense and geopolitics are relatively significant as a driving force: Much of radio and television structure is traceable to the needs of the state during conflict. Broadcasting policies were highly influenced by World War I, World War II and the Cold War. Satellite communications in part were shaped in the Sputnik era as a zone of cooperation and competition between the United States and the Soviet Union. The Internet famously began as a project of the U.S. Department of Defense, with design features built in to protect the system against the danger of nuclear damage.

The relationship of the military to system architecture is important for the general theme of this chapter. Many coups begin with the seizure of the broadcast media. The military sees control of narrative in the most sharply instrumental way. For example, in Thailand, the military portrays its place as the trusted keeper of the monarchy, and believes the media system should project a view not inconsistent with that view; in Pakistan, Egypt and Turkey, the military has similarly contributed to a construction of the institution as a historical embodiment of the state. Militaries – typical of major forces in the society – are significantly interested in how innovations in media architecture affect government functioning. Increasingly, they are interested in how media shape stability at home and attitudes at home and abroad. Both civilian and military agencies may intervene to improve the communication practices of a target society to enable it to move from fragile to functional or authoritarian to more democratic. The military agenda may be more concerned with the short-term consequences of destabilization or protection during active missions, as was the case with the U.S. command in Afghanistan. The history of reorganization of media systems during a military occupation (in Germany, Japan, Bosnia-Hercegovina and Iraq, for example) provides important examples of architectural strategies for the design of comprehensive media structures at transitional moments.

More directly, in conflict zones and hard-case transitions, the various powers, often including the domestic or intervening military, seek to address the information environment in its theaters of operation. If a goal is stability, or the strengthening of fragile societies so that the nominal government has a chance to govern, obtaining the right strategic narrative is significant. Caring about these narratives is perceived, in some quarters, as a way of reducing conflict. For General Wesley Clark, responsible for much of the NATO-Kosovo campaign, a well-crafted information war, earlier commenced and effectively conducted, might have been preferable to the bombing campaign that was actually implemented. "Achieving information dominance over an adversary will decide conflicts long before resort to more violent forms of warfare is necessary."[16]

Champions of public service broadcasting – descendants of Lord Reith – are another source of drive for architectural solutions.[17] The BBC and state

---

[16] See Julian Borger, "Cyberwar Could Spare Bombs; Nato Commander Wesley Clark Boosts the Case for Telecom Assaults with a Vision of How They Might Have Been Used in Kosovo," *Guardian*, November 5, 1999.

[17] The European Convention on Human Rights affects the power of a state to implement a system that structurally shapes an internal market. One early European case that established limits was *Informationsverein Lentia and others v. Austria*, which decided, under the European

counterparts in Europe turned radio from a hobbyist's delight into a national or state enterprise with significant cultural and nation-building characteristics. For several key decades, the major architects of radio were in these great national systems; they saw themselves as part of a global movement, furthering a public service model of the medium. The U.S. commercial model, with the national networks as chief architects, were not so significant a competitor in the global arena for system design in the first decades of the twentieth century, but the reshaping of the system as essentially commercial has proceeded apace, partly because of long-term planning and legal and lobbying interventions that weakened commitment to a public and publicly financed sector. Often, the interests of commercial broadcasting see themselves as the norm and the foundation on which broadcast systems in democratic societies should be built.

Communications satellites had their origins in science fiction, with the inventive writer Arthur C. Clarke as the conceptual inventor. In the 1950s and 1960s, exemplary centers of research, such as Bell Labs, developed a vision and designed a plan for their implementation. Indeed, the role of strategic innovation by these intense research and development engineering arms of national telecom monopolies can hardly be overestimated. Later, communications satellites became an information technology that had a comprehensive plan or vision that arose from the U.S. government itself as it sought to shape an international approach to the new distribution mechanisms.[18]

An interesting art form for these articulations of strategic design is the set of national commissions: examples proliferated in the United States, the UK and elsewhere, from the 1940s onward. These sought to consider the future of incipient information technologies, how they should be designed and their potential impact on society. In 1965, the Carnegie Corporation in New York City established a national commission to study what kind of legislation and what kind of strategy was desirable for the future of public service broadcasting in the United States.[19] That report, bolstered by interventions from the Ford Foundation, set a U.S. model for elite-level, somewhat pluralistic inquiries into the architecture of media and communications policy. A broad-based,

---

Convention, against the then-Austrian broadcasting law that vested a monopoly over radio in the national broadcasting system allowing for no licensing of private stations.

[18] See Joseph N. Pelton, Robert J. Oslund and Peter Marshall, eds. *Communications Satellites: Global Change Agents* (Mahwah, NJ: Lawrence Erlbaum Associates, 2004); See also Monroe Price, "Satellite Broadcasting as Trade Routes in the Sky," in *In Search of Boundaries: Communication, Nation States and Cultural Identities*, eds. Joseph M. Chan and Bryce T. McIntyre (Westport, CT: Ablex Publishing, 2002).

[19] Stephen White, "Carnegie II: A Look Back and Ahead," *Public Telecommunications Review* 5, no. 2 (July/August 1977).

wide-lensed successor was the 1968 President's Task Force on Telecommunications Policy, which made recommendations on the breakup of the telephone monopoly and sought comprehensively to deal with federal issues related to media and society. Fast on its heels was the 1972 Sloan Commission on Cable Communications, focused primarily on the burgeoning future. These were all efforts – partly modeled on British prototypes engaged in periodic review of the BBC – to gain high-level, disinterested, multi-disciplinary perspectives on the role information technology could play. Some of these had public or governmental involvement or were initiated by government; others were products of "the great and the good," public-spirited individuals bringing larger perspectives to significant public choices.[20]

THE INTERNET AND STRATEGIC ARCHITECTURE

I turn, as an example of a debate involving strategic architecture, to the clashing conceptions of Internet design articulated by the United States and China. Both countries have a great deal at stake internally in terms of the evolution of Internet system design, and both seek to project their views on an international stage. I use two statements about the future of the Internet, one from the United States, one from China, to explore these questions of design: a 2010 speech by then-U.S. Secretary of State Hillary Clinton and a China-originated Internet White Paper issued not long afterward. These are presented as visions of what future generations of the Internet should look like, but they are also presented as visions about the society that the Internet would impel or reinforce. This competition is illustrative of a modern phenomenon: Those advocating change in communications policy, both nationally and globally, have enmeshed their conceptions in various technological, social and political categories to improve the chances that these policies will be adopted. They have sought to "hard-wire" their ideas of speech and society into evolving structures.

The U.S. "Internet Freedom" Strategy

In January 2010, Secretary Clinton delivered a much-acclaimed speech called "Remarks on Internet Freedom" at a temple of free speech, the

---

[20] On the British side, for example, the role of the Peacock Committee was central, yielding Alan Peacock, "Report of the Committee on Financing the BBC," Cmnd. 9824 (London: HMSO, 1986). Also see Tom O'Malley and Janet Jones, eds., *The Peacock Committee and UK Broadcasting Policy* (Basingstoke: Palgrave Macmillan, 2009).

Newseum in Washington, DC.[21] As an exercise in global framing, the talk was a dramatic effort to define proper structuring of the Internet in a global setting. The speech threw down a gauntlet: "Both the American people and nations that censor the Internet should understand that our government is committed to helping promote Internet freedom," and this requires that the U.S. government fight for a global policy consistent with these views.[22] Left somewhat vague was what Internet freedom would actually mean in terms of system implementation. In 2006, the Bush Administration had already established a Global Internet Freedom Task Force (GIFT). The Clinton State Department, renaming GIFT as the NetFreedom Task Force, bureaucratically provided an upgraded framework to make the Internet – and U.S. policy concerning it – a priority in bilateral and multilateral discussions and to develop grant programs, policy initiatives and other steps to further that goal.

The Secretary's Newseum presentation featured the earmarks of a "new information" enthusiasm, celebrating the glories of the technology: "The spread of information networks is forming a new nervous system for our planet. . . . Now, in many respects, information has never been so free. There are more ways to spread more ideas to more people than at any moment in history. . . . And even in authoritarian countries, information networks are helping people discover new facts and making governments more accountable."[23] The speech contained the normal duality of benefits and dangers, the litany of grounds for concern (including child pornography and national security). The speech articulated a ground for exporting a form of communications architecture.

Secretary Clinton's argument depended on a tree of logic in which U.S. interests are served by the increase in democratic values in states throughout the world. A long-standing theory holds that a world that is more dependably democratic is more stable, possibly more prosperous, and less likely to lead to conflict with other democracies. Related to this is the belief that openness to information, and press freedom more specifically, is linked to democracy, as a system of information diffusion that empowers individuals, leads to greater accountability and improves or enhances the demand side for democratic

---

[21] Hillary Clinton, "Internet Freedom," January 21, 2010. Clinton gave a second Internet freedom speech a year later at The Hague. See "Secretary Clinton on Internet Freedom," December 8, 2011.

[22] See, for example, Adam D. Thierer and Clyde Wayne Crews, eds., *Who Rules the Net?: Internet Governance and Jurisdiction* (Washington, DC: Cato Institute, 2003).

[23] Clinton, "Internet Freedom." For a critique of the prevailing Internet freedom rhetoric, see Evgeny Morozov, *The Net Delusion: The Dark Side of Internet Freedom* (New York: Public Affairs, 2011).

governance. "Internet freedom" is, at least in part, shorthand for a series of policies concerning the Internet that would advance these democratic values and expedite more democratic political outcomes. It entails a commitment to an "enabling environment," one that asserts the rule of law and may in fact respect it.[24]

A second strategy for an "Internet freedom" agenda – not necessarily inconsistent with this first one – is an economic one, with at least two branches that implicitly favor U.S. economic output. First, an "Internet freedom" agenda may be an umbrella for expanded demand for approaches and products developed by American suppliers (or transnational companies with strong U.S. and Western ties). An "Internet freedom" rationale encourages a system for the diffusion of information that is highly consistent with a freer market in goods and services – a market that is also beneficial to a liberalized economy. For example, as satellite services transformed modes of supplying information, they created broad new markets both for video programs and for consumer goods advertised or promoted on the new channels of distribution. This was a market in which American entertainment providers had an historic advantage. The same, of course, is potentially true for the Internet. In this sense, an "Internet freedom" agenda is also an agenda for a robust transnational economy in which the United States considers it has a stake.

Finally, an "Internet freedom" agenda feeds into a pronounced vision of opening what, in Chapter 1, I categorized as cartels in significant markets for loyalties. Many entities, many organizations, many "sellers" in the search for expanding constituencies of allegiances have an interest in an infrastructure that offers them easier access to publics. An "Internet freedom" policy, generally speaking, facilitates access by such entities – at least providing the technical capacity for entry. The United States (and other governments) may have their own reasons to reach target publics, as do global NGOs with passionate agendas, or religious entities that wish to compete with those systems of belief that are more established and protected. A policy that furthers "Internet freedom" enlarges the possibility of such entry. Indeed, the special definition of strategic communication that I provided in Chapter 1 – a transnational effort to reach audiences and shift their perspectives on matters significant to their identity – is dependent

---

[24] For this notion, see Monroe E. Price and Peter Krug, "The Enabling Environment for Free and Independent Media," in *Media Matters: Perspectives on Advancing Governance and Development from the Global Forum for Media Development*, ed. Mark Harvey (Paris: Internews Europe, 2006).

on innovative ways to gain access.[25] "Internet freedom" furthers such a structure.

Clearly, Secretary Clinton's speech was playing on the anxiety that a great opportunity for free expression would be lost if the United States in concert with others was not vigilant. The Internet provided the long hoped for chance for a liberating technology, one that had the potential to increase education, serve as the basis for stronger citizenship and advance democratic values. And "freedom" is, itself, the U.S. narrative or brand (or has been most consistently in recent decades). "Internet freedom" in this sense implies some vindication for American approaches, American aspirations. "Internet freedom" as an idea exports both a legal structure and a culture of expression that, at least on the surface, favors American narrative. It implies the structuring of a competitive environment for entry and reception in which U.S. interests have historically done well. And the alternative – more closed systems – can be seen as encouraging an environment in which counter-narratives have privileged if not exclusive access.[26]

How does one make such a vision, incomplete and aspirational as it is, operational? Clinton's speech created the prospect of a new design element, a potential international "right to connect." This would be a high-minded right that sought to bring rhetorical grandeur to the proposal and use entitlement discourse to ground a policy approach. Creating a "right" is an example of deploying international norms as a persuasive underpinning for a strategic outcome. By highlighting a movement toward a "right to connect" (or an obligation to ensure a "freedom to connect"), or, in other guises, a right to communicate,[27] the U.S. government would establish a public and external framework in which steps toward the Internet freedom structure would be seen as almost mandatory.

At the heart of the U.S. position seemed to be this architectural point, which was immediately subject to multiple interpretations: "We stand for a single

---

[25] Some activists have accused U.S.-based corporations of profiting from censorship and filtering software exported to "authoritarian" regimes, even as the U.S. government funds an industry of anti-censorship software. See Sami Ben Gharbia, "The Internet Freedom Fallacy and the Arab Digital activism," *nawaat.org*, September 17, 2010.

[26] See Rebecca MacKinnon, *The Consent of the Networked: The Worldwide Struggle for Internet Freedom* (New York: Basic Books, 2012).

[27] The "right to communicate" was first articulated in the 1960s by Jean d'Arcy. See Jean d'Arcy, "Direct Broadcast Satellites and the Right to Communicate," *EBU Review* 118 (1969). See also Desmond Fisher, *The Right to Communicate: A Status Report* (Paris: UNESCO, 1982). More recently, William J. McIver, Jr., William F. Birdsall and Merrilee Rasmussen have discussed the right in the context of the Internet. See William J. McIver, Jr., William F. Birdsall and Merrilee Rasmussen, "The Internet and the Right to Communicate," *First Monday* 8, no. 12 (2003).

Internet where all of humanity has equal access to knowledge and ideas." Combining the "single Internet" idea with the "right to connect" provides the basis for a legal model, where the Internet should not be splintered into many national Internets, each with its own rules of entry and separate regulatory frameworks reflecting differences among national publics. What was desired would be "One Internet" with overwhelming access. Gaining a vision and encapsulating it within a pithy term can be an element of strategy – a strategy of mobilization of influence. The articulation of strategy sometimes requires the exclusion of complex details, which might detract from the appeal of the more clearly stated idea. As we shall see, it is this feature, the idea of "One Internet," that pits the U.S. position directly in contrast with that of China.

In terms of strategy, the Clinton speech was the public launch of a global campaign. A significant element of what makes this strategic is building an international consensus for the vision. Kenneth Corbin, reporting on a speech by the then-State Department guru, Alec Ross, could write that the "Department has made Internet censorship a key pillar of its foreign policy and now factors the issue into its diplomatic relations with every other nation."[28] Ross argued that "Internet freedom has gone from being something that's a piece of what could at best be called a piece of foreign policy arcanum – a little thing that a handful of people work on – to something becoming increasingly central in our foreign policy." The field of engagement was wide, but troublesome: "2009 was the worst year in history in terms of Internet freedom. ... There are now literally dozens of countries with less-than-stellar internet freedom records. And it's increasingly the case that governments view the Internet as less something built on a single end-user-to-end-user principle than something that can be sort of built to spec, that looks and feels and works more like an intranet than an Internet."

A strategy must be attentive to its many parts and create what counts as an acceptable agenda. For example, an "Internet freedom" strategy would require further policy on standards – for controls, for pricing, for content – and on the legal enabling environment on which an open Internet depends: what liability rules are imposed on Internet Service Providers or other intermediaries, the discouragement of licensing at any level, the repeal of laws concerning criminal libel, and so forth. There would be areas in which the U.S. government had policies inconsistent with what it was recommending abroad, issues where it was not necessarily beyond criticism for its own melding of restrictive

---

[28] Kenneth Corbin, "Net Censorship Central to U.S. Foreign Policy," *Benton Foundation*, June 12, 2010.

and open efforts. These include issues concerning cyberwar and cyberse-curity[29] and the demanding debate over protection of intellectual property on the Internet.[30]

A public conversation in February 2011 between then-Assistant Secretary of State Michael Posner and Leslie Harris of the Center for Democracy and Technology dealt candidly with inconsistencies and challenges in fostering a coherent strategy.[31] Would there be universal standards and how would they be enforced? Who would referee this world? In the conversation, Harris said, "We have to figure out some kind of global governance bodies that don't force us into a race to the bottom." Here was another area, Harris stated, where an American vision might collide with other perspectives:

> There are some calls around the world for governance bodies, like the UN, where we would be negotiating what works on the internet or what ought to work with countries who have very, very different values. . . . I'm hoping that in the first instance, that we can reach agreement with other democratic governments on what we believe the right policy principles are, so that we can start demonstrating the way that the Internet should be governed cross borders. But the questions of who should manage the Internet in a global environment is the thorniest and the biggest challenge.

Posner, too, noted:

> We have, I think, a range of anxieties about throwing this issue and many others into the United Nations. We believe in the United Nations; it has a lot of important roles to play. But we have great trepidation that if this became a UN-sponsored initiative, all of the most – all of the governments that have the greatest interest in regulating and controlling content and protecting against dissident speech in their own countries would be very loud voices.

The explicit global debate about architectural strategy and the role of the United States within it is captured in this discussion between Posner and Harris. How contested approaches are interpreted is markedly important for

---

[29]   Indeed, the rise of externally-directed rhetoric on Internet freedom in the United States has more or less coincided with a rise of internally-directed concerns about cybersecurity and the need for additional protection and surveillance measures. See, for instance, former NSA director in Mike McConnell, "Mike McConnell on how to win the cyber-war we're losing," *Washington Post*, February 28, 2010.

[30]   This was the case with the PIPA and SOPA bill controversies in 2011 and 2012. See, for instance, Mark A. Lemley, David S. Levine and David G. Post, "Don't Break the Internet," *Stanford Law Review Online* 64 (2011). This debate explicitly aligned with similar struggles over perceived inconsistencies in "Internet freedom" over the international ACTA agreement: David Jolly, "A New Question of Internet Freedom," *New York Times*, February 5, 2012.

[31]   Michael Posner and Leslie Harris, "Conversation with America: The State Department's Internet Freedom Strategy," *U.S. Department of State*, February 18, 2011.

the next-generation Internet. The United States had a formative role in the early history of the Internet and the role of national security institutions in shaping its foundations.[32] Critics argue that the Internet has been a creature of various U.S. strategies in the past, and the "Internet freedom" design is primarily a way to try to sustain influence on architecture through a re-articulation of goals. The building of a coalition for maintaining a "freedom agenda" for the Internet gained a new set of challenges in the post-Snowden environment. A new historical moment, and the need to develop a new constituency for Internet regulations, requires regaining trust, especially on the part of Washington policy proponents.

Elements of the bureaucratic embodiment of the U.S. strategy are useful to note. In addition to making the condemnation of online censorship a plank of its diplomatic work, the State Department established monitoring and reporting mechanisms to produce a more reliable picture – as in its annual Human Rights Reports[33] or the largely federally funded Freedom House reports on Internet freedom.[34] The Department accentuated its support for grassroots efforts advocating for Internet freedom or expressing dissident views in blogs and other online forums. It offered funding for research and study in how groups in repressive societies use the Internet and how Internet opportunities can be extended and, most directly, provided funding for the production and distribution of circumvention software to avoid filtering in societies deemed unfree.[35] It supported a Freedom Online Coalition and an activated Internet Governance Forum that celebrated multistakeholderism. It encouraged the Global Network Initiative (GNI), an entity for companies to come together with NGOs to further social responsibility objectives.[36]

---

[32] See, for example, Jonathan Zittrain, *The Future of the Internet and How to Stop It* (New Haven, CT: Yale University Press, 2008).

[33] "Human Rights Reports," *U.S. Department of State.*

[34] "Freedom on the Net," *Freedom House.*

[35] "Internet Freedom: Fact Sheet," *U.S. Department of State*, February 15, 2011; Fergus Hanson, "Internet Freedom: The Role of the U.S. State Department," *Brookings*, October 25, 2012. This U.S. approach to fostering "Internet freedom" has contributed to a competitive market for resources among activists and resistance movements. See, for instance, Clifford Bob, *The Marketing of Rebellion: Insurgents, Media, and International Activism* (Cambridge: Cambridge University Press, 2005).

[36] Established in 2008, GNI "is modeled on previous voluntary efforts aimed at eradicating sweatshops in the apparel industry and stopping corruption in the oil, natural gas and mining industry. As with those efforts at self-regulation, this one came at a time when Internet companies were seeking to polish their image and potentially ward off legislation." See Verne G. Kopytoff, "Sites Like Twitter Absent from Free Speech Pact," *New York Times*, March 6, 2011. Google, Yahoo! and Microsoft were charter corporate participants.

The China Internet White Paper

Beginning again with the premise that large-scale strategic players seek to seal their visions in favorable infrastructures, China's architectural approach to the Internet should be contrasted with that of the United States. Viewed together, what seems to be emerging is a global competition over influence on infrastructure. I focus on a document called the China Internet White Paper,[37] released in June 2010, which, compared to the U.S. position as declared by Secretary Clinton is more impersonal, a product more of a bureaucracy than of a single campaigning figure and a tradition of advocacy. The White Paper is clearly a product of careful deliberation: polished, clearly manicured and presentable for a substantial international audience. Given the timing, it seems to be a response to the American initiative. Like the American position (Secretary Clinton's speech and its sequel), it is ultimately addressed to an international audience, an element in building a competing international approach.

China's argument in the White Paper, its distinct selling point, is a position attractive to many governments. China stresses the important – indeed necessary – role of the state, the deep significance of national sovereignty as a means of asserting rules and imposing obligations. The White Paper claims both to enlarge the field of expression and emphasize industrial policy (the way in which the Internet expands and is an engine of growth), but, significantly and distinctively, primarily advances the economic. For China, the appropriate architecture of the Internet is not measured mainly by its "openness" but rather by the extent of its integration into society, its technological qualities, its reach and its widespread use. For China, as outlined in the White Paper, the country's record with respect to the Internet is one of pride and achievement.

According to its self-characterization, the Chinese Internet, far from being an example of repression, stands as an example of expanded opportunities for citizenship and productivity. The White Paper heralds China's Internet accomplishments and denotes the volume of citizen use. It celebrates industrial policy. It highlights the achievement of goals in the country's successive Five Year Plans. Here, then, is the essence of China's advocacy of its model: "To build, utilize and administer the Internet well is an issue that concerns national economic prosperity and development, state security and social

---

[37] Information Office of the State Council of the People's Republic of China, "White Paper: The Internet in China," *China.org.cn*, June 8, 2010. Also see Rebecca MacKinnon's excellent analysis, at "China's Internet White Paper: Networked Authoritarianism in Action," *RConversation*, June 15, 2010.

harmony, state sovereignty and dignity, and the basic interests of the people."[38] To this end, administration and management, not autonomous free market growth, are the key to making the Internet successful in society. Administration and management are the antidotes to anxiety. They are what allow China to create growth while simultaneously maintaining control over the national narrative.

From the perspective of China, this set of goals and achievements demonstrates why national legal regulation is warranted, indeed central:

> The Chinese government has from the outset abided by law-based administration of the Internet, and endeavored to create a healthy and harmonious Internet environment, and build an Internet that is more reliable, useful and conducive to economic and social development. ... China advocates the rational use of technology to curb dissemination of illegal information online. Based on the characteristics of the Internet and considering the actual requirements of effective administering of the Internet, it advocates the exertion of technical means, in line with relevant laws and regulations and with reference to common international practices, to prevent and curb the harmful effects of illegal information on state security, public interests and minors.

This is the formulation – one written, obviously, to appeal to other states and one that legitimates system management. It establishes a bias with which many other states, and their leaders, might concur: "Within Chinese territory the Internet is under the jurisdiction of Chinese sovereignty. The Internet sovereignty of China should be respected and protected. Citizens of the People's Republic of China and foreign citizens, legal persons and other organizations within Chinese territory have the right and freedom to use the Internet; at the same time, they must obey the laws and regulations of China and conscientiously protect Internet security."[39]

It is not only in this emphasis on exercise of sovereignty of course, that the China-originated design for the Internet differs from the "One Internet" vision articulated by the U.S. Department of State. Yet that is a significant distinction. Each of the two countries seeks to maintain the initiative, to influence the shaping of global and national Internet policies. But they do so in obviously different ways with different consequences. The U.S. position embraces and features the elements of Article 19 of the Universal Declaration of Human Rights that promise the right to receive information regardless of frontiers and advocate universal principles for free expression

[38] Information Office of the State Council of the People's Republic of China, "White Paper."
[39] Ibid.

within borders. This position, as interpreted by many of its champions, discourages the sovereign from filtering or eliminating speech that comes from outside one's borders. And the American position celebrates ways Internet architecture has contributed to innovation and economic growth.

The assertion of sovereignty in the White Paper pushes toward recognition of interests and values other than freedom of expression as enunciated by governments.[40] The tendency of the United States to disfavor the United Nations as a decision-maker in setting such values and standards has already been mentioned; in contrast, the Chinese White Paper calls for "the establishment of an authoritative and just international Internet administration organization under the UN framework through democratic procedures on a worldwide scale." As the White Paper says:

> China holds that the role of the UN should be given full scope in international Internet administration. China supports the establishment of an authoritative and just international Internet administration organization under the UN system through democratic procedures on a worldwide scale. The fundamental resources of the Internet are vitally connected to the development and security of the Internet industry. China maintains that all countries have equal rights in participating in the administration of the fundamental international resources of the Internet, and a multilateral and transparent allocation system should be established on the basis of the current management mode, so as to allocate those resources in a rational way and to promote the balanced development of the global Internet industry.[41]

Comparing Approaches

The contest for Internet governance has become a quasi-Olympic sport. Neither the Clinton statement nor the White Paper anticipated the way attention would turn to the Internet, not only as a site for freedom, but as a site for surveillance and monitoring. Nor is it clear how competition between the two models on that issue will evolve. There will be serious and continuous jousting as the United States and China and allies of both find opportunities

---

[40] On September 29, 2011, Wang Chen, head of China's State Council Information Office (SCIO), spoke in the UK at the Fourth UK-China Internet Roundtable. During his opening remarks, Wang noted the importance of "sovereign jurisdictions" over the Internet in various countries and urged his counterparts to refrain from using "network freedom" to seek "network hegemony." See "The Fourth UK-China Internet Roundtable," *Chinadaily.com.en*, September 29, 2011.

[41] Information Office of the State Council of the People's Republic of China, "White Paper."

for contesting governance approaches.[42] In 2012, the site for contestation was the World Conference on International Communication (WCIT) in Dubai, held to review existing international telecommunications regulations. The United States saw the debates leading up to the WCIT as threatening a movement of Internet governance, away from mechanisms such as ICANN – the entity that governs Internet names and numbers – that are technical, engineer-dominated, and designed, at least until recently, as under U.S. management. The apprehension by those countries associated with a "freedom coalition" was that governance would tilt away from what is called a multistakeholder approach toward increasing intervention through the ITU or other international organizations. In 2012, there was a collapse in consensus around such a shift. The final document published by the ITU included, as an aspiration, that "all governments should have an equal role and responsibility for international internet governance,"[43] but this seemingly anodyne language was portrayed as code for a potential attack on existing arrangements. Even proposals for change that, in other circumstances, might have been interpreted as constructive were warily received. A provision, for example, on regulating spam was seen as a Trojan horse for a broader system of content controls for the Internet.

This exercise in competitive system design has outcroppings in contexts other than the Internet, as both the United States and China are interested in encouraging adoption of their view in different fora for influence and trade purposes. One such strategy of the Chinese government, and its associated companies, has been to "[enhance] their direct involvement in the telecommunication and media markets in Africa,"[44] Ethiopia being a prime example. The Chinese government has also provided significant support to state broadcasters in selected countries, such as Kenya and Zambia. Finally, China has worked to expand the reach and content of its international broadcasters, including China Central Television (CCTV) and China Radio International (CRI). The emphasis on technology and system design is supplemented by other efforts to bolster the Chinese presence. In a study of how China's media and telecom-related policies in Africa compare to those of the United States and Europe, Oxford's Programme in Comparative Media Law and Policy tracks how in recent years China has rapidly become an important player in the media sector (not just the Internet) in many African countries. Its economic success

[42] *Laura De Nardis, The Global War for Internet Governance* (New Haven, CT: Yale University Press, 2014).

[43] "Final Acts: World Conference on International Telecommunications," WCIT 2012, March 15, 2013.

[44] Iginio Gagliardone, Maria Repnikova and Nicole Stremlau, "China in Africa: A New Approach to Media Development?" *Oxford: Centre for Socio-Legal Studies*, 2010, 1.

and the growth of media players and users within China "have quietly promoted an example of how the media can be deployed within the larger political and economic strategies of developing states, moving beyond the democratization paradigm promoted in the West." The Oxford study argues that heavy investments in media and information and communication technologies "can go hand-in-hand with a tight control over them, posing a lesser challenge to local governments and to political stability."[45] As the report concludes, "Chinese actors prefer to frame their activities in the media sector as forms of collaboration and exchange, aimed at encouraging mutual understanding, at strengthening diplomatic and economic ties, and at counterbalancing the negative reporting of both China and Africa in Western media."[46]

The two powers – and increasingly others – continue to market versions of these competing ideas of the Internet. The Organization for Economic Co-operation and Development (OECD) has framed the future of the Internet in terms of innovation and the capacity to drive economic growth.[47] The White House issued an International Strategy for Cyberspace, designed to "build an international environment that ensures global networks are open to new innovations, interoperable the world over, secure enough to support people's work, and reliable enough to earn their trust."[48] Federal policy would "encourage an environment in which norms of responsible behavior guide states' actions, sustain partnerships, and support the rule of law." Google has invested in supporting the U.S. position, including in the publication of its Transparency Report, which tracks government requests for removal of data or for user data.

It is hardly adequate to describe the clash over the future of the Internet as a duel between the United States and China. The world is neither composed of a single superpower nor bipolar. Other models and approaches to system architecture exist. Brazil bid strongly to shape the governance debate with NetMundial in 2014, Iran seeks to implement a "halal Internet," structured to conform to a particular view of national and religious morals and Shari'a jurisprudence. Such an Intranet would constitute a severe and comprehensive architecture of management, a strong version of what, in earlier Internet days, was called a "walled garden" approach. Alexey Sidorenko has written of a

---

[45] Ibid., 1.

[46] Ibid., 2.

[47] See "OECD Council Recommendation on Principles for Internet Policy Making," OECD, December 13, 2011; NGOs raised objections to the Recommendation on the ground that it gave too much weight to policies that might be restrictive. See Monika Ermert, "OECD Faces Concerns Over Its Internet Policy Principles," *Intellectual Property Watch*, June 28, 2011.

[48] Howard A. Schmidt, "Launching the U.S. International Strategy for Cyberspace," *The White House Blog*, May 16, 2011.

sophisticated means of structuring the Internet in Russia.[49] Rohozinski and Deibert emphasize the "Russianness" of the "Runet."[50] They point out that, unlike much of the Internet, which remains dominated by English and dependent on popular applications and services that are provided by U.S.-based companies, such as Google, Yahoo! and Facebook, Runet is a self-contained linguistic and cultural environment with well-developed and highly popular search engines, Web portals, social network sites and free e-mail services. As Sidorenko highlights, the increasing activity of the government makes the Internet environment not only "more Russian," but also more state-affiliated. The new initiatives, such as the Cyrillic domain, not only contribute to further the "Russianness" of Runet, but also to implement a higher level of state influence. Secondly, only platforms and software that are supported by the government are used in the educational system. Consequently, they become part of the socialization process for the new generations of "digital natives."

The future of the Internet will be a function of how these and other contesting, often comprehensive strategic architectures struggle and are received globally. I have focused on China and the United States because of their deep investments in fashioning the outcome of these debates. But other states, in Europe, Latin America, the Middle East, Asia and Africa will continue to gain entry into this debate and find issues that are significant to them as part of their strategies of communication. In the concluding chapter, I return to this debate and ways in which the 2013 Snowden revelation and other factors reshape approaches to system architectures.

---

[49] Alexey Sidorenko, "Quick Overview of Russian Blogosphere in 2009–2010," *Global Voices GV Citizen Media Summit 2010*, May 13, 2010. Also see Alexey Sidorenko, "Russian Digital Dualism: Changing Society, Manipulative State," *Russie.Nei.Visions* 63 (2011). For more on control of the Russian Internet, see Ronald J. Deibert and Rafal Rohozinski, "Control and Subversion in Russian Cyberspace," in *Access Controlled: The Shaping of Power, Rights, and Rule in Cyberspace*, eds. Ronald J. Deibert et al. (Cambridge, MA: The MIT Press, 2010).

[50] This term is widely used within and outside Russia to denote the Russian-language Internet (both inside and outside the country) as well as the Internet in Russia.

7

Soft Power, Soft War

If we were to rank traditional strategic communicators in terms of output and purpose, states would be among the strongest practitioners. Public diplomacy is the banner under which many forms of state-sponsored persuasion fly.[1] That is the late-twentieth century term usually reserved for the efforts by one government to reach and affect publics in the territory of another. In this overall process, states use many tools, including state-sponsored international broadcasting, such as the Voice of America, the BBC World Service, Iran's Press TV, CCTV 9 (part of China's increasing efforts abroad) and RT (formerly Russia Today).[2] States also deploy clandestine radio stations that emerge unknown and unwanted across borders[3] and, more benignly, cultural exchanges that use art, travel and education as a way to increase influence.

Almost to the level of cliché, much has been written about "soft power" in this regard. Joseph Nye, the father of this term, has frequently described the concept as a combination of national culture, political ideals and policy through which states "attract" individuals, groups and governments in other states to the positions and culture of the projecting entity.[4] Which instruments and approaches constitute the instruments of soft power or of public diplomacy – what should be included under these umbrellas and what belongs in another conceptual category – is hotly disputed among practitioners and theoreticians. Soft power can be very soft or surprisingly aggressive. From the perspective of the target society, exercises of soft power can be happily tolerated

---

[1] See Nicholas Cull, *The Decline and Fall of the United States Information Agency* (New York: Palgrave MacMillan, 2012) for one case study.

[2] See, for instance, Michael Nelson, *War of the Black Heavens: The Battles of Western Broadcasting in the Cold War* (Syracuse, NY: Syracuse University Press, 1997).

[3] Lawrence C. Soley and John Nichols, *Clandestine Radio Broadcasting: A Study of Revolutionary and Counterrevolutionary Electronic Communication* (New York: Prager, 1987).

[4] See, for instance, Joseph S. Nye Jr., "Public Diplomacy and Soft Power," *The Annals of the American Academy of Political and Social Science* 616, no. 1 (2008).

and are often reinforcing of the society's own goals. But the situation is different when the sending society transmits what it declares as the height of enlightening information, but the target society (or its self-preserving government) sees as a hostile, debilitating intrusion. When is the exercise of strategic communication describable not merely as soft power but as something more controversial? Such questions warrant a more complex analytical evaluation.

I have characterized strategic communication as, most dramatically, an external source investing in methods to alter basic elements of a societal consensus. In this chapter, I focus on Iran as a case study in this conceptual border area of the softness of power; I examine circumstances where this process is considered as systematically reducing the target government's legitimacy. The government of Iran, particularly during the Ahmadinejad era, held that it was the object of a concentrated, directed and strategic series of information-related actions (through international radio and other means) undertaken by the United States and the West. The purposes of these efforts can be placed on a spectrum (with various objectives in the mind and effort of different players), and extend from "strengthening civil society" to "reinforcing domestic discontent" to regime change.

Officials and theorists in Iran sought to draw a line between soft power and "Soft War" – claiming that the latter characterization was more descriptive of events. For the Islamic Republic, Soft War was defined by them as the strategic use of non-military means to achieve objectives such as regime change, an objective that might otherwise be obtained through conventional weaponry. In July 2011, Intelligence Minister Heidar Moslehi stated, rather typically: "we do not have a physical war with the enemy, but we are engaged in heavy information warfare with the enemy."[5] The discourse about the proposed distinction between soft power and Soft War might contribute to the theory of strategic communication. How is such a Soft War articulated by the target, and how are the contours of free expression implicated as the emphasis flows more to "war" than to the "softness" of the equation? When Iran characterized these external efforts as a Soft War, what did it mean and how did it conceptualize the shift?

The drama of the Ahmadinejad years and Iran's ideological conflict with the United States may recede with the election of Hassan Rouhani as president. American policy may alter and paranoia may diminish. But by studying the Iran case, one might be able to identify the supposed elements that lead to a target state's perception of a persistent and disciplined threat to its stability and its capacity to govern. Examining Iran's response or counter strategy would allow the description of a bureaucracy of defense: the shaping of

---

[5] "Iran Adopts Aggressive Approach Toward Enemies," *Tehran Times*, July 18, 2011.

cultural redoubts and the equivalent of soft fortresses and propaganda. It would show the relationship between a defensive and an offensive posture in a Soft War context. Iran during this period presents an exceptional locus to study this evolving discourse and the articulated response. There are few states for which there has been more continuing external concern and involvement with the nature of authority and those who are exercising control. It is a site where there have been frequently implied, often explicit, efforts to use forms of intervention to shape, reshape, reinforce or destabilize the political status quo both from within and from without. These have included an externally driven coup, investment in the sustainability or reputation of the Shah, the bitter period of the hostage crisis, efforts at rapprochement, external support for various factions in election campaigns and more generalized and intense information intervention after the 2009 elections.

Certain conflicts (famously the Spanish Civil War) have been test zones for the tools of conventional war, for new technologies in hot wars (new ordnance, new armored vehicles and new modes for targeting). And certain conflicts offer test zones for modes of strategic communication, such as new information technologies. Iran has been such a test bed, including for the use of circumvention technologies and the study of the effects of social media and satellite-related modes of receiving information. There are, of course, ample precedents before Iran for the large-scale use of information techniques as an adjunct to conflict or even as an alternative to conflict. The history of propaganda is an encyclopedia of such efforts.[6] International broadcasters in the West often point to the collapse of the Soviet bloc as a triumphant example of a persevering investment in international broadcasting and similar mechanisms as altering opinion and softly preparing a target society to be a more intense demander of democratic change. But rarely since the Cold War and never in the era of social media has there been such a full blown governmental response and reaction to such intervention as in Iran – a national rallying to a war footing, as if it were a hot war. It is this public articulation and reaction that can reveal for the observer what kind of steps governments take when they consider themselves under this kind of attack.

This conceptualization of attack has its roots in the 1979 Islamic revolution. The revolution positioned itself as a homegrown response to the Shah, who was seen as a decadent, Westernized (and therefore un-Islamic) puppet installed by Western operatives and intelligence agencies after their orchestration, in 1953, of a coup d'état to overthrow then Prime Minister Mohammad

---

[6] See Nicholas Cull, David Culbert and David Welch, *Propaganda and Mass Persuasion: A Historical Encyclopedia from 1500 to the Present* (Santa Barbara: ABC-CLIO, 2003).

Mossadegh. The revolutionary rhetoric, still salient and sustained thirty-five years later, is situated as a bulwark against those seen to be meddling in Iran's domestic affairs, with the regime imagined as the righteous defender of Islam and caretaker of a moral society. Even those who are not supporters of the regime are familiar with this trope of legitimacy, derived from the fact that the popular uprising was voluntary, homegrown and reflective of the population's desire to purge corruption and immorality from the ranks of society by empowering the clergy. Consistent with this view of its history, Iran voiced support for the Arab Spring in 2011, suggesting that the events across the Arab World were "an Islamic awakening" similar to Iran's 1979 revolution.[7] It could celebrate change in Egypt and Tunisia at the same time that it considered similar efforts at home, such as the Green Movement following the disputed 2009 election, as outcroppings of foreign-spawned illegal intervention.[8]

THE CHARACTERIZATION OF SOFT WAR

There is a language of conventional war – its weapons, objectives, modes of measuring the effectiveness of battles and formulae for bringing such a war to conclusion. This language has a long international tradition about the use of force, when it is authorized and when it is justified. The language of conventional war is preoccupied with distinctions such as those between fighting armed forces and ordinary citizens or civilians. The language of conventional war contains limits, often in treaty formulations like those of the Vienna Conventions. There is no law-based vocabulary counterpart for a Soft War, however, no elaborated discourse of acceptable methods and articulated limits. Statements by Iranian officials, hyperbolic as they might be, can provide insight into the possibilities of such a discourse. For instance, consider the language of the Islamic Development Organization of Iran, an institute created by the Iranian regime after 1979 to "promote Islamic revolution values" both internally and externally. The IDO defined Soft War as:

> Any kind of psychological warfare action and media propaganda which targets the society and induces the opposite side to accept the failure without making any military conflict. The subversion, internet war, creation of radio-television networks and spreading the rumors are the important forms

---

[7] Ayatollah Ali Khamenei said, "Today's events in the north of Africa, Egypt, Tunisia and certain other countries have another sense for the Iranian nation. They have special meaning. This is the same Islamic awakening which resulted in the victory of the big revolution of the Iranian nation." Saeed Kamali Dehghan, "Tehran Supports the Arab Spring ... But Not in Syria," *Guardian*, April 18, 2011.

[8] Reza Aslan, "Cairo's Protests Reverberate in Tehran," *The Atlantic*, February 9, 2011.

of Soft War. This war intends to weaken the ... thought processes of the given society and also causes the socio-political order to be annihilated via the media propaganda.[9]

In 2009, Ali Mohammad Na'ini, then deputy head of the *Basij-e Mostaz'afin* (in a way, a state-related militia, an organization subordinate and loyal to the Iran Revolutionary Guards and Ayatollah Khamenei), had put this in the context of the 1979 Islamic revolution.

The main principle of that revolution was... the ability of the leadership to arouse an entire nation. ... The main aim behind the Soft War is to force the system to disintegrate from within in view of its values, beliefs, its main fundamental characteristics, and its identity. Any system, especially a system that is based on certain beliefs and values, owes its identity and its existence to those beliefs and values. It is based on the models and principles on the basis of which it continues its political, social and economic life.[10]

According to Na'ini, the deep strategy behind this particular iteration of the Soft War – i.e. relating to Iran – was to "force the system to disintegrate from within." The targets are not physical, but rather, he argued, the society's "values, beliefs, its main fundamental characteristics, and its identity." What is central in this Iranian definition of the tools of disintegration is the basic logic that a value system is central to national identity, and placing some critical element of that value system in question can lead to progress toward the Soft War objective. Altogether, and this seems to be the essence, Soft War proceeds by seeking to destroy the effectiveness of a system's ideological framework. If the society's organizing model can be put in doubt, "it will weaken the different pillars of the society." Such "infiltration" of "the different intellectual, mental and spiritual layers of the society" would undermine the invaluable element of public trust, and the "main ideas of [the] political system" would begin to unravel. That will increase instability; the "instability and lack of trust in turn will result in civil resistance."[11]

This form of articulation of Soft War by Iranian governing authorities and commentators helps explain the country's response. In an effort to "brand" the Soft War, to find a name for the organization of the Western offensive, the term "cultural NATO" was crafted. It is a phrase that encapsulates a quasi-military approach from the West and implies a coordinated activity within

---

[9] "Soft War Reasons Against Islamic Republic of Iran," *Islamic Development Organization,* January 2, 2010.
[10] Ali Mohammad Na'ini, interview by Ali Shirin, "Military Official on 'Soft War' that Iran is Allegedly Facing," *BBC Monitoring International Reports,* November 28, 2009.
[11] Shirin, "Military Official."

an alliance (through the NATO reference) but one that acts with the velvet glove of "culture." To gain a sense of the Iranian perception of a "cultural NATO," I slightly paraphrase and consolidate elements of its depiction or projection, not to legitimate the concept but rather to explain how it has been used.

After 1991 and the end of the Cold War, in the Iranian reading of events, the United States sought widely to impose dominion in various economic and cultural areas. What followed, as the Islamic Republic sees it, was a concerted effort that sought to affect the "thought, idea and culture of nations," rather than military targets. Cultural NATO was described as superior to efforts dependent on force; its functions were "long-term, convenient and inexpensive," while military alternatives were "short-term, troublesome and more expensive." The policy of cultural NATO was to "obtain the nation's beliefs and trusts, while the purpose of military attack is to occupy the land and obtain the main economical resources and centers." In a military conflict, "the damages and losses are tangible and observable"; in cultural NATO, "damages and destructions are not tangible and they are not reconstructed easily." In a conventional war, "the human losses especially in the front of holy defense under the title of martyrdom are valuable and permanent," while, in a cultural NATO, it is minds and sentiments that are damaged.[12]

Cultural NATO, in the Iranian construct, is seen as a collective effort to capture the target nation's beliefs and trust for the purposes of exploiting them. According to the Islamic Development Organization (IDO):

> The plan of "Cultural NATO" which has been underscored and noted by the Supreme Leader, consists of the offensive line of the enemy and their effort in order to enter into the cultural, artistic and media arenas so that they deal a black picture against Iran. The main purpose of cultural NATO is to destroy the unity and inseparable connection of the nation which has resisted and tolerated during the three decades with all pressures, shortcoming and imperfections.[13]

Tellingly, the sweeping claims include the following: "One of the purposes of cultural NATO is to put the national-religious culture of the target society on the margin so that [the external entities hold] in hand the control of the world's affairs via the domination of [the target society's] desires."[14] Iranian analysts thus framed the Soft War, along with the idea of a cultural NATO, as containing a coordinated set of efforts together seeking to enlarge discontent in the society. In this framing, economic sanctions reinforce a range of

---

[12] "Soft War Reasons."
[13] Ibid.
[14] Ibid.

information-related measures, and vice versa. The deployment of the media is accompanied by engagement with non-governmental organizations. This is seen as accomplished through a set of psychological operations, subtle in some cases, quite bold in others, all adjusting to shifts in attitudes in Iran. Iranian discourse includes an explicit listing of the imputed approaches, including the exploitation of tribal and national differences or the fostering of civil disobedience in student gatherings, often through Persian-speaking radio-television channels developed abroad that reach into Iran by satellite.

In constructing this theology of a Soft War, Iranian analysts identified their litany of "Western talking points," considering them, together, as an assault on Iranian values. The claim was that the West – or the architects of Soft War – were using various radio and television platforms to reiterate the following charges, and by doing so would undermine societal confidence. These charges (independent of which of the points were fully justified) included a) inculcating the idea that Iran's nuclear technology is not solely for peaceful purposes; b) generating a media atmosphere that reinforces the idea that Iran supports terrorism and with that in mind interferes in Iraq, Lebanon and elsewhere; c) presenting a "biased analysis" of the internal situation of Iran in terms of economics and politics; d) representing and promoting discontent concerning such subjects as human rights, women's rights and "aggravation of trade and social exactions by some press and internal parties of Iran;" e) down-grading government implementation of policies, indicating, for example, that "performance of some plans ... limits women's freedom and rights" and f) emphasizing "confrontation among the superior heads of Islamic system" and repeating and inculcating patterns of "war of power in Islamic Republic."[5] Whether these continue to be U.S. talking points – and how discourse with Iran changes after possible arrangements on nuclear issues – is yet to be determined.

TECHNIQUES OF ATTACK IN A SOFT WAR

This, then, is a complex order for a Soft War – identifying the signal values of a society, creating a strategy for undermining them, having that strategy penetrate various levels of society and doing so in such a way as to subvert public trust and create instability. Iran's construction of the Soft War imputes to the United States and the West a sophisticated and effective arsenal: foreign manipulation of civil society through a variety of subsidies and inducements, "cultural invasion," use of psychological operations, deployment of international

---

[5]   Ibid.

broadcasting and intervention in regulation of content on the Internet (specifically through the encouragement of circumvention technologies).

One major preoccupation of Iran, as its officials described the implementation of a Soft War, was financial and other support by the U.S. government and European counterparts for elements of Iranian civil society. Since 1979, the Islamic Republic has characterized many internal dissenters (and often mere participants in civil society activities) as "proxies of the United States and its allies, working to weaken the political system."[16] This preoccupation has escalated in recent years and includes systematic charges of links between U.S. civil society groups, primarily NGOs, and individuals and counterparts in Iran (I discuss NGOs as strategic communicators and government responses more generally in Chapter 9). For example, Iran authorities arrested Western-based scholars visiting Iran like Ramin Jahanbegloo (in 2006) and Haleh Esfandiari (in 2007) on suspicion of their assistance to Washington-based think tanks and human rights groups.[17] In 2010, authorities in Iran labeled sixty international groups and media organizations as "Soft War agents" and forbade Iranians from working with or receiving aid from them. These included think tanks, universities and broadcasting organizations identified as being part of a concerted effort to bring down the state's Islamic system. The contact ban was articulated as a response to what was described as the systematic undermining of the Islamic system. As Iran's government saw it, Western-sponsored individuals and groups were reaching out to influential "special groups," including experts, artists and academics, under the cover of cultural and scientific exchanges. The Islamic Republic News Agency (IRNA) quoted one official as saying that "Our revolution has become a target to be overthrown by the intelligence services of some countries, particularly America and Britain, and they have established soft invasion and overthrow strategies against the Islamic Republic of Iran. They have allocated extraordinary formal budgets to fulfill this aim."[18]

In Iran's construction, during the Ahmadinejad era, of a harsh and destabilizing pattern of strategic communication, a generally outdated but lingering focal point for Iranian government complaints was a controversial entity called the Iran Democracy Fund (IDF), a U.S. government-established source of grants and contracts to fund activities related to the Islamic Republic.[19]

---

[16] Nima Adelkhah, "Iran Integrates the Concept of the 'Soft War' Into its Strategic Planning," *Terrorism Monitor* 8, no. 23 (2010).

[17] Ibid.

[18] Robert Tait, "Iran Bans Contact with Foreign Organisations, Including the BBC," *Guardian*, January 5, 2010.

[19] See Stephan de Vries, "United States Policy on 'Democratizing' Iran: Effects and Consequences," *Democracy and Society* 8, no. 1 (2011).

The IDF was created in 2006 during the George W. Bush administration, when Congress approved $66 million of a $75 million administration request. Much of this funding went to international broadcasters, Radio Farda and Voice of America Persian. More controversial, however, according to the National Iranian American Council (NIAC), "was the $20 million provided to MEPI [Middle East Partnership Initiative] for 'democracy programs in Iran.'"[20] Sidestepping the suggestion that the project was furthering regime change, a 2008 Congressional explanation suggested that the focus of the program was not on Iran and its internal politics, but rather on Iran's role in the region. That statement recommended the State Department "use an unspecified amount 'to support groups, organizations, and individuals in the Middle East who adhere to democratic principles and who may counter in a non-violent manner the meddling of Iran in the domestic political affairs of neighboring countries.'"[21]

Prominent Iranian-American groups argued that the U.S. approach was too explicit and thus counterproductive. In 2008, a letter was sent to the new administration by distinguished representatives of the Iranian diaspora seeking the closure of the Fund. According to one blogger, the Iranian democracy fund was initiated by the Bush administration in an effort to topple the clerical regime in Tehran by financing Iranian NGOs. But, the blogger averted, the fund only hindered the actions of Iranian NGOs as they were now accused of working to overthrow the government with the help of the United States.[22] Trita Parsi, founder and president of NIAC, said, "'the money has made all Iranian NGOs targets and put them at great risk. While the Iranian government has not needed a pretext to harass its own population, it would behoove Congress not to provide it with one.'"[23]

I have already mentioned the augmented use of international broadcasting as central to the Soft War in Iran's eyes. For the purposes of this discussion, it matters less how these broadcasters and grantees conceived of their own motives, and more what the then Iranian officials imputed to them. From Iran's perspective, the international broadcasts provided yet another mode of reinforcing the narratives that, for the Iranian authorities, seemed designed to undermine legitimacy and foster dissent. Among the many foreign government-sponsored broadcasters, Radio Farda, Voice of America and

---

[20] Emily Blout, "Questions Remain about Iran Democracy Fund," *National Iranian American Council*, January 23, 2008.

[21] Ibid.

[22] Sahar Zubairy, "Barack Obama Does Not Care About Iranian People?" *Foreign Policy Association Blog*, October 29, 2009.

[23] DeVries, "United States Policy," 8.

BBC Persian were the most important.[24] In Iran's analysis, the intensification of international broadcasting directed at its population was somewhat more comprehensive and therefore more sinister than what usually occurs as the ordinary extension of soft power.[25]

The Iranian perspective on international broadcasting was set forth in a 2009 book published by the Bureau of Media Studies and Planning at Iran's Ministry of Culture and Islamic Guidance. This book claimed, referring to Radio Farda, that "The most significant task of the media hostile to the Islamic republic is creating a rift between the [Iranian] regime and its government."[26] Masoud Mohammadi, the book's author, argued, according to an RFE/RL account, that the international broadcasters had consciously prefabricated hostile and critical post-2009 election coverage. In his view, Radio Farda and other Persian-language media based outside Iran preplanned their coverage and coordinated with the mass demonstrations that greeted President Mahmoud Ahmadinejad's victory; they knew beforehand, Mohammadi argued, that Ahmadinejad would be accused of fraud. "Months before Iran's 10th presidential elections in June 2009, the directors of such networks had planned to use this opportunity to promote the project of creating instability in the country."[27] Surveying output, Mohammadi pointed to international broadcasters' tendency to over-report individuals most noted for dramatic change and to encourage popular dissent as evidence of their bias. Radio Farda, according to his findings, interviewed the Nobel Peace laureate Shirin Ebadi 118 times over an unspecified two-year period. Journalists Mashallah Shamsolvaezin and Issa Saharkhiz were interviewed 149 times and 106 times, respectively, over the same period. The point here is not the accuracy of the claim, but the nature of the Iranian perception.

Government-sponsored services from the West were not the only presumed participants in the Soft War. Farsi1, a satellite entertainment channel broadcasting from Dubai, became immensely popular in Iran and was said to be changing attitudes among the public.[28] Farsi1 was jointly owned by the MOBY

---

[24] In addition, Al Jazeera is seen as part of a foreign conspiracy, as are private external satellite services that are beamed into Iran.

[25] A useful example of Iranian media analysis of BBC Persian from a strategic perspective was a panel discussion among three Iranian media experts held in Tehran in August 2009. See Raja News, "Iranian Experts on BBC's Coverage of Iranian Election," *BBC Monitoring International Reports*, August 10, 2009.

[26] Robert Tait, "Radio Farda an Agent of the West's Soft War Against Iran, Book Says," *RFE/RL*, August 9, 2010. See also: "اسلامی جمهوری علیه سایت هزار 18 فعالیت," *Fars News Agency*, June 9, 2013, http://www.farsnews.com/newstext.php?nn=9004060828.

[27] Tait, "Radio Farda."

[28] Ken Auletta, "The Networker: Afghanistan's First Media Mogul," *The New Yorker*, July 5, 2010.

Group[29] and News Corporation. The popularity of Farsi1, tied with anxiety over satellite television in general, was the subject of much excoriation among Iranian authorities, with Mohammad Taghi Rahbar, head of the clerical faction in the Iranian parliament, accusing Farsi1 of airing content that "seeks to destroy the chastity and morals of families and encourage young Iranians to have sex and drink alcohol."[30] Magazines devoted entire issues to disparaging Farsi1's purported ulterior motives,[31] while others blamed the channel for a rising divorce rate across Iran.[32] In late November 2010, the Farsi1 website itself was hacked by Iran's Cyber Army, which posted a warning to the "allies of Zionism" that "dreams of destroying the foundation of the family will lead straight to the graveyard." Earlier in the year, authorities attempted to jam the satellite used by the channel.[33]

Other perceived tools of the Soft War included financing of circumvention tools to facilitate access for Iranians to information. What has been previously articulated by the U.S. government as a project for advancing Internet freedom was claimed in Iran as an element of the regime change effort. In 2012, the Minister of Communications and Information Technology, Reza Taghipour, was subjected to U.S. sanctions and blamed by the United States for ordering the jamming of satellite television broadcasts and restricting Internet connectivity, according to a statement from the U.S. Department of State.[34]

THE ISLAMIC REPUBLIC'S RESPONSE TO THE SOFT WAR

I have sought to provide some insight into how a Western communications strategy is perceived in a target society. I have also tried to show how the adoption of the term Soft War helped provide a justification for Iran's argument that it was on an information-related war footing. This set of events provides an opportunity to examine how Iran as a target society fashions a defensive strategy in addition to an offensive strategy of censorship and

---

[29] The privately-owned MOBY Group was founded by the Mohseni family in Afghanistan in 2003. It is partly owned by News Corporation.

[30] Samar Namizikhah, "Satellite TV Dramas Take Iran by Storm," *Institute for War and Peace Reporting*, September 3, 2010.

[31] Thomas Erdbrink, "In Iran, What's Forbidden is In – and On Rupert Murdoch's Farsi1 TV Channel," *Washington Post*, June 26, 2010.

[32] "Of Divorces, 15% Due to Network," *Jahan News*, June 9, 2013.

[33] Dexter Filkins, "TV Channel Draws Viewers, and Threats, in Iran," *New York Times*, November 19, 2010.

[34] "US Sanctions Iranian Minister Behind Jamming TV Broadcasts, Blocking Internet," *RTT News*, November 9, 2012. See, on satellite jamming, Small Media, "Briefing: Satellite Wars: Why Iran Keeps Jamming," *Tehran Bureau*, November 20, 2012.

accompanying repression. The concept of a Soft War in which Iran is the target was so central to Iran's identity in the Ahmadinejad period and became such an integral part of Iran's strategic defense planning that it produced an elaborate governmental response, with sizeable funding and the creation of a Soft War cabinet.[35] Considering itself at war meant the formation of a strategy, the creation of a new kind of bureaucracy of conflict and the motivation for innovation and experimentation in responsive techniques. This response included not only a reorganized officialdom, but also plans for an Intranet with increased capacity for the government to reach its population.

The Bureaucracy of Soft War

Having conceptualized an ongoing, large-scale Soft War attack, including the concept of a cultural NATO, it is predictable that the Islamic Republic would take on its own war footing and organize for a projected counter-strategy, reflected in the bureaucracy or operational aspects of response at an institutional level. In its own articulation of this response, the Iranian discourse provides that "in order to confront the Soft War, . . . it is necessary that the role of each governmental institution is determined and explicated and capability of the security organizations is reinforced in both internal and international arenas."[36] The Supreme Leader of the Islamic Revolution, Ali Khamenei, himself took an explicit, high profile interest in institutional responses to the Soft War. He is depicted as exhorting "the students, professors of universities and artists . . . to foil the threats of the enemy." Western threats, he claimed, invoke a classic method – "Showing the future dark" – to inculcate fear, disturb the populace, and exhaust the "main forces" through the creation of doubt and hesitation in their principles and accomplishments.[37] In these reports, the Supreme Leader is quoted as addressing the university faculties, saying, for example, "you should give the student hope so that they do not see the great accomplishments of the country as worthless and valueless." Students should see themselves as "the insider commanders of a soft [war] front."[38]

One example of an institutional response was Iran's Ministry of Defense and Armed Forces Logistics, which in 2011 established a special military force, a "Unit of the Soft War" (*Setad-e Jang-e Narm*). This unit, largely made up of members of the *Basij*, was, on behalf of the military, responsible for Soft War

---

[35] Adelkhah, "Iran Integrates."
[36] "Soft War Reasons."
[37] Ibid.
[38] Ibid.

operations, including some cultural activities and "psychological operations."[39] The unit had the objective of confusing and subsequently disrupting
foreign-organized soft attacks, perhaps by jamming and other similar techniques. In another example, in May 2010, according to a Jamestown Foundation
Report, the Iranian *Majlis* (parliament) ratified a bill setting aside substantial
funds for provincial councils for establishing "Soft War camps" and for the
Supreme Cultural Revolution Council to produce pro-government art and
film. To foster understanding and improve strategy, conferences and instruc-
tional programs were set up to help analyze how the regime could effectively
advance its activities on the Internet and in the cultural and educational
domains.[40]

Nima Adelkah has written, concerning education and the Soft War, that:

> Since one of the main Soft War battlefields is in the educational domain, an
> attempt is being made to reacquaint the young with the ideals of the revolu-
> tion (Payvand, September 6, 2009). The institutionalization of various Basij
> centers in elementary schools is reminiscent of the early revolutionary years
> of the 1980s, when the newly established Islamic Republic sought to instill the
> new ideology among the younger population. . . . . In many ways, the thrust of
> the new ideological campaign can be described as a form of "cultural
> revolution" that includes the involvement of artists, intellectuals and poets
> as agents of "truth" who can "distribute" (or propagate) such ideals through
> cultural means.[41]

Iran's efforts to reorganize or innovate in the broadcast media sphere were also
significant. The objective here was not merely to advance the state ideology,
but to expand various media outlets that could rival and "neutralize the effect
of anti-Islamic Republic media."[42] The 2007 launching of Press TV, an
English-language 24-hour news channel, set the stage for the rise of a new
type of state media competing on a global scale with Sunni Arab channels
such as Al Arabiyah and Western channels such as CNN and the BBC.[43]

---

[39] Adelkhah, "Iran Integrates."
[40] "Soft War Reasons."
[41] Adelkhah, "Iran Integrates."
[42] "Iran Urged to Loosen Hold on BBC Persia," *Press TV*, April 19, 2009. This article discusses a
      2009 report, produced by the Institute for Political Studies in Iran's Parliament Research
      Center, which recommends that the government take a less stringent approach to foreign
      media outlets.
[43] "Iran Officially Launches HispanTV," *IRDiplomacy*, February 1, 2012. In 2013, following the
      addition of the IRIB to the U.S. Treasury Department's "specially designated nationals list,"
      French satellite provider GlobeCast removed HispanTV from satellites reaching Latin
      America. See "French Company GlobeCast Takes Iran's Hispan TV Off Air," *PressTV*,
      June 9, 2013.

In November 2009, the Iranian Revolutionary Guard Corps (IRGC) announced its plan to begin a new press agency called Atlas, modeled on international news agencies like Al Jazeera. In May 2010, the strategic studies center of the Expediency Discernment Council convened a meeting to look into the "covert aims" of Persian language satellite TV directed from abroad, and Farsi1 in particular. Speakers at the meeting noted the "extraordinary welcome" these TV stations had received from viewers in Iran. Many media experts became highly critical of the Iranian state-run national station, the Islamic Republic of Iran Broadcasting, for making programs so unappealing to Iranian audiences that it drove them into the arms of Farsi1.[44] Partially in response, in 2011, Defense Minister Ahmad Vahidi announced the inauguration of a new Iranian-designed satellite called Tolou ("Rise"), which would expand Iran's global media capacities along with its military defense capabilities.[45] As Former IGRC commander Yahya Rahim Safavi put it, using a military metaphor, "We can block the enemy's cultural onslaught by using our own culture."[46]

In addition to these efforts, the Ahmadinejad government dedicated manpower and resources toward developing the Iranian Cyber Army, mentioned earlier, an organization to implement larger designs to control the flow of information both entering and exiting Iran. Well-funded and with access to a huge manpower pool, the ICA developed hacking techniques to disrupt the then political opposition, as demonstrated when the ICA disrupted prominent reformist websites.[47]

Toward a Protected "Intranet"

Among responses to the idea of a Soft War, the most total approach is to control incoming information and affirmatively enrich or populate the space according to revolutionary precepts.[48] Reza Marashi, among others, has written about the Islamic Republic's plans to create a "halal Internet," or fenced off Intranet, designed to accomplish parts of this set of tasks. Marashi recognized the government's long-term vision as reinforcing and invigorating a peculiarly Iranian Islamic culture and ensuring that the Internet affirmatively contributes to that vision (rather than detracts from it). Marashi stated that the

---

[44] "People Are Forced to Watch Satellite," *Aftab News*, May 30, 2011.
[45] "Iran to Launch New Satellite in Feb.," *PressTV*, January 16, 2012.
[46] "Advanced Technology Can Fight Soft War," *PressTV*, March 8, 2010.
[47] "Pro-Iranian Hackers Hit Twitter and Opposition Websites," *BBC News*, December 18, 2009.
[48] In March 2012, Iran set up the Supreme Council for Virtual Space, seen as one of the strongest efforts to date to control the Internet. See "Iran's Supreme Leader Sets Up Body to Control the Internet," *BBC News*, March 7, 2012.

Iranian decision-makers of the time sought "to increasingly quarantine their population by dividing this international system into a fragmented national network. And while foreign-inspired virus attacks command the attention of policymakers and pundits in the West, the Islamic Republic's long-term strategy is slowly succeeding."[49] According to Marashi, first, the Islamic Republic would control network infrastructure in Iran – "literally the 'plumbing' that facilitates the existence of internet, mobile, and landline communication networks." Second, the government would control network carriers – mobile phone operators, Internet service providers, global telecom carriers, and Iranian telecom companies. Increasing technological capacity thus remains one of the Islamic Republic's "defense" requirements for a sustained conflict.

Marashi saw the government as seeking to master packet switching technologies so it would be more capable of checking information sent and received via the Internet: "this would enable the government to block traditional circumvention mechanisms (such as VPNs) created to bypass filtering." Finally, the government sought to domesticate the Internet through other steps: a) by requesting Iranian companies "relocate websites to domestic data centers, and ... [by] examining the feasibility of creating a national email account;" b) by building "indigenous search engines and email accounts" and c) "by building filtration mechanisms into the infrastructure." Together these would provide government control over the physical infrastructure of the Internet and assist the government to "increase its control over the flow of information *within* Iran, but also information coming *in and out*."[50]

Experimenting with "Offensive" Measures

The strategy of information management in a Soft War includes many elements of control. Tactical features of Iran's Soft War deal with active affirmative content measures, some of the most important of which involve the use of the Internet. Tehran viewed (and may still view) social sites such as Facebook, YouTube and Twitter as elements of a cyber warfare threat to the Islamic Republic. Rumors, the government has perceived, are spread online to "stir up" discord within Iran.[51] Along with reactive measures such as filtering and blocking access to various sites, Iran's approach became one of proactive management of the flow of information. These included "establishing a 'national data center'" and "limiting and supervising the activities of dissidents

---

[49] Reza Marashi, "The Islamic Republic's Emerging Cyber War," *National Iranian American Center, Iran Working Paper Series* 3 (2011).
[50] Marashi, "The Islamic Republic's Emerging Cyber War," 2.
[51] Adelkhah, "Iran Integrates."

supported by the United States."[52] The offensive measures also extended to much more active production of programming, as the Islamic Republic expands state influence over cyberspace and other media outlets to spread pro-government propaganda.[53] Iranian officials include in the discourse of management, various techniques to shore up an internal defense by bolstering public satisfaction. These include efforts: a) to improve the "performance of the deprived and frontier territories' development in various dimensions such as poverty, insecurity, inflation, unemployment and traffic;" b) to expand civil freedoms in the framework of the constitution along with the necessary awareness in order to prevent possible threats; c) to reinforce cultural and educational substructures; d) to supervise and control non-governmental organizations; e) to increase the capacity of the security organizations; f) to improve the effectiveness of the country's administrative system; and g) to employ governmental and political elites with the purpose of preventing them from being attracted by external views.[54] As the *Basij* official, Na'ini, put it:

> In order to confront the Soft War, the main strategy is to increase the soft power of the system. In other words, this battlefront requires its own tools and weapons. Its model of operation is also different. We must increase our capabilities in the field of Soft War. . . . We should also have a clear strategy and programme for confronting it. In order to fight against a Soft War we need special methods and models and we must accept the special require-ments of this battle too. . . . We must increase our media, cultural and propaganda power, and our ability to persuade others, to engage in producing movements and strengthening our defensive psychological operations. We must define the field of play in the Soft War, and we must get out of our present defensive mood. We must make good use of media capabilities and cyber opportunities. We must become productive and must produce new ideas. We must influence public opinion and different groups, and must shape movements.

There were also efforts at coordination in the arts, evident in Iran's Soviet-style development plans that included the setting of goals in the cultural area. Under this development plan, "all state-run cultural organizations and media partic-ularly Ministry of Culture and Islamic Guidance, Islamic Republic of Iran's Broadcasting (IRIB) and Islamic Propagation Organization" are persuaded

---

[52] Ibid.

[53] See, for example, information on a pro-government blogging competition: "Iran Holds its Own Blogging Competition," *Deutsche Welle*, April 1, 2011; and Elizabeth Flock, "Iran Holds Pro-Government Blogging Competition," *Washington Post*, April 1, 2011. Also see pro-government tweets and official Facebook pages: "Iran Pro-Regime Voices Multiply Online," *Wall Street Journal*, July 3, 2009.

[54] "Soft War Reasons."

"to produce works in cyberspace, [and] organize and strengthen such virtual space."[55] Claiming that the Soft War cannot be fought purely through a "political approach," Ayatollah Khamenei called on Iranian artists to present "the truth" through a "full-fledged and influential artistic manner."[56]

STRATEGIES OF INFORMATION MANAGEMENT

The case of Iran and the Soft War provides an example of the complex operation of the model of the market for loyalties. Iran sought, at least in the Ahmadinejad period, through the use of law, force, technology and subsidy, to maintain a cartel of acceptable purveyors in a struggle to keep allegiances. Elements of government action, through a variety of techniques, limited the capacity of competitors to enter. Foreign governments, sometimes working with non-governmental organizations and others, in a countervailing way, used law, technology and subsidy to seek to break the cartel – to find space for their own favored entities to be able to reach Iranian audiences. In Iran, the existence of a cartel and efforts to break it took the shape of competing efforts to create or limit the activities of civil society. There were many constraints; for example, While Shi'a culture, non-Islamic Iranian culture and Islamic Republic culture offer "ample material to create sources of soft power that are attractive within Iran and internationally ... the regime's limitations on freedoms inside Iran as well as its recycling of primary currencies from the first decade of revolution and war prevent innovation in this area."[57]

Soft War is about modes, principally from outside, for breaking through the established market, deploying extraordinary, often innovative measures, aggressively differentiated in content and purpose from soft power. As a process, it is more than a set of moves and counter-moves. It is also a study in governmental organization – here a study of both the Iran side and its counterparts among those supplying strategic voices, in the United States, the United Kingdom and elsewhere. We have seen in the course of the chapter a reorganization of government in Iran to mobilize, organize, censor, monitor

---

[55] "Budget Bill Lacks Fund to Counter US Soft War," *KhabarOnline*, March 10, 2011.
[56] "Khamenei Wants to Enlist 'Influential Artists to Fight in Soft War,'" *Payvand Iran News*, September 6, 2011.
[57] Farzan Sabet and Roozbeh Safshekan, "Soft War: A New Episode in the Old Conflict Between Iran and the United States" (Philadelphia: Iran Media Program, 2011), 20. Sabet and Safshekan's exploration of the Iranian regime's "hard" and "soft" responses to a perception of a Soft War against the West notes that while the regime's hard responses are often ad hoc and disorganized, the regime's real failure has been in its inability to generate successful soft responses. This is largely because these efforts "are not monopolized by the state but are mainly produced by civil society," which has been severely repressed by the state.

and police outcomes. In Iran's eyes, Soft War is an ongoing experiment in hardware and software, in content and delivery systems and in the relationship between control through information and the potential use of force. It is a study in transformation of technologies: using international broadcasting and its era of satellites and transmitters, and then the Internet with its associated environment of circumvention, cybersecurity and altered approaches to a market for loyalties.

The Iran experience and response to its perception of a Soft War leads to a final point of analysis: a shift in strategic understanding of government steps often grouped, externally, under the heading of censorship. Censorship is often cast in terms of a series of actions, often arbitrary, to deny basic citizen rights to express oneself, rights promised under international norms. Censorship could be thought of as episodic and reactive, rather than as an integrated strategic response to the management of information flows. Censorship in this theater of conflict – in the mindset of the leadership of the Islamic Republic – became a component of a wholesale effort to reorient the mix of images, to "correct" against what was deemed threatening. In what might be called a "total Soft War," all aspects of the system of understanding and indoctrination are in play: the arts, the media, the educational system. All can be deemed a part of the battlefield with an effort to "reacquaint the young with the ideals of the revolution."[58] The Iranian model, by increasingly focusing on the production of information, on the one hand, and surveillance on the other, knits censorship, filtering and arrest into a complex and comprehensive approach. Particularly in authoritarian states such as Iran, "'censorship' ... is not just about expurgating or restricting the flow of information, but also about the strategic promotion of discourses or practices that seek to impose discipline and order over networks of communication, and the construction of knowledge favorable to the stability of state power."[59]

In this chapter, I have sought, as mentioned, to see "strategic communication" not from the perspective of the progenitor, but from the perspective of the receiver. This is hardly because one perspective is more accurate than the other. Rather it is because a focus on the counter-view provides more insight into transnational interactions in processes of persuasion. The question of how and when a policy of intervention changes from soft power to one that is

---

[58] Adelkhah, "Iran Integrates."

[59] Babak Rahimi, "Censorship and the Islamic Republic: Two Modes of Regulatory Strategies for Media in Post-Revolutionary Iran," *Middle East Journal* (forthcoming). Rahimi describes Soft War as the most aggressive of the proactive strategies, with the aim of producing and reproducing "elaborate and complex divisions of governance over the management and regulation of media and, by extension, the public sphere."

perceived as Soft War is significant, partly because of the nature of counter-strategies that are triggered and angers that are fostered. In the context of Iran, where the larger narrative changes – as Iran and the United States try fitfully to reorder and rebuild their relationship – approaches to Soft War may recede, once again, into mutual exercises in soft power.[60]

[60] Dr. Annabelle Sreberny of SOAS published useful comments on an earlier version of this chapter. See Annabelle Sreberny, "Too Soft on 'Soft War,'" *International Journal of Communication* 7 (2013), Feature 801–804, https://www.mysciencework.com/publication/show/1623473/talking-soft-about-soft-war

8

Religions and Strategic Communication

Religious groups provide an extraordinary focus for observing patterns and behaviors in strategic communication. In Chapter 1, I described how sellers of allegiances compete against one another for market share, fight to preserve their position or aggressively maneuver to enter and expand. Instances of the strengthening or weakening of a religious hold on popular modes of thinking, often across national borders, become hallmark cases of ways to influence public sentiment on matters related to significant aspects of cultural formation. Religions, and those who seek to limit or expand their influence, have the kind of consensus-shifting or basic influence-related goals I have characterized as attributes of strategic communication. They often engage with elements of belief central to the target society. Much of modern politics revolves around the extent to which certain religious actors can expand their sway, unite or separate from the political realm and increase their footprint and reach. Multiple terrains exist where efforts to expand influence are met by efforts to block such expansion, where monopolies and oligopolies over religious experience are maintained or are subject to bitter attack.[1] Ultimately, much of this interaction, struggles to expand followed by struggles to restrict or limit, becomes a matter of communication or restraints on communication. Religious communication is associated with a transcendent force, a force with a claim to authority higher than that of other forms of speech or influence. Because it has the capacity to motivate large-scale attitudes, because it is so basic to issues of identity, religious speech raises important challenges to regulation and control.

Religious strategic communicators bring a special passion to their task. They have the motivating force of being divinely inspired. Some religious

---

[1] For a sweeping historical perspective on communication, religion and "monopolies of knowledge," see Harold Innis, *Empire and Communications* (Toronto: University of Toronto Press, 1950), especially chapters 3 and 6.

entities are satisfied with their share in a market for allegiances and want to be left alone, while some are institutionally committed to expand and compete.[2] States, and religious groups themselves, seek to use force, law, subsidy, technology and other techniques to place boundaries on this process. Many governments and religious entities are fully committed to engaging in cartel-shaping activities, a dynamic process in which entities seize the moment, where there is an opening, to reshape existing arrangements for exercising strategic opportunities. Religions, of course, in union with governments, can buttress state power. But transnational religious movements – fervent, sometimes apocalyptic, sometimes deeply political – can also become perceived threats, precariously destabilizing with the proclamations and teachings of religious figures more and more labeled and associated with terror. The implications for considerations of speech and regulation are, of course, profound.

Religious competition is deeply and intensely about persuasion and belief. How does one square a commitment to freedom of expression with policies that manage efforts at dramatically changing shares in religious markets? Freedom of speech principles often assume that expressions and beliefs associated with religion are merely a subcategory of the universal right to receive and impart information and ideas and should be safeguarded under the broad and noble umbrella of protected expression. But the implications of religious development – ties to states, challenges to dominion, relationships to national security – create tensions that bring religious freedom and freedom of expression principles into nervous conflict. This chapter explores the play of these techniques as aspects of the positioning in strategic communication both to demarcate and limit influence and to expand it. I relate these efforts to a background of international principles of human rights, including freedom of speech and freedom of religion.[3]

The strength and influence of religions in the competition for loyalties changes over time. In many cases, the assertion of religious rights challenges traditions of state authority, and states seek to maintain the patterns of control that have long existed. Consider the long and torture-filled history of missionaries, for example, and efforts in receiving societies to limit the presence, the functioning and the persuasive field of action for them. How should such histories be described in the annals of strategic communication? Under what conditions are states privileged in shielding their societies from external

---

[2] Brian J. Grim and Roger Finke, *The Price of Freedom Denied: Religious Persecution and Conflict in the Twenty-First Century* (Cambridge: Cambridge University Press, 2011).

[3] See Paul M. Taylor, *Freedom of Religion: UN and European Human Rights Law and Practice* (Cambridge: Cambridge University Press, 2005).

influences? As religion becomes an integral aspect of defining international movements and presents increasing threats to national security, preexisting customs or identities, states have adjusted their reactions and their discourse. They have modified restrictions on the propagation of messages by competing religious groups and the advance of messages that malign or diminish religions. The very identification of belief and practice of religion as a preferred right in international norms supplies a basis for arguing that enforcing an existing monopoly or restriction is both ennobled and suspect. Interpretations of religious rights can celebrate and reinforce a state-established religion at the same time as they tolerate or, indeed, demand pluralism and the exercise of religious freedom. In terms of the expressive aspect of religions and their advocates, the task of limiting the persuasive forces seems increasingly complex. Can a state ban or regulate sermons of a certain kind or restrict proselytizing? Can it limit entry into its borders of imams, priests or missionaries on the basis of their aggressively persuasive capabilities? Can it make it more onerous for certain religious actors, especially transnational ones, to enter the market?

In addition to competing among themselves, religions, as they so frequently point out, also compete with the force of secularism. For this reason, just as they may limit the effectiveness of competitive creeds, they wish to use the power of the state to act against forms of popular culture. This may be through informal (though quite coercive) influence on their adherents or by using law and force to shift the tenor of the society as a whole. The religious establishment may consider that vigilance is essential at every point so that the goals of the religious community are not subverted. It is the risk of being undermined that governs behavior, the fear that unguarded openings will lead to corruption of the young and unwanted and effective competitors for fashioning belief and behavior. As one example of this, which I discuss later, many religious denominations have sought to influence the use of Internet filtering to advance their point of view.

One could hypothesize several models of the relationship of the state to religious influence within it. For simplicity's sake, think of three historical archetypes of religion's place in a single-state context: a religious monopoly within a state, a state dedicated in law and practice to plural religious practices, and a state that is ruthlessly anti-religious in its imposition of secularism.[4] Each of these paradigms would imply a different view of religious communication. Taking just one element of regulation, relating to religious broadcasting, we can consider the following implications. A monopoly state – one with an

---

[4] This line of thinking grew out of a conversation with Professor Brendan O'Leary of the University of Pennsylvania.

established and dominant religion – may preclude all other religions from the use of powerful electronic media, providing the established religion with a monopoly itself (a variation on this would be a strong and small cartel). Over time, a slow atrophy may occur because of the lack of a disciplining influence in the form of competition. The second model might be thought of as carrying out pluralism in broadcasting (I discuss the Dutch example later in the chapter). Rules would exist, perhaps even limiting new entrants, but the intention would be to be inclusive, fair and non-discriminatory at least for existing players. The third model would seek to maximize secularism by looking at religions as fierce competitors whose role in the public sphere should be minimized, if not prohibited or subject to degradation. In all three cases, state control over religious communication is subject to various threats; a monopoly can be predictably difficult to maintain, but so can any particular desired version of pluralism.[5] Indeed, all modes of design are more complex in a multi-channel, Internet-rich and satellite-driven world. Where entry barriers have weakened, stability in fixing markets falters. And force, intimidation, banning and surveillance become tools more frequently used.

The Arab Spring and its wider aftermath can be seen as a vast cross-regional effort to use crises to alter patterns of entry, and particularly entry by religious entities, into the competition for allegiances. In Egypt, if violently and fitfully, this process involved the resurgence – and reaction to that resurgence – of the Muslim Brotherhood as a politically connected religious movement after years of being banned or restricted from popular involvement. In Syria, violent conflict involved the undoing or narrowing of the Baathist-Alawite hegemony and the effort at a Sunni restoration. A more powerful Iran is feared, in part, because of its capacity to create a Shi'ite corridor enfolding parts of Syria and, with Hezbollah, Lebanon. The meteoric rise of the Islamic State of Iraq and the Levant (ISIS) implies the aggressive creation of a transregional caliphate, undoing old political borders and consequent religious arrangements, Throughout the region, there is the dire threat to Christian groups, including the Copts in Egypt.

The process of state efforts to shape the comparative power of particular religions is not limited to the Middle East or to countries with less-developed traditions of freedom of expression and religion. Portions of Europe are tremulous with concerns about the expansion of virulent Islam or Islamism and the impact of its practices on national identities; various efforts, blunt and

---

5   See Russell Blackford, *Freedom of Religion and the Secular State* (Malden, MA: Wiley-Blackwell, 2012).

subtle, are initiated to limit market share for "extremist" perspectives.[6] Soft approaches – educational, promotional and media-focused – are deployed to limit growth. Governments seek to determine feasible and appropriate ways to encourage "moderate Islam" in response to a growing and transnational set of Arab and Muslim networks labelled disruptive.[7] Schools, television channels, travel, sermons are all studied to determine how messages and trans-border output may be modulated.[8] And the drama of large-scale changes in religious influences is hardly restricted to Islam. Christianity is a triumph of the expansion of influence. One could reflect on its growth in South Korea, where the power of Christianity became substantial over a long period of considerable attention.[9] Africa can be seen as a series of contested zones where traditional African religions, Catholicism, Mormonism and various forms of evangelical and Pentecostal Christianity vie for adherents and wrestle with the host state to enlarge or limit influence.[10] Latin America has also been a battleground on which transnational religious movements have struggled for dominance; witness, for example, the election of Pope Francis.

The possibilities for thinking about religion-related entities themselves as strategic speakers are endless. Turbulence and instability shake up existing cartels in ways that alter the religious power structure. What is significant is the amount of coercion necessary to maintain a particular cartel arrangement, and the patterns of exclusion and inclusion. The long-existing efforts to suppress

---

[6] See case studies of European countries in chapters 5–10 of Roel Mejier and Edwin Bakker, eds., *The Muslim Brotherhood in Europe* (Oxford: Oxford University Press, 2013). See also Joel S. Fetzer and J. Christopher Soper, *Muslims and the State in Britain, France, and Germany* (Cambridge: Cambridge University Press, 2005).

[7] There is no adequate definition of "moderate Islam," nor, perhaps, can there be. It is generally a projection of what qualities certain adherents and many who are outside the religion project as desirable (adherence to democratic values, certain kinds of conformity to human rights norms, spurning of violence, adjustments to modernity). I use the term mainly to describe government and group reactions designed to prefer these emphases of belief and practice over others. See M. A. Muqtedar Khan, *Debating Moderate Islam: The Geopolitics of Islam and the West* (Salt Lake City: University of Utah Press, 2007). An instrumental approach is found in Angel Rabasa et al., *Building Moderate Muslim Networks* (Santa Monica, CA: RAND, 2007).

[8] See, for instance, Robert W. Hefner and Muhammad Qasim Zaman, eds., *Schooling Islam: The Culture and Politics of Modern Muslim Education* (Princeton, NJ: Princeton University Press, 2010).

[9] James H. Grayson, *Early Buddhism and Christianity in Korea: A Study in the Emplantation of Religion* (Leiden: Brill, 1985).

[10] See, for instance, Paul Freston, *Evangelicals and Politics in Africa, Asia and Latin America* (Cambridge: Cambridge University Press, 2004); Arye Oded, *Islam and Politics in Kenya* (Boulder, CO: Lynne Reinner Publishers, 2000); Richard H. Elphick and T. R. H. Davenport, eds., *Christianity in South Africa: A Political, Social, and Cultural History* (Berkeley: University of California Press, 1997).

the political participation of the Muslim Brotherhood in Egypt, mentioned earlier, provide one example in which an authoritarian government needed the use of force and surveillance and the management of the electoral processes to hold fast to patterns of permitted involvement.[11] Governments are not always adequately aware of when pressures are so great that the cartel must open to new entrants, and covetous and ambitious religious rivals are not always appreciative of prevailing arrangements slowly to allow pluralism. Disruptive moments, moments of political transformation, become opportunities for producers of religious allegiances, or state sponsors of such producers, to change the rules or take other actions to break an existing cartel or alter an existing balance.[12] Such times provide a special set of circumstances both from outside and among internal groups competing for salience – a key moment in which various religions and states struggle to shape or influence the outcome of these deliberations. Freedom of expression and freedom of religion norms will be invoked, and complex interventions – diplomatic, military, technological and financial – will serve to influence whether Christians can live peacefully and practice their religion in a newly arranged Iraq or Syria or Egypt. External pressures will affect how much room there will be for plural Islamic practices, women's rights and strong elements of secular traditions. These issues will be iterated in numerous decisions: who is eligible to run for office (or which religious manifestations are barred from participation in election campaigns); what relationship there is to forms of campaign funding and support from abroad; what kind of moral, normative and even legal authority religion accrues; and what relationship there is between a formal acceptance (or rejection) of pluralism and actual practice.

PARADIGMS AND WORLD-VIEWS

The well-known freedom of expression paradigm is one in which "religious speech" is a subcategory of a larger, identifiable category called "speech" and in which, under international standards, maximum protection is to be afforded.

[11] See Mohamed Fahmy Menza, *Patronage Politics in Egypt: The National Democratic Party and Muslim Brotherhood in Cairo* (London: Routledge, 2012). In this case, the struggle to suppress the Muslim Brotherhood in Mubarak's Egypt played out across a variety of media platforms. While the state sought to diminish the Brotherhood's influence over targeted broadcast programming, the Brotherhood used new media platforms, such as YouTube and Facebook, to disseminate their religious views. See Karim Tartoussieh, "Virtual Citizenship: Islam, Culture, and Politics in the Digital Age, *International Journal of Cultural Policy* 17, no. 2 (2011).

[12] For a study of this process in Latin America, see Paul Freston, ed., *Evangelical Christianity and Democracy in Latin America* (Oxford: Oxford University Press, 2008).

An inspiration of this baseline of "modernization" is the Enlightenment and its ideal of the secular free thinker, able to speak and act independent of constraint by government. Linked to this is the idea of government acting independent of a dominant religion or of religion acting, in some circumstances, effectively as if it were its own government. Equally rooted is the principle that a dissenting or innovative or competing religion should be able to assert itself without state interference. The modern project can be seen as honoring societies more plural than monopolistic, where power is diffused among religions (as well as political parties). Of course, these abstract rights do not easily map themselves on to the practices that occur in the tumultuous shifts in religious and political markets.[13] Indeed, the way current narratives play themselves out contributes to the constant redefinition of free speech and religion. In China, the state requires that it, not Rome, appoints bishops of the Catholic Church.[14] In Myanmar, the brutal perception of Rohingya Muslims as "foreign" fractures their relationship to the Burmese public sphere. In Tunisia, the French (and the West generally) seek to bring soft efforts to bear to foster a political Islam that is deemed "moderate."[15] Religion becomes a more significant factor in national security, both offensively and defensively.[16] With the stakes so high, it is hardly surprising that governments continue to address the impact of religious activity, no matter what their constitutions or treaty commitments say.

A complex example (now somewhat obsolete) of government-enforced cartelization of religious communication involves the Netherlands in the mid-twentieth century and before. I have discussed, in Chapter 6, how the mode for achieving such cartelization was pillarization, the term used to characterize the profound Dutch solution for regulating a multicultural society.[17] Various aspects of life – churches, political parties, trade unions,

---

[13] See Jonathan Fox, *An Introduction to Religion and Politics: Theory and Practice* (London: Routledge, 2013), 10.

[14] Mark Juergensmeyer, *Global Rebellion: Religious Challenges to the Secular State, from Christian Militias to al Qaeda* (Berkeley: University of California Press, 2008); Yoshiko Ashiwa and David Wank, eds., *Making Religion, Making the State: The Politics of Religion in Modern China* (Stanford, CA: Stanford University Press, 2009); Richard Madsden, *China's Catholics: Tragedy and Hope in an Emerging Civil Society* (Berkeley: University of California Press, 1998).

[15] For a contemporary discussion, see United States Institute of Peace, "Tunisian Debate over Islam, Rights in Constitution Illustrated at USIP Event," May 14, 2013. For background on historical confrontations between Islamic interests and the state, pre-Arab Spring, see Mohamed Elhachmi Ḥamdi, *The Politicisation of Islam: A Case Study of Tunisia* (Boulder, CO: Westview Press, 1998).

[16] See Jonathan Eberhardt Shaw, "The Role of Religion in National Security Policy Since September 11, 2001," *Carlisle Paper*, February 2011.

[17] Ben Spiecker and Jan Steutel, "Multiculturalism, Pillarization and Liberal Civic Education in the Netherlands," *International Journal of Educational Research* 35 (2001).

hospitals, scouting organizations, and broadcasters and newspapers – were divided into pillars. There were originally three pillars – Catholic, Protestant and Socialist – but over time, particularly in the broadcasting arena, fragmentation occurred and a variety of other groups, including atheists, gained pillar status. Each such pillar was allocated time on the broadcasting channels, roughly in proportion to their strength in the general public. The associations that represented the existing "pillars" fought entry by new entities that would strenuously compete with them. Ultimately, as I have indicated, technology (and changes in European Union law commanding access) allowed the ready entry of competitors in the previously tight market of allegiances, and spelled the decline of the cartel.[18] But rather than an external religious force, one of the most effective disrupters at work was popular music broadcast from stations on pirate ships. Another significant example of cartelization occurred in Lebanon after its civil war commenced in the mid-1970s.[19] During the conflict and in the absence of state power, a large number of radio and television stations were created in what amounted to a proliferating open market. As part of the settlement to the conflict, the number of television stations was dramatically reduced, and access to audiences was restricted to each of the major militia and religious participants, including Christians, Sunnis and Shi'ites. Regional pressures (from Syria, Iran and Saudi Arabia) also played a role in the exclusion of some religious communicators. Many stations now operating owe their existence to this settlement.[20]

THE INTERNATIONAL RELIGIOUS FREEDOM
ACT AND STATE INTERVENTIONS

Among the types of state activity to buttress or alter a cartel is the action of one state intervening in the production of religious allegiances in another state – for example, trying to facilitate entry for a particular religion or, conversely, to make entry more difficult. One could ask what stake the United States has in the working of the market for religious loyalties in Egypt or Syria or Mali or Indonesia. In the post-9/11 "War on Terror," the United States and others acted in support of what officials and politicians have called "moderate Islam" and in diminishing the power of certain strains of fundamentalism. The U.S. government, for example, has sought (often indirectly) to encourage more

---

[18] See Hans Knippenberg, ed., *The Changing Landscape of Europe* (Amsterdam: Het Spinhuis, 2005).
[19] Marwan Kraidy, *Hybridity, or the Cultural Logic of Globalization* (Philadelphia: Temple University Press, 2005).
[20] Ibid.

Enlightenment-friendly forms of Islam and forms of Islamic education in Pakistan and Afghanistan. It has sought to block certain Islamic charities that fund more extreme *madrasas*, and that are marked for their links to terror. Partly reflecting domestic interests, the United States has claimed a stake in protecting Christian groups abroad (in Nigeria, in China and elsewhere).[21]

One way to illustrate the spectrum of intervention is the United States' International Religious Freedom Act of 1998 (IRFA), the vehicle by which the United States articulates a belief in universal human rights principles regarding freedom of religion. Based on moral, pragmatic and ideological claims, the government, under the legislation, has responsibilities to identify potential violations and take some, relatively soft, remedial actions. Although the statute is fervently neutral as to which religious practices are to be protected, its origins point to a vital interest in the defense of Christian groups, some engaged in evangelical activity abroad and facing persecution, abuse, violence, criminal actions and other major forms of discouragement.[22] This legislation is relevant to the larger theme of influencing markets for loyalties because it commits the U.S. government, and the State Department, to seek to alter a local cartel in terms of enlarging the scope for religious practice and persuasion. The statute advances religious freedom, as (more or less) defined in international documents, with a significant gloss of U.S. interpretation.[23] IRFA compels the executive branch to document and take certain actions where religious freedom is denied in foreign states. The U.S. perception of religion in society – as captured by IRFA and its annual reports – emphasizes the capacity to change one's religion as a necessary right. Citing the diversity of religions in the United States, IRFA's Advisory Committee has presented American pluralism and flow as a virtue, featuring the ability of individuals to express themselves through religious change.

IRFA can be seen, then, as placing a U.S. imprimatur on international standards that permit existing religious groups to function and new entrants to arise in foreign markets for loyalties. IRFA can be seen as an exercise in strategic communication, with American religions themselves acting strategically by using their domestic influence to bring U.S. economic and other power to bear to compel such foreign markets to function in a more open

---

[21] See Liora Danan and Alice Hunt, *Mixed Blessings: U.S. Government Engagement with Religion in Conflict-Prone Settings* (Washington, DC: The CSIS Press, 2007).

[22] Allen Hertzke, *Freeing God's Children: The Unlikely Alliance for Global Human Rights* (Oxford: Rowman and Littlefield, 2006).

[23] This is an interesting set of standards because the United States has not always adhered to all the relevant international agreements that are said to govern interpretation of the statute. See Dominique Decherf, "Religious Freedom and Foreign Policy: The U.S. International Religious Freedom Act of 1998," June 8, 2001.

manner. Among its mandates are that the Department of State prepare national reports that survey how states are said to violate religious freedom as it is defined or approximated by the law. The annual U.S. State Department International Religious Freedom Reports chronicle areas where the Department considers that standards are in need of adjusting – where practices in particular countries are subject to criticism. These include prohibitions and restrictions on proselytizing, prohibitions on having and distributing certain tracts or religious material, prohibitions on the entry of foreign clergy and prohibitions on any private use of broadcast frequencies, much less religious ones.

I quote from the 2011 reports to provide some example of how the range of interests and the complex practices are noted as part of a process to honor or shame. For example, the 2011 Report on the Kyrgyz Republic noted that:

> In February 2009 the then minister of education signed a decree that officially bans students from wearing religious clothing, particularly the hijab (traditional Islamic headscarf worn by women) in public schools. In March 2009, after local NGOs and parents gathered signatures in protest of the decree, it was changed from an official ban to a recommendation. During the year, several Islamic organizations including Mutakallim, Dil Murok, and Sumaia protested some schools' use of this recommendation as a basis to refuse admission to girls wearing headscarves. As a result, the new education minister, Kanatbek Sydykov, presented the protesting organizations with a semi-official letter specifically stating that "headscarves are not prohibited" in schools. The organizations then distributed the letter to the schools, and the issue appeared to be resolved. Nonetheless, the decree "recommending that hijabs not be worn to school" was not reversed.[24]

Or, from the country report on India for that year:

> Despite the national government's continued rejection of Hindutva (Hindu nationalism), a few state and local governments continue to be influenced by Hindutva. During the year, some states passed laws based on Hindu religious beliefs that restrict the religious freedom of minority groups. For example, on September 29, Gujarat passed a bill which prohibits cow slaughter and requires a permit for transporting cows. The law mandates a seven-year jail term for anyone directly or indirectly involved in the slaughter, storage, transportation, or sale of cow or cow products. Critics argue that such laws deprive Muslims, Christians, and lower castes of livelihoods, a source of nutrition, and the right not to observe Hindu religious restrictions.[25]

---

[24] U.S. Department of State, "International Religious Freedom Report for 2011: Kyrgyz Republic."
[25] U.S. Department of State, "International Religious Freedom Report for 2011: India."

The India report also recalled that

> In 2007 Andhra Pradesh enacted the Propagation of Other Religions in the Places of Worship or Prayer (Prohibition) Law. The law allows the state to prohibit the propagation of one religion near a place of worship or prayer of another religion. Thus far, the state has identified only Hindu religious sites for this protection. Punishment for violations of the act can include imprisonment up to three years and fines up to 5,312 rupees ($125). To date there have been no prosecutions under the act. A fact-finding team from the National Commission for Minorities found that the prohibition was not in line with the constitution's protections of freedom of religion, noting that the IPC [Indian Penal Code] had provisions sufficient to deal with offenses committed in places of worship.[26]

PROSELYTIZING, CONVERSION AND THE MARKET FOR LOYALTIES

As these reports suggest, an often-employed mode of maintaining "stability" in the cartel of religious loyalties is to restrict or manage efforts at proselytizing and conversion and punish deviations.[27] Regulation of proselytizing is a case study in the structuring of cartels as well as an example of the complexity of relying on rights-related jurisprudence alone. From a human rights perspective, proselytizing has several faces. It is speech at its most fundamental: the articulation of ideas most important to the speaker and possibly of redemptive significance to the receiver. At the same time, proselytizing can be perceived as disruptive or subversive of existing arrangements among providers of allegiances – inconsistent with a state's hegemonic perception of its national identity or invasive of a religion's internal binding principles.

As states vary in their disciplining of these market-shaping techniques, external players invoke international norms to favor particular outcomes. The relevant language of the human rights documents on the issue of proselytism is deceptively simple, and masks long-standing disputes (particularly those dealing with vulnerabilities, inducements and the exercise of power). Article 18 of the International Covenant on Civil and Political Rights (ICCPR) states that:

1. Everyone shall have the right to freedom of thought, conscience and religion. This right shall include freedom to have or to adopt a religion or belief of his choice, and freedom, either individually or in community

---

[26] Ibid.

[27] For an influential essay, see David A. Snow and Richard Malachek, "The Sociology of Conversion," *Annual Review of Sociology* 10 (1984).

with others and in public or private, to manifest his religion or belief in worship, observance, practice and teaching.

2. No one shall be subject to coercion which would impair his freedom to have or to adopt a religion or belief of his choice.

3. Freedom to manifest one's religion or beliefs may be subject only to such limitations as are prescribed by law and are necessary to protect public safety, order, health, or morals or the fundamental rights and freedoms of others.

Section 2 of the Article seems to limit the right of proselytizers to use "coercion" as a means of inducing conversion or exercise of "choice." This has led to a discourse, including in the decisions of the European Court for Human Rights, of what should be considered coercion.[28]

An overriding and effective norm that privileges the right to convert seems a victory for the freedom to speak and believe. But enforcing this norm can also be read as favoring certain religions over others. Defending or qualifying the right to proselytize (or the right to be converted or to hear arguments for change) affects the ability of states to maintain or change a given cartel in the market for loyalties. Guaranteeing rights to convert quite obviously establishes a norm that encourages greater competition and somewhat favors religions or sects within religions that are committed to active proselytizing.[29]

There are states that regulate such conversion practices, either formally or informally, as a commitment to the existing religious cartel. Informal agreements may exist between or among religious entities that tolerate some degree of conversion advocacy but also suggest limits on the practice. Greece, Afghanistan, Pakistan and certain of the states of Central Asia and Malaysia[30] all provide case studies of regulation of efforts to convert.[31] Informal or formal

---

[28] The ICCPR has been amended on this issue, differentiating it from the 1948 Universal Declaration of Human Rights. The significance of the change is subject to debate. In the 1948 version, "religious freedom" explicitly included the freedom to "change" one's religion, but in the later version (of the ICCPR) the word "change" disappeared. Freedom, instead, became the "freedom to have or to adopt" a religion or belief. Perhaps this was a subtle effort, adopted under pressure from newly decolonized states, to make it clear that maintaining religious beliefs was a value equivalent to altering them.

[29] For one approach to these questions, see Tad Stahnke, "Proselytism and the Freedom to Change Religion in International Human Rights Law," *Brigham Young University Law Review* 1 (1999).

[30] See Dian Abdul Hamed Shah and Mahd Azizuddin Mohd Sani, "Freedom of Religion in Malaysia: A Tangled Web of Legal, Political, and Social Issues," *North Carolina Journal of International Law &Commercial Regulation* 36, no. 3 (2011).

[31] For the Greek case in particular, see Johannes A. van der Ven and Hans Georg Ziebertz, eds., *Tensions Within and Between Religions and Human Rights* (Leiden: Brill, 2012). Also see, for a Russian example, John Witte Jr. and Michael Bourdeaux, *Proselytism and Orthodoxy in Russia* (New York: Orbis Books, 1999).

punishment for apostasy is a companion aspect; Christian groups and others invoking human rights norms have fought to bring pressure on states that impose sanctions (including death) on converts.[32] Different contexts yield varying regulatory environments, ranging from China, with its current emphasis on its version of secularism, to Russia, with its Orthodox tradition, to Central Asia and Africa, where tribal and clan traditions bring varied consequences if norms relating to conversion are violated.[33]

The issue of regulating conversion practices and other techniques for favoring some market-building steps for favored groups was and remains an important one in Russia, the Ukraine and other post-Soviet societies. In 1997, by an overwhelming vote, the Russian parliament passed a bill establishing two categories of religious institutions, "traditional" and "nontraditional." Traditional religious communities, legally referred to as religious "organizations," were defined as those with an established presence in Russia of fifteen or more years. They included Orthodoxy, Judaism, Islam and Buddhism. Under the statute, these entities have – though there is some debate about this – a privileged status that allows them, among other things, to run radio and television stations. Roman Catholic, Baptist and breakaway or dissident Russian Orthodox denominations, even those that have been in Russia longer than fifteen years, were classified instead as religious "groups" and have not enjoyed the same bundle of rights, including the right to run broadcasting outlets.[34] Catherine Wanner, who has written about comparative Russian and Ukrainian post-Soviet approaches to this question, has argued that although "the aim of the law was to restrict 'totalitarian sects' and 'dangerous religious cults,'" the law in fact could be said to have discriminated "against less-established religious groups, such as Jehovah's Witnesses and Mormons, by making it difficult for them to establish institutional bases."[35] These approaches could be seen not only as a competition among religious entities but within a larger environment of competition for allegiances. At the fall of the Soviet Union, the Protestant fundamentalist denominations were

[32] See, for example, Abdullah Saeed and Hassan Saeed, *Freedom of Religion, Apostasy and Islam* (Aldershot: Ashgate Publishing, 2004).

[33] For a survey of such efforts from various religious perspectives, see John Witte Jr. & Richard C. Martin, eds., *Sharing the Book: Religious Perspectives on the Rights and Wrongs of Proselytism* (New York: Orbis Books, 1999). Also see Stahnke, "Proselytism and the Freedom to Change."

[34] Catherine Wanner, "Missionaries of Faith and Culture: Evangelical Encounters in Ukraine," *Slavic Review* 63, no. 4 (2004): 738. See also Zoe Knox, *Russian Society and the Orthodox Church: Religion in Russia after Communism* (London: Routledge, 2013).

[35] Wanner, "Missionaries of Faith and Culture," 738. Also see the studies in *Emory International Law Review* 12, no. 1 (1998).

perceived as aggressively anti-communist, which gave the movement a special immediate appeal. The ideological vacuum left by the collapse of communism as a viable worldview and a source of individual and collective meaning was replaced, according to Wanner, by a "religious-based orientation to self and society."[36] Indeed, Wanner claims, "the disorientation prompted by sweeping social change as the Soviet system began to fall apart caused some to embrace religion as an anti-Soviet alternative, as a new moral compass to guide their ideas and behavior amidst social confusion and economic collapse."[37]

Wanner placed these religion-ranking statutes in the post-Soviet national identity context. "Ukrainian government and cultural leaders remain obsessed by the growth of nontraditional religious groups, meaning neither Orthodox nor Greek-Catholic. The growing presence of foreign missionaries in Ukraine buttressing these new religious institutions strains the ideal of Ukrainians as a unified ethno-religious people and complicates the process of nation building." The desire to rein in proselytism, especially by foreigners and by foreign-imported nontraditional religious groups, was "palpable" among government leaders and even among the population at large.[38]

What each religious organization or group considers appropriate in its effort to expand is definitely an aspect of the competition. Self-regulation (by the group or by the cartel) limits the mode of expansion. Religious entities that prohibit proselytizing or that impose strong ethical limits on the proselytizing activities of their adherents can be compared with those whose standards allow more aggressive efforts at conversions. Furthermore, host states have different interpretations of what constitutes "coercion" in proselytizing activities. A useful insight into the complex legal and ethical questions relating to national regulation and self-regulation of proselytizing appears in an essay by Mark Elliott called "Evangelism and Proselytism in Russia: Synonyms or Antonyms?" published by the Overseas Ministries Study Center. Sensitive to national regulation that minimizes or eliminates inducements that are inconsistent with ethical religious practice, Elliott reaffirms that proselytism is acceptable "as long as it falls short of … coercion, material inducement, invasion of privacy, and preachments to captive audiences."[39] Commenting on post-Soviet Russia in the somewhat raw 1990s, he argues:

[36]   Wanner, "Missionaries of Faith and Culture," 733–734.
[37]   Ibid., 734.
[38]   Ibid., 740–741.
[39]   Mark Elliott, "Evangelism and Proselytism in Russia: Synonyms or Antonyms?" *International Bulletin of Missionary Research* 25 (2001): 74. See also United Nations General Assembly, "The Declaration on the Elimination of All Forms of Intolerance and Discrimination Based on Religion or Belief" (November 25, 1981).

Increasingly the xenophobic Russian Orthodox Church sees not only such manipulative charity but all Western Protestant compassionate ministries and communications as illegitimate material inducements. Moscow Patriarchate Department of External Relations representative Alexander Dvorkin ... deplores all manner of Western Christian ministry in the former Soviet Union, including "the furnishing of humanitarian aid, English lessons, education, and employment ... the use of television, newspapers, and other mass media to propagate the faith and the organization of loud and insensitive crusading carnivals." In 1996 Metropolitan Kyrill of Smolensk and Kaliningrad bitterly complained to a World Council of Churches Conference on World Mission and Evangelism meeting in Brazil about the "hordes of missionaries" in Russia who "came from abroad with dollars" in a "crusade ... against the Russian Church," preaching on radio and television "in order to buy people." Metropolitan Kyrill contended, "This work is not Christian mission, it is spiritual colonialism." Similarly, throughout the 1990s Patriarch Alexis II decried the "massive influx" of "well-organized and well-financed" missions of "foreign proselytizing faiths," "zealots" in search of "new markets."[40]

Later efforts demonstrated experiments in cooperation in Russia. In 2005, Alexis II, then Patriarch of Moscow and All Russia (head of the Russian Orthodox Church), issued his definition of what constituted appropriate understandings with his counterpart in Rome, stating: "Cooperation with the Roman Catholic Church must exclude the forms of proselytism (i.e. the Vatican spreading its influence to what the [Russian Church] sees as its canonical territory) that have been pursued recently."[41]

Strategies of communication, including methods for encouraging or fighting conversion, differ by medium, time and place. One can look across religions and religious groups at long-term strategies for the use of different media; and one can look across national boundaries at regulation of specific technologies of persuasion. Broadcasting has been the obvious medium to study, although in contexts concerning religion far beyond proselytizing.[42] Religious broadcasting – assignment of channels, regulation of content – has turned, in large part, on how the powers within a state see the channel, whether they view it as serving to undergird or reaffirm religious faith or,

---

[40] Elliott, "Evangelism and Proselytism," 73.

[41] "Russian Patriarch: Cooperation Does Not Imply Proselyte Activities," *RIA Novosti*, June 08, 2005.

[42] See Stewart M. Hoover, *Religion in the Media Age* (London: Routledge, 2013); Birgit Meyer and Annelies Moors, eds., *Religion, Media, and the Public Sphere* (Bloomington: Indiana University Press, 2005).

rather, as a more aggressive agent of change, designed fundamentally to alter the mix of allegiances.[43]

An example within the United States from the 1930s reflects the process of market division, holding the power of the relatively new medium in safe hands.[44] Soon after the National Broadcasting Company was created (and in anticipation of government concern), its owners formed an advisory committee to guide in the development of programs in various fields, including religious broadcasting. A standing committee was charged with providing time or opportunities for the benefit of the "three great religious communions" and no more. Among the principles adopted (as a surrogate for regulation) were the following:

> The national broadcasting company will serve only the central or national agencies of great religious faiths, as for example, the Roman Catholics, the Protestants, and the Jews, as distinguished from individual churches or small group movements where the national membership is comparatively small.
>
> The religious message broadcast should be nonsectarian and nondenominational in appeal.
>
> The religious message broadcast should be of the widest appeal; presenting the broad claims of religion, which not only aid in building up the personal and social life of the individual but also aid in popularizing religion and the church.[45]

This approach – establishment-oriented and exclusive – extended to all the networks and, with tacit government approval, remained the dominant approach on the main broadcast channels for decades. But there was a revolt through radio and later American televangelism. Especially in the last third of the twentieth century, opposition grew to this audiovisual cartel of the dominant religious orders. Passionate sects and individuals sought out underused channels (UHF for example). They built support by portraying themselves as marginalized and victimized, deprived of opportunities to practice and extend their faiths. They accused the Federal Communications Commission of enforcing unconstitutional limitations on their use of frequencies. They created lobbying groups and mastered the idiosyncrasies of the U.S. political system. Decades of strategic effort resulted in a radically effective capacity

---

[43] See Jim McDonnell, "From Certainty to Diversity. The Evolution of British Religious Broadcasting since 1990," in *Faith and Media: Analysis of Faith and Media: Representation and Communication*, eds. Hans Geybels, Sara Mels and Michel Walrave (Brussels: Peter Lang, 2009).

[44] Spencer Miller, Jr., "Radio and Religion," *Annals of the American Academy of Political and Social Science* 177 (1935).

[45] Tona J. Hangen, *Redeeming the Dial: Radio, Religion, and Popular Culture in America* (Chapel Hill: University of North Carolina Press, 2002), 25.

to use broadcasting and, later, the new technology of satellite by religious figures. Their transformation of media and its consequent impact on the American polity is an oft-told tale.[46]

Broadcasting is intrinsically manipulative, and some practices of persuasion by radio or television – those that promise cures, perhaps those that defraud or even overclaim – may be inconsistent with ethical and legal standards and have been subjected to state regulation as coercive under international standards.[47] One scholar has written that, "especially where they are in a majority, non-proselytizing religions often seek to use broadcasting regulation to limit the capacity of minority religions to gain converts from among adherents of the majority religion. Majority religions have done so in the past by seeking to influence regulation of broadcasting in a manner that limits the access of minority religions to the media or by increasing their own share of time on the media."[48]

Attention shifts somewhat to the Internet as another medium that states, particularly oppressive regimes, attempt to regulate in hopes of controlling transnational (and local) religious flows.[49] Dawson and Cowan conclude that the Internet is not, in terms of their studies, yet a significant instrument for proselytizing.[50] They argue, however, that it may be a medium for intensifying beliefs, rendering some who are already faithful more intensively engaged and susceptible to mobilization. The Chinese attempt to control the content of the Falun Gong movement on the Internet provides an example of governmental response. The Falun Gong, or Falun Dafa, is a deeply controversial movement that began in China in 1992 and has been led from the United States by

---

[46] The story is told in various places: Jeffrey K. Hadden, "Regulating Religious Broadcasting: Some Old Patterns and New Trends," in *The Role of Government in Monitoring and Regulating Religion in Public Life*, eds. James E. Wood Jr. and Derek Davis (Waco, TX: J. M. Dawson Institute of Church-State Studies, 1993); Jeffrey K. Hadden and Anson Shupe, *Televangelism: Power and Politics on God's Frontier* (New York: Henry Holt, 1988). As to whether there was a deliberate effort by mainstream religious organizations to keep evangelical programs off the primary airwaves, Hoover demurs. He argues that the evangelicals insisted on preaching doctrine, while the mainstream groups went along with an FCC and network preference for "broad truths." See Stuart Hoover and Douglas K. Wagner, "History and Policy in American Broadcast Treatment of Religion," *Media, Culture and Society* 19, no. 1 (1997).

[47] For an early and interesting exploration of these themes in the U.S. context, see Jonathan Weiss, "Privilege, Posture and Protection: 'Religion' in the Law," *Yale Law Journal* 73, no. 4 (1964).

[48] Rodney K. Smith, "Regulating Religious Broadcasting: Some Comparative Reflections," *Brigham Young University Law Review* 4 (1996).

[49] Rudiger Lohliker, *New Approaches to the Analysis of Jihadism: Online and Offline* (Göttingen: V&R Unipress, 2012).

[50] Lorne L. Dawson and Douglas E. Cowan, *Religion Online: Finding Faith On the Internet* (London: Routledge, 2013).

its founder Li Hongzhi. Falun Gong has grown in China and elsewhere partially because of the movement's adroit use of the Internet, which has allowed Li to create a passionate diasporic community of adherents. To control the spread of the Falun Gong, which the Chinese government considers potentially or actually destabilizing, the Chinese government strategically deploys Internet filtering among many extremely harsh measures to ensure that information about the movement is blocked.[51]

Efforts to regulate religious content as a way of limiting the impact of disfavored groups are hardly limited to China. Distribution of information about Christianity has been widely hampered.[52] Pakistan has blocked, or required Internet intermediaries to block, "blasphemous content," the breadth of this term signaling the tight control the government retains over the circulation of religious messages online.[53] In some settings, Christian groups as well as others, religious and not, have advocated the use of filtering to create what they consider a more protected Internet. In Australia, for example, such groups have successfully lobbied for laws requiring the availability of a "clean feed," in which pornography and other offensive content has been blocked. As Brian Simpson notes, commenting on Australian developments, pro-choice websites and sites advocating for gay rights have been deemed "offensive content," providing certain Christian groups an additional tool in their long-standing struggle against what they see as evil aspects of secularization.[54]

SERMONS, INCITEMENT AND BLASPHEMY LAWS AS A LOCUS FOR REGULATION

The use of law and regulation to block or encourage particular religious perspectives takes many other forms – for example, rules punishing or regulating hate speech where the hate is directed at religions.[55] Proscribing hate speech or blasphemy puts a tax on a religion's critics. A more contemporary technique is to provide some immunity or comfort for a calumnized group, in part to reduce isolation and extremism within its ranks. One example involves

---

[51] See David Ownby, *Falun Gong and the Future of China* (New York: Oxford University Press, 2008).

[52] See Robert Faris and Nart Villeneuve, "Measuring Global Internet Filtering," in *Access Denied: The Practice and Policy of Global Internet Filtering*, eds. Ronald Deibert et al. (Cambridge, MA: The MIT Press, 2008).

[53] Deibert et al., eds., *Access Denied*.

[54] Brian Simpson, "New Labor, New Censorship? Politics, Religion and Internet Filtering in Australia," *Information and Communications Technology Law* 17, no. 3 (2008).

[55] Michael Herz and Peter Molnar, eds., *The Content and Context of Hate Speech: Rethinking Regulation and Responses* (Cambridge: Cambridge University Press, 2012).

British laws seeking to reduce the maligning of Islamic entities. The Racial and Religious Hatred Act 2006 provisions criminalized incitement of religious hatred in a way designed to protect vulnerable religious beliefs and practices. Within the market for loyalties paradigm, this is not the usual case in which the anti-blasphemy law exists to protect the dominant religion. It is, rather, an instance in which there is interest in maintaining a version of plurality, of giving a sense to an embattled group that their market share is not wholly endangered, of creating an environment in which competition is civil rather than vicious.

A little-studied but significant example of formal and informal regulation to affect religious communication involves control of sermons or those who give them.[56] In a way, this is not surprising; government tends to regulate those media exercises that are potentially the most challenging to the existing order (and statements from the pulpit have demonstrated this potential). Many religious orders "self-regulate," assuring that those conducting sermons do so in ways that conform – roughly speaking – to church orthodoxy. Where the religious order is sufficiently centralized and where there is an understanding between the government and the religious hierarchy on which messages are tolerated, that may be adequate comfort for the authorities. But frequently, the state is more deeply involved. For example, in Jordan imams have been hired and trained by the state and their messages are tightly monitored to prevent the dissemination of revolutionary or anti-government ideas.[57] Ehteshami and Wright affirm this pattern elsewhere: "In Kuwait there is strict regulation and monitoring of the mosques by the Ministry of Islamic Affairs which sets tight guidelines on what imams are allowed to discuss in their sermons."[58] They point out that in Qatar imams are civil servants and that exacting authority is also exercised in Saudi Arabia.[59] In October 2011, fifty imams from mosques across Morocco demonstrated in Rabat complaining about the tight controls the government imposed on them. Imams claimed that they

---

[56] For an excellent essay on regulation of sermons, see Curt Hessler, "Keeping the Faith," *The New Yorker*, October 7, 2013.

[57] See Quintan Wiktorowicz, *The Management of Islamic Activism: Salafis, the Muslim Brotherhood, and State Power in Jordan* (Albany: State University of New York Press, 2001).

[58] Anoushiravan Ehteshami and Steven Wright, *Reform in the Middle East Oil Monarchies* (Sussex: Sussex Academic Press, 2011), 57. The complex relationship between imams and public officials in Dagestan and Tatarstan is explored in Galina Yemelianova, "Islam and Power," in *Islam in Post-Soviet Russia*, eds. Hilary Pilkington and Galina Yemelianova (London: RoutledgeCurzon, 2003).

[59] The 2010 International Religious Freedom Annual Report to the U.S. Congress describes Saudi Arabia's system of strict control over sermons and what they say as potential violation of religious freedoms. See U.S. Department of State, "2010 Report on International Religious Freedom: Saudi Arabia," September 13, 2011.

were given government-prepared sermons that they were ordered to deliver on Fridays without deviation from the text.[60]

The arrest and deportation to the United States of the British imam Abu Hamza is a manifestation of similar patterns in Europe, an example of a state reaction to arguably destabilizing forms of discourse originating from within the mosque.[61] As an Australian paper put it, somewhat dramatically:

> The role of the 47-year-old Egyptian-born cleric in radicalising the men responsible for Britain's worst mainland terror atrocity, the London suicide bombings, can be revealed. So, too, can the extraordinary influence Hamza and the Finsbury Park mosque had over some of the world's most notorious terrorists. For in the six years the hook-handed former mujahidin fighter was preaching his anti-Western sermons in North London, it became a breeding ground for terrorism under his controlling power. He is suspected of helping recruit and influence hundreds of British Muslims and of facilitating their journeys to terror training camps – trips often orchestrated and supported by a criminal network run through the mosque.[62]

In the United States, a peculiar form of regulation took place in the wake of the 2001 attacks. The Department of Justice discovered that the Wahhabi sect – a conservative, fundamentalist branch of Sunni Islam – had informally obtained a virtual monopoly position among chaplains in federal and key state prisons and, in the government's view, was using that power to recruit prisoners to the faith. What followed was a successful effort not only to break the monopoly but to virtually ban the sect from participating in that particular market for loyalties. Here is an excerpt from U.S. Senator Charles Schumer explaining the context during Congressional hearings:

> Let me give you an example of how Wahhabism has wreaked some degree of havoc in my own backyard in New York State. For 20 years the New York State Department of Corrections employed Warith Deen Umar as one of its chaplains, eventually appointing him administrative chaplain of the New York Department of Correctional Services. A strict believer in Wahhabi Islam, Umar was responsible for the hiring and firing of all chaplains in the New

---

[60] "Moroccan Imams protest government control," *AP*, October 10, 2011.

[61] In one reaction, in 2004, the Spanish Prime Minister suggested registering imams and regulating what they preached. See Ben Sills, "Spain Seeks to Control What Imams Preach," *Guardian*, May 3, 2004.

[62] David Williams and Ben Taylor, "Evil Incarcerated," *The Mercury*, February 11, 2006. For a contextual account, see Frank Foley, *Countering Terrorism in Britain and France: Institutions, Norms and the Shadow of the Past* (Cambridge: Cambridge University Press, 2013); Anneke Meyer, "Moral Panics, Globalization and Islamophobia: The Case of Abu Hamza in *The Sun*," in *Global Islamophobia: Muslims and Moral Panic in the West*, eds. George Morgan and Scott Poynting (Farnham, Surrey: Ashgate, 2012).

York State prison system, exercising complete control over personnel matters. But last year Mr. Umar was banned from ever again entering a New York State prison after he incited prisoners against America, specifically preaching to inmates that the 9/11 hijackers should be remembered as martyrs.

Many of the clerics Umar hired during his tenure have reportedly echoed his sentiments in sermons before many of New York State's 13,000 Muslim inmates, as well as – and this is the amazing point – impeding their freedom of religion by denying these prisoners access to materials and imams used by more moderate forms of Islam. ... When my office researched further, we discovered that New York's prisons were not the only ones that had been penetrated by this kind of Wahhabi zealotry. The U.S. Federal Bureau of Prisons uses two groups to select imams who administer to Muslim inmates: the Graduate School of Islamic and Social Sciences, whose offices are right across the river in Northern Virginia, and the Islamic Society of Northern America. ... Both of these groups appear to have disturbing connections to Wahhabism and terrorism. ... These organizations have succeeded in ensuring that militant Wahhabism is the only form of Islam that is preached to the 12,000 Muslims in federal prisons. That is against the American view of pluralism. If there are some in the prisons who want Wahhabi ministers that's one thing, but for every Muslim to be forced to have a Wahhabi minister, that is wrong, incorrect and against the American way. And these imams flood the prisons with anti-American, pro-bin Laden videos, literature, sermons and tapes. They destroy literature sent to the prisons by more moderate Shia and Sunni organizations and prevent imams that follow these traditions from speaking to prisons.[63]

It was an ironic turn in regulation of the market for loyalties. The Wahhabi clerics had found a way to develop a near monopoly in one sector of American life. In reaction, the Justice Department changed the rules concerning appointment and broke the cartel that governed entry into the prison chaplaincy.

CONCLUSION

The purpose of this chapter has been to place religious entities and their competitors, groups vying for allegiances in complex markets for loyalties, within an account of strategic communication. Among these entities are forceful and committed organizations reaching across borders, seeking to challenge and upend the status quo, and much is at stake in terms of global values as these contests between belief systems take place. Satellite imams and

---

[63] Senator Schumer, "Hearing of the Terrorism, Technology and Homeland Security Subcommittee of the Senate Judiciary Committee: Terrorism: Growing Wahhabi Influence in the United States," *Federal News Service*, June 26, 2003.

televangelists and a legion of religious leaders have significant ambitions, not only to gain adherents but also to alter certain political arrangements and bolster others, to change the world. They become innovators, too, in the use of media to achieve their objectives. Their involvement in cartel-formation has provided many negotiated outcomes (explicit or implicit), often allowing states and religions to coexist, but sometimes deepening and embedding conflict. My account concentrates on how states engage in shaping and regulating competition among religious groups. We see how parties perceive religious fervor as competition for the core ideas of the state, particularly in states where a traditional commitment to secular centrality is challenged by demographic and belief-related shifts. As strengths of particular religions become dominant (or threatening), tension mounts in terms of control of the narrative of the state, even its narrative of legitimacy. Each state's religious formation and religious tendencies also exist in a global environment. We have seen how these strategic communicators in one state often have a serious impact on the political and security structure in another state.

Many understandings of religious communication, including the under-standings discussed in this chapter, emphasize the power of a religion's core meaning and the circumstances that make its set of ideas appealing. This chapter opens up, however, a different perspective, a counter-analysis that links the growth of religious influence to the impact of additional com-municative opportunities. Here Roger Finke and Laurence Iannaccone are instructive. Largely based on their chronicle of the hothouse American religious experience well before the twentieth century, they set out an inter-esting proposition: The growth of various new faiths and the decline of the old ought not to be attributed wholly or largely to "altered desires, perceptions, or circumstances."[64] They assert, rather, that "the most significant changes in American religion derive from shifting supply, not shifting demand. Colonial revivalists, Asian cult leaders and contemporary televangelists all prospered when regulatory changes gave them freer access to America's religious marketplace."[65] For Finke and Iannaccone, it is changes in the incentives and opportunities provided to religious producers that contribute so substantially to expansion or contraction among faiths, not "some sudden shift in the material or psychological state of the populace."[66]

Here is how they see the hand of government: "The market model views churches and their clergy as religious producers who choose the

---

[64] Roger Finke and Laurence R. Iannacconne, "Supply-Side Explanations for Religious Change," *Annals of the American Academy of Political and Social Sciences* 527 (1993): 28.
[65] Ibid., 27.
[66] Ibid., 28.

characteristics of their product and the means of marketing it. Consumers in turn choose what religion, if any, they will accept and how extensively they will participate in it. As in other markets, government regulation can profoundly affect the producers' incentives, the consumers' options and the aggregate equilibrium."[67] For them, for example, "the so-called Great Awakenings" of the periods 1730–1760 and 1800–1830 succeeded "when restrictions on new sects and itinerant preaching diminished. Early American religion flourished in response to religious deregulation."[68] Finke and Iannaccone called successful innovating preachers, like the Grand Itinerant, George Whitfield, "unregulated competitors in the religious marketplace, foreign competition that threatened the privileges and profits of a domestic cartel."[69]

This dynamic of sudden competition helps explain movements in the Middle East, as shrewd strategic communicators, such as the Islamic State (ISIS), mine new opportunities to enter, proselytize and build support.[70] Revolution, uprising, occupation – all, sometimes just for a split second, create the opportunity for rapid entry and substantial change in the structure of the market. Temporarily, there may be a kind of deregulation, or regulation of a different sort, opening a space where competitors for allegiances, religious entities among them, seek to create a new equilibrium and exercise pressure on the state to enforce it. Religions, as strategic communicators, are on the watch for these critical apertures, these changes in structure that allow for a supply of alternatives to change. Similarly, strategic communicators consider here, as elsewhere, how international norms of freedom of expression and freedom of religion can be used to deregulate barriers and facilitate opportunities for entry. And, of course, we have seen the broad restructuring of supply that has been the consequence of the vast expansion of channels for distribution, by satellite, by cable and by Internet.

This chapter has concerned entities passionate about faith and its consequences. I turn next to the field of non-governmental organizations, a zone filled with groups passionate about an array of intensely significant matters, where constituencies are formed and where advocacy and its successes have important political consequences. These groups – environmental, political and humanitarian – seek, like religions, to influence hearts and minds. How and whether their capacity to communicate is regulated, and by whom, has led to questions of great contestation.

---

[67] Ibid., 28.
[68] Ibid., 29.
[69] Ibid., 32.
[70] Scott Shane and Bell Hubbard, "ISIS Displaying a Deft Command of Varied Media," Newyork Times, August 30, 2014.

9

Regulating NGOs in the Market for Loyalties

I turn to non-governmental organizations (NGOs) as one of the most interesting and important categories of "sellers of allegiances" in a complex transnational market for loyalties. These groups, while functioning within a relatively opaque formula of international, political and civil rights, have become vital innovators in the process of reshaping attitudes and affecting behaviors around the world. They champion a wide range of issues, such as health, the environment and human rights. These issues have frequently been underrepresented in the public sphere, and their advocacy is often suppressed or muted. Many NGOs seek to gain traction for their causes by building support not only in the societies which gave birth to them, but in the external societies whose texture must also be affected if solutions are to be globally meaningful. Recent developments underscore how financing of such groups and other forms of government involvement affect the strategic response of target states to their effectiveness. Chapter 10, dealing largely with the Beijing Olympics of 2008, examines some techniques used by NGOs to advance their points of view.

NGOs have emerged as increasingly influential and visible entities in the public realm and as key actors in international debates, at times rivaling governments or acting as their proxies in terms of impact on certain issues. The category implies serving a particular significant social purpose, often humanitarian, that is altruistic and change-oriented.[1] In fact, the category includes groups with very diverse objectives, varied along a political spectrum, varied by form of organization and by relationship to governments. Unlike

---

[1] For a discussion on the breadth of approaches taken by NGOs, see Clifford Bob, *The Global Right Wing and the Clash of World Politics* (Cambridge: Cambridge University Press, 2012). Also see, for the evolving relationship between NGOs and activism/humanitarianism, W. Lance Bennett, "Social Movements beyond Borders: Understanding Two Eras of Transnational Activism," in *Transnational Protest and Global Activism: People, Passions and Power*, eds. Donatella Della Porta and Sidney George Tarrow (Lanham: Rowman & Littlefield, 2005).

businesses, NGOs are generally not profit-oriented, though they may be large and prosperous; unlike states, they ordinarily have no special status within the international system. As they push to become more successful players, these groups rely on the general adoption of a model of access, a model that implies the acceptance of certain international norms that give them greater opportunity to function in local and global markets. Many of these NGOs are engaged in strategic communication as I have defined it. They seek public support, often for positions deemed unorthodox by segments in the receiving society or by its government. In this context, global strategies can offer what Margaret Keck and Kathryn Sikkink describe as a "boomerang effect," allowing groups to circumvent domestic indifference or pressure by transferring debate to the international level and also positioning NGOs as truly important strategic actors in the global arena.[2]

My focus in this chapter shifts from the strategies and actions of the transnational entities, the NGOs themselves, to the reactions of governments where these entities operate (in this regard, the perspective here is similar to that in Chapter 7, which examined Iran's reaction to what it believed was a Soft War). These governmental reactions attribute particular kinds of effectiveness to the NGOs, impacts often claimed by the NGOs themselves.[3] Unthreading the impact that NGOs, including large transnational NGOs, such as Human Rights Watch or Amnesty International, play in this process is immensely difficult. Scholars have tried to correlate the level of activity of NGOs to changes in various democracy indices.[4] Public opinion can be tracked in the target society to determine the influence of NGO efforts. Blogospheres can be mapped to determine the density of impact on ideas and networks of influence.[5] Many were the studies that attributed increased demand for democratic governance during the color revolutions to the work of civil society.

NGOs, usually, stand for values that reflect treaty-accepted positions. Many are advocates for rights set forth in the Universal Declaration of Human Rights

[2] Margaret E. Keck and Kathryn Sikkink, *Activists Beyond Borders: Advocacy Networks in International Politics* (Ithaca, NY: Cornell University Press, 2004), 12.

[3] See, e.g., Claude E. Welch, *NGOs and Human Rights: Promise and Performance* (Philadelphia: University of Pennsylvania, 2001); Scott Calnan, *The Effectiveness of Domestic Human Rights NGOs: A Comparative Study* (Leiden: Brill, 2008).

[4] Helmut Anheir, *Civil Society: Measurement, Evaluation, Policy* (London: Earthscan, 2004); Alnoor Ebrahim, *NGOs and Organizational Change: Discourse, Reporting, and Learning* (Cambridge: Cambridge University Press, 2003). USAID issues a CSO Sustainability Index for civil society organizations, which scores various nations for the capabilities of NGOs and governments' affordances for them. E.g.: http://www.usaid.gov/europe-eurasia-civil-society/cso-sustainability-2012.

[5] See John Kelly and Bruce Etling, "Mapping Iran's Online Public: Politics and Culture in the Persian Blogosphere," *Berkman Center for Internet & Society*, April 5, 2008.

and similar documents. These are often justifiably, elegantly and passionately set forth using methods of strategic communication. For many of these goals, and in many circumstances, NGOs see the need to change not only government agendas but also popular opinion that influences those agendas. In understanding the role of NGOs in strategic communication, it helps to identify two broad categories (although many groups blur the lines). These categories, somewhat simplified, are *campaigning* and *service*. NGOs that are committed to a large idea – such as promoting conformance to human rights norms – are often called "campaigning NGOs" and must build local or home constituencies for their vision. These organizations may be seeking, for example, to raise consciousness of human rights globally, or to create support in one state (e.g., the United States) to bring pressure to bear for greater adherence to particular objectives in another state (e.g., Myanmar). Other organizations are effective advocates for environmental change, as is the case with Greenpeace or the World Wildlife Federation. For many of these NGOs, since mobilization is a key weapon in their arsenal, communication is central. Greenpeace, among many organizations, provides videos on its website for use by publications, mirroring the tactics and sophistication of corporate and government PR to get their messages across in the media. Amnesty International's Urgent Action Network has long used communication strategies to put pressure on influential government officials in response to human rights violations (for example, through targeted letter-writing campaigns), highlighting the fact that campaigning is not mere publicity. Indeed, many NGOs have taken on the functions of news media, establishing mechanisms for gathering and diffusing information on the issues important to them.[6]

In addition to campaigning NGOs, there are those that can be characterized more as "service" entities (though some of the most accomplished NGOs fit both categories). Medical and children's charities are archetypal in this category; one example is Doctors Without Borders, which provides medical assistance, particularly in areas of prolonged violence, conflict and natural disaster. If these service entities have a communications strategy, it may be to try to differentiate the message in the society in which they work (where they may wish to keep a low profile) from the societies from which they gain financial support and where knowledge of their work in general is essential for survival. In this respect, much of their communication is simply public relations for fundraising purposes. They often need to reinforce, communicatively, their role as neutral actors. Although many NGOs are studiously

---

[6] See the online series "NGOs and the News," *Nieman Journalism Lab*, http://www.niemanlab. org/category/ngo-journalism/.

apolitical (or deeply believe that they are), they can be politicized by the mere act of being involved in a contentious situation – as seen, for example, in the expulsion of Concern Worldwide and other NGOs (and kindred organizations like UNICEF) from areas of Somalia controlled by the Islamist group al-Shabaab.[7] Proximate are groups committed to conflict resolution or conflict avoidance, particularly in areas of strong historic divisions. For instance, groups such as Search for Common Ground create social marketing and entertainment education efforts, including video soap operas, to bring greater harmony and understanding to environments that face extreme poverty and economic inequality or are chronically strife-ridden.

Campaigning and service NGOs face very different struggles when they enter complex markets for loyalties in an attempt to achieve their strategic goals. From a persuasion perspective, service NGOs sometimes have it slightly easier, as they may be seen not as countering or critiquing existing political arrangements – even if what they seek to accomplish exposes regime deficiencies – but rather as solving a problem. For instance, aside from simple service provision, their objective might be to engender large-scale behavior change in fields such as health, an agenda that may be supported by the target country's government as well. Even as governments have become more restrictive in their approach to NGOs, especially foreign-funded ones, they have tended to give those engaged in service delivery more leeway than those engaged in furthering human rights or democracy issues. Campaigning NGOs, and particularly those engaged in democracy promotion, have typically faced more significant obstacles. South Africa presents one example where NGOs focused on preventing the spread of AIDS, or on alleviating AIDS-related suffering, had to compete in forums of public opinion and civil society in order to gain governmental permission to provide services.

DEMOCRACY PROMOTION

Of particular interest in this chapter is the significant subset of NGOs, both service and campaigning, aimed at fostering democratic processes, a cluster of activities often referred to as "democracy promotion."[8] These NGOs are noteworthy not only because of their idealism and their representation of a set of Western goals, but also because they frequently arouse anxious trepidation

---

[7] Clar Ni Chonghaile, "Al-Shabaab Bans Aid Agencies in Somalia and Raids Offices," *Guardian*, November 28, 2011.

[8] A classic in marking out the territory is Marina Ottaway and Thomas Carothers, eds., *Funding Virtue: Civil Society Aid and Democracy Promotion* (Washington, DC: Brookings Institution Press, 2000).

among the powerful in the societies affected. The consequences of the rights they advocate can be perceived in target states as assaults on an often entrenched status quo. In the world of persuasion, it is sometimes difficult to disentangle the goals of a democracy-promoting NGO from a panoply of other strategic interests, including donor, state or even commercial interests. Some leading NGOs that have engaged in democracy promotion receive funding (often a large percentage) from the government in their home country. In highly regulated local markets for allegiances – and certainly in those that the target society strives to police entry to – efforts to challenge effective NGOs are increasingly fierce. The resulting global struggle surrounding the importance, positioning and establishment or delegitimation of these NGOs takes place in the halls of the United Nations, in Washington and European capitals, and in the states across the world where contentious political changes attract the interest of multiple stakeholders.

Democracy promotion encompasses strengthening civil society, improving election processes, enhancing access to information and providing related education and training. It also includes assistance in building a media system that fosters a citizenry capable of meaningful participation in elections or a press that can act as a check on government. The hope is that, in doing so, NGOs increase demand for appropriate democratically inclined outcomes among the elite and general public. This effort involves, often, advocacy of international norms that favor NGOs' inclusion in these great debates: furtherance of the rule of law, free press, lack of censorship and other emblems of healthy civic engagement. As a result, democracy promotion comes close to a classic form of strategic communication. Democracy promotion is contentious not only because of the purpose – encouraging more widespread democratic institutions – but because of its underlying method: providing resources in support of a particular approach can have the consequence of altering opinion in a target society so as to yield substantial political and social change. And that contentiousness becomes accentuated when the resources behind democracy promotion are external and transnational in origin. To be sure, much democracy promotion is apparently technical, such as assistance in the mechanics of monitoring elections, establishing the machinery of elections, understanding alternatives in regulating campaigns and reviewing alternative requirements for candidate eligibility.[9]

The Arab Spring and its complicated consequences have underlined the increasing importance and increasing controversy over the role of democracy

---

[9] See, as an example of complexities, Mark Weisbrot, "Why American 'Democracy Promotion' Rings Hollow in the Middle East," *Guardian*, January 31, 2012.

promotion NGOs.[10] Although it has been standard practice to debate how transformative a role "the street" and civil society played in the protests in the Middle East and North Africa, international NGOs took some degree of credit for the processes. The *New York Times* published an account with this emphasis: "The United States' democracy-building campaigns played a bigger role in fomenting protests than was previously known, with key leaders of the movements having been trained by the Americans in campaigning, organizing through new media tools and monitoring elections." According to this account, groups and individuals directly involved in the revolts and reforms – such as the April 6 Youth Movement in Egypt, the Bahrain Center for Human Rights, and grassroots activists – received training and financing from groups like the International Republican Institute (IRI) and the National Democratic Institute (NDI) both of which are funded by the U.S. Congress (and neither of which are technically NGOs, though they are similar in form and activities). Freedom House, an organization well-known for its ranking of countries in terms of their implementation of free press principles and in providing assistance in achieving such goals, was also credited for its role.[11]

Not surprisingly, "the work of these groups often provoked tensions between the United States and many Middle Eastern leaders, who frequently complained that their leadership was being undermined."[12] Cables released by WikiLeaks indicate that American officials "assured skeptical governments that the training was aimed at reform, not promoting revolutions."[13] In Bahrain, officials had barred a representative of the National Democratic Institute from entering the country, concerned that political training "disproportionately benefited the opposition," according to a January 2010 cable.[14] In Yemen, "officials complained that American efforts to promote democracy amounted to 'interference in internal Yemeni affairs.'"[15] Gamal Mubarak, the former president's son, was described in an October 20, 2008 cable as "irritable about direct U.S. democracy and governance funding of Egyptian NGOs."[16] In September 2006, Mahmoud Nayel, an official with the Egyptian Ministry of Foreign Affairs, complained to American Embassy officials about the U.S. government's "arrogant tactics in promoting reform in Egypt."[17] Transnational

---

[10] Shahram Akbarzadeh et al., *American Democracy Promotion in the Changing Middle East* (London: Routledge, 2013).

[11] Ron Nixon, "U.S. Groups Helped Nurture Arab Uprisings," *New York Times*, April 14, 2011.

[12] Ibid.

[13] Ibid.

[14] Ibid

[15] Ibid.

[16] Ibid.

[17] Ibid.

NGOs found themselves treading a fine line. Were they to claim even partial credit for the fall of Mubarak, they would confirm the fears and apprehensions of other governments about these NGO and NGO-like strategies systematically to work with populations to develop leadership. If they denied their role, they would lose an opportunity to celebrate their skills, advertise their potential and justify contributions and awards from governmental and private donors.

The relationship of these NGOs to their financial backers and sponsors flared into significance in late 2011 and early 2012. Government officials of the post-Tahrir Square Egyptian military government raided international and Egyptian civil society organizations, and the Egyptian offices of Freedom House, NDI and IRI. Prosecutors charged these entities with violating Egyptian law concerning registration, non-payment of taxes and functioning without a license (especially relevant because they had foreign funding). But in the background were implications that the organizations were doing more than providing technical assistance on how to conduct or monitor elections or enhance institutions of governance.[18] So palpably combustible was the context that some employees of the indicted organizations sought asylum in the American Embassy, and representatives of the U.S. Congress threatened to withhold more than a billion dollars of annual U.S. aid to the Egyptian military. The immediate crisis dissipated, but the underlying anxieties continued.[19]

The Carothers Analysis and International Norms

The reactions in the Middle East illustrate how the activities of particular NGOs and other entities in specific markets for loyalties of interest bring free expression norms into play and highlight the often awkward efforts of governments to manage the activities of external entities within their boundaries. The Egyptian case became a marquee episode in a global discussion about the role of NGOs, their financing and their sponsorship. The NGOs involved there complained that the Egyptian government's actions violated international norms protecting freedom of expression and association.

Thomas Carothers, the consistent and perceptive chronicler of the process of NGO assistance for democratic transitions, has written extensively about different moments in the history of these NGO activities. In his account, the high-water mark of democracy promotion – at least until the recent Arab

[18]   Evan Hill, "Egypt Dossier Outlines NGO Prosecution," *Aljazeera.com*, February 26, 2012.
[19]   For more on the investigation, see "Backgrounder: The Campaign Against NGOs in Egypt," *POMED*, February 10, 2012.

Spring – was the period of color revolutions and the political turmoil in the Balkans in the 1990s and early 2000s. That triumphal period began, in the late 1990s, with efforts against Prime Minister Vladimír Mečiar of Slovakia and President Franjo Tudjman of Croatia. Carothers quantified support for the campaign against President Slobodan Milošević of Serbia by American and European pro-democracy groups as reaching somewhere between $60 and $100 million. As the 2000 elections unfolded there, many unconnected pieces came together. "With Western help, Serbian civic groups convinced large numbers of ordinary citizens to bet on change and engage in the electoral process; the opposition parties performed better than they had in the past; and independent monitoring efforts laid bare Milosevic's effort to override the results. The outcome was the autocrat's ouster in a largely peaceful 'electoral revolution.'"[20] Many of the NGOs involved were domestic, operating with support from transnational NGO allies.

Carothers has posed a provocative argument concerning the presence of these NGOs and related entities in foreign countries and the strategic dimensions that influence their behavior:

> There are relatively coherent international norms about democratic political practice, embodied in a raft of multilateral and regional agreements. But there is no well-settled body of norms about acceptable forms of involvement in democratization across borders. In fact, the line between reasonable and unreasonable restrictions on outside political aid is not at all clear. Simply pushing other governments to follow U.S. or Western standards in this area will not help much. To the extent there are generalized standards, they generally allow less space for outside influence than Western democracy promoters usually seek. Would Washington countenance the presence, during elections, of foreign organizations – especially ones funded by a powerful, possibly hostile government – that underwrite and help carry out voter-education campaigns, the training of and provision of material aid to political parties, parallel vote counts, and citizen-mobilization efforts?[21]

"Democratization across borders" is both supremely important and a challenge in terms of global architecture of rights and privileges. Managing the timing, intensity and effectiveness of domestic political change is simultaneously within the remit of national governments and their citizenry and an area of concern for a state's neighbors, its diaspora and global powers. It hardly requires a sophisticated analytic frame to predict that governments in societies

[20] Thomas Carothers, "The Backlash against Democracy Promotion," *Foreign Affairs* 85, no. 2 (2006): 61.
[21] Ibid., 65.

targeted by NGOs that challenge the basis of their power will seek to limit NGO entry or effectiveness.

Transnational NGOs challenge the status quo; states react vigorously to assert control and defend against what they perceive to be destabilization. From Slobodan Milošević onward, these organizations have attracted the attention of authoritarian leaders and other entrenched interests. As Carothers has noted, after two decades of steady expansion in democracy-building programs around the world and the impacts of that agenda "a growing number of governments [were] starting to crack down on such activities within their borders. Strongmen – some of them elected officials – began to publicly denounce Western democracy assistance as illegitimate political meddling. They started expelling or harassing Western NGOs and prohibiting local groups from taking foreign funds – or started punishing them for doing so."[22] Responses have included requiring NGOs, both local and transnational, to register (or re-register) and to disclose funding sources and their list of purposes. The aim is to limit the nature and scope of the activities they can engage in and the foreign funding available to them.[23] Often it is, as well, to stigmatize the group as alien and non-patriotic.

Antagonisms and Restrictions

The investigation and prosecution of democracy promotion organizations in Egypt in early 2012 was just one example of such a reaction. Also in 2012, in Russia, Vladimir Putin, faced with an invigorated opposition and a much more robust set of protests than anticipated, used the election to criticize foreign governments for "meddling" in national affairs and involvement in Russian political processes,[24] in part through foreign funding of non-governmental groups. He argued that then–U.S. Ambassador Michael McFaul had been chosen specifically because of his prior work with civil society and was deploying his expertise to push forward an improper involvement in the Russian election cycle. In July 2012, President Putin signed into law a controversial bill forcing foreign-funded non-governmental groups involved in political activity to register as "foreign agents" in Russia, with the consequence of onerous disclosure and reporting requirements and heavy

---

[22] Ibid., 55.
[23] See, for example, "Uganda: Government Should Drop NGO Registration Renewal Process," *Article 19*, September 19, 2013. See also Karla Simon, "Dissolution Dos and Don'ts," *The International Journal of Not-for-Profit Law* 2, no. 2 (1999).
[24] See "Putin Warns Foreign States over Meddling in Russian Affairs," *PressTV*, December 12, 2012.

penalties for infractions.[25] Even public opinion research organizations were affected.[26] In September of the same year, the Russian government expelled the USAID mission.[27] The Putin government claimed that USAID was inter- fering in internal Russian political processes through its support of human rights and election-related organizations.

These relatively recent crackdowns can be added to a catalogue, compiled by Carothers and others, of earlier and ongoing state reactions to transnational support for civil society democracy promotion efforts. In 2004, Robert Mugabe expelled a string of Western NGOs from Zimbabwe and constrained or closed down local groups that received external support, especially from the West. In 2005, Ethiopia did the same with respect to IRI, NDI and the International Foundation for Electoral Systems (IFES). While the official reason for the expulsion was that the groups had failed to properly register,[28] President Meles Zenawi linked the decision to events in Europe, stating on Ethiopian tele- vision that "there is not going to be a 'Rose Revolution' or a 'Green Revolution' or any color revolution in Ethiopia after the election."[29] Shortly afterwards, in neighboring Eritrea, the government enacted a law restricting NGO activities, prohibiting the receipt of funds from the United Nations and bilateral organ- izations and imposing minimum operating capital requirements of $1 million for local organizations and $2 million for international organizations.[30] According to Carothers, Eritrean authorities asked USAID to cease all oper- ations in the country, stating that they were uncomfortable with the agency's activities, which included promoting citizen participation in economic and political life.[31]

Also in 2005, the Uzbek government "stepped up scrutiny of foreign and local NGOs promoting democracy in the country in the wake of the fall of the government in neighboring Kyrgyzstan,"[32] as well as the rose and orange revolutions in Georgia and Ukraine. These efforts demonstrated to authorities

[25] "Russia: Controversial NGO bill becomes law," *BBC News*, July 21, 2012.
[26] See, for example, Ellen Barry, "Russian Polling Group Says it May Close," *New York Times*, May 20, 2013.
[27] "Russia Expels USAID Development Agency," *BBC News*, September 19, 2012.
[28] AFP, "Ethiopia expels US-funded pro-democracy groups ahead of elections," *reliefweb*, March 31, 2005.
[29] Carothers, "The Backlash against Democracy Promotion," 58.
[30] "Eritrea Curbs Non-Government Organizations," *Sudan Tribune*, May 30, 2005; "Eritrea Reportedly Expels USAID," *BBC Monitoring*, July 30, 2005. Eritrea's reaction could be viewed not just as a response to NGO activity, but more broadly as a reaction, on Eritrea's part, to perceived favoritism by international groups to Ethiopia.
[31] Carothers, "The Backlash." Also see Thomas Carothers, *Critical Mission: Essays on Democracy Promotion* (Washington, DC: Carnegie Endowment for International Peace, 2004).
[32] "Uzbekistan: Government Takes Democracy NGO to Court," *IRIN*, April 6, 2005.

the consequences of NGO efforts to help reshape a market for loyalties. IRIN quoted an Uzbek political analyst as saying, "Now, following the popular uprising in neighboring Kyrgyzstan … which toppled President Askar Akayev, the Uzbek government will take extra measures to prevent such an uprising in the country."[33] The previous year, Uzbekistan, by denying re-registration, had closed down the offices of foundations linked to the Open Society Institute (OSI) and other democracy-promoting international NGOs, and had issued warnings to foreign-originated entities not to support local opposition movements.[34]

Divisive concern about the activity of foreign-funded NGOs also has a long history in Ukraine, already a place of tension between the European-leaning West and the often Russian-leaning East. In December 2003, the sitting government introduced legislation to investigate foreign support of NGOs, a response to allegations of involvement by external governments to affect election outcomes. The adoption of the legislation came on the heels of a November parliamentary resolution claiming that the external financing of NGOs had "reached mass proportions, and it amounts to direct interference in the internal affairs of Ukraine." Some politicians, reflecting existing divisions, asserted that this required a more thorough look at the activities of foreign-sponsored groups that might influence the 2004 presidential elections.[35] In 2011, Ukraine's Security Service (SBU) was reportedly "investigating foreign funding for NGOs" because of suspicion that "this money will be used for political activity in Ukraine."[36] Of course, later events, including the annexation of Crimea and the clashes of government troops with separatists, put NGO activity in a new perspective, in which democracy promotion would take on greater importance for the government in Kiev.

The approach of Robert Mugabe in Zimbabwe provides insight into the implementation of a particularly purposive and brutal strategy. In 1995, the government had passed the Private Voluntary Organizations (PVO) Act, under which NGO officials could be removed from their administrative duties whenever "it is necessary to do so in the public interest."[37] Despite the

[33] Ibid.
[34] "Uzbek Government Closes Down Open Society Institute Assistance Foundation in Tashkent." *Eurasianet.org,* April 17, 2004. For more on NGOs in Central Asia, see Scott Horton and Alla Kazakina, "The Legal Regulation of NGOs: Central Asia at a Crossroads," in *Civil Society in Central Asia,* eds. M. Holt Ruffin and Daniel Waugh (Seattle: University of Washington Press, 1999).
[35] Taras Kuzio, "Ukrainian Politicians Put the Squeeze on Civil Society," *RFE/RL,* May 18, 2011.
[36] Ibid.
[37] Government of Zimbabwe, "Private Voluntary Organizations Act," 2002.

restrictions, NGOs continued to operate, often receiving foreign assistance and funding. In 2000, civil society organizations, in a massive "NO vote" campaign led by the National Constitutional Assembly (NCA), helped defeat the Mugabe-led government's proposed new constitution. Mugabe was angered by the support that leading foreign donor agencies like USAID, the Swedish International Development Cooperation Agency (Sida), the UK Department for International Development (DFID) and others had provided to the civil society campaign. The government denounced the near universal funding of civil society organizations by foreign governments as an infringement on Zimbabwe's sovereignty. Indeed, President Mugabe was one of the most virulent critics of Western donor support to local pro-democracy movements. Britain's then–prime minister, Tony Blair, foregrounded the Mugabe government's apprehension by announcing in the British parliament that his government was working behind the scenes with the opposition movement in Zimbabwe to effectuate regime change.[38]

As anticipated, the government in Harare responded with a host of repressive measures meant to silence and reduce the space for non-state actors. Apart from limiting and complicating interpersonal communication via mass public meetings, the government largely took control of all radio and television programming and banned human rights NGOs' access to mass media outlets. Authorities also targeted local activists behind the effective advocacy and communication campaigns in Zimbabwe, utilizing measures that included force and arrests.[39]

The government stocked its arsenal of repression with various pieces of legislation, including the Broadcasting Services Act (BSA), the Public Order and Security Act (2002), the Access to Information and Protection of Privacy Act and the 2004 Non-Governmental Organisations Bill. All of these laws shrank the space for the activities of civil society and the perceived opponents of the government and violated fundamental human rights enshrined not just in the Zimbabwean Constitution, but also in the African Convention on Human and People's Rights, the United Nations Convention for the Protection of Human Rights and Fundamental Freedoms and many other instruments to which Zimbabwe is a party. The Public Order and Security Act restricted freedom of assembly and required that organizations notify the police if a meeting was to be held; it also gave the Zimbabwean police force

---

[38] Jeevan Vasagar, "Mugabe Paints MDC as Blairite Cronies," *Guardian*, March 26, 2005. Blair's remarks were made to the UK House of Commons in June 2004.

[39] Michael Wines, "Zimbabwe to Outlaw Groups That Promote Human Rights," *New York Times*, December 10, 2004. Similar sanctions continue a decade later: "Zimbabwe Police Ban Radios, Crack Down on NGOs," *IRIN*, February 26, 2013.

excessive powers to ban and disrupt public gatherings. The police did not hesitate to exercise these powers against civic organizations and the opposition. Restrictive broadcasting legislation, parts of which were later held unconstitutional, resulted in highly limited operational space for NGOs, leaving only privately owned print media houses, alternative media platforms such as Facebook, and foreign-based radio stations to work with the organizations. The level of restriction continued to vary partly dependent on electoral strategies and external pressure.

A strenuous, massive debate in Israel, where many international and national NGOs are involved, provides further understanding of the interplay between NGO efforts, sources of funding and the reaction of the state – this time in a more open, contentious and active society. The question of what standards should exist and in what form is a feature of the Israeli debate, which highlights the difficulty of identifying what Carothers calls "the line between reasonable and unreasonable restrictions on outside political aid."[40]

In terms of efforts to shape public opinion, few issues could be more controversial than the global debate, and the debate within Israel, over the characterization of the war in Gaza and the policies of settlement and occupation. At the center of the controversy were NGOs functioning in Israel, particularly ones that received funding from donors abroad. These included Human Rights Watch, the New Israel Fund and B'Tselem, groups that had been engaged in long-term support and advocacy for democratization and civil rights in Israel and the Palestinian Territories. External interest and support – including funding that often originated from international bodies outside Israel, such as the European Commission and American foundations, along with diasporic communities – had been a constant in financing efforts on significant issues relating to the Middle East peace process.

The situation was complicated by the role of a non-state actor, NGO Monitor, which was generally associated with the "right" in Israel – advocates of settlement and a hard line in negotiations. NGO Monitor claimed its goal was to make the role of NGOs more transparent and their actions more open to scrutiny by the Israeli public. It focused its efforts primarily on those NGOs that criticized purported breaches of human rights and international law by the Israeli state, essentially arguing that these NGOs were, in a sense, anti-Israel. It characterized the key NGO players (such as B'Tselem) as "extremely powerful and influential, particularly with respect to human rights and development issues in the Arab-Israeli conflict. Their reports, protests and

---

[40] Carothers, "The Backlash," 66.

lobbying activities have a dominant impact in shaping global attitudes and terms of reference."[41] According to NGO Monitor,

> The vast resources at the disposal of these self-proclaimed humanitarian NGOs allow for large staffs who produce an immense volume of reports, press releases and media interviews, turning them into primary sources for journalists, researchers, and government policy makers. The amplifying effect of these public pronouncements has often framed the terms of public discourse and strongly influences the crafting of policy. NGOs are in a dominant position to offer the supply to meet the demand for quick and focused information on what Prof. Irwin Cotler has called the new secular religion of human rights.[42]

NGO Monitor, at least in the heat of the moment, saw these groups as presenting a threat to the country by leading to an altered perception of Israel internationally and potentially destabilizing the status quo through their influence in shaping the global narrative.

In a 2009 report, NGO Monitor identified in its rhetoric the key markets these entities were influencing. First, domestic:

> As a democratic country with an open and pluralistic political system and facing a largely hostile external environment, Israeli society is particularly vulnerable to manipulation by externally funded NGOs. Outside political influence of this kind resonates throughout civil society. This hidden foreign intervention infringes on the sovereignty and independence of Israel by unbalancing the political process, and interfering with the policies of the elected government and the mainstream Zionist majority.[43]

Then, international:

> In the international arena, the same NGOs submit statements to United Nations frameworks such as the Human Rights Council, run major media campaigns, and spearhead lawsuits in various countries. Using the tens of millions of shekels, euros, and dollars they receive each year, the externally

---

[41] See "Memorandum Submitted by the NGO Monitor," *parliament.uk*, November 2003. This is an earlier version of the NGO Monitor Mission Statement submitted to the UK Parliament and is itself a commentary on the organization. It shows that one of the key objectives of NGO Monitor was to maintain an appearance of neutrality. This is not to say that NGO Monitor was not neutral or that its reports were not accurate but that an international *appearance* of neutrality was of key strategic value.

[42] Ibid.

[43] "Trojan Horse: The Impact of European Government Funding for Israeli NGOs," NGO *Monitor*, November 23, 2009. I am quoting this for its rhetorical implications. These are the justifications stated by NGO Monitor. They could, of course, be criticized on several grounds, including selective objection to foreign funding in a society where many entities receive global support for more favored interventions.

funded NGO network is far more powerful than other Israeli organizations that do not enjoy similar support from foreign governments.[44]

The project that possessed elements of the Israeli right, in and out of government, was how to curb these NGOs, how to lessen their impact, how to limit their capacity to be effective in strategic communication around the most sensitive issues in Israeli society – how, in short, to limit their participation in the market for loyalties.

"Ethical guidelines" proposed by NGO Monitor demonstrate the perils for freedom of expression norms when NGO activity is seen as a threat to a state or group of powerful interests. Under the proposed guidelines, NGOs would implement broad "transparency, accountability, tolerance, and civility" principles.[45] These are hardly controversial at first glance. But their speech-related implications would be severe. In adumbrating on the meaning of these guidelines in the context of Israel, NGO Monitor stated that the proposed "guidelines" would have forbidden "use of language or accusations of 'apartheid,' 'ethnic cleansing' and similar terms of demonization against Israel or Israelis." They would have barred linking Israel to "'war crimes' or 'crimes against humanity' . . . based on gross distortions of international law." They would have prohibited advocating for boycotts, divestment and sanctions, or engaging in what NGO Monitor calls "'Lawfare' – legal threats or actions against Israeli officials abroad." And they would have restricted supporting "UN-related activities that "use double-standards, single-out Israel . . . [and] opposition to Israel's status as a Jewish and democratic state, including calling for the elimination of the Jewish framework."[46]

The not-so-velvet glove of self-regulation was reinforced by members of the Knesset, the Israeli parliament, which in July 2011 sought to enact controversial legislation known as the "anti-boycott bill."[47] This bill would have provided authority for lawsuits and other penalties for NGOs and similar entities. The prism of actions affected by this legislation would be narrower than that of the guidelines, but the consequences greater. The drafters established a unique category of zones for special attention. Advocating boycotts and delegitimation and favoring the imposition of sanctions persisted as a trio of general concerns. Claims, including those beyond actual damages, would be available for a public call for a boycott – economic, cultural or academic – against Israel or its

[44] Ibid.
[45] "Ethical Guidelines for Political Advocacy NGOs," *NGO Monitor*, July 4, 2011.
[46] Ibid.
[47] See Lahav Harkov, "Anti-Boycott Bill Becomes Law after Passing Knesset," *The Jerusalem Post*, July 11, 2011; Charly Wegman, "Israeli Left Condemns Controversial 'Boycott Ban' Law," *AFP*, July 14, 2011.

West Bank settlements. While the law was ultimately put in abeyance, it serves as a useful guide to the steps groups within a society may use to block or limit advocacy by their competitors. It also demonstrates how competitors in a market for loyalties seek to shape general principles of free expression.

RAMIFICATIONS

Treatment of NGOs, especially democracy promotion NGOs, will be a crucial indicator of strategic communication in the next several years. Here, in strong contrast, is the claim of sovereignty against the increasing transnational flows of influence. Here is both the assertion of control over local modes of political participation and global efforts, governmental and non-governmental, for more intense participation in the decision-making process regardless of boundaries. Deployment of NGOs with external (largely Western) governmental and private funding continues to rise. Globalization offers opportunities for civil society groups to achieve their goals through increased media access and global connections. Diasporas, stronger, better-funded and often with complex governmental ties, have definite opinions about political outcomes in their homeland and are willing to dedicate their own resources and pressure the governments where they have local impact.

NGOs become committed to an interpretation of international (and national) norms and to strategic architectures of the media that provide them with adequate leeway for effectively advocating policies they favor. In terms of structure, transnational NGOs generally favor "Internet freedom" (meaning fewer barriers to access) and, in television, a multi-channel universe that expands the numbers of outlets, facilitated by altered technologies such as satellite-to-home and satellite-to-cable. The development of a global infrastructure that allows for broader, less impeded dissemination of NGO messages becomes a collective goal. The strengthening of international free speech norms works to break seller cartels, providing a space for new voices in the market for loyalties. Too little attention is given to aspects of patronage in analyzing the flow and regulation of communication. Yet strategic communicators are often identified, labeled and understood through the patterns by which they are funded. NGOs have had a golden period of growth, influence and effect. Increasingly, however, their results and their impact have yielded pushback, sometimes brutal.[48]

---

[48] For instance, see new regulations introduced by China in March 2010: Meg Davis, "[Commentary] China's New Nonprofit Regulations: Season of Instability," *Asia Catalyst*, June 14, 2010; Karla W. Simon, "Recent Developments in Chinese Law Affecting CSOs/NGOs,"

Ultimately, the NGO democracy promotion episodes touch on problems of authority and law itself. These problems are of importance to all strategic communicators – those seeking to enter a market and those acting in reaction. In the last analysis, what both NGOs and strategic communicators desire is a widespread clarification of "international norms" or "best standards," so as to protect them in the future. Invoking international norms where there is not a shared commitment can be a hollow exercise. This is especially true where a democracy promotion mindset uses such norms as euphemisms of self-justification. The home society of the NGOs – the United States, United Kingdom or elsewhere – develops, through its own framework, a set of purposes and techniques that are linked to international norms, even in an international context that is darkly hostile and frequently inconsistent with these efforts. The rupture between the state of origin and the state of application deprives the effort of some legitimacy.

The rise of social media and new technologies adds another layer to the struggle between NGOs seeking to be effective and host governments evaluating modes of support and resistance. In order to adapt to this changing environment and maintain influence in the market for loyalties, NGOs engaged in democracy promotion have to expand their knowledge, expertise and capacity with respect to social media tools, such as Facebook, Twitter and the Internet more generally, in order to gain entry into existing information-controlling cartels. The existence of these still new techniques can deepen anxieties in host societies and accelerate monitoring and supervision. NGOs become increasingly adept at the opportunities social media present (often more nimble at such opportunities than governments or other entities). They become test cases for defining the scope, limits and privileges in the transnational space for entities that are innovatively funded and constructed.

International Center for Civil Society Law, June 2010. In Iran, the Ahmadinejad government banned contact with a large number of NGOs. "Iranian Intelligence Ministry Lists 60 'Enemy' Organizations," *Payvand Iran News,* January 5, 2010. The full list can be found, in Persian, at *JamejamOnline,* http://www1.jamejamonline.ir/newstext.aspx?newsnum=100863901101.

10

Strategic Platforms

In this chapter, I turn to the 2008 Beijing Olympics to demonstrate how strategic communicators shape opportunities to project their messages and how others then try to wrest control, piggy-back or hijack those opportunities. The Beijing Olympics is a useful case study because it represented a huge investment by China in establishing its story of itself globally. The very idea of China as an international actor – what it is, what role it should play, how it would exercise its power – was and remains a subject over which there is global contestation. Before and during the Olympics, China recognized the potential for a large-scale narrative transformation. The Beijing Summer Games is an example of massive investment to alter attitudes: to reposition China, by changing perceptions both of the domestic population and a global public. How successful this effort was is beyond the scope of this book.[1] In this chapter, I explore a strategic nuance: how the process of projection and counter-projection took place. I consider the Olympics to be an example of a "platform," a locus (often informal) where contests for attention occur.

Creating and exploiting platforms is often a response to the complexity of modern communications flows. Much of the work in Daniel Dayan and Elihu Katz's canonical work, *Media Events*, is about the communications-related aspects of creating and exploiting such platforms. Thinking about these scaffolds for performance is also a way of understanding the complex relationship between infrastructure and freedom of expression discourse. The effectiveness of expression depends, frequently, on access to a platform where the organizer has a substantial capacity to control entry and use and produce access to

---

[1] For a pre-Olympics viewpoint, see Susan Brownell, *What the Olympic Games Mean to Beijing* (Lanham, MD: Rowman & Littlefield, 2008) and Monroe E. Price and Daniel Dayan, eds., *Owning the Olympics, Narratives of the New China* (Ann Arbor: University of Michigan Press, 2008). See also Kevin Caffrey, ed., *The Beijing Olympics: Promoting China: Soft and Hard Power in Global Politics* (London: Routledge, 2011).

sympathetic receivers. Platforms may be a way of finding an effective space to consolidate a state's vision of itself and to crowd out the competition of alternate statements. But global civil society groups and others also have an understandable hunger to exploit such platforms, either to create them or to take advantages of already existing fora to advance their own political and commercial messages.

China's bid to host the 2008 Olympics in Beijing was from the start an illustration of the perceived importance of investing in a vehicle for narrative transformation. In this sense, this chapter relates to the issues discussed in Chapter 3. China recognized the enormous legitimacy-conferring quality of the Olympics and the benefit of linking China's "coming out" into global power with this unique quadrennial event. It is difficult to capture fully China's desired "narrative of legitimacy." In part, the projection would be of benign power, a legitimacy refurbished by projecting wealth used wisely. Unlimited capacity and strength would be coupled with a sub-narrative that issues of domestic tension and threats to stability were minor or under control. Achievement in sport would be a metaphor for China's standing in the family of nations. The Beijing Olympics would mark the beginning of what might become the century of China.

At the same time, China also understood that in addition to attracting pervasive global attention, there is a contradiction: the Olympics is a site for image production that is heavily controlled and policed, but it is also a site where efforts to capture dramatically the narrative are pervasive. Strategic communicators face a world of cunning competitors, and the Olympics reveals the complexities of maintaining ownership and management. The Games are marked by efforts of free riders or interlopers to seize the opportunity to perform in a global theater of representation. One infamous appropriation was the terrorist attack at the Munich Olympics. Each Olympic Organizing Committee is haunted by Munich; the elaborate planning is to some extent about mechanisms for avoiding its repetition. Beijing might also have become a magnet for violent displays. It certainly became a robust lure for advocacy groups and transnational NGOs – disparate groups that make up the global civil society critical of China – to shift the impact of the Games in terms of global public opinion.

PLATFORMS AND THEIR USES

For the purposes of this analysis, I consider a "platform" to be any mechanism that allows for the presentation of information in a way that facilitates its promotion and accessibility and aids its legitimacy. The term implies a sense of solidity and a locus for action, but platforms also exist in the electronic universe, or simply as the relationships or links between various entities. Platforms have enormous value if they are successful in attracting large, indeed massive, audiences and serving the needs of their sponsors, whether they are selling goods or ideas or have the potential to do so. One can consider newspapers and broadcasting as not only "media" but as historic platforms, and the process by which various groups gain access and influence with them has, of course, been much studied.[2] In this chapter, however, what I wish to emphasize is the appropriation of already-created platforms by those who seek new opportunities to deliver messages and pathways to persuade. A task for strategic communicators is understanding which platforms exist and what it takes to construct new ones. But a sub-task is understanding which entities can subvert holders of platforms and how they do so to undermine the communications strategy of those who have invested in them.

This phenomenon of platforms exists in a world in which much clamoring for attention – to sell goods or alter political attitudes – encounters too few effective channels to reach the desired audience. Furthermore, the existing channels are often tightly controlled and present significant barriers to entry. In much of the twentieth century, media systems were designed so that issues would be articulated, framed and discussed largely within national boundaries, and the residue of that system persists. Increasingly, however, issues such as human rights, environmentalism and even the impact of domestic political choices are seen with respect to their vast transnational implications. The interests and actions of civil society and other groups shift from a national to a global level. The rise of social media reinforces that approach. These passions are all the more frustrated by the fact that, despite new technologies, transnational groups are often blocked from entry (purposely or merely because of patterns of scarcity) into domestic media systems. As a result, these groups seek new ways of reaching widely distributed elites (and masses).

There is, of course, a very long history of alternate modes of gathering audiences together through various mechanisms that allow persuasive messages to be articulated and widely diffused. Demonstrations, marches, strikes or manifestations are exemplary. In the last several decades, global civil society groups have organized huge concerts, terrorists have caused immense catastrophes and political figures have staged gatherings of dignitaries, all widely differing efforts to create an opportunity for significant audiences to experience arguments or assertions that would not otherwise come to their attention,

---

[2] Kathryn C. Montgomery, *Target, Prime Time: Advocacy Groups and the Struggle over Entertainment Television* (New York: Oxford University Press, 1989).

or not with such emphasis. Media coverage of such events plays a major role in bringing them to the attention of the public. In the era of the Internet and social media, there is significant energy devoted to the interplay between platforms (marches, for example) and the adroit use of new technologies. The blogosphere and the capacity to become a viral phenomenon becomes a way to reinvent platforms.

Because of the ever-present danger of appropriation, one defining characteristic of significant platforms is the effort to fence access to them from unwanted or unremunerating users. The Seattle 1999 World Ministerial Conference of the World Trade Organization was a teaching moment in this regard: a hallmark event, though not Olympics-related, that exemplified the exploitation of a platform created for one general narrative (furthering one vision of world trade relationships) to convey quite another (the injustice of existing economic patterns). In the Internet world, cybersecurity technology involves the elaborate process of protecting sites from being seized by others.

But what about platforms as ephemeral as the Olympic Games? They can be protected through physical modes of security, which limit those who may actually enter the Olympic facilities or who receive press accreditation for coverage. They can be protected through assertion of intellectual property and contractual rights, using highly developed legal mechanisms to enjoin or impose significant costs on those who seek to be free riders. The International Olympic Committee (IOC) sets terms for the uses of the platform (and limitations on those uses) by the organizers, the sponsors and the athletic federations. Because of commercialization and the costs of sponsorship, sponsors – whether they are selling soda, burgers or large-scale perceptions about citizenship, consumption and identity – fight to guard the platform from competitors.[3] Most subtly, platforms are protected through intense management of narrative and response – who can tell what story – so as to avoid efforts to subvert or countermand the intended purpose.

Although the Olympics provides an opportunity to examine efforts at platform appropriation and the response to such actions, it also presents some fundamental problems. First, there is a built-in ambiguity as to the "ownership" of the Olympics platform. In some Games, the platform has belonged more to the International Olympics Committee, and in some more to the Organizing Committee; in recent Olympics, ownership is increasingly a combination of these two. Further ambiguity is added as the host city or

---

[3]   Michael Payne, *Olympic Turnaround: How the Olympic Games Stepped Back from the Brink of Extinction to Become the World's Best Known Brand* (Westport, CT: Praeger Publishers, 2006). Also see Jason K. Schmitz, "Ambush Marketing: The Off-Field Competition at the Olympic Games," *Northwestern Journal of Technology and Intellectual Property* 3, no. 2 (2005).

country seeks to control part of the narrative. For China, while 2008 was the *Beijing* Olympics, it presented a major opportunity for the country as a whole to tell its stories at home and abroad.

Because ownership of the platform is multiple and ambiguous, so is the question of the platform's dominant or accepted narratives.[4] Narratives can be complementary (indeed reinforcing), in competition with or in contradiction to the accepted narrative. I use the term "complementary" for uses in which the appropriator gains benefits without hurting the interests of those who invested in or ostensibly controlled the platform. For example, cities other than Beijing in China wished to use the Olympics to promote their value as tourist destinations. Large commercial entities – including major sponsors – also sought to propagate a vision of China (or a particular sense of "One World, One Dream") that is distinct from what the Beijing Organizing Committee for the Games of the XXIX Olympiad (BOCOG) or the regime sought to propagate, emphasizing, for example, China's advances in health technology or in science, as opposed to its achievements in athletic prowess or, subtly, in military power. The theme of Johnson & Johnson's campaign, as one of the core sponsors for the Beijing Olympics, was "Golden Touch, Golden Mom," an idea that strongly tied the Olympics to the idea of motherhood in Chinese culture.

Alongside these complementary narratives, there were major and minor "competitive" efforts to undermine the dominant narratives of the Beijing Olympics and, via a kind of jiu jitsu, to create images of China that were less favorable, or to use the Olympics for some wholly different purposes. Just as China used the 2008 Games to influence public opinion at home and abroad, many advocacy groups and other interests – both inside China and internationally – used the occasion to deflect this official representation. These groups fought for space in U.S. and global media, mainstream and not, to reinforce China's flaws and weaknesses, all issuing body jabs against the depiction of the new Colossus.

From the point of the view of the organizers of the Olympics and the Olympics establishment, both the complementary and competitive user pose problems. Both categories of users are "free riders," sometimes involved in what might be more gently called piggy-backing on, rather than hijacking,

[4] William J. Morgan, "Cosmopolitanism, Olympism, and Nationalism: A Critical Interpretation of Coubertin's Ideal of International Sporting Life," OLYMPIKA: *The International Journal of Olympic Studies* IV (1995); John Hoberman, *Darwin's Athletes: How Sport Has Damaged Black America and Preserved the Myth of Race* (Boston: Houghton Mifflin Co., 1997); Robert K. Barney et al., eds., *Global and Cultural Critique: Problematizing the Olympic Games. Fourth International Symposium for Olympic Research* (London, Ontario: International Centre for Olympic Studies, The University of Western Ontario, 1998).

the platform. Free riders threaten the exclusivity of the platform and the underlying marketing theory that yields compensation for the IOC. Even when the free rider does not damage the Games or its family of participants, the IOC has an interest in capturing the economic benefits, thus internalizing the benefits of the Games and protecting those who pay for the privilege. It is a widely told tale that at the 1984 Olympics, Fuji was an official sponsor, but Kodak was a principal advertiser of both U.S. television broadcasts of the Games and named supporter of the U.S. track team. In 1992, at the Barcelona Olympics, official sponsors, including Reebok, paid $700 million, but it was Nike that sponsored the press conference when the U.S. basketball team won a gold medal. Increasingly, legislation, at the behest of the IOC, restricts and bans such practices. For the 2012 London Olympics, legislation prevented any business making reference to the 2012 Olympics in its promotions unless it was an official sponsor.[5] There is a specific rhetoric that captures the commercial appropriation of the endorsed and official narratives. "Ambush" or "parasite" marketing refers to the efforts by a company, not an official sponsor of the Olympics, who appears to have that status by centering its advertising campaign around the event.[6] These commercial appropriations are a way of thinking about the greater stories of the Olympic platform: Because so much is spent, because the economy of the Olympics depends upon controlling them, and because there are lawsuits with extensive explanations, struggles in this sphere are well articulated.

THE PROBLEM OF THE "BASE NARRATIVE"

To have a category of the subversive, there must be an idea of what it seeks to displace. Hijacking assumes a base narrative that is shunted aside. And that raises the question of who owns or controls the platform – for example, whether, as adverted to earlier, the platform in the case of the Beijing Olympics belonged to the IOC or the Beijing Organizing Committee for the Olympic Games (BOCOG) or China or the commercial sponsors or the great transnational broadcasters, like NBC. One could go further and argue that the Olympic platform was long ago seized from a purer Olympic past by commercial interests (at least since 1984) or by various incarnations of the IOC, which, it has been argued, has not always been a true bearer of the Olympic torch. John Hoberman, who has used "amoral universalism" as a

---

[5] House of Commons, *London Olympics Bill*, Session 2005–2006.
[6] Schmitz, "Ambush Marketing." Also see Robert N. Davis, "Ambushing the Olympic Games," *Villanova Sports and Entertainment Law Journal* 3, no. 2 (1996).

descriptor of the IOC's approach in the past, has written, in an interview for this chapter, that:

> I have read Coubertin's major works and analyzed them in *The Olympic Crisis* (1986), and I have no doubts about the authenticity of his idealism and his good intentions about achieving world peace through international sport. The problem, from my perspective, is that a lot of the wrong people have wielded power over the 'movement' from even before Coubertin passed from the scene in 1937 – viz. the Nazi Olympics and my account in 'Toward a Theory of Olympic Internationalism' (1995) of who played influential roles in 1936 and how they acquired them. So the question here is whether the IOC has played politically wholesome roles in international diplomacy in the past, and whether, in the light of this past, they are capable of doing so now.[7]

For Hoberman, it is precisely an absence of historical understanding that renders the current acceptance of the dominant narrative of the Olympic tradition possible. Only this ignorance allows the positive glow in which NBC and corporate sponsors, who underwrite the Games, to thrive.

> It is clear that the Olympic ideology satisfies a deep yearning for globalism (in the key of sentimentalism). The Olympic 'movement' (along with Esperanto and the Red Cross) is one of the late 19th century internationalisms that has actually survived and succeeded. The difference is that ceding the Olympic Games to the sports entertainment industry has inevitably resulted in multiple forms of corruption from which the Esperantists and the Red Cross people – shielded from temptation – remain happily immune.[8]

It is against this perspective that one might examine the process of competition to define the Olympic narrative. In this regard, I borrow from James Nafziger's analysis of the traditional interplay between the Olympics and the processes of legal and political change.[9] Nafziger and other scholars argue that pursuit of certain ideals is strongly consistent with the Olympic ideal. For example, they invoke the Olympic Charter and its aspirations that render as incompatible with the Olympic Movement "any form of discrimination with regard to a country or person on grounds of race, religion, politics, gender or otherwise."[10] Here the dominant Olympic narrative is the promotion of harmonious interaction among peoples and states and the cultivation of international dialogue. Advocates of this approach point to the role of the IOC in the

[7] James Hoberman, email exchange with the author, November 15, 2007.
[8] Ibid.
[9] James A. R. Nafziger, "International Sports Law: A Replay of Characteristics and Trends," *American Journal of International Law* 86, no. 3 (1992).
[10] *Olympic Charter*, International Olympic Committee (Laussane, Switzerland: International Olympic Committee, 2013), 11.

decision to urge the North and South Korean teams march together at the opening ceremonies of the 2000 Sydney Olympics. This event was trumpeted as a symbol of a renewed effort to cooperate and was commended as representative of the Olympic goal of camaraderie and peaceful relations.[11] Olympic officials also encouraged North and South Korea to use the 2006 Asian Games as a chance to mend diplomatic relations, despite a growing rift between the two over North Korea's recent missile launches and nuclear test, by forming a joint team for the first time.[12] When the two countries announced their intentions ultimately unreachable, to complete together in 2008, the decision (which ultimately proved unsustainable) was applauded by the IOC. A spokesperson announced: "Today marks a milestone in the completion of this important project for the two Koreas and the Olympic movement."[13]

Coursing through Olympic history are aggressive instances of using the platform as a bargaining tool to criticize norm-related behaviors of certain states. A prevailing example of using international sports events to advance the cause of human rights was the IOC's campaign to abate racial discrimination and apartheid in South Africa. Between 1964 and 1991, the IOC, recognizing that apartheid was "in contravention of the Olympic Charter," not only precluded South Africa from competing in the Olympic Games; it urged all International Federations to exclude South Africa from participating until South Africa abandoned the policy.[14] By imposing penalties for its practice, "the IOC rightly subordinated the Olympic goal of widespread international sports participation to the more fundamental principles of international human rights law."[15] Individual states also have used the platform of the Games for evidently propagandistic purposes that are intended to enhance national prestige. A well-known example of this kind is the USSR's boycott of the Games from 1912 to 1952 because of its "bourgeois and capitalist" nature. The United States boycotted the Moscow Olympics in 1980 to protest the Soviet invasion of Afghanistan and the

---

[11]　"Olympic Spirit: North, South Korea March Together in Ceremonies," *Sports Illustrated*, Sept. 15, 2000.

[12]　Choe Sang-Hun, "Two Koreas to Compete as Single Nation at Olympics," *New York Times*, November 1, 2005. Despite efforts by the IOC and the two National Organizing Committees, diplomatic tensions prevented North and South Korea from competing as a single team at the 2006 Asian Games, although they did march together at the opening ceremony.

[13]　"One More Step Towards Joint Korean Team," *People's Daily Online*, Sept. 7, 2006. The countries were ultimately unable to agree on the details of a joint team and did not march together in the opening ceremonies. See Mark McDonald, "In Olympic Infighting, The Koreas Take the Gold," *New York Times*, July 2, 2012.

[14]　*Mexico Declaration*, Association of National Organizing Committees (1984).

[15]　Paul Mastrocola, "The Lords of the Rings: The Role of Olympic Site Selection as a Weapon Against Human Rights Abuses: China's Bid For the 2000 Olympics," *Boston College Third World Law Journal* 15, no. 1 (1995).

Soviets retaliated in kind with respect to the 1984 Olympics in Los Angeles. The 1936 Berlin Olympics was a horrifying abuse of the Olympic ideal, exploited by the Nazi regime to strengthen its hold at home while providing foreign spectators and journalists with a picture of a peaceful, tolerant Germany. For rejecting a proposed boycott of the 1936 Olympics, the United States and other western democracies were charged by many within their own countries with acting in violation of international norms.[16]

The Games can also serve as a more positive forum. Nafziger recalls:

> At the end of the Cold War, the Olympic Movement helped end a sort of negative ping-pong in the form of reciprocal boycotting by the United States and the Soviet Union, joined by their national allies, of each other's Olympic venues. With governmental support initiated by the IOC, the national committees of the two countries signed an antiboycott and cooperative agreement that was adopted by their Governments in an early hint that the Cold War was drawing to a close.[17]

There are abundant examples of the interrelationship between the machinery of the Olympics and national narratives. Upon the establishment of the People's Republic of China in 1949, the International Olympic Committee ruled that Taiwan's Olympic committee would represent China; after the PRC gained the Chinese seat at the United Nations in 1971, the IOC recognized Beijing's Olympic committee. The conflict over representation gained another level of complexity when Taiwanese athletes were allowed to compete, but only as part of the "Chinese Taipei Olympic Committee." Under the formal arrangement, the Taiwanese entrants were prohibited from using Taiwan's national symbols, such as Taiwan's flag; the national anthem of Taiwan would not be sung when its athletes won medals.

In this sense the IOC moves between a more positive notion of Olympian harmony and global cooperation, and a claim of interventionist achievement and "amoral universalism," to use Hoberman's term. Often, the IOC claims a practice in forwarding Olympic goals that seeks to avoid the political. For example, soon after China was awarded the 2008 Games, Jacques Rogge, president of the IOC, said, "The IOC is not a political body – the IOC is a sports body. Having an influence on human rights issues is the task of political organisations and human rights organisations. It is not the task of the IOC to get involved in monitoring, or in lobbying or in policing."[18] And in 2006, Rogge's chief of staff wrote a letter to a protesting Tibetan group, the

---

[16] David Clay Large, *Nazi Games: The Olympics of 1936* (New York: W.W. Norton, 2007).
[17] Nafziger, "International Sports Law," 497.
[18] New Boss to Cut Olympic Growth," *BBC Sport*, August 27, 2001.

International Campaign for Tibet, rejecting the Tibetans' appeal that the IOC bring pressure to bear on China. Of course, the spokesperson said, a Beijing Olympics could play a positive role "in China's changing social and economic fabric," but "We believe your demands fall unquestionably well outside the remit of our organization."[19] A broad perspective – linked to the history of the IOC – sees the Olympics as a mode for moving a society, and the host city itself, "forward" along a number of dimensions. It is that part of the legitimated narrative that has provided justification for civil society groups and others to consider seeking partial control of the platform. Their advocacy would be not only an ethical use of the Olympics moment, but wholly consistent with historic Coubertin-like objectives. For many, it is this history that undermines the contention that the intended narrative of the Olympics should only have to do with sports and performance, and any attempt to inject broader social or political meaning and impact is an intrusion, a side effect of the extravaganza. Political impact is inevitable.

COMPETING NARRATIVES, CIVIL SOCIETY AND THE BEIJING OLYMPICS

What made the 2008 Olympics somewhat different from its predecessors was the specific context in the twenty-first century: the rise of China and Asia generally and the increased complexity of issues and players involved in the Olympic process. Beijing was not only the most expensive Games and the Games with the largest potential audience, it was also the Olympics with the most substantial hopes and plans for geopolitical change. The *China Daily* wrote that "Comparing the Olympic spirit and China's quest for a harmonious society, one sees clearly that the aspirations of the Chinese people and the ideas of the Olympic movement have so much in common with respect to interactions between people, between people and society and between man and nature."[20] The official slogan for the Games, "One World, One Dream," encapsulated this theme of harmony and, in the way of rebranding, sought to crowd out competing narratives of China, such as China as repressive, China as exploitative, China as a menacing international power. In the run-up to the Games, Chinese scholars were commissioned to scour the foreign press to determine what was written about the PRC and whether the Games were being portrayed as a moment of potential glory or as symptomatic of larger social and economic flaws and political differences.

---

[19] Charles Hutzler, "Hunger Strike Sends IOC into Tough Situation," *AP*, February 26, 2006.
[20] Qin Xiaoying, "Harmonious Confluence of Ideas at Olympics," *China Daily*, July 18, 2007.

This objective of redefining China became subject to the organized efforts of various proponents from civil society within China and without. What in the past constituted primarily a debate among governments and national groups was further transformed and complicated as the battle over representation in the Olympics expanded and intensified. The major players in this new competition were the increasingly global and increasingly effective NGOs, a group I discussed in Chapter 9 as distinguished by notably sophisticated strategies for leveraging power. With their political acumen and reach, these civil society groups had become important entrants in the struggle over the way Beijing was interpreted. In short, the 2008 Olympics took place at a moment when an expanding civil society sphere was organizing more effectively and communicating globally, and the event provided an ideal opportunity for the relevant actors to mobilize support for their various causes and appeals. The civil society organizations taking up the issue of the Olympics included general human rights advocates and groups specifically concerned with issues of religion and press freedom. There were groups involved in China's relationship with Tibet and entities with specific public agendas, such as environmental organizations and opponents of China's one-child policies. This emerging global society used a variety of venues to mobilize, to generate support and to achieve prominence. They set up as foils BOCOG, the IOC, China and the advertisers and sponsors of the 2008 Games. They enlisted their national parliaments. And, in so doing, these civil society actors became the functional equivalents of the official sponsors, seeking the looming billboard of the Games to attract audiences and loyalties for their views and to reshape the Olympics as an agent for change.

Although it is impossible to chart the various modes of shifting the agenda of the IOC (and through it China) completely or exhaustively, some examples should help to convey how these groups aggregated to form a kind of global civil society and how, in competing and different ways, they sought to exploit the platform to shape an agenda around the Olympics. Most of these efforts to open up a kind of public sphere – whether coordinated or isolated – involved individual NGOs and various entities of influence. Campaigns were designed especially to bring pressure to bear on the IOC and China. Transnational NGOs used a variety of techniques and addressed them to a wide range of individuals and entities. They used electronic petitions to activate their members as intermediaries. They attempted to assert pressure on groups, including the IOC, directly and through sponsors with vested interests in the country, such as Coca-Cola and other companies. They acted as clearinghouses of information on human rights abuses, keeping track of developments and reporting on the activities of other human rights groups regarding China and the Olympics. They reached out to publics in the United States and Europe to bring pressure on governments, sports federations, sponsors and individual athletes. They stressed continued media pressure on China as a way to directly embarrass or shame the relevant parties into improving their records.

Among the various Christian groups, to take one example, seeking to make their claims part of the Olympics agenda was the Cardinal Kung Foundation, which asserted its ties to and advocated for the underground Roman Catholic Church in China, detailing China's record of religious persecution in an attempt to include religious freedom on the Olympic change agenda. In testimony to the U.S. Congress and in letters to President Hu Jintao, the Foundation sought to invoke the Olympic aura, describing the "current Chinese government religious policy" as the direct opposite of the Olympic goal of friendship, decency and solidarity, and calling on China to prove that the country "is honoring the spirit of the Olympic Games."[21] Groups concerned with issues in Tibet were particularly active. In 2006, a group of Tibetan cyclists held a freedom rally in New Delhi to protest Chinese rule and to appeal to the Indian government to help resolve the Tibet issue for its own security. When a Uyghur activist (and Canadian citizen) was extradited from Uzbekistan to China and jailed, lawyers and family members attempted to exert pressure on the Canadian government to influence China by invoking the Olympic values. In cases such as these, the Olympic spirit becomes a kind of symbolic or disembodied code that is employed as an instrument of rhetorical power.

Some of the themes or tropes of these entities can be identified in a letter issued on August 7, 2006 by an international coalition of human rights organizations, including Olympic Watch (a human rights monitoring association created especially to focus on the Games), Reporters Without Borders, the International Society for Human Rights, Solidarité Chine and Laogai Research Foundation. The letter maintained that "The IOC has the obligation to protect the Olympic ideals of 'harmonious development of man,' 'human dignity' and 'peace,' and to prevent the political propaganda abuse of the Games." It alleged that "the IOC has refused to face the reality in which Beijing 2008 is to take place," charging current IOC leadership with being "either too cynical, or too incompetent, or both, to protect the Olympic ideals and take a clear stance on the continuing human rights abuses in China." The group called on National Olympic Committees and individual athletes "to start discussing ways how they can protest the conditions under which the

---

[21] "The Persecution of the Underground Roman Catholic Church in China: Testimony of Joseph M.C. Kung," *Cardinal Kung Foundation*, January 31, 2007; "Two Priests Arrested in China," *Catholic News Agency*, February 27, 2006.

2008 Games are to take place." As to implementation, the letter suggested that "At a minimum, the IOC could demand that the Beijing Organizing Committee of the Olympic Games not be personally linked to the perpetrators of human rights violations, the Chinese Communist Party." It recommended that National Olympic Committees organize boycotts, stage peaceful protests in Beijing during the Games, include Chinese, Tibetan and Uyghur exiles in their teams and delegations and visit human rights defenders in prison. Corporate sponsors were urged to "show their commitment to corporate social responsibility by making it clear to the IOC and to BOCOG that their business philosophy does not condone propaganda abuse of the Games and human rights violations."[22]

MOBILIZING TO GAIN GLOBAL ATTENTION

I close this chapter by focusing on two specific strategic campaigns of civil society to use the Olympics platform to shift allegiances on significant questions: to intensify foreign pressure on domestic policy in China regarding labor standards and foreign policy – in particular, China's then-relationship with Sudan and Darfur. The first example involves a campaign that stretches across several Olympics, and the second involves one that was targeted specifically at 2008. Each example shows modes of organizing to use the Olympics platform to gain global attention. Each illustrates – even in the relatively early days of social media – processes of mobilization by strategic communicators and the transnational character of such mobilization.

PlayFair Alliance

The PlayFair Alliance, a group with foundations in the international labor movement (among other bases), had been engaged in a long-term effort to improve working standards for children and others. Begun before the Athens Games, as the "Play Fair at the Olympics Campaign," it claimed to be the "biggest ever global mobilisations against inhuman working conditions."[23] Somewhat reconstituted for Beijing, the PlayFair Alliance demonstrated modes of highlighting a narrative – the exploitation of child labor – drawing upon lofty and explicit Olympic goals. PlayFair skillfully used the rhetoric of the Olympic movement, including the IOC Code of Ethics, and mastered the intricacies of the IOC and national licensing agreements. In short, like others,

[22] "Two Years Until Beijing 2008: IOC Fails, Activists Call on Athletes, Sponsors to Act," *Olympic Watch*, August 7, 2006.
[23] PlayFair 2008, *No Medal for the Olympics on Labour Rights*, n.d.

it appropriated an officially proclaimed narrative of Olympic decency and then sought to hold those involved to their articulated high standard. The platform was not only the 2008 Olympics themselves but also the rhetoric of the IOC.

The efforts resulted in a report, published in June 2007, which sought to document the illegal use of child labor in China's manufacture of the Olympic-related mementos that were under license to BOCOG. The report provoked an instant reaction from Chinese authorities, prepared for crisis management, in which they announced that local officials would be punished, law-violating businesses sanctioned, and illegal contracts immediately terminated or modified.

One of the striking features of the report is the way in which it shows how traditional IOC aspirations can be deployed to create a frame for altering narratives. Quoting directly from the IOC's Code of Ethics, PlayFair invoked the following principles:

> 1. Safeguarding the dignity of the individual is a fundamental requirement of Olympism.
>
> 5. The Olympic parties shall use due care and diligence in fulfilling their mission. They must not act in a manner likely to tarnish the reputation of the Olympic Movement.
>
> 6. The Olympic parties must not be involved with firms or persons whose activity is inconsistent with the principles set out in the Olympic Charter and the present Code.[24]

The report detailed the Alliance's efforts, since 2003, to discuss with the IOC the conditions under which Olympic-branded sportswear is produced. In response to requests for meetings, the IOC commented "that it condemns the practice of unfair labour practices, which are contrary to the spirit and ideals of the Olympic movement," but that day-to-day licensing is managed by the 202 National Olympic Committees around the world, and "The IOC has no direct involvement with regards to such contracts."[25] PlayFair's report also referenced a 1998 cooperation agreement signed between the IOC and the International Labour Organisation (ILO) that focused on respect for social justice in the labor field. In that agreement, "the IOC and the ILO undertake to encourage activities in pursuit of this objective, particularly those which contribute to the elimination of poverty and child labour."[26]

---

[24] Ibid.
[25] Ibid.
[26] Ibid.

PlayFair understood the implications not only for the IOC story, but for the China narrative as well. For China, much was at stake in terms of the relationship between the Olympics and changing global perceptions of the quality of domestically produced goods. The stated "mission" of the Beijing 2008 Licensing Programme was to promote the brand image of the Beijing Olympic Games and the Chinese Olympic Committee (COC) – that is, to "express the unique culture of China and Beijing by offering an array of traditional cultural products; to make a strong effort to involve Chinese enterprises in Olympic licensing; to showcase Chinese products and build the brand image equation that conveys a quality message, i.e. 'Made-in-China = High Quality;' and to raise funds for the Beijing 2008 Olympic Games."[27] Both before and after the Olympics, concerns over quality of goods regularly plagued China. PlayFair's effectiveness should be seen in a long running effort concerning labor standards in a global economy that reverberates through factory tragedies in Bangladesh and minimum wage debates in the United States. For the major establishment players – the IOC and China – the lessons would be fairly standard: survey vulnerabilities in advance, be careful with what you claim; seek to ensure that actions are as consistent as possible with principles and promises; and understand what other strategic actors will seek to do and what platforms they will utilize. PlayFair went on to launch similar campaigns at the 2010 Africa World Cup and the 2012 London Olympics.

The "Genocide Olympics"

There is no gold medal for the NGO narrative that comes closest to hijacking, usurping or piggy-backing on the immense investment in the Olympics. But if there were, one of the competitors for the 2008 award might be Eric Reeves, an English professor at Massachusetts' Smith College and longtime Sudan activist, who created the accusatory concept of the "Genocide Olympics" as a way of influencing China's dealings with Sudan. Reeves' was a classic effort to seize the platform and to use the social and financial capital invested in the Olympics in order to turn it to the advantage of an NGO policy advocate "free rider." It is useful to trace the intense history of this effort and its implications for the earlier discussion of platforms.

Many have remarked on China's close resource-related relationship with countries of marginal stability and democracy, seen to be partly an imperative of the country's growing domestic economy and need for oil and other

---

[27] "Beijing 2008 Olympic Games Licensing Programme," *Chinese Olympic Committee*, March 27, 2004.

reserves. A prominent example in this arena is Sudan. Since the mid-1990s, China National Petroleum Corporation (CNPC), one of China's national oil companies, had been the dominant player in both exploration and production in Sudan's oil reserves. Human Rights Watch and others charged that China's involvement in oil exploration was marked by complicity in gross human rights violations, including clearances of the indigenous populations in the oil regions and direct assistance to Khartoum's regular military forces. In addition, China has purchased a great share of Sudan's oil exports, and these revenues are a major source of financial support for the Sudanese government. These policies have undermined the effectiveness of sanctions imposed by other global players.

Most important and relevant to the subject of Reeves' use of the Olympics platform was international concern about widespread killing and displacement in the Darfur region and the specific role of China in this crisis. In September 2004, the UN Security Council adopted a resolution threatening Sudan with oil sanctions if it did not stop atrocities in the Darfur region. China abstained. In August 2006, China abstained again in a vote on Resolution 1706 that provided for the transfer of responsibility in Darfur to the United Nations from the African Union.[28] Many advocates felt that China was shielding Sudan in its refusal to consent to the entry of UN forces.

The public efforts to pressure Sudan, and countries that could influence Sudan, were substantial. What was particularly relevant, however, was the leveraging of the 2008 Olympic Games as a method of bringing additional pressure to bear. Eric Reeves' "re-branding" of the Beijing events as the "Genocide Olympics" was a kind of asymmetric image warfare, which also proved to be a highly effective mode of mobilizing support for his position. From the outset, the most salient characteristic was Reeves' rhetorical strategy, deploying the evocative and immediately understandable phrase, "Genocide Olympics." This elegant and powerful formulation effectively juxtaposed two complex worlds that are not readily associated with each other. The phrase assaulted and awakened the reader, and invited further inquiry. It was a phrase that, for some readers, played on deep and abiding concerns about China and the 2008 Games that could not otherwise be easily summarized and compressed. The brilliance of this two-word phrase was what gave the project its initial momentum.

Reeves was able to build on Beijing's own contribution to the notion of multiple sorts of Olympics. As part of its expansive claims for the Olympics,

---

[28] "Security Council Expands Mandate of UN Mission in Sudan to Include Darfur," *United Nations Security Council*, August 31, 2006.

BOCOG chose the "One World, One Dream" motto to convey the idea of simultaneous and overlapping Olympics, Olympics that asserted and followed certain themes: a Green Olympics, a People's Olympics and a Hi-Tech Olympics. The Green Olympics would emphasize harmony, mutual promotion of man and nature and China's commitment to sustainable development. The People's Olympics would promote an internally harmonious society, facilitate the formation of a peaceful international environment and emphasize solidarity between East and West.[29] The Hi-Tech Olympics would, according to BOCOG, "be a window to showcase [China's] high-tech achievements and innovative capacity."[30] In another, slightly more worrisome interpretation, however, the Hi-Tech Olympics provides an "arena to exhibit the comprehensive power and the highest level of the scientific and technological development of China."[31] Playing against the quasi-hyperbole of Beijing's claims, the coining of Reeves' phrase was a small act of rhetorical hijacking.

The second reason the phrase was so striking was that it broke through the dense layers of complexity about Darfur, atrocities, geopolitics, oil and weapons trading. The phrase "Genocide Olympics" was issued and introduced to a global audience that understood something horrible was proceeding in Darfur and that there had been numerous seemingly ineffectual attempts to resolve the crisis. There was, as is often the case, a generalized hope for a new solution that could be understandable and workable. By fixing responsibility on China and suggesting a potential solution, the concept of "Genocide Olympics" had staying power. It gathered, under a single banner, much of the accumulated discontent, anxiety and suspicion about China and human rights.

Reeves' public and transparent campaign made it possible to document and analyze what he proposed to do and how his small campaign exploited great platforms such as the Games. Reeves had long experience as a Sudan activist; his website, www.sudanreeves.org, carried many of his writings and analyses on this subject. He had spent eight years fully devoted to Sudan-related questions. And he had always used newspapers, radio and other means to keep his views in the public eye. When Reeves turned to the Olympics as a platform for mobilization, he met with the *Washington Post* editorial board and convinced them to write an editorial that had "Genocide Olympics" in its

---

[29] Before 2006, the "People's" Olympics was called the Humanistic Olympics. However, the awkward phrasing of this term, as well as its semantic signals to related concepts, such as humanitarian, resulted in a change to the People's Olympics. The problems might have been even greater without this change.

[30] "Concepts of the Beijing Olympic Games: Green Olympics, Hi-tech Olympics, People's Olympics," *BOCOG*, August 5, 2005.

[31] Hua Meng, "An Analysis of the Role of National Culture in 2008 Beijing Olympic Games," 2004.

title (the first such publication of the term).[32] He wrote an opinion piece in December 2006 in the *Boston Globe* about his proposed campaign. In March, Reeves appeared again in the *Boston Globe* – this time as a subject of a story – with an account of his campaign, which he launched with an email manifesto sent in February, an "Open Letter to Darfur Activists."[33]

The manifesto is interesting for its differing modes of achieving the goal of hijacking the Olympics for secondary purposes. The letter challenged current NGO techniques for citizen actions regarding Darfur:

> Enough of selling green bracelets and writing letters. . . . It's time, now, to begin shaming China – demanding that if the Beijing government is going to host the premier international event, the Summer Olympic Games of 2008, they must be responsible international partners. China's slogan for these Olympic Games – "One world, one dream" – is a ghastly irony, given Beijing's complicity in the Darfur genocide. . . . The Chinese leadership must understand that if they refuse to use their unrivaled political, economic, and diplomatic leverage with Khartoum to secure access for the force authorized under UN Security Council Resolution 1706, then they will face an extremely vigorous, unrelenting, and omnipresent campaign to shame them over this refusal.

In opposition to the established means of exploiting the Olympics platform, Reeves suggested that a boycott of the Games would not be the most effective technique:

> It is important to remember that this should not, in my strongly held view, be a campaign to boycott the Olympics: a boycott would defeat the whole purpose of the campaign, and be deeply divisive. Moreover, if a boycott were successful (extremely unlikely) the political platform from which to challenge China would disappear.

Reeves' aspiration, rather, was for the use of the Olympics platform to engender a global, grassroots movement. He intuited the bigger the platform (and the Olympics is certainly among the biggest), the greater the room for major uses by the appropriator:

> There is tremendous scope for creative advocacy here, and for the deployment of diverse skills and energies: linguistic, internet, communications, graphic design, advocacy writing, and organizational. What happens, for example, if 1,000 students and advocates demonstrate before the Chinese embassy in Washington, DC, declaring with banner, placards, and T-shirts

---

[32] "China and Darfur: The Genocide Olympics," *Washington Post*, December 14, 2006.
[33] Kevin Cullen, "Genocide Games," *Boston Globe*, March 25, 2007.

that China will be held accountable for its complicity in the Darfur genocide? What happens if such demonstrations are continuous, and grow, and take place outside China's embassies in other countries? in many other countries? What happens if everywhere – everywhere – Chinese diplomats and politicians travel they are confronted by those who insist on making this an occasion for highlighting China's role in the Darfur genocide?[34]

Almost immediately, there was rapid diffusion of the idea. Reeves gave interviews to NPR and other broadcast outlets. Even a French presidential candidate, François Bayrou, called for a potential boycott of the Olympics if China did not assist in altering Sudan's stance.[35]

Then celebrity intervened. The actress Mia Farrow, and her son, Ronan, published an opinion piece in the *Wall Street Journal*.[36] Reeves had had long discussions, as a kind of tutor on Darfur, with the senior Farrow who was serving as a good-will ambassador for UNESCO and a committed Sudan activist before the essay's publication. The essay, not surprisingly titled "The 'Genocide Olympics,'" repeated much that was in Reeves' campaign manifestos and analyses:

> State-owned China National Petroleum Corp. – an official partner of the upcoming Olympic Games – owns the largest shares in each of Sudan's two major oil consortia. The Sudanese government uses as much as 80% of proceeds from those sales to fund its brutal Janjaweed proxy militia and purchase their instruments of destruction: bombers, assault helicopters, armored vehicles and small arms, most of them of Chinese manufacture. Airstrips constructed and operated by the Chinese have been used to launch bombing campaigns on villages.[37]

Then the Farrows introduced a new point – one that also likely originated with Reeves – that turned the rhetorical heat up by more than a few notches. They aimed a verbal volley at the producer Steven Spielberg, who had been contracted to orchestrate and produce the opening and closing ceremonies for the 2008 Olympics. "Does Mr. Spielberg really want to go down in history as the Leni Riefenstahl of the Beijing Games? Do the various television sponsors around the world want to share in that shame? Because they will.

[34] Eric Reeves, "An Open Letter to Darfur Activists and Advocates," *Sudan Tribune*, February 11, 2007.

[35] Jamey Keaton, "Olympics Boycott Call Made at Rally, 3 candidates in France Seek to Pressure China," *AP/South Florida Sun Sentinel*, Broward edition, March 22, 2007, 17A.

[36] Mia Farrow and Ronan Farrow, "The Genocide Olympics," *Wall Street Journal*, March 28, 2007.

[37] Ibid.

Unless, of course, all of them add their singularly well-positioned voices to the growing calls for Chinese action to end the slaughter in Darfur."[38]

Bringing Spielberg into the frame seemed instantly to alter the dynamic of the campaign. In a sense, it meant, for Reeves, a slight loss of control of the narrative. All of a sudden, this was now a Hollywood celebrity campaign. A great reputation (Spielberg's) seemed on the line. Diffusion spiked as more and more newspapers carried elements of the story. *The Washington Times*, a frequent critic of China, found the Olympic platform a suitable vehicle for their views. Nat Hentoff wrote:

> It astonishes me that the same Mr. Spielberg so admirably founded the Shoah foundation that records the testimony of the survivors of the Nazi Holocaust. How can he fail to make any connection with Shoah and the holocaust in Darfur? . . .
>
> The Farrows also ask whether "the various television sponsors [of the Beijing Olympics] want to share in that shame" of the host's complicity in genocide along with such American corporate sponsors of the games as Johnson and Johnson, Coca-Cola, General Electric and McDonald's.[39]

By mid-2007, the campaign sparked by Reeves and reinforced by Farrow was gaining even greater visibility. The world's largest mutual fund, Fidelity Investments, slashed its stake in PetroChina amid pressure to sell shares in companies doing business in Sudan.[40] In May, more than 100 members of the United States House of Representatives sent a joint letter to Chinese President Hu Jintao urging him to use his influence with the Sudanese government. The letter concluded on a Reeves-like note: "It would be a disaster for China if the Games were to be marred by protests. . . . Already there are calls to boycott what is increasingly being described as the 2008 Genocide Olympics."[41]

Athletes also joined the campaign. A reserve basketball player on the Cleveland Cavaliers, Ira Newbie, inspired by an article about Reeves in *USA Today*, convinced his teammates to join in a plea to the government of China: "We, as basketball players in the N.B.A. and as potential athletes in the 2008 Summer Olympic Games in Beijing, cannot look on with indifference to the massive human suffering and destruction that continue in the Darfur region of Sudan."[42] And in July, Joey Cheek, a speed-skating medalist from the 2006 Winter Olympics, delivered to the Chinese Embassy in Washington

---

[38] Ibid.

[39] "Khartoum's Enablers in Beijing," *Washington Times*, April 16, 2007.

[40] "Fidelity Prunes its Stake in PetroChina," *Wall Street Journal*, May 17, 2007.

[41] "Lantos, House Colleagues Send Strong Message to Chinese President, Demand Action on Darfur," May 9, 2007.

[42] Howard Beck, "Cavalier Seeks Players' Support for Darfur," *New York Times*, May 16, 2007.

42,000 signatures on a petition from the Save Darfur Coalition. He proposed leading a group of American and Chinese athletes on a trip to Sudan. A column in the *New York Times* celebrated his idealism.[43]

The consequences of the *Wall Street Journal* essay by the Farrows, and the efforts by others who joined in the campaign, demonstrated that the launching of a campaign does not guarantee control of how it will be carried and diffused. Reeves' narrative was carefully constructed and phrased, with specific objectives and specific means of persuasion. It was to be a grass roots-supported narrative, with a broad international base. It would engage and energize people around the world concerned with Darfur (and the relationship between Sudan and China). The option of boycott as remedy would be sidelined. However, the publication of the *Wall Street Journal* piece subtly shifted the campaign. Mia Farrow's fame launched the concept of tarring 2008 as the "Genocide Olympics" to a wider audience. But despite (or perhaps because of) the success of Reeves and others who initiated the campaign, control of the narrative had been weakened. At the outset they could influence almost every related element in seizing the Olympics platform. Now the platform of Darfur and the Olympics had plural authors.

A different tale began to be told, and, in a way, the shaming appeared to have consequences. China (and Steven Spielberg) sought to regain control of the narrative. In mid-April 2007, Spielberg's spokesperson, Marvin Levy, announced that the producer had written a four-page letter to Hu Jintao, urging him to take further action regarding Sudan and Darfur. At the same time, China – while denying there was any connection to the Genocide Olympics campaign, or to Spielberg's letter – announced that it was sending a special ambassador to Sudan. These events led to a journalistic denouement – at least a temporary one – on the front page of the *New York Times*, in an April 13 story by Helene Cooper that realigned the Olympics narrative, placed Steven Spielberg in a good light, and also shifted the dynamic for evaluating the government of China by suggesting positive political movement.[44] The story was entitled "Darfur Collides With Olympics, And China Yields." The following day, the story was republished in the *International Herald Tribune*, with the headline "China acts on Sudan after Hollywood push."[45] Not long after,

---

[43] Harvey Araton, "Good Guy is Forgotten in Bad Week for Sports," *New York Times*, July 31, 2007.

[44] Helene Cooper, "Darfur Collides With Olympics, and China Yields," *New York Times*, Diplomatic Memo, April 13, 2007.

[45] Reeves sought to keep the pressure on Spielberg. See Eric Reeves, "Artists Abetting Genocide," *Boston Globe*, April 16, 2007: "What are the obligations of artists in the face of genocide? Spielberg and the others are at two removes from the ethnically targeted killing in Darfur; they are helping with the Olympics that China's government cares so much about, and China is helping Khartoum. But how do we assess degrees of complicity in the ultimate human crime?"

Sudan agreed to the increased entry of UN peacekeepers (followed by the UN authorization of a hybrid African Union/UN peacekeeping force in July).[46] The narrative of a Genocide Olympics had accomplished its limited purpose, a platform for attention to Sudan.

In July 2007, two scholars from Harvard, one of whom had previously worked with the Chinese government, wrote an op-ed piece for the *Boston Globe*, later reprinted in the *International Herald Tribune*, criticizing "some in the West" who were labeling Beijing 2008 the Genocide Olympics.[47] "Is China really turning a cold shoulder to the humanitarian crisis in Darfur," they asked, or, as they suggested, "has the explosive charge of complicity in genocide blinded observers to China's aid and quiet diplomacy in Sudan?" It continued: "In the face of increasing pressure from the international community, China may consider bolder options," but "China's principle of exerting influence but not interfering and imposing is consistent with African practice, and the final political decision will have to be made by Africans." A few days later Liu Guijin, China's special envoy to Darfur, criticized American politicians who, he suggested, had "unfairly played up the Darfur issue to burnish their moral credentials amid the presidential election campaigns." Those who linked Darfur with the Olympics "were either ignorant of reality or steeped in obsolete cold war ideology."[48]

CONTROLLING THE NARRATIVE

There is hardly a more important set of narratives for the twenty-first century than those concerning the role of China in the world and as an internally governing power. As a consequence, there are few narratives that so many actors seek to shape with such fervency. In this chapter, I have concentrated on global civil society groups, but this narrative-shaping effort is clearly a process in which multiple other bodies have a stake as well; for states, religions, corporations and large-scale movements, the 2008 Olympics represented a great opportunity, and both the IOC and China were mindful of this fact. No subsequent Olympics has presented such a powerful platform nor such an attractive one to capture for purposes of pointed and effective strategic communication.

[46]   Howard LaFranchi, "Why Sudan is Now Allowing UN Troops in Darfur," *Christian Science Monitor*, April 18, 2007. See also United Nations, "The United Nations and Darfur: Fact Sheet," August 2007. Despite these developments, Spielberg announced that he would resign as artistic director.

[47]   Jason Qian and Anne Wu, "Playing the Blame Game in Africa," *International Herald Tribune*, July 24, 2007.

[48]   Mure Dickie, "China Defends its Stance on Darfur," *Financial Times*, July 28, 2007.

The drama of constructing representations of China has underscored what might be called the jurisprudence of platforms: who constructs them and who has access, the modes of controlling their use or defending them, and the modes of seeking access. Over decades, the way of thinking of traditional platforms has evolved and is continuing to change. There are ways of conceptualizing the structure of broadcasting and the press, thinking about certain public spaces and even zones of transnational discourse. Effective speech often requires platforms, but in a world of new technologies old platforms dissolve while new ones come into being. We have little sense of the role these scaffolding enterprises play in a full conception of speech and society. But ultimately, a theory of strategic action must address these less tangible aspects of infrastructure.

In all these instances, beneath notions of rules and practices, there is the issue of who has what degree of control over the narratives that define our lives. As advocacy groups seek new platforms to advance their messages, it becomes crucial to understand the mechanisms by which these activities take place. The Beijing Olympics offered a site that can aid in this understanding, that illustrates the dynamic of competing themes and that underscores the role of platforms in making those competing themes more or less effective.

11

Strategic Communication and Satellite Channels

I turn to a relatively arcane subject: regulating the use of satellite transponders to reach across national boundaries and significantly affect target audiences. Techniques of supervision related to satellite positions in geostationary orbit, the use of their transponders and the efforts to manage the signals have been an exercise in governing seemingly ungovernable phenomena. In the last three decades of the twentieth century, a vast infrastructure of communication satellites – new trade routes in the sky, as I have called them[1] – was built. Strategic communicators – commercial, religious, ideological – were provided new opportunities, new apertures for entry into previously closed markets. A combination of state industrial policies and, later, private entrepreneurship shaped the nature of these structures and set the backdrop for experimentation with potential uses of the new transmission opportunities by new players that would alter existing information flows. Strategic communicators – often delivering powerful and polarizing messages, even menacing and hate-filled – find their way onto satellites. Often this is a result of the relatively invisible and laissez-faire mode of leasing time on the transponders that satellites carry and downlinking those signals direct to homes or to cable operations in territories within the satellite footprint.

Gaining transponder leasing rights has been a matter, especially in the United States, of private negotiation, not an appeal to administrative author-ities. No overarching international scheme of regulation has emerged. What did occur is significant; in the absence of such an overall regulatory scheme, patterns of "informal governance" arose. These informal practices frequently resulted in ad hoc, often ragged policies, hidden repression and novel arrange-ments. In such a system of informal governance, paradoxically, what constitutes

[1] Monroe E. Price, "Satellite Broadcasting as Trade Routes in the Sky," in *In Search of Boundaries: Communication, Nation States and Cultural Identities*, eds. Joseph M. Chan and Bryce T. McIntyre (Westport, CT: Ablex Publishing, 2002).

"freedom of expression" can get lost.[2] Because of the challenge of governing the ungovernable, and regulating the unregulable, the history of satellite regulation has been something of a dress rehearsal for the current Internet debate, in which battles over the question of the resilience of state control have grown sharper and more contested.

STRATEGIC ARCHITECTURES AND THE UNITED NATIONS

Even in the system's relative infancy, the potential that satellites held for assaults on national understandings of media control was well understood. By the mid-1960s, when the promise (or threat) of satellites was just past the science fiction phase, the truly transnational potential of the new technology became quite clear. As a result, there were furious efforts to establish a system that would preserve some version of the existing order, in which broadcasting was organized along national lines. One way to do this was to keep total control of satellites and the transponders on them in government hands, and that was the initial strategy. A new kind of entity, international in character and coordinated with the UN, was developed, under U.S. leadership, to control the new technology. INTELSAT was composed of an international board that would govern satellite construction, launch and operation. These were comfortable hands for assuring which users could take advantage of the increased capacity for distribution without unduly violating national boundaries and cultural norms.

With the multiplication and privatization of satellites and their transponders, the major powers lost exclusive control over the new technology. One result was an increased demand for regulation. The threat to the existing order of states as strategic communicators was becoming clearer. An early, ambitious and acrimonious forum concerning the design of a system of international standards for direct-to-home satellite signals involved the United Nations, which undertook an extensive debate that ended in tatters in the 1970s.

This UN debate casts light on contemporary issues of sovereignty and regulation. As now occurs in the debate over the operation and regulation of the Internet, the sending of a signal from one country into the territory of another could be looked at both as a triumph of free expression and as a potential violation of national sovereignty. Not surprisingly, satellite discussions took place against the historical background of terrestrial broadcasting

---

[2]   See Lisa Parks and James Schwoch, *Down to Earth: Satellite Technologies, Industries, and Cultures* (New Brunswick, NJ: Rutgers University Press, 2012).

regulation. There, the general rule had been that in medium- and long-wave there should be management of broadcasting signals so that national borders were respected and what might be called "intended spillover" was minimized. Now, in both the UN and UNESCO, similar ideas were debated from the late 1960s to the early 1980s.[3]

A principal forum was the UN Committee on the Peaceful Uses of Outer Space (COPUOS). Members of COPUOS's working group argued for "a prohibition on broadcasts beamed from satellites by one State to others without the explicit prior consent of the Government concerned through bilateral or multilateral agreements."[4] In a related UNESCO draft declaration, the Soviet Union, supported by many developing countries, fought for a similar requirement; the USSR claimed that it desired to limit political propaganda, while others were more concerned with the impact on economic development and cultural heritage. These arguments were closely linked to debates concerning the "New World Information and Communication Order," an effort that emerged during the 1970s and 1980s to address imbalances in global communications between developed and developing nations. The United States argued that it could not, consistent with the U.S. Constitution, impose restrictions on producers or distributors of programming who sought to send signals from the United States to other countries. With several allies, American opposition successfully blocked the UN initiative.[5] In 1982, the UN General Assembly passed the non-binding Resolution 37/92, entitled "Principles Governing the Use by States of Artificial Earth Satellites for International Direct Television Broadcasting."[6] These principles were hortatory only.

While the explicit principle of requiring "prior consent" of the receiving countries was abandoned, paragraph 8 of the document provided that

---

[3] For details of debates on the prior consent requirement in particular and regulation of direct broadcasting by satellite in general, see Kathryn M. Queeny, *Direct Broadcast Satellites and the United Nations* (Alphen aan den Rijn: Sijthoff & Noordhoff, 1978), Kaarle Nordenstreng and Herbert I. Schiller, eds., *National Sovereignty and International Communication* (Norwood, NJ: Ablex, 1979), and Jon T. Powell, *International Broadcasting by Satellite – Issues of Regulation, Barriers to Communications* (Westport, CT: Quorum Books, 1985).

[4] United Nations, General Assembly, Committee on the Peaceful Uses of Outer Space, Working Group On Direct Broadcast Satellites, Report Of The Second Session Of The Working Group (UN Doc. A/AC. 105/66), August 12, 1969, 7. See also Broadcasting from Satellites, U.N. GAOR Comm. on Peaceful Uses of Outer Space, 2d Sess. 32–34, U.N. Doc. No. A/AC.105/PV.62 (1969) (discussing Soviet position); Marika N. Taishoff, *State Responsibility and the Direct Broadcast Satellite* (London: Pinter, 1987).

[5] See Frank Stanton, "Will they Stop our Satellites?" *New York Times*, October 22, 1972.

[6] The resolution was adopted on December 10, 1982. One hundred and seven countries voted for the resolution, thirteen voted against and thirteen abstained.

states should bear responsibility for activities in the field of international direct television broadcasting by satellite carried out by them or under their jurisdiction. This reflected the alternative approach developed during the UN and UNESCO debates: a set of internationally agreed-on standards with the originating country being responsible that no signal emanating from it would violate them. The principles adopted by the General Assembly provided that "A State which intends to establish or authorize the establishment of an international direct television broadcasting satellite service shall without delay notify the proposed receiving State or States of such intention and shall promptly enter into consultation with any of those States which so requests."[7] The Assembly resolution was advisory only and had few consequences.

This UN debate is significant, even though it did not yield binding law; the main approaches still haunt current discussions concerning satellite signals and have echoes in Internet debates. An example is the endurance of the idea of prior consent even in the face of Article 19's right of an individual to receive and impart information regardless of frontiers. Mei Ning Yan characterizes China's policies in the satellite sphere as determinedly implementing a prior consent rule as best it can, achieving that result not by a process of "global governance" but by old-fashioned, strong-handed and persistent national regulation. Professor Yan quotes the Chinese strategy as based on a complex version of "a single satellite in the sky, a single network on the ground."[8]

[7]   United Nations General Assembly, "Principles Governing the Use by States of Artificial Earth Satellites for International Direct Television Broadcasting," December 10, 1982.

[8]   Mei Ning Yan, "China and the Prior Consent Requirement: A Decade of Invasion and Counter-Invasion by Transfrontier Satellite Television," *Hastings Communication & Entertainment Law Journal* 25 (2003): 268. China has demonstrated some flexibility in the application of this principle, often informally, either through turning a blind eye to significant use of satellite receiving dishes in certain areas, allowing cable carriage of specified foreign satellite-delivered channels, or permitting carriage of specific channels only in privileged sites (such as international hotels). While this approach requires a complex monitoring and filtering system and control of backbone entry of data into China with respect to the Internet, the issue is somewhat simpler for satellites. It requires control of satellites with footprints over its territory, coupled with regulation and banning of satellite dishes. China cannot similarly control what signals are carried to third countries, but makes efforts to do so by exercising informal pressure on satellite operators in their leasing capacity.

China uses its economic power as a major customer to encourage satellite operators not to carry disfavored program channels: those perceived by China as threatening, deceptive or potentially violating stability. A celebrated episode (partly because of the publicity-gaining capacity of the affected actors) involved the efforts of China to limit distribution of NTDTV, which deems itself an insistent commentator and critic of the government of China and the Communist Party. China's characterization of the channel is quite different – the authorities consider it an instrument of the banned Falun Gong. China threatened to withdraw business from satellite companies that agreed to carry NTDTV. Most of the pressure involved Eutelsat, the French broadcast regulatory agency (CSA) and the French government. See "Chinese-language NTDTV Harassed by Beijing," *Reporters Without Borders*, May 25, 2004.

THE INFORMAL ORDER OF SATELLITE COMMUNICATIONS

Prior to the 1990s, broadly speaking, to the extent that there were transnational broadcasting issues of great political significance, they largely involved the residual short-wave radio efforts of the Cold War. Then great changes occurred. These included the founding of Al Jazeera in 1996 and the proliferation of Middle East satellite channels, and the NATO bombing campaign of 1999, which included a focus on the effort of Serbia to reach Serbians worldwide by satellite. The new regional and global political impacts of satellite transmissions began to attract renewed attention.

In this emerging dynamic, old modes of discussing freedom of expression were enriched. The proliferation of satellites meant that the language of Article 19 of the International Covenant on Civil and Political Rights, conferring rights to receive and impart information "regardless of frontiers," was suddenly meaningful as an implementable possibility. Those with strategic communication responsibilities globally had to reconsider the way in which the opportunities of this technology could be used. Application of rules became more conceptually difficult as well, as remote speakers entered distant societies, sometimes in violation of broadly held local cultural norms.

The following sections touch on several significant cases in this history and demonstrate how strategic communicators interact in the satellite realm, some seeking to enter markets for allegiances and some seeking to bar entry. I have chosen an eclectic set of examples of the problem, Med TV, Geo TV and Al Jazeera America, as they navigate the difficult landscape of gaining access into a non-systematized world. Because of a paucity of transparent government decisions, what we know about these transactions depends greatly on journalistic accounts and information gleaned from websites. What emerges from this anecdotal analysis is a window into the interactions between content providers and instruments of power. To use the word "governance" to describe the relationship of states to the content of satellite signals is an exercise in hyperbole. The strategies of entry – starting up, producing programming, leasing time – exist against efforts, often desperate, by states or regional and international entities to intervene when a crisis exists or is perceived to occur.

Med TV, Kurdistan and Narratives of Legitimacy

Many elements of the earlier-mentioned interactions are present in the development of Med TV, an international Kurdish satellite channel established in

London. Med TV was to be a "virtual Kurdistan," binding through imagery, advocacy and inspiration Kurdish populations in Turkey, Iraq, Iran, Syria and elsewhere. Med TV was to be the satellite fulfillment of the Kurdish dream, providing a culturally enriching mix of news, entertainment and education aimed at a transnational, distributed community, claimed to be 35 million, and engaged in rediscovering and redefining Kurdish nationhood. The channel had the task of reaffirming the Kurdish language and reinforcing Kurdish culture. Naomi Sakr captured this view, calling Med TV a "kind of Kurdistan in space," as it provided a unifying function in the absence of a Kurdish homeland or single territorial base.[9]

The channel was seen, by pre-Erdogan Turkey, as an assault on the country's Ataturk-inspired secularism and monocultural assumptions. Turkish officials claimed that Med TV was the media arm of the Kurdistan Workers' Party (PKK), the separatist Kurdish force engaged in armed conflict with Turkish government troops, deemed by Turkey a significant threat to the integrity and unity of the country.[10] For the Turkish government of the time, this narrative was secessionist and Med TV was a foreign intrusion, disturbing local forms of regulation and seeking to foment instability and violence.

Med TV was an example of the new satellite world. Its legal home was in the United Kingdom, and it was to British institutions that it answered. But its target audience was in Turkey, for the most part, and, because of satellite technology and direct-to-home broadcasting, it could largely evade formal Turkish regulation. Ankara acted with limited success to suppress Med TV's domestic reception, for example banning the purchase and mounting of satellite dishes that could specifically obtain Med TV's signals.[11] Faced with an inability to fully control the signal's entry, Turkey tried another technique, available as a result of Med TV's use of Eutelsat transponders for distribution.

[9]　Naomi Sakr, "Frontiers of Freedom: Diverse Responses to Satellite Television in the Middle East and North Africa," *Public/Javnost: Journal of the European Institute for Communication and Culture* 6, no. 1 (1999): 102–103.

[10]　"Turkey Calls on USA to End MED-TV Broadcasts," *BBC Summary of World Broadcasts*, August 30, 1996; "MED-TV Off the Air After UK, Belgian Police Raids," *BBC Summary of World Broadcasts*, September 27, 1996; "Turkish Premier Discusses MED-TV with Tony Blair," *BBC Summary of World Broadcasts*, December 19, 1997; A. Hassanpour, "Med-TV, Britain, and the Turkish State: A Stateless Nation's Quest for Sovereignty in the Sky," Unpublished paper presented at the Freie Universität Berlin, November 7, 1995.

[11]　For example, its transmission was originally on a satellite that directed its signal from a different location from the more commonly viewed Eutelsat satellites. Med TV viewers had to turn their satellite dishes in a different direction from those receiving the Eutelsat originated satellite, one that carried traditional Turkish entertainment channel services. The authorities could see the difference in the position of the dish and could use that information to harass the Med TV viewers. To protect its viewers, Med TV had to shift, therefore, to the more commonly viewed bird in the sky.

Under Eutelsat's internal rules, the satellite's transponders were (loosely) con-trolled by public agencies in EU member states; many of the states that controlled those agencies had good bilateral relations with Turkey. Turkey sought, in relevant European capitals, to deny Med TV leasing rights. Over time, Med TV was unceremoniously bounced from transponder to transponder.

One solace – an anchor, as it were – was Med TV's British license. Whatever the channel's political goals, the choice of a relatively secure legal and political system had been a vital one for its independence. This became one of Med TV's most important achievements. Acceptance in the UK meant, generally, under EU law, that the programming should not be restricted by administrative agencies in other member states. This led to a third Turkish approach; Turkish officials mounted an extensive campaign to pressure the British government to withdraw Med TV's license as a means of closing the producer down.

Turkish officials contended that Med TV was a "political organization" and therefore, under United Kingdom legislation, precluded from obtaining a British license. The British government denied the impact of such pressures, claiming that neither the Foreign Office nor the Prime Minister's Office would ever interfere with the independence of the regulator. Nonetheless, after many complaints to the government and the Independent Television Commission (now part of Ofcom) in February 1998, the ITC penalized Med TV for a total fine of approximately $150,000. The proceedings indicated the contorted nature of free expression conditions in these unusual circumstances. According to the Commission, despite formal warnings, three broadcasts of Med TV had violated the impartiality requirements of the ITC's programming code. In one breach, according to the Commission, a "40 minute long programme consisted entirely of a political rally organized by the PKK. . . . No context was supplied and there was no balancing material."[12] In a second breach of impartiality requirements, Med TV "seemingly endorsed" the on-camera condemnation of a U.S. list of terrorist organizations. A third transgression of the ITC's rules, that of the neutrality of its journalists, involved "'personal comments' from a Med TV journalist in the field, namely a description of the more pro-government Kurdish Democratic Party as 'treach-erous and murderous.'"[13] In 1999, the ITC withdrew the license, finding that the station had too often violated standards of objectivity and impartiality.[14]

---

[12] "Med TV Fined for Serious Breaches of ITC Code," BBC *Summary of World Broadcasts*, February 6, 1998.

[13] See Monroe E. Price, "What Price Fairness?" *Media Studies Journal* 12, no. 2 (1998).

[14] According to Sir Robin Biggam, the ITC's chair: "Whatever sympathy there may be in the United Kingdom for the Kurdish people, it is not in the public interest to have any broadcaster use the UK as a platform for broadcasts which incite people to violence. Med TV have been

Soon thereafter, Med TV, in its then incarnation, closed down, but the effort to nourish a "Kurdistan of space" continued, with ongoing efforts by Ankara to disturb satellite transponder leasing by Med TV's successors. In 2013, as Turkey and the PKK announced a plan for reducing historic frictions and the potential for conflict, it appeared that some goals of the channel had been partially vindicated.[15] And in the ongoing fallout of war in Iraq, an independent or autonomous Kurdistan seemed increasingly likely.

Geo TV: International Relations and "Free Media Zones"

The Med TV case involved a strategic communicator based in one state seeking to influence a target population living elsewhere. I turn now to a case in which international relations and the invocation of international norms more openly affected regulation of the chain of facilities around satellite transponders, especially the uplink facilities. Geo TV was and remains a major Urdu satellite service feeding cable systems and operating direct-to-home programming for households in Pakistan. Its main production capacity and uplink is located in Dubai's Media City – established by the Gulf state to serve as a home to a new industrial gathering of media companies. There, the offices of the media channel would be, generally, free to flourish – free, particularly, of the constraints of Pakistan, where the footprint of the satellite signal landed.

Channel programmers like Geo TV could consider Dubai a kind of switching or linking station. Signals would be uploaded from there for delivery to the desired satellites, which would then downlink them to the targeted audience. In November 2007, following a fiercely contested presidential election and consequent unrest over the tallying of the results, then president of Pakistan Pervez Musharraf declared a state of emergency. Under new media restrictions that were imposed as part of the emergency declaration, Geo TV and other local and international television channels were temporarily ordered removed from cable systems. While many channels defiantly continued to transmit information online, only Geo continued to be available on television sets because of its direct-to-home television signals through the satellite transponder serviced from Dubai.

given many opportunities to be a peaceful voice for their community; to allow them to continue broadcasting after such serious breaches would be to condone the misuse of the UK's system for licensing broadcasters." See "UK Regulator Revokes Kurdish Med TV's License," *BBC News*, April 23, 1999.

[15] The 2012 treatment of Iran's Press TV by Ofcom presented echoes of the Med TV dispute. See "Iran's Press TV Loses UK License," *BBC News*, January 20, 2012; Geoffrey Alderman, "Suppressing Press TV is Deplorable," *Guardian*, January 24, 2012.

Reflecting the fragility of these immunity arrangements, on November 17, after conversations between the Musharraf government in Pakistan and officials in Dubai, the UAE government ordered the discontinuance of its uplink service to Geo TV.[16] This was a dramatic and important move. Statements issued by the UAE government and Dubai Media City suggested the sensitivity of the step. A government statement tried to play the UAE's strategic role both ways: "the United Arab Emirates has always played a positive and constructive role in international affairs," but "neutrality has been a key principle of its foreign policy." The UAE argued it had been a consistent advocate of international law and an active contributor to peace and stability in the region. But, "in light of the current sensitive state of affairs in Pakistan, the UAE can only assume its responsibility and maintain its neutrality."[17] A Dubai Media City statement, issued simultaneously, offered its rationale: "As an entity within the UAE, Dubai Media City would also observe the broad principles of the country's foreign policy and prevent the broadcast of news and material that would undermine those principles. Geo TV and ARY Digital [another Pakistani television network] are respected business partners in Dubai Media City for several years. Our relationship with them has been strong and friendly. We are in discussion with them with regard to the broadcast of their news components and we are confident we will resolve this matter in the best way possible to protect their interests and those of the UAE."[18] The suspension was brief. On November 30, after Musharraf became a civilian president and there was notice that the state of emergency would soon be lifted, Dubai again agreed to allow the uplinking of Geo TV.[19]

---

[16] Geo TV continued to distribute information online. The day after closing, the company briefly showed its Internet site on a large screen mounted in downtown Islamabad. The showing was discontinued after intervention by the police. See "Pakistan: Islamabad Police Halt Large Screen Showing of Geo News TV," *BBC Monitoring World Media Monitor*, November 20, 2007.

[17] Amir Wasim, "UAE Admits Stopping Geo, ARY Broadcast," DAWN, November 18, 2007.

[18] Ibid.

[19] "Analysis: Broadcasters Welcome in Dubai, But Not Their Domestic Politics," *BBC Monitoring World Media Monitor*, November 20, 2007. The trenchant BBC Monitoring World Media Analysis chronicled other instances when the UAE had removed or disabled services that were to originate in Dubai's Media City, including one from Iran: "In 2005, former speaker of parliament Mehdi Karrubi was one of the candidates defeated by Mahmud Ahmadinezhad in Iran's presidential election. Frustrated with what he saw as the lack of airtime allowed to those with reformist views, he announced plans to launch a television channel called Saba TV. The intention was to produce the channel's programmes in Iran and then have them sent to Dubai for transmission. But on the day of the planned launch, the person carrying the tapes for the inaugural broadcast was not allowed to disembark at Dubai airport and the whole project was called off. In an interview with the US-funded Radio Farda earlier this year, Aminah al-Rustamani of Dubai Media City said … the UAE did not permit

The Geo TV tale is an important one for understanding the politics of strategic communication in a transnational environment. First, there is the growing idea of finding "free zones" for foreign broadcasters – a recognition that a business can be built on providing relief from harsh forms of media regulation. The Geo TV case dramatizes the interplay of politics, technology and at least some deference by the sending country to the desires of the receiving state. It presents the complex discussions among states concerning the carriage or barring of signals originating elsewhere or destined for another location. Here, Dubai inferred a foreign policy commitment to consider the governmental preferences of the state to which a signal was directed. It was an example of negotiations between countries to limit participants in the market for loyalties. The idea of a free media zone did not escape unscathed. Eight months after the original incident, Dubai informed Geo TV that it might lose its license if it did not drop two news shows that aggressively supported the Pakistani lawyers' movement for reinstatement of deposed judges.[20] Accommodation and adjustment became part of the culture of the zone.[21]

Al Jazeera, the United States and Access to Cable Carriage

Much of the strategic history of access by programmers to audiences can be told through the story of Al Jazeera. Later in this chapter, I indicate some of the difficulties the Qatari channel faced in gaining satellite transponder opportunities in the Middle East. But there was another complexity, relevant to the issue of maneuvering for access in an unclear structural environment. Satellite signals are at their most disruptive when they bypass local regulators and go direct to homes. In some contexts, the United States being one, the predominant way of receiving satellite originated signals is through a local cable system. Gaining access to satellite transponders is not sufficient. The consent of cable system owners – often an oligopoly and often tied to government formally or

any Iranian political publications or broadcasters to operate because it did not want to strain relations between the two countries."

[20] "Dubai Asks Geo TV to Drop Shows or Lose Licence," *Times of India*, June 13, 2008.

[21] In May 1999, with Slobodan Milosevic seeking alternative modes of distribution for Serbian signals, the Israeli Spacecom company agreed to broadcast Yugoslav television and radio program via the AMOS satellite. By the time the U.S. administration recognized what had occurred, the satellite had managed to operate for days, superseding the transmitters that were one of the first targets of the NATO bombers. In July, the United States gently reminded Israel that the Israel Aircraft Industries, which owned 25 percent of Spacecom's shares, had the status of a subcontractor for the U.S. Department of Defense, a status that might be endangered if AMOS did not discontinue broadcasts "aimed at delegitimizing the residents of Kosovo." "(RTS Said Taken off Amos Satellite After US pressure," BBC Summary of World Broadcasts, July 16, 1999). AMOS complied.

informally – is necessary. In the United States, Al Jazeera had difficulty in gaining carriage both on satellite-to-home systems and also on cable systems that were needed for retransmission. Al Jazeera English, which, in the United States, morphed in 2013 into Al Jazeera America, could hire space on transponders, but the final link to the home was difficult to achieve.

The network could achieve Internet streaming in the United States for its Al Jazeera English channel (AJE) and there was no official effort at blockage, By the summer of 2006, however, it appeared that, despite the channel's rigorous efforts, there were only a very few cable or other adoptions, one example being a provisional agreement to carry the English language channel on the satellite-to-home Dish Network. Dish Network's commercial director told *Broadcasting & Cable* that Dish only offered the network carriage on an Arabic tier, not appealing to a wide audience. After the start of the Arab Spring, it was clear that AJE was producing important television. Still, carriage on American satellite and cable systems was sparse, almost nonexistent. In February 2011, during the Arab Spring, the *New York Times* sought to evaluate the uptake of Al Jazeera English on U.S. cable and direct broadcasting channels.[22] The reporter found that AJE had developed informal networks of distribution; for example, some public broadcasting stations carried the service as a digital sub-channel. Link TV, a nonprofit available on DirecTV and Dish Network, pre-empted other programming to show Al Jazeera for extended periods of time during the Arab Spring.[23] YouTube started promoting a live stream of the channel, supplementing the channel's own web stream.[24] The noncommercial broadcaster MHz Worldview expanded the number of hours that Al Jazeera English was simulcast each day.[25] But an informal poll of cable and satellite companies in the United States by the *Times* showed restrictive results. The *Times* asked whether they carried Al Jazeera English, "whether they were considering adding the channel in light of the events in Egypt and whether they had heard from customers who were requesting access to the channel." A typical response came from Comcast: "We do not currently carry Al Jazeera English as a cable channel, but we do carry it as part of a multicast feed from a public broadcaster in the Washington, D.C. area, and we understand they may have multicast agreements with other broadcasters."[26] Verizon's response was a bit more detailed, but similar: "Verizon FiOS

[22]   Brian Stelter, "Al-Jazeera Finds New Paths in U.S.," *New York Times*, February 1, 2011.
[23]   See http://www.linktv.org/.
[24]   See http://www.youtube.com/user/AlJazeeraEnglish and http://english.aljazeera.net/watch_now/.
[25]   "MHz Worldview Broadcasts Extended Al Jazeera English Live Coverage from Egypt," *MHz Networks*, n.d.
[26]   Stelter, "Al-Jazeera Finds New Paths."

TV offers a robust international offering, but that does not currently include Al Jazeera English. We receive requests for many channels, including Al Jazeera English, and we make those requests part of our decision-making process. For example, we've received requests for other Middle Eastern channels like Rangarang, Kuwait TV and ART, all of which we carry. We'll continue to evaluate additions to our FiOS TV lineup against expressed customer interests as well as other factors." Other systems gave similar responses.[27]

In August 2011, AJE gained footing on New York's large Time Warner Cable network but in a most unusual way. It made an arrangement with an entrepreneurial minor broadcast channel, WRNN-TV, which had a "must carry" arrangement with cable systems and also had obtained digital channels as part of their operation. WRNN's Rise Channel gave more than twenty-three hours to Al Jazeera English in a permissible sublet of the channel. The arrangement gave the channel grudging access to more than 2 million homes. It was still a jerry-built arrangement but one that caused grumblings by those who considered it "Terror Television," at the worst, or more biased than was suitable.[28]

In 2013, Al Jazeera, drawing on the vast reservoir of Qatari wealth, acquired the low-impact news-related satellite channel, Current TV, owned by a consortium led by Albert Gore. Through this transaction, Al Jazeera essentially obtained, at a very high premium, access to 40 million U.S. cable homes and a shot at greater legitimacy.[29] A new channel, titled Al Jazeera America, was the vehicle created to provide the Qatar-based network a fresh start in the United States.[30] As a result of that foothold, Al Jazeera America gained more cable system penetration, although not with all major U.S. cable systems. Interestingly, its programming strategy was to be more intensely attuned to "local America" than was the competitor it sought to emulate, CNN. Internationally, Al Jazeera was becoming more of a global institution with global credibility, global influence and global reach. Qatar had achieved a strategic goal, becoming an even greater and more significant actor in developments in the Middle East and North Africa region and undergirding that status with a powerful international broadcasting presence.

---

[27] Ibid.

[28] Stewart Ain, "Concern Over Al Jazeera English Network Here," *The Jewish Week*, August 9, 2011.

[29] Brian Stelter, "Al Jazeera Seeks an English Voice where Al Gore Failed," *New York Times*, January 2, 2013. Following the announcement of the acquisition, Time Warner Cable, which reaches 12 million households, announced that it would drop the low-ranked Current TV (and thus Al Jazeera America) from its lineup. See Michael Calderone, "Time Warner Cable Drops Current TV Upon Sale to Al Jazeera," *Huffington Post*, February 1, 2013.

[30] For an example of the immediate negative reports, see Cliff Kincaid, "Gore's Deal now a Major Scandal," *Accuracy in Media*, March 8, 2013.

IMPLICATING SATELLITE GOVERNANCE

Two other examples are useful: Al Zawraa, a channel developed in the wake of the Iraq War, and Al Manar, identified with Hezbollah. Both these examples illustrate efforts to intervene and block entry at the point where the channel seeks transponder use. These cases are about the search for "choke points" or bottlenecks where power can be exercised. Both cases also illustrate the process by which a legal system plays catch up with technological developments.

Al Zawraa

Al Zawraa started as a terrestrial broadcast channel in Iraq, licensed by the post-Saddam liberalizing authority, with an audience-pleasing entertainment format. Its evolution must be seen in the context of the struggle by an occupying power, together with officials of the new Iraq, to manage information flows in a post-conflict environment.[31] Owned by Mishan Al Jaburi, a leader of the Sunni Arab Front for Reconciliation and Liberation, the channel over time became intensely politicized. It transformed into what Ibrahim al-Marashi and others have called insurrectionist television,[32] playing, among other things, repeated videos of jihadist bombings with footage of attacks against the United States and multinational forces. In November 2006, the Iraqi government ordered the station to be closed down and its offices in Iraq shuttered on charges of "inciting violence and murder."[33]

Banned from using transmitters in Iraq, Al Jaburi staked the future of the channel on a satellite strategy, leasing channels on Egyptian-owned Nilesat. The channel's campaign intensified, broadcasting what one observer called "a blend of pro-insurgent propaganda, video clips of attacks on Coalition forces and calls for violence against Iraqi Shi'is and the Iraqi government." It featured "audio messages from the Islamic Army of Iraq, an insurgent group dominated by the Iraqi Ba'th Party loyal to former president Saddam

---

[31]   Monroe E. Price, Douglas Griffin and Ibrahim al-Marashi, *Toward an Understanding of Media Policy and Media Systems in Iraq: A Foreword and Two Reports*, CGCS Occasional Paper Series, Number 1 – May 2007 (Philadelphia: Center for Global Communication Studies, Annenberg School for Communication, University of Pennsylvania).

[32]   Ibrahim al-Marashi, "The Dynamics of Iraq's Media: Ethno-Sectarian Violence, Political Islam, Public Advocacy, and Globalization," *Cardozo Arts & Entertainment Law Journal* 25, no. 1 (2007).

[33]   Andy Sennitt, "Iraq: US Blacklists Al-Zawraa TV," *BBC Monitoring*, January 10, 2008.

Husayn."[34] An American blogger described showing the Al Zawraa feed to U.S. soldiers and Iraqis:

> The images include destroyed mosques, dead women and children, women weeping of the death of their family, bloodstained floors, the destruction of U.S. humvees and armored vehicles, and insurgents firing mortars, RPGs, rockets and AK-47s. Juba, the mythical Iraqi sniper, was featured prominently. ... The "mujahideen" are portrayed as "freedom fighters," and are seen going through "boot camp training." Attacks from across the country were shown, including in Abu Ghraib, Ramadi, Fallujah, Baiji, Baghdad and elsewhere.[35]

This was a form of what I called, in Chapter 5, "asymmetric communication." Al Zawraa became the voice of a relatively weak player finding technological holes and opportunities to enter the Iraqi market for allegiances, using an Egyptian satellite as its technology of choice. Where could the offended powers find relief? Angered U.S. officials began discussions with the Egyptian government to urge them to terminate the Al Zawraa transponder lease on Egypt-controlled Nilesat. A report on Cairo's *Al-Misriyun* newspaper website in early 2007 said the U.S. ambassador in Cairo had asked Egyptian Information Minister Anas al-Fiqi to "pull the plug on the channel," on the pretext that it constituted the last weapon in the hands of those he described as the Sunni "rebels" in Iraq. The minister initially declined the ambassador's request, arguing that the broadcasting of the channel was purely an apolitical business transaction. Ultimately, threats made by supporters of the Shi'i Al-Mahdi Army (affiliated with Muqtada al-Sadr) to attack and kill members of the Egyptian diplomatic mission in Baghdad if the channel was not struck constituted enough pressure to drive Egypt to backtrack.[36] Superficially, Nilesat officials continued to resist the pressure and persist in the argument that carriage was merely a contractual matter. The Nilesat chair was reported as saying in *Al-Masry Al-Youm* that "Satellites do not monitor the channels they are carrying. Accordingly, the Egyptian satellite should not be part of the dispute regarding the channel. It is the right of whoever is hurt by the material broadcast by Al-Zawraa to respond through their channels or media."[37]

---

[34] Peter Feuilherade, "Egypt Row Brews Over Iraqi Sunni Channel Al-Zawraa on Nilesat," *BBC Monitoring*, January 9, 2007.
[35] Bill Roggio, "Al-Zawraa: Muj TV," *The Long War Journal*, December 10, 2006; Bill Roggio, "Al-Zawraa Responds to Muj TV," *The Long War Journal*, December 25, 2006.
[36] Feuilherade, "Egypt Row Brews."
[37] Ibid.

With the threat of being ejected from Nilesat, Al Jaburi claimed the station would soon be carried "on three satellites from European countries."[38] By late January, Al Zawraa was observed to be broadcasting via the Saudi-owned Arabsat and France-based Eutelsat.[39] In February, the Nilesat transmission was closed after Nilesat accused the station of technical interference with other channels;[40] in April, the French regulator required Eutelsat to stop transmission over Eutelsat's transponders, claiming that the station's broadcasting of propaganda was in breach of France's 1881 law of freedom of the press and of the September 30, 1986 law prohibiting stations from incitement to hate and violence for reasons of religion or nationality.[41] Finally, on January 9, 2008, Al Jaburi and Al Zawraa were placed on the U.S. sanctions list and precluded from any financial transactions with U.S. citizens or companies, a category with global implications.[42] According to *Intelligence Online*:

> On Jan. 9, the U.S. Treasury published a list of several individuals and entitles subject to financial sanctions for backing Iraqi insurgents. Among them was the Iraqi politician Misham Al Jabouri and the satellite television channel he runs out of Damascus, *Al Zawraa*. Since October, 2006, the station continually ran messages and video clips shot by Sunni Baa'thist militia in their fight against American troops in Iraq. . . .
>
> Starting from last spring, only the Pan-Arab operator Arabsat, which is majority-owned by Saudi Arabia, continued to broadcast Al Zawraa via its *Badr3* and *Arabsat 2B* satellites. The State Department complained in vain to Riyadh before opting for a more aggressive strategy. In March, the frequency on which Al Zawraa broadcasted on Badr 3 (11747 Mhz) was constantly jammed, forcing the station to cease its programs before switching to another frequency (11765 MHz).[43]

Al Zawraa was a minor player, a nuisance. But its wily efforts to remain irritatingly visible maddened Iraqi and U.S. officials. The level of official frustration with Al Zawraa, and the inability to locate and deny production

---

[38]   Lawrence Pintak, "War of Ideas: Insurgent Channel Coming to a Satellite Near You," *USC Center on Public Diplomacy*, January 10, 2007.

[39]   See "Iraqi Sunni Al Zawra TV Now Carried on Saudi Based Arabsat," *BBC Worldwide Monitoring*, January 26, 2007; "Iraqi Sunni Al Zawra TV Now Broadcasting on European Satellite," *BBC Worldwide Monitoring*, January 31, 2007.

[40]   "Egypt Takes Militant Iraqi Channel Off Air," *Daily Star*, February 26, 2007.

[41]   Government of France, "Décision n° 2007–293 du 3 avril 2007 mettant en demeure la société Eutelsat SA," May 20, 2007.

[42]   See "Treasury Designates Individuals, Entity Fueling Iraqi Insurgency," *U.S. Department of the Treasury*, September 1, 2008.

[43]   "U.S. Pulls Plug on Insurgent TV," *Intelligence Online*, January 17, 2008.

facilities or access to distribution facilities, was resolved with the dramatic step of placement on the sanctions list.

Al Manar and Sovereignty

I end this litany of disruptive examples with the complex story of Al Manar, the Hezbollah-related broadcasting station based in Lebanon.[44] In the 1990s and after, Al Manar expanded vigorously from Lebanon to include satellite distribution of channels targeting Arabic populations throughout Europe and beyond. Significantly, it deployed on a satellite owned and adminis- tered by France-based Eutelsat. Because of its function as the voice of Hezbollah, Al Manar was always in the cross hairs of state and non-state actors seeking to block its access to a global market and reduce its effective- ness. In 2004, Al Manar was accused, in Paris, of distributing anti-Semitic programming through its satellite channel in violation of French standards. Much can be said of the merits of this claim, but the point here involves the structure of reaction. Al Manar originally presented a jurisdictional and governance crisis. Because the channel did not originate in France, nor indeed in the EU, the question arose whether France had the power to restrict its distribution.

Enacting special legislation, the French Parliament bestowed on the Conseil Superieur de l'Audiovisuel (CSA) – the general broadcasting regulation agency – explicit authority to prosecute, but questions were raised about the legality of that action. The CSA president, while expressing dismay about the controversial programming, highlighted the difficulties presented to the agency when dealing with channels established outside the European Union. A Eutelsat press release stated that the organization shared the CSA's "indignation expressed on (the) broadcasting of racist programmes," while making it clear that Eutelsat itself had no right of censure over the channels it carries.[45]

---

[44] The relationship between Al Manar and Hezbollah has been described as follows: "In 1991, shortly after Hezbollah actively entered the Lebanese political scene, Al Manar was launched as a small terrestrial station. Although legally registered as the Lebanese Media Group Company in 1997, Al Manar has belonged to Hezbollah culturally and politically from its inception. Today, the terrestrial station can reach Lebanon in its entirety and broadcasts programming eighteen hours daily. Moreover, Al Manar's satellite station, launched in 2000, transmits twenty-four hours a day, reaching the entire Arab world and the rest of the globe through several major satellite providers. One of the satellite providers which have transmitted Al Manar has been the French satellite Hot Bird 4, owned by the Eutelsat Satellite organisa- tion." See "EU Rules and Principles on Hate Broadcasting: Frequently Asked Questions," *European Union*, March 17, 2005.

[45] "Cooperation Between Eutelsat and the CSA," February 3, 2004.

A month later, however, the CSA announced a new theory. It asserted that because the channel was uplinked to Eutelsat and Eutelsat is a French company, the broadcasts (or at least the satellite carrier) were susceptible to regulation. This was a substantial volte-face. The CSA and Eutelsat began a policy of cooperation to check television channels transmitted by Eutelsat (but originating outside the EU) for conformity to European legislation. In relatively short order, the CSA requested the Conseil d'Etat to order Eutelsat to stop transmitting Al Manar. By late 2004, Al Manar obliged voluntarily.

As in the Al Zawraa case, invoking national security became decisive. In 2004, Al Manar was also placed on the U.S. Terrorist Exclusion List and subjected to all the sanctions consequent to that status (including making it impossible for U.S. providers of satellite leasing time to deal with the channel).[46] Yet the issues concerning Al Manar continued to reverberate, partly because of efforts by Israel and by U.S. activist groups to block the channel in countries around the world.[47] Those who condemned Al Manar tracked the channel and its efforts to expand, bringing public pressures to bear wherever in the world Al Manar sought to deliver a signal. Organized monitors in Washington and elsewhere devoted substantial resources to policing Al Manar's efforts to diffuse its message on various platforms and to persuading governments to block it.[48]

SATELLITE ACCESS AND INSTITUTIONAL ADJUSTMENTS

The strategic encounter between Al Manar and France occurred several decades after the first murmurs of concern about satellite regulation occurred in the United Nations. But the experiences of the 1990s and the early years of the new millennium had presented aggravated examples of efforts, using satellite signals, not only to bring disruptive and potentially destabilizing ideas to new markets, but to do so where regulatory approaches were poorly developed or conceptualized. This was not necessarily a question of censorship, broadly defined. It also involved conceptualizing international norms, institutions and frameworks for decision. Two examples – one from Europe and one from the Middle East – illustrate the issue.

---

[46] "Addition of Al-Manar to the Terrorist Exclusion List," *U.S. Department of State*, December 28, 2004.

[47] Franklin Lamb, "Australia Rejects Israeli Ordered Media Censorship on Al-Manar," *Foreign Policy Journal*, December 20, 2010.

[48] An example of the effort is Avi Jorisch, *Beacon of Hatred: Inside Hizballah's Al-Manar Television* (Washington, DC: Washington Institute for Near East Policy, 2004).

The European Union

The Al Manar case became an intermediate step in terms of efforts to shape a systematic approach to satellite-carried channels, a concerted European response to signals that come from outside the EU. In March 2005 (after the Al Manar decision), EU officials recognized that difficulties would arise if it were only up to those few states with jurisdiction over satellite providers to police what might be generically called hate speech issues. Better coordination among the states would be essential. The bureaucracy declared that "The free movement of TV broadcasting services in the EU is governed by rules that aim to promote the growth of an EU-wide market in broadcasting and related activities. . . . Freedom of expression and of the Media on the one hand and respect for human dignity on the other hand are essential values underlying the EU rules. . . . Member States shall ensure that broadcasts do not contain any incitement to hatred on grounds of race, sex, religion or nationality."[49] But how would these potentially conflicting goals be harmonized? Which member state would assert authority, or would each member state impose its own rules over these trans-community signals?

Complicated arrangements ensued to embody these European principles. It is normally the responsibility of the "country of origin" member state to regulate satellite channels. If, as was the case with Al Manar, the satellite channel originates in a third country outside the EU, different rules apply.[50] After 2007, the rules were broadened so that more states had the possibility to regulate. By March 2006, the regulators in the member states had supported the Commission's proposal to launch a new Cooperation Forum to implement their "commitment to combat clear cases of incitement to hatred in broadcast and audiovisual media services whilst scrupulously respecting the Fundamental freedoms enshrined in the EU Charter of Fundamental Rights and the need for judicial scrutiny of such interventions by broadcast regulators."[51]

From the perspective of strategic communication, the EU approach marked a point of critical self-perception. It acknowledged that the existing system of regulating satellite channels had a substantial gap and that that gap should be addressed. Officials realized that disruptive users of satellite technologies could easily break national boundaries, enter the public sphere

[49] "EU Rules and Principles."
[50] Among other texts, see Lyombe S. Eko, *New Media, Old Regimes: Case Studies in Comparative Communication Law and Policy* (Lanham: Rowman & Littlefield, 2012).
[51] "European Broadcasting Regulators Strengthen Their Cross-Border Cooperation Under the Television Without Frontiers Directive," *European Union*, March 24, 2006.

despite an emergent and common set of standards and make the assertion of state power difficult. The result was European in style: inclusive, consultative and baroque. In its European fashion, the result claimed both to be consistent with principles of freedom of expression while ensuring that a signal's journey from communicator to target audience should be, in specified subject matter areas, subject to review and modification, channeling and blocking.

The Arab Satellite Broadcasting Charter

The European solution – allowing existing authorities to be more effective in policing channels of communication – was a significant moment in the little understood history of transponder regulation for another reason: It influenced policies elsewhere. The European example was crudely copied. The rather half-hearted effort to establish and enforce an Arab Satellite Broadcasting Charter stands as an example of a cartel seeking to police voices that had the potential to disrupt existing authorities. The Charter, initiated before the Arab Spring, was an attempt to render more formal the existing awkward, behind-the-scenes negotiations over what signals and programs should or should not be carried on regionally controlled satellites. It would be superimposed on an existing pattern of satellite signal delivery dominated by Egypt and Saudi Arabia through their ownership and control of Nilesat and Arabsat, respectively.

In February 2008, ministers of information of the Arab League met to develop a regional document that would reduce the increasing dangers that widely open skies were posing to closed political systems.[52] Their unusual meeting – there had been few if any similarly regional agreements – was an indication of deep anxieties. The meeting reflected great frustration occasioned by the extraordinary abundance of satellite signals that were reshaping flows of information in the region.[53] The ministers were guilty of strategic nostalgia: seeking to restore a pattern in the region where almost all broadcast programming was controlled at the state level. The wall of information control that had long undergirded their states was crumbling.

These ministers of information were particularly concerned by the damage to the status quo that had already occurred because of the programming

---

[52] See "Arab Satellite Broadcasting Charter: Principles for Regulating Satellite Broadcasting Transmission in the Arab World (Unofficial Translation)," *Arab Media & Society*, February 2008.

[53] See "Arab TV Broadcasters Face Curbs," *BBC News*, February 12, 2008.

of Al Jazeera. What brought them together that February, what virtually united them, was the effectiveness of the Qatari network. Certainly, some Arab states had previously barred the sale of receiving dishes to control the impact of satellite programming; in some contexts there was a climate of intimidation for receiving certain signals. But the arrival of Al Jazeera in 1996 brought a sea change. By aggressively covering politics in many Middle Eastern capitals, Al Jazeera was able to tap into a regional audience hungry to receive more thorough news about their leaders, to the immense frustration of the Arab states.[54] The channel was further legitimated because its source was regional, professional according to global standards and supported by a Qatari base.

One can infer the fears that gave birth to the Charter by reading the regional standards that the signatories articulated. The Charter went far beyond the system of its mild European counterpart. The satellite providers in the region were directed, according to the Charter, not to accept programming that would "jeopardize social peace, national unity, public order and general propriety."[55] Under the Charter (similar to the European resolution), the satellite entities were to adopt standards requiring them to abstain from inciting hatred or ethnic, color, racial or religious discrimination and from broadcasting any material that would incite violence and terrorism (interestingly, differentiating between terrorism and "resisting occupation"). But then it veered to capture a larger and more regionally relevant agenda. The Charter discouraged providers from broadcasting anything that would insult God, revealed religions, prophets, *mazhabs* (religious schools) and religious symbols (with the groups included not fully identified); from broadcasting and programming any material that included obscene scenes or dialogue or pornography; from broadcasting any material that would encourage smoking or alcohol drinking; and from describing crimes of any form or kind in a tempting way, implying that the crime or its predators are heroes or justifying the crime's motives. The satellite providers were instructed to protect children from anything that would abuse their physical, mental or ethical growth or corrupt their manners or encourage wrongdoings and to comply with the religious and ethical values of the Arab society to maintain its familial ties and social integrity.[56]

Additional notes melded modernization with ancient concerns. The satellite broadcasters, according to the Charter, were to furnish "the largest

---

[54] Marc Lynch, *Voices of the New Arab Public: Iraq, Al-Jazeera, and Middle East Politics Today* (New York: Columbia University Press, 2006).

[55] "Arab Satellite Broadcasting Charter."

[56] Ibid.

number possible of programmes and services to maintain the Arab identity and the Islamic culture and values and to highlight the Arab contribution to human civilization,"[57] and were to promote dialogue and understanding among different cultures. And there was an umbrella of political regional integration to the Charter in the call for satellite agencies to "maintain Arab identity against the negative impact of globalization and reaffirm the specificity of the Arab world."[58] Satellite providers would consider ways of "enriching the character of the Arab citizen" and reinforcing "integrity and intellectual, cultural, social and political development."[59] The Charter, consistent with a penchant for stability, articulated a policy of avoiding the broadcast of "anything that would contradict or jeopardize Arab solid-arity."[60] And, of course, carried channels were not to insult leaders or national or religious symbols.

The Charter could be seen as giving additional political cover to sclerotic governments that wished to impose more restrictions, governments that would soon see the kinds of activities that they feared might occur in an era of freer expression and media-driven mobilization. Early on, there were accounts that the Charter served to justify additional restrictions in Mubarak's Egypt in contracts for the use of Nilesat; such restrictions would also be imposed on the use of production facilities in media cities in Egypt and elsewhere. But the Charter was so cumbersome as to be ineffective, and certainly, post–Arab Spring it became a distant relic in the ensuing political turmoil. From the outset, Qatar and Lebanon did not agree to be included in the cartel; Qatar, of course, because of its relationship with Al Jazeera and Lebanon because of its history of producing popular and adventurous satel-lite channels for the region.[61] In retrospect it can be seen as a precedent for "soft regulation"; standards were designed as a "code of honor," a matter for self-regulation rather than state enforcement. The concerns articulated would continue to inform the actions of regional governments,[62] even

---

57   Ibid.
58   Ibid.
59   Ibid.
60   Ibid.
61   For an enlightening introduction to satellite programming in the region, see Marwan Kraidy, "Arab Satellite Television, Between Regionalization and Globalization," *Global Media Journal* 1, no. 1 (2002).
62   In the Syrian conflict, in 2013, echoes of the Charter debate arose; the Arab League, which then opposed the Assad regime, resolved that the two main Arab satellite TV providers, Arabsat and Nilesat, should block all official Syrian government channels. The rationale was that Syrian media were consistently "misleading." The National Syrian Media Council issued a statement that the Arab League decision was "a blatant interference in Syria's internal affairs, an

post–Arab Spring, and the notes that it struck would reemerge in subsequent regulatory approaches.[63]

CONCLUSION

I have sought to recite a truncated pocket of reactions to the opportunities provided by satellite technologies, as entities, large and small, jostled to innovate and take advantage of regulatory lacunae. This is a story of how content disrupters maneuvered where there was no comprehensive legal regime and incumbents, including existing state powers, sought to protect their turf. In the early days of satellite communication, dreams and plans oscillated between imagined technologies of freedom and formal and informal mechanisms of state control. Satellite regulation on a global or even a regional level proved daunting; commercial leasing of transponder space overwhelmed content control. It is a study in capitalism as a facilitator of an architecture of information distribution. States have had to resort to a variety of direct and indirect techniques to manage access to which signals land in their territory and reach their populations.

Where is freedom of expression in this debate? The examples I have used in this chapter demonstrate the fragility, almost the absence, of law as a mode of discriminating between expression that should be free and expression that is marked as too hateful or destabilizing. What I have illustrated here is a system in which formal law – even formal agreements among countries – hardly describes the range of actions concerning sensitive content on satellites and cannot adequately capture the norms that are emerging. The debate over satellite signal distribution originally was marked by free expression rhetoric and passions as well as explicit concerns over

unprecedented assault on the freedom of the media in the Arab world and a brazen attempt to conceal the reality of what is happening in the Syrian territories." Writing for the Abu Dhabi-based paper *Al Ittihad*, UAE journalist Ahmed Al Mansouri criticized Syrian broadcasting for its steady narrative seeking to delegitimize the opposition: "Most of their coverage is basically a reporting of the unchanging rhetoric of Syrian officials: Syria is a target of a conspiracy, and terrorists and armed groups paid by Gulf states are trying to undermine the country's security and stability. ... The managers of Arabsat and Nilesat have a moral responsibility here ... because the question is no longer about respecting freedom of speech, it's about responding to channels that promote deadly propaganda, which innocent Syrians pay for with their lives." See "Blocking of Syrian Television is Justified," *National*, June 6, 2012.

63 It may also be seen as a harbinger of efforts at regional standard-setting. Shortly after the Arab Charter was adopted, a similar but rather more informal mechanism was proposed for the Euro-Mediterranean Partnership (EuroMed), a regional grouping comprising relevant EU member states and proximate Middle East and North African countries. See "Agreed Conclusions of the Third Euro-Mediterranean Conference of Ministers of Culture," *Euromed*, May 29–30, 2008.

sovereignty. In a sense, that has been reduced to a series of commercial undertakings, inter-state understandings and novel political arrangements. Satellite distribution has become a complex history of interactions among strategic communicators, often shielded from pervasive institutional review. Future writers will see, in this history, a preface or rehearsal for the jurisdictional, technological and institutional challenges presented by the Internet.

12

Strategies of Closure, Markers of Anxiety

I have titled this book *Free Expression, Globalism and the New Strategic Communication*. But what, in the end, is "new" about this process, or put differently, what is *significantly* new? Mass efforts at persuasion are hardly unknown, nor is assiduous use of whatever technology becomes newly available. What differentiates the present is an accumulation of factors. Newness resides in a combination of elements, including global scale, the multipolarity of clashing narratives and the extraordinary nature of the technology that strategic communicators can exploit. Among these are novel combinations of techniques that ambitious communicators deploy in advancing their objectives: strategic diagnostics, strategic narratives and the building of strategic architectures. Current embodiments of strategic communication are also "new" because of the explosion of data available for analysis and because of the social media techniques for instrumentalizing that data. Dizzying and confounding asymmetries give rise to sudden ascendancies for newly coined or long-suppressed viewpoints.

And there is one additional level of newness, not new as in unheralded, but new in application and intensity. Given the sharply competing innovations for the media and communications infrastructure, there is intense competition for Daniel McCarthy and others "technological closure."[1] Closure is a prize because, if and when it occurs, what was subject to debate becomes accepted as a norm. Technological closure exists when, in McCarthy's phrase, the innovation or process "no longer strikes its users as interesting or novel."[2] In this sense, obtaining closure can be the highest challenge to strategic communicators. It is, in a sense, acceptance of the strategy itself. Strategic

---

[1] Daniel R. McCarthy, "Open Networks and the Open Door: American Foreign Policy and the Narration of the Internet," *Foreign Policy Analysis* 7, (2010): 90. McCarthy draws on Andrew Feenberg, *Critical Theory of Technology* (Oxford, Oxford University Press, 1991).
[2] McCarthy, "Open Networks," 90.

communicators seek closure around ideas of freedom of expression, around ideas of history and legitimacy, and, of course, over the deployment of the technologies themselves.

Technological closure occurs differently in different societies. The audience for closure might be a floating group of global policy wonks; it might be members of an active public sphere or it might be citizens resigned to the decisions of their government. But the essence of technological closure is that the way of thinking about the processes becomes taken for granted.[3] It this very quality – the taken for grantedness – that is a significant source of power of the arrangement. Technological innovations are dependent for effectiveness, in part, on a constructed vision of political and social arrangements, often elaborate and often historically rooted. The goal – for strategic communicators – is to obtain deep and long-term support for their mode of thinking about an approach to media.

Partly, this means that what is "new" about strategic communication is no single factor or characteristic, but the aggregate of influences. The new strategic communication encompasses the disruptive technologies, the rise of social media, the capacity to aggregate these and other approaches. These become building blocks of an intense era for transnational instruments of elite persuasion and mass information. How they are amassed and deployed is significant for understanding power and international relations in a globalized world. It is too early fully to fathom the stakes of the move to a new level of engagement in the structure of information flows, but the vector and direction become observable. And the stronger, more global, more strategic the communication, the more complex the challenge to principles of freedom of expression. Changes and transmutations in strategic communication both advance ideas of free expression and complicate them. The strategic element is gaining assurance that a particular approach is the surviving, hopeful, possibly dominant one. An approach to understanding this evolution involves the prism of technology and closure.

This schema for the acceptance of technological systems is useful for this book. Societies are attempting both to instill norms and disrupt them. Surveillance and security are examples of this. Around what set of practices should a norm be established? in the face of newly perceived evils, Western governments huddle to reexamine what was assessed as adequate. A continuing set of skirmishes exists to bring Internet governance to some settled stage, and competing tropes are repeatedly invoked to justify one approach or another. States, businesses, civil society and international governmental organizations all seek to steer the debate. Each group seeks to produce an

---

3   Ibid.

enveloping and comforting account of the technology and its role in society that is strategically relevant and that supports a particular governing approach.

Principles of freedom of expression can be understood in this framework of competing entities seeking to shape an overall approach that becomes settled and accepted. It was a long process, over centuries, for a nuanced understanding of freedom of expression to evolve that was specific to a print society, one featuring primarily newspapers and books. And even there that consensus had regional and otherwise limited circumscription. The last half of the twentieth century saw efforts to settle ideas and institutions for the electronic media and their relation to freedom of expression. These were decisions often cabined in specific language relating to scarcity of spectrum or the power of television images on children. A consensus on these matters was hard to achieve and, of course, is still ongoing (relating, for example, to the role of public service media or depictions of sexual activity and violence). Article 19 of the International Covenant on Civil and Political Rights and Article 10 of the European Convention were efforts, episodically successful, to reach consensus on approaches to transfrontier communications. The requisite consensus on the governance of new information technologies, including social media and the Internet and its governance, may not yet be at hand. So dramatic, so disruptive are events, ranging from the reorganization of the book industry to the reconfiguration of mobilization and protest, that once more or less agreed-upon freedom of expression positions become open to question.

INTERNET GOVERNANCE

I return, once more, to ways the U.S. State Department and the White House – in competition with those proposing other systems – have sought to make "Internet freedom" the conclusive narrative of a global Internet. Hardly alone, and building on the extraordinary success of technology advances, these government officials emphasize how a minimally encumbered Internet can be the imagined fulfillment of hopes for free expression, human rights and democracy. Creating and establishing that hopeful narrative of legitimacy has been a long-term effort requiring the work of not only government and civil society but of transnational companies like Google, as well as academics and others.

Gaining acceptance of this narrative also shapes the international norm and with it ways of thinking about ensuring freedom of expression. The benefits of legitimacy are conferred when for a particular technology, like the Internet, there is "the stabilization of an artifact and the 'disappearance' of problems."[4]

---

[4]   Ibid, citing Pinch and Bijker 1987:44; Feenberg 1999:97.

This condition only occurs, as McCarthy and others suggest, when relevant social groups see important definitional issues as being more or less resolved. Additional institutions, as a consequence, would then more likely fall into line and act according to the desired standard. The lesson is extremely useful and for closure to occur, the proper cultural and symbolic understandings must be nourished and sustained.

Controlling the high ground of contention does not solve all problems, but it provides sweep and direction. Achieving a level of acceptedness softens the circumstances in which additional issues are treated. Closure could make it more likely that certain companies would be absolved of intermediary liability. Closure could reduce exceptions for rights to receive and impart information. Closure might help resolve difficult questions over jurisdiction. General settlement around the Internet freedom agenda almost automatically incorporates attitudes toward global Internet governance, including the role of civil society and a more limited role for agreements among states (identified in Internet governance parlance as multilateralism).

And it is here that, as a study in strategic communication, the disclosures, in 2013, of depictions of massive global surveillance by the United States and its National Security Agency become relevant. By then, the open Internet or Internet freedom narrative was ascendant, but had not yet been perfectly and globally accepted as the "natural" and settled narrative. Much progress had been made in that direction; at least in the minds of its proponents, the freedom narrative had become the widely accepted, perhaps default account of what an Internet should be, with every new measure (such as those involving domain names, net neutrality, filtering, transparency and privacy) evaluated in terms of conformity to that prevailing narrative. China and Russia, Brazil and Iran were states for whom a counter-narrative remained vital and contesting.

Revelations of broad internal and extraterritorial surveillance produced a partial check on progress in establishing Internet freedom as the established norm. The inference arising from accounts of the NSA (an inference long suggested yet never realized so powerfully) was that the new technologies, even while advancing freedom of expression goals, could also be an instrument for subverting the very same objectives. Persistent surveillance, made possible by the structure of the Internet, could be seen as potentially undermining rights to receive and impart information. The global "One Internet" concept was, in some way, hoisted by its own petard. Advocates had built much of the argument for the Internet – as they saw its design – on the normative value of human rights in the struggle against alternative conceptions of the new technology. The Internet had been engineered for free flow; that was its bias.

Now, cruelly, the arguments for "One Internet" and seamlessness could be turned against its dedicated supporters. Approaches that were hailed as "technologies of freedom" became tarred, at least for the moment, as engines of surveillance. International trust as a foundation for thousands of public and private arrangements was eroded, and the potential for closure around the Internet freedom narrative declined, although there were rapid efforts at repair. Too great were the questions at stake for the narrative setback to be conclusive. Yet Internet governance became subject to the unsettled status of greater re-examination.

These events also demonstrated how much of international discourse and much strategic communication is based on a suspension of disbelief (in this case the willingness to take for granted the benign face of the new technologies and the collective wish for the opiate quality of closure). The surveillance disclosures impaired what might have continued as virtually unquestioning support for relatively unquestioned innovation. Now, words that signified one thing before the disclosures had somewhat different implications after. Altruism, industrial optimism and concepts of freedom all became recrystallized or remixed, affected by the shifting waves of public information and ensuing debate.

Brazil sought to assume a mantle of leadership. At the UN and in speeches at home, President Dilma Rouseff offered her own vision of the Internet. One suggested element, for example, might be requiring foreign-based Internet companies to maintain data centers inside Brazil. This step, not realized, would have been consequential in that these foreign companies would be governed by Brazilian privacy (and presumably other) laws. Asserting sovereignty in this way, as Brazil proposed, would trigger an alternate narrative pathway to closure, one that was attractive for many states opposed, often for troubling reasons, to the "One Internet" umbrella of ideas.

Asserting sovereignty is hardly novel. Here, again, what is specifically unusual is the context in which sovereignty is asserted – a world of data transmission, servers and complex software codes. In a sense, much of the history of all media regulation is composed of relinquishing and reasserting sovereignty over technologies that have transnational potential. As I indicated in earlier chapters, this was true of radio, of television and of satellite. And it is true of the Internet. One way to describe a set of responses to the objective of the transnational involves what might be called "domestication:" quite complex and sometimes desperate efforts to take what would be a disruptive technology and, essentially, make it perform, to the extent possible, according to the norms that bound deliverers of information that preceded it, often confining the technology's impact within extant political borders. Domestication defeats innovation, but it can serve the needs of those in power. Domestication does not need to be complete. There is always some level of uncontrollable change. A government seeking to domesticate new media entrants often singles out preferred beneficiaries who receive the advantages of new technologies while denying them to the populous as a whole. It may merely slow adoption, but otherwise be sensitive to the demands of the public.

How does domestication take place? Domestication can take place by bilateral agreement. A long-ago agreement between Mexico and the United States is a relatively minor example, in which each country arranged to place transmitters so they would have minimal impact on the spectrum allocation of the other (the effort was not wholly successful).[5] Domestication takes place by international treaty, for example through the ITU, which has its rules concerning purposeful "spillover" or transmitted cross-border projection of a broadcast signal. Domestication takes place through informal pressures, one state upon another, or pressure by a state against a lessor of transponder space on a satellite. It proceeds by seeking to create technological borders, as in the proposed Intranet in Iran.

There is a full-court press, in fora around the world, to instill what should become generally agreed approaches to the Internet, a hoped for closure. Civil society, through such mechanisms as the Internet Governance Forum and other offshoots of the United Nations' World Summit on the Information Society, engage with states, corporations and international governmental organizations to influence the outcome. Cyberwar and cybersecurity issues loom as a trumping aspect of debate. From this cauldron of discussion, way stations of accommodation and patterns of governance will evolve.

STRATEGIC COMMUNICATION AND SOCIAL MEDIA

How we think about social media and free expression can be subjected to this closure-related analysis as well. There has been a generally optimistic naturalization of these innovations. Social media are represented, particularly in the West, as usually beneficial, with narrowly construed exceptions (for child pornography, for example, or Holocaust denial or, more broadly, hate speech). Social media, as represented, hits all the categories for furthering freedom of expression. It is celebrated for its potential for amplifying individual autonomy and for expanding deliberative opportunities. Yet, for YouTube, Facebook and similar entities, there is a danger that the march toward a satisfying

[5]   Agreement Concerning Frequency Modulation Broadcasting in the 87.5 to 108 MHz Band, November 9, 1972.

naturalization in which these powerful players are seen as benign could be pushed back, forcing more emphasis on the challenges, Here the danger is not necessarily or only potential bullying on Facebook, exposure to child pornography or hate speech. In many contexts, social media are seen as disruptive of local cultures and local political arrangements, an instrument of intrusion by external forces. Closure is impeded by a complex and hazardous set of choices: if management of content is desirable, what should the division of authority be among the jurisdictional state, the user, and the companies along the chain of passage of information? More attention is given to considering how transparent Internet-related companies, particularly the Internet service providers, are, how sensitively they adhere to human rights and freedom of expression requirements and how protective of privacy they are.

There are related factors in play: apprehension about the relationship of the social media entities and the data they control. What seems to be in process, particularly with social media, is a profound reworking of the relationship between the sender and the receiver of information. On an increasingly large scale, a key feature of a seemingly ordinary exchange is gaining the unknowing or unwilling surrender of personal data. That data, in comprehensive and integrated abundance, allows strategic analysis and consequent action without the subject's formal or meaningful consent. This is part of the same massive shift from a communications model of mere transmission and receipt (if there can be said to be such a model) to a context of studied surveillance and interaction.

These developments have important – but as yet still little-explored – implications for the concepts of free speech and free expression. Speech is enlisted as a cover for a process of data generation and use in which the superficial exchange of information masks the principal basis for the transaction, namely the analysis of feedback data. A shift takes place away from explicit free expression concerns to privacy and notions of consent. Think of the use of these new techniques – social media particularly – as a kind of bait (or clickbait to expand on the vernacular). The goal of the strategist is to prod a subject to provide data that is fodder for use, to provoke a subject not so much to respond literally but to register with sufficient and sufficiently relevant data for processing and mobilization of one kind or another. The strategist can use the data to identify and categorize the recipient and make him or her a candidate for further useful interactions and manipulations. Retrieved data will help determine whether the person exists in a special category for surveillance or whether he or she should be the target of the marketing of products or ideologies.

The intellectual machinery for determining which elements of these transactions are "speech," and which are not, is not yet developed. Every aspect of personhood, the data-producing aspects of being and motion, become elements of expression. Or should these manifestations be otherwise categorized? One reason for confusion is whether the practice of identification and use of information differs materially from the way in which speech normally works, where A puts forth a provocative statement that engages B, B responds, and more speech leads to potential persuasion. Perhaps there should be a category of "speech as bait" that is qualitatively different, offerings for which the consistent and only motive is to elicit a mechanical or data-related response. There are other problems with closure. The technology is so ubiquitous, its impact so pervasive, that there is a public cloaking of closure by the automated processes of consent-based denial. The ordinary user clicks the "I agree" button, confounded, confused or so as to avoid any real consideration of the risks and conditions that the operator of a site denominates as the default setting. Final closure does not exist because of inadequate comfort with this process.

CLASHING NARRATIVES

The ultimate contestation involves narratives and their incorporation in strategies of power. The narratives of consequence here create or question new approaches to legitimacy as well as retaining or delegitimatating old ones. These are often narratives on the edge of conflict or of the destabilization of regimes. Ukraine in 2014, for example, was a cauldron of bristling and combatting narrative claims. The European Union and the United States projected EU-leaning reflections of reality, sometimes backing their strategic narrative with arms; Moscow responded not only with counter-narratives but with support for the use of force. "Separatists," "rebels," privately funded militias, all operated, violently, in the service of various versions of the truth. There were levels within levels: Russian Orthodox and Ukrainian Orthodox clerics enacted a parallel version of the chronicled differences. Thousands died and history was dismembered in a staggeringly clumsy upheaval. The realities among sundered tanks and white-clothed Russian vans were frequently out of kilter with public statements and the competing efforts at generating narratives (often called lies and untruths) stemming from Washington and Paris, Moscow and London, and even Vilnius and Riga. This was competition for redefining Russia's sphere of influence, about the disruption of post-Soviet arrangements, reinforcing fearful questions concerning already tenuous arrangements concerning citizenship, language and borders in the region.

In the Middle East in 2014, where many narratives were, if possible, of even more ancient origin, the binding nature of pre-existing narratives was being sorely tested. What was Syria, what was Iraq, what value was there to boundaries drawn a century before in European capitals and what to make of the existential threats of the Islamic State in Iraq and Syria (ISIS) and its proclamation of a new caliphate? Indeed, stuttering nomenclatures revealed the voids of meaning. Confusion had already reigned over who could agree to what narrative to unseat Syria's Assad. The Kurds, in 2014, saw more opportunity for their hope for a larger, more autonomous, perhaps independent Kurdistan. And a new "coalition of the willing" was hastily assembled to establish a very specific strategic narrative: what should occur to the Islamic State in Iraq and Syria (ISIS) with economic, diplomatic and military power wheeled out to realize the desired objectives? In relation to Israel and the Palestinian Authority, in the wake of the 2014 Gaza war, the strategic narrative of the "two state solution" was in doubt anew. Asymmetries both of force and information warfare led to the recasting, retelling and reframing of Zionism within Israel, in Middle East capitals, and in the United States and Europe.

I have written earlier of the ongoing narrative of a China redefined internally and globally. This has been one of the grand and textbook exercises of strategic communication of our time, and each day sees some playing out of its development and transformation. There is the narrative of China in Asia, its relation to Japan, the Republic of Korea, to Vietnam, Cambodia and Myanmar. There is the narrative of China in Africa. And there is the super narrative of China and the United States and the competing stories they tell the world. Anbin Shi, a faculty member at Peking University, is representative of one perspective on this competition. He asserts that "The long-awaited Spenglerian prophecy of 'the decline of the West' has turned into reality. ... Not surprisingly, the end of the American dream, ... coincides with the emergence of the Chinese Dream..." For Shi, the Chinese dream "significantly diverges from the American dream [in] the perception of the relationship between the self and the other. The American dream is more of an individualist fulfillment than a collectivist goal and agenda. The outcome of American dream is incarnated in a "Great-Gatsby-styled" ascension for an individual, as well as the emergence of the U.S. as the one and the only superpower in the 21st century." In contrast, the Chinese dream, Shi claims, is more attractive to the developing countries, because China, as the world's most populated nation, is rising with "the rest." Indeed, these deeply personalizing, psychological interpretations of national approaches can be applied across a ground that is totalizing in its intensity. And in its totalizing, the pathways to compromise, to strategic narratives of resolution, seem increasingly narrow.

The melding of narrative and the architectures of information flow must be emphasized, as I have described earlier. Narratives are housed in adjusted, sometimes dramatically adjusted, architectures. In his talk about China, Shi discussed this element of implementation of the idea of the "China Dream:

> It is no mere surprise that an ambitious "going abroad" campaign has been implemented since 2009 to counteract the Western media portrayal of China as a mystic player and a rogue donor in the global community. Among others, six media organizations at the "central" level, namely, Xinhua News Agency, People's Daily, China Central Television (CCTV), China Radio International (CRI), China Daily, and China News Service, have become the major beneficiaries of this campaign with tremendous investment and significant expansion of their global reach.

There is a general gearing up for a heightened competition to propagate global narratives. The professionalization and spread of Al Jazeera, including the investment in Al Jazeera Africa, Al Jazeera English and (now) Al Jazeera America, is a major sign of Qatar's commitment to a vehicle that can be used strategically if the opportunity arises. There are other examples: I have referred to the effort behind RT (formerly Russia Today) as a vehicle that can make occasional and long-term narratives about Russia as a player in the complex world more understandable, more accessible, and more attuned to the Kremlin's perspective. Neither China's "going abroad policy" nor Russia or Qatar's media investments are unprecedented. But in sophistication or ambition, in uses of technology, in scope and scale or potential, they represent elements of what is "new" about strategic communication. They combine careful attention to strategic architectures with close supervision of changing narrative opportunities. The Islamic State is backhandedly praised for its information competences, for the use of modern methods for medieval messages.[6]

Throughout this book, a key aspect has been assessing what techniques states have deployed to shift or preserve a particular position in local or regional or global markets for loyalties. We have seen how manipulation of narratives remains a major way to alter, retain and expand allegiances. And we have seen that it is hardly states alone that are engaged in this process of nervously making, preserving or purposely changing markets for loyalties. The relation of these actors to strategic architectures also demonstrates how the new combinations affect principles of freedom of expression. Many strategic communication approaches rely on international norms to justify their global extensions – either as grounds for delivering information to those denied it domestically, as a claim against restrictive practices, or as a general celebration

---

[6]   David Carr, "With Videos of Killings, ISIS Sends Medieval Message by Modern Method," *New York Times*, September 7, 2014.

of a world in which information can be received and imparted regardless of frontiers. Strategic architectures also determine ways to avoid law and legal principles affecting expression by embedding them in software or hardware. In copyright, protectionism now becomes part of the code that accompanies data as much or more than it is a consequence of legal rights and privileges. Structural intervention alters the debate, removing elements of argument over entitlements and restrictions from public discussion. Words and images are more and more subject to private limitations in flow; and states, in their architecture of access to publics, manage routing, manage speed, manage access to servers. The point is that visible and contestable moments where a state is seen formally to censor will become fewer and fewer as additional and new structural arrangements are substituted as controls.

ANXIETIES OF POWER, ANXIETIES OF LOSS

I have reflected on a dichotomy that runs through almost all discourse concerning media and free expression: While destiny seems to lie with the freedom to receive and impart ideas regardless of national boundaries, it would be naïve to see the world as a place where information moves without various forms of restriction.[7] This tension between the anxieties of hope and the anxieties of power is one that, I think, continues to haunt. These are times when vast breakthroughs in information freedom seem ever present and tantalizingly secure. But these are times, as well, when the reorganization of information and society tighten and the world seems to approximate 1984, an Orwellian dystopia, with vast new potential for public control. *Media and Sovereignty* was published in the shadow of 9/11. The ever intense emphasis on national security – and its uses by various governments – had rendered more complex the line between aspiration and reality. The Internet has boomed, though unevenly, satellite distribution has become ubiquitous, social media has blossomed, but mechanisms for control have kept pace, often enveloping and utilizing the new technological opportunities presented by the new advances. Destiny, our constant companion, seems to lie both with enhanced transnational flows of information and with vigorous state resilience.

Anxieties proliferate. The Pakistani author Yasser Latif Hamdani has written, from his vantage point, that "Governments everywhere, be they western democracies or authoritarian regimes or an amalgam of both, are deathly afraid of the power of the internet, this invisible, indivisible and intangible free

---

[7] Monroe E. Price, *Media and Sovereignty: The Global Information Revolution and its Challenge to State Power* (Cambridge, MA: The MIT Press, 2002), 3.

realm that they wish to cordon off and limit within their borders." It is true: Information threatens power. Knowledge destabilizes. But Hamdani downplays the anxiety associated with hope by presenting too sunny a prognosis. "Every attempt," he boldly predicts, "by any state that tries to either limit or monitor the internet will eventually fail terribly." His basis for this prognosis is appealing but not necessarily substantiated. "The road to progress and prosperity," he writes, "lies in ensuring that all our citizens are granted equal access to information freely and without any surveillance. Internet freedom is going to be the key indicator in human freedom and human rights. Let us not allow ourselves to be sold off or manipulated any longer by those conniving powers that be, which wish to exercise control over our thoughts and minds."[8] Hamdani's are stirring sentiments, but the complexities that stand in the way of the realization of this claim are daunting.

Twin anxieties of hope and power not only persist but greatly influence policy and behavior. In a world of anxieties, the demand for strategic communication becomes sharper, with the desire for planning, intervention and certainty often overwhelming the capacities for openness, spontaneity and immunity from supervision. Strategic communicators often seek more effective architectures to control the flows of information; strategic communicators increase the demand for pervasive and subtle diagnostic capacities. And the search for more convincing narratives increases as well. They play on the rhythmic divide between aspiration and reality. These anxieties have as their feedlot the gaps between the promise of unencumbered transnational information flows and the urge for cordoned zones of regulation.

Much of what takes place is rooted, then, in the anxiety of those in power as new media contribute to a severe uncertainty of status and existential questions about the stability of governance. And much is rooted, as well – often for a wholly different sector of society – in the lurking concern that the promised fruits of liberation, the much vaunted hopes for the new media, hopes for social advance, political democratic development and so much more, will come crashing to the ground.

A healthy realization of freedom of expression requires an enabling environment that is relatively free of the most disabling of these anxieties. For freedom of speech to flourish requires a specific kind of closure concerning media technologies: one that celebrates more speech and does not fear it. The understandable persistence of concerns about the dangers and failed promises of media corrode. They reinforce a belief that power and geopolitics – more

---

[8]   Yasser Latif Hamdani, "Comment: Stockholm Internet Forum Yasser Latif Hamdani," May 27, 2013.

than principle – determine the execution of speech-related policy, and that media interventions are strategic, instrumental and consequential, not altruistic. The prevalence of these anxieties renders analysis and policymaking increasingly convoluted. It leads to an overly defensive and sometimes aggressive approach – sometimes a spurious self-reporting of positive developments; at times a whistling in the wind that indices of freedom are increasing while dangers are manifest. And anxieties cause false assessments of particular contexts, even a caricatured representation of reality that may serve political or therapeutic goals. Anxieties can result in punitive or harsh measures as one way of coping when circumstances do not fit the desired mold where the porousness of boundaries is a perceived danger.

My effort, then, has been to locate and identify new challenges to the way free expression principles play out in a geopolitically complicated and technologically changed world. Even if the overriding fact is that freedom of expression is a matter of principle, that principle is generally encased in a set of formulae, rules, practices and rhetoric developed over centuries and locally differentiated (sometimes dramatically). The resulting canons are significant and vital and must be sustained through a clear and valued set of standards. But the great clashing narratives – reflecting fundamental differences in the way society should be organized and what purposes drive it – will increasingly produce different models for what constitutes free expression. Conceptions of freedom of expression will multiply, but those who live in speech-favored societies will know that some realizations of free expression are far superior to others.

Globalization has its discontents. Globalization – which has the amazing capacity to enact an exuberant, irresistible flow of music, images, words and ideas transnationally – also, in the fear and concern that it generates, instigates resistance by states and others who wish to maintain control. Besides, globalization is a convenient word that masks a significant phenomenon: "freedom" becomes, in the context of the global, not just more speech, not just freer speech, but the juggling of forces, the creation of opportunities for some and harsh and brutal competition for others.

It is almost impossible to adequately map substantial shifts in the course of expression in the world. It would be a great achievement to say that freedom of expression is on the rise. There are noble attempts like the measures of Freedom House to take national and regional temperatures on the question. Maps have been fashioned that show vast swaths of the globe moving from not free to freer or in the opposite direction. Countless are the efforts to quantify what aspects of intervention by what entities result in the furtherance of more public goals concerning speech and expression. In the chapters of this book,

I have not dealt with the metrics of free expression.[9] What I have sought to do, instead, is to capture emerging patterns of global expression, largely attending to the rising force of and emphasis on strategic communication (particularly as I have defined the term). I have tried to demonstrate the increasing tension between the practices of strategic communication and the theories underlying free expression. Not surprisingly, this review has reflected areas of deep unease and worrisome justifications for abuse of basic human rights. All times, all eras, have their challenges to concepts of free speech. For future policy developments to be constructive, we need to understand the particular set of current challenges. There is an elegance and dignity to our traditional modes of constructing and advocating free expression practices. But if shifts take place that undermine those articulations, they must be foregrounded and acknowledged.

Societies have been confounded before by the promise of a cornucopia of speech only to be consumers of a narrow range or disappointed by the recurrence of restriction. I have tried to show how the institutional borders of the great adventure in free expression are fraying. I have described the anxiety that seems to mount that the grand opportunity for a much freer, more substantively fascinating life-world of expression is simultaneously being real-ized and vanishing. The point of expanding free expression is to achieve goals: individual self-realization, a more democratic society, the opportunity for an informed citizenry to engage in meaningful deliberation. In this current age of strategic communicators, achieving these simply stated goals appears to be even more difficult than hoped. The strategies pursued are many. But a suitable goal is increasing the occasions when the consequence is an enhanced citizenry capable of achieving meaningful participation in public affairs. It is for that reason that scholars scurry for evidence that there has been a Twitter Revolution or an effective "Internet incident" in China or elsewhere.

This is, then, a book about the conflict between traditional ways of thinking about freedom of expression and the consequences of a world of speech and persuasion organized through strategic communication. The technologies of speech and society are constantly being transformed, and the geopolitics of information flow alter daily. I suggested at the outset of this book that the circumstances for free expression, in this context, can be compared to manag-ing mathematical formulae: Disturb one factor and all other factors become subject to adjustment. Ideas of freedom of expression are part of a delicate ecology – mysterious to almost all of us – but one that depends on many

---

9   Elsewhere I have expressed my concerns about the feasibility and reliability of such measures. See Susan Abbott, Monroe E. Price and Libby Morgan, eds., *Measures of Press Freedom and Media Contributions to Development* (New York: Peter Lang Publishing, 2011).

factors, many assumptions, many conditions of literacy, stability, access and opportunity. Principles of freedom of expression rest on certain institutional foundations. And if corrosion and transformation in those foundations are not adequately understood and addressed, the bases or justifications for the principles will be undermined. Without attention to the specific institutions that undergird much of free speech, its jurisprudence weakens. I have canvassed certain of these institutions and assumptions: the state as the cauldron for deliberation and political choice; a corpus of laws fairly enacted, constitutionally rooted and properly enforced; common grounds for civility that may be necessary to facilitate or permit a free expression environment; rough equality of opportunity for access to information and the capacity to effectively express oneself. Each of these and more is an area for complex controversy, as those engaged in strategic communication, and societies at large, seek to shape, channel and manage the drama of expression, individual and group, self-generated and mobilized – a drama that sets the stories of our time.

Bibliography

Abbott, Susan, Monroe E. Price and Libby Morgan, eds. *Measures of Press Freedom and Media Contributions to Development*. New York: Peter Lang Publishing, 2011.

Abdul Hamed Shah, Dian and Mahd Azizuddin Mohd Sani. "Freedom of Religion in Malaysia: A Tangled Web of Legal, Political, and Social Issues." *North Carolina Journal of International Law & Commercial Regulation* 36, no. 3 (2011): 647–678.

Adelkhah, Nima. "Iran Integrates the Concept of the 'Soft War' Into its Strategic Planning." *Terrorism Monitor* 8, no. 23 (2010).

Akbarzadeh, Shahram, James Piscatori, Benjamin MacQueen and Amin Saikal. *American Democracy Promotion in the Changing Middle East*. London: Routledge, 2013.

Al-Marashi, Ibrahim. "The Dynamics of Iraq's Media: Ethno-Sectarian Violence, Political Islam, Public Advocacy, and Globalization." *Cardozo Arts & Entertainment Law Journal* 25, no. 1 (2007): 95–140.

Altai Consulting. *Afghan Media – Three Years After*. March 2005, http://www.altaicon sulting.com/docs/media/2005/II-2.Internews_Assessment.pdf

Altai Consulting. *Afghan Media in 2010: Synthesis Report*. October 13, 2010, http://www.altaiconsulting.com/docs/media/2010/Afghan%20Media%20in%202010.pdf

Anheir, Helmut. *Civil Society: Measurement, Evaluation, Policy*. London: Earthscan, 2004.

Antoniades, Andreas, Ben O'Loughlin, and Alister Miskimmon. "Great Power Politics and Strategic Narratives." *Center for Global Political Economy*, Working Paper No. 7, March 2010.

Archetti, Cristina. "Terrorism, Communication and the War of Ideas: Al-Qaida's Strategic Narrative as a Brand." Paper presented at the International Communication Association (ICA) annual convention, Singapore, June 22–26, 2010.

Armstrong, Robert. *Broadcasting Policy in Canada*. Toronto: University of Toronto Press, 2010.

Arsenault, Amelia and Manuel Castells. "Conquering the Minds, Conquering Iraq: The Social Production of Misinformation in the United States – A Case Study." *Information, Communication & Society* 9, no. 3 (2006): 284–307.

Ashiwa, Yoshiko and David Wank, eds. *Making Religion, Making the State: The Politics of Religion in Modern China*. Stanford, CA: Stanford University Press, 2009.

Atkins, William. *The Politics of Southeast Asia's New Media*. London: Routledge, 2002.

Baker, C. Edwin. *Human Liberty and Freedom of Speech*. Oxford: Oxford University Press, 1989.

"The Media That Citizens Need." *University of Pennsylvania Law Review* 147, no. 2 (1998): 317–408.

Media, Markets, and Democracy. Cambridge: Cambridge University Press, 2002.

Barnett, Roger W. *Asymmetrical Warfare: Today's Challenge to U.S. Military Power*. Washington, DC: Brassey's Inc., 2003.

Barney, Robert K., Kevin B. Wamsley, Scott G. Martyn, and Gordon H. MacDonald, eds. *Global and Cultural Critique: Problematizing the Olympic Games. Fourth International Symposium for Olympic Research*. London, Ontario: International Centre for Olympic Studies, The University of Western Ontario, 1998.

Basurto, Xavier and Elinor Ostrom. "Beyond the Tragedy of the Commons." *Economia delle fonti di energia e dell'ambiente* 52, no. 1 (2009): 35–60.

Benkler, Yochai. *The Wealth of Networks: How Social Production Transforms Markets and Freedom*. New Haven, CT: Yale University Press, 2007.

Bennett, W. Lance. "Social Movements beyond Borders: Understanding Two Eras of Transnational Activism." In *Transnational Protest and Global Activism: People, Passions, and Power*, edited by Donatella Della Porta and Sidney George Tarrow, 203–226. Lanham, MD: Rowman & Littlefield, 2005.

Blackford, Russell. *Freedom of Religion and the Secular State*. Malden, MA: Wiley-Blackwell, 2012.

Blanchard, Margaret A. *Exporting the First Amendment: The Press-Government Crusade of 1945–1952*. New York: Longman, 1986.

Bob, Clifford. *The Global Right Wing and the Clash of World Politics*. Cambridge: Cambridge University Press, 2012.

Braman, Sandra. *Change of State: Information, Policy, and Power*. Cambridge, MA: The MIT Press, 2009.

Briggs, Asa. *The BBC: The First Fifty Years*. Oxford: Oxford University Press, 1986.

Brownell, Susan. *What the Olympic Games Mean to Beijing*. Lanham, MD: Rowman & Littlefield, 2008.

Caffrey, Kevin, ed. *The Beijing Olympics: Promoting China: Soft and Hard Power in Global Politics*. London: Routledge, 2011.

Calnan, Scott. *The Effectiveness of Domestic Human Rights NGOs: A Comparative Study*. Leiden: Brill, 2008.

Carey, James W. "Space, Time, and Communications: A Tribute to Harold Innis." In *Communication as Culture: Essays on Media and Society (Revised Edition)*, 109–132. New York: Routledge, 2009.

Carothers, Thomas. *Critical Mission: Essays on Democracy Promotion*. Washington, DC: Carnegie Endowment for International Peace, 2004.

"The Backlash against Democracy Promotion." *Foreign Affairs* 85, no. 2 (2006): 55–68.

Clarke, Richard A. and Robert Knake. *Cyber War: The Next Threat to National Security and What to Do About It*. New York: HarperCollins, 2010.

Collins, Richard. *Culture, Communication, & National Identity: The Case of Canadian Television*. Toronto: University of Toronto Press, 1990.

Comor, Edward A. *Consumption and the Globalization Project: International Hegemony and the Annihilation of Time*. New York: Palgrave Macmillan, 2008.

Comor, Edward and Hamilton Bean. "America's Engagement Delusion: Critiquing a Public Diplomacy Consensus." *International Communication Gazette* 74, no. 3 (2012): 203–220.

Crawford, Susan. *Captive Audience: The Telecom Industry and Monopoly Power in the New Gilded Age*. New Haven, CT: Yale University Press, 2013.

CRTC Broadcasting Public Notice. 'Requests to add al Jazeera to the lists of eligible satellite services for distribution on a digital basis,' CRTC 2004–51, July 15, 2004.

Cull, Nicholas, David Culbert and David Welch. *Propaganda and Mass Persuasion: A Historical Encyclopedia from 1500 to the Present*. Santa Barbara, CA: ABC-CLIO, 2003.

Decline and Fall of the United States Information Agency. New York: Palgrave MacMillan, 2012.

Danan, Liora. "*Mixed Blessings: U.S. Government Engagement with Religion in Conflict-prone Settings*." *CSIS Report*, August 2007.

D'Arcy, Jean. "Direct Broadcast Satellites and the Right to Communicate." *EBU Review* 118 (1969): 14–18.

Davis, Robert N. "Ambushing the Olympic Games." *Villanova Sports and Entertainment Law Journal* 3, no. 2 (1996): 423–442.

Dawson, Lorne L. and Douglas E. Cowan. *Religion Online: Finding Faith On the Internet*. London: Routledge, 2013.

Deibert, Ronald J. and Rafal Rohozinski. "Control and Subversion in Russian Cyberspace." In *Access Controlled: The Shaping of Power, Rights, and Rule in Cyberspace*, edited by Ronald J. Deibert, John Palfrey, Rafal Rohozinski and Jonathan Zittrain, 15–34. Cambridge, MA: The MIT Press, 2010.

Della Porta, Donatella and Sidney Tarrow, eds. *Transnational Protest and Global Activism*. Lanham, MD: Rowman and Littlefield Publishers, 2004.

DeNardis, Laura. "Hidden Levers of Internet Control: An Infrastructure-Based Theory of Internet Governance." *Information, Communication & Society* 15, no. 5 (2012): 720–738.

The Global War for Internet Governance. New Haven, CT: Yale University Press, 2014.

De Sola Pool, Ithiel. *Technologies of Freedom*. Cambridge, MA: Belknap Press, 1983.

In Technologies without Boundaries, Edited by Eli M. Noam. Cambridge, MA: Harvard University Press, 1990.

Deutsch, Karl W. *The Nerves of Government: Models of Political Communication and Control*. London: Free Press of Glencoe, 1963.

De Vries, Stephan. "United States Policy on 'Democratizing' Iran: Effects and Consequences." *Democracy and Society* 8, no. 1 (2011): 7–10.

Dewing, Michael. "Canadian Broadcasting Policy." Background Paper 2011–39-E. Ottawa: Library of Parliament, 2012.

Downie, Leonard Jr. and Michael Schudson. "Reconstruction of American Journalism." *Columbia Journalism Review*, October 19, 2009, http://www.cjr.org/reconstruction/the_reconstruction_of_american.php?page=all

Drezner, Daniel W. "Does Obama Have a Grand Strategy? Why We Need Doctrines in Uncertain Times." *Foreign Affairs*, July/August 2011.

Ebrahim, Alnoor. *NGOs and Organizational Change: Discourse, Reporting, and Learning*. Cambridge: Cambridge University Press, 2003.

Eccarious-Kelly, Vera. "Political Movements and Leverage Points: Kurdish Activism in the European Diaspora," *Journal of Muslim Minority Affairs* 22, no. 1 (2002): 91–118.

Ehteshami, Anoushiravan and Steven Wright. *Reform in the Middle East Oil Monarchies*. Sussex: Sussex Academic Press, 2011.

Eko, Lyombe S. *New Media, Old Regimes: Case Studies in Comparative Communication Law and Policy*. Lanham: Rowman & Littlefield, 2012.

Elliott, Mark. "Evangelism and Proselytism in Russia: Synonyms or Antonyms?" *International Bulletin of Missionary Research* 25 (2001): 72–76.

Elphick, Richard H. and T. R. H. Davenport, eds. *Christianity in South Africa: A Political, Social, and Cultural History*. Berkeley: University of California Press, 1997.

EUROPA 2005. "EU Rules and Principles on Hate Broadcasts: Frequently Asked Questions," http://europa.eu/rapid/pressReleasesAction.do?reference=MEMO/05/98&format=HTML&aged=0&language=EN&guiLanguage=en

Faris, Robert and Nart Villeneuve. "Measuring Global Internet Filtering." In *Access Denied: The Practice and Policy of Global Internet Filtering*, edited by Ronald Deibert, John Palfrey, Rafal Rohozinski and Jonathan Zittrain, 5–28. Cambridge, MA: The MIT Press, 2008.

Feenberg, Andrew. *Critical Theory of Technology*. Oxford: Oxford University Press, 1991.

Fejes, Fred. *Imperialism, Media and The Good Neighbor: New Deal Foreign Policy and United States Shortwave Broadcasting to Latin America*. Ablex Publishing: Westport, CT, 1986.

Fetzer, Joel S. and J. Christopher Soper. *Muslims and the State in Britain, France, and Germany*. Cambridge: Cambridge University Press, 2005.

Finke, Roger and Laurence R. Iannacconne. "Supply-Side Explanations for Religious Change." *Annals of the American Academy of Political and Social Sciences* 527 (1993): 27–39.

Fisher, Desmond. *The Right to Communicate: A Status Report*. Paris: UNESCO, 1982.

Fiss, Owen M. "Why the State." *Harvard Law Review* 100 (1987): 781–794.
    Liberalism Divided: Freedom of Speech and the Many Uses of State Power. Boulder, CO: Westview Press, 1996.

Foley, Frank. *Countering Terrorism in Britain and France: Institutions, Norms and the Shadow of the Past*. Cambridge: Cambridge University Press, 2013.

Fox, Jonathan. *An Introduction to Religion and Politics: Theory and Practice*. London: Routledge, 2013.

Foxley, Tim. "The Taliban's Propaganda Activities: How Well is the Afghan Insurgency Communicating and What Is It Saying?" *SIPRI Project Paper*, 2007.
    "Countering Taliban Information Operations in Afghanistan." *Prism* 1, no. 4 (2010): 79–94.

Freedom House. "Freedom on the Net." http://www.freedomhouse.org.

Frederick, Howard H. *Cuban-American Radio Wars: Ideology in International Telecommunications*. Westport, CT: Ablex Publishing, 1986.

Freston, Paul. *Evangelicals and Politics in Africa, Asia and Latin America*. Cambridge: Cambridge University Press, 2004.

Freston, Paul, ed. *Evangelical Christianity and Democracy in Latin America*. Oxford: Oxford University Press, 2008.

Gagliardone, Iginio, Maria Repnikova and Nicole Stremlau. "China in Africa: A New Approach To Media Development?" *Oxford: Centre for Socio-Legal Studies*, 2010.

George, Cherian. *Freedom from the Press: Journalism and State Power in Singapore*. Singapore: NUS Press, 2012.

Giddens, Anthony. *Social Theory and Modern Sociology*. Cambridge: Polity Press, 1987.

Gofas, Andreas and Colin Hay, eds. *The Role of Ideas in Political Analysis: A Portrait of Contemporary Debates*. London and New York: Routledge, 2009.

Grayson, James H. *Early Buddhism and Christianity in Korea: A Study in the Emplantation of Religion*. Leiden: Brill, 1985.

Grim, Brian J. and Roger Finke. *The Price of Freedom Denied: Religious Persecution and Conflict in the Twenty-First Century*. Cambridge: Cambridge University Press, 2011.

Haas, Peter. "Introduction: Epistemic Communities and International Policy Coordination." *International Organization* 46, no. 1 (1992): 1–35.

Habermas, Jürgen. *The Structural Transformation of the Public Sphere*. Cambridge, MA: The MIT Press, 1991.

Hadden, Jeffrey K. "Regulating Religious Broadcasting: Some Old Patterns and New Trends." In *The Role of Government in Monitoring and Regulating Religion in Public Life*, edited by James E. Wood Jr. and Derek Davis, 179–204. Waco, TX: J.M. Dawson Institute of Church-State Studies, 1993.

Hadden, Jeffrey K. and Anson Shupe. *Televangelism: Power and Politics on God's Frontier*. New York: Henry Holt, 1988.

Hallin, Daniel C. and Paolo Mancini. *Comparing Media Systems: Three Models of Media and Politics*. Cambridge: Cambridge University Press, 2004.

Hamdi, Mohamed Elhachmi. *The Politicisation of Islam: A Case Study of Tunisia*. Boulder, CO: Westview Press, 1998.

Hangen, Tona J. *Redeeming the Dial: Radio, Religion, and Popular Culture in America*. Chapel Hill: University of North Carolina Press, 2002.

Hassanpour, A. "Med-TV, Britain, and the Turkish State: A Stateless Nation's Quest for Sovereignty in the Sky." Unpublished paper presented at the Freie Universitat Berlin, November 7, 1995.

Haworth, Alan. *Free Speech*. London: Routledge, 1998.

Hayden, Craig. *The Rhetoric of Soft Power: Public Diplomacy in Global Contexts*. Lanham: Lexington Books, 2012.

Hefner, Robert W. and Muhammad Qasim Zaman, eds. *Schooling Islam: The Culture and Politics of Modern Muslim Education*. Princeton, NJ: Princeton University Press, 2010.

Helmus, Todd, Christopher Paul and Russell W. Glenn. *Enlisting Madison Avenue: The Marketing Approach to Earning Popular Support in Theaters of Operation*. Santa Monica, CA: RAND, 2007.

Hertzke, Allen. *Freeing God's Children: The Unlikely Alliance for Global Human Rights*. Oxford: Rowman and Littlefield, 2006.

Herz, Michael and Peter Molnar, eds. *The Content and Context of Hate Speech: Rethinking Regulation and Responses*. Cambridge: Cambridge University Press, 2012.

Hesmondhalgh, David. *The Cultural Industries*. London: SAGE, 2007.

Hirschman, Albert O. *Exit, Voice, and Loyalty: Responses to Decline in Firms, Organizations, and States.* Cambridge, MA: Harvard University Press, 1970.

Hoberman, John. *Darwin's Athletes: How Sport Has Damaged Black America and Preserved the Myth of Race.* Boston: Houghton Mifflin Co., 1997.

Hoover, Stuart and Douglas K. Wagner. "History and Policy in American Broadcast Treatment of Religion." *Media, Culture and Society* 19, no.1 (1997): 7–27.

Hoover, Stewart M. *Religion in the Media Age.* London: Routledge, 2013.

Horton, Scott and Alla Kazakina. "The Legal Regulation of NGOs: Central Asia at a Crossroads." In *Civil Society in Central Asia*, edited by M. Holt Ruffin and Daniel Waugh, 34–56. Seattle: University of Washington Press, 1999.

Hoskins, Andrew, Akil Awan and Ben O'Loughlin. *Radicalisation and Media: Connectivity and Terrorism in the New Media Ecology.* London: Taylor and Francis, 2011.

Howard, Philip N. *New Media Campaigns and the Managed Citizen.* Cambridge: Cambridge University Press, 2005.

Howard, Philip N. and Muzammil M. Hussain. *Democracy's Fourth Wave? Digital Media and the Arab Spring.* Oxford: Oxford University Press, 2013.

Humphreys, Peter J. *Mass Media and Media Policy in Western Europe.* Manchester: University of Manchester Press, 1996.

Huntington, Samuel L. "The Clash of Civilizations?'" *Foreign Affairs* 72, no. 3 (1993): 22–49.

Innis, Harold. *Empire and Communications.* Toronto: University of Toronto Press, 1950. *The Bias of Communication.* Toronto: University of Toronto Press, 1951.

International Religious Freedom Act of 1998. Public Law 105–292, October 27, 1998.

Jorisch, Avi. *Beacon of Hatred: Inside Hizballah's Al-Manar Television.* Washington, DC: Washington Institute for Near East Policy, 2004.

Juergensmeyer, Mark. *Global Rebellion: Religious Challenges to the Secular State, from Christian Militias to al Qaeda.* Berkeley: University of California Press, 2008.

Kalathil, Shanthi and Taylor Boas. "Internet and State Control in Authoritarian Regimes: China, Cuba, and the Counterrevolution." *Carnegie Endowment Paper* no. 21, July 2001.

Karst, Kenneth. "Boundaries and Reasons: Freedom of Expression and the Subordination of Groups." *University of Illinois Law Review* (1990): 95–149.

Katz, Daniel and Floyd H. Allport, *Student Attitudes.* Syracuse, NY: Craftsman, 1931.

Katz, Elihu. "Publicity and Pluralistic Ignorance: Notes on 'The Spiral of Silence.'" In *Public Opinion and Social Change*, edited by H. Baier, H. M. Kepplinger and D. A. Reumann, 28–38. Weisbade: Westdeutscher Verlag, 1981.

Keck, Margaret E. and Kathryn Sikkink. *Activists Beyond Borders: Advocacy Networks in International Politics.* Ithaca, NY: Cornell University Press, 2004.

Kelly, John and Bruce Etling. "Mapping Iran's Online Public: Politics and Culture in the Persian Blogosphere." *Berkman Center for Internet & Society*, April 5, 2008.

Khan, M. A. Muqtedar. *Debating Moderate Islam: The Geopolitics of Islam and the West.* Salt Lake City: University of Utah Press, 2007.

Knippenberg, Hans, ed. *The Changing Landscape of Europe.* Amsterdam: Het Spinhuis, 2005.

Knox, Zoe. *Russian Society and the Orthodox Church: Religion in Russia after Communism.* London: Routledge, 2013.

Kogen, Lauren and Monroe E. Price. "Deflecting the CNN Effect: Public Opinion Polling and Livingstonian Outcomes." *Media, War & Conflict* 4, no. 2 (2011): 109–123.

Korthals Altes, Willem F. "European Law: A Case Study of Changes in National Broadcasting." *Cardozo Arts & Entertainment Law Journal* 11, no. 2 (1993): 313–335.

Kraidy, Marwan. "Arab Satellite Television, Between Regionalization and Globalization." *Global Media Journal* 1, no.1 (2002).

Hybridity, or the Cultural Logic of Globalization. Philadelphia: Temple University Press, 2005.

Lamb, Franklin. "Australia Rejects Israeli Ordered Media Censorship on Al-Manar." *Foreign Policy Journal*, December 20, 2010.

Large, David Clay. *Nazi Games: The Olympics of 1936*. New York: W.W. Norton, 2007.

Lemley, Mark A., David S. Levine and David G. Post. "Don't Break the Internet." *Stanford Law Review Online* 64 (2011): 34–38.

Libicki, Martin C. *Cyberdeterrence and Cyberwar*. Santa Monica, CA: RAND, 2009.

Livingston, Steven. *Clarifying the CNN Effect: An Examination of Media Effects According to Type of Military Intervention*. Research Paper R-18. Cambridge: Joan Shorenstein Center on the Press, Politics and Public Policy, John F. Kennedy School of Government, Harvard University, 1997.

Lohliker, Rudiger. *New Approaches to the Analysis of Jihadism: Online and Offline*. Goettingen: V&R Unipress, 2012.

Lugo-Ocando, Jairo, ed. *The Media in Latin America*. Berkshire: Open University Press, 2008.

Lyn, Carolyn A. and David J. Atkin. *Communication Technology and Social Change: Theory and Implications*. Mahwah, NJ: Lawrence Erlbaum Associates, 2007.

Lynch, Marc. *Voices of the New Arab Public: Iraq, Al-Jazeera, and Middle East Politics Today*. New York: Columbia University Press, 2006.

MacKinnon, Rebecca. *The Consent of the Networked: The Worldwide Struggle for Internet Freedom*. New York: Basic Books, 2012.

Madsden, Richard. *China's Catholics: Tragedy and Hope in an Emerging Civil Society*. Berkeley: University of California Press, 1998.

Maoz, Ifat and Menahem Blondheim, eds. Special Issue: Media Coverage in Asymmetric Conflict. *Dynamics of Asymmetric Conflict* 3, no. 2 (2010).

Marashi, Reza. "The Islamic Republic's Emerging Cyber War." *National Iranian American Center*, Iran Working Paper Series 3, 2011.

Marvin, Carolyn. *When Old Technologies Were New*. New York: Oxford University Press, 1988.

Mastrocola, Paul. "The Lords of the Rings: The Role of Olympic Site Selection as a Weapon Against Human Rights Abuses: China's Bid For the 2000 Olympics." *Boston College Third World Law Journal* 15, no. 1 (1995): 141–170.

Mattelart, Armand. *Multinational Corporations and the Control of Culture: The Ideological Apparatuses of Imperialism*. Brighton: Harvester Press, 1979.

Mayer-Schonberger, Viktor and Kenneth Cukier. *Big Data: A Revolution That Will Transform How We Live, Work, and Think*. Boston: Houghton Mifflin Harcourt, 2013.

McCarthy, Daniel R. "Open Networks and the Open Door: American Foreign Policy and the Narration of the Internet." *Foreign Policy Analysis* 7, no. 1 (2011): 89–111.

McCauley, Clark and Sophia Moskalenko. "Recent U.S. Thinking About Terrorism and Counterterrorism: Babysteps Towards a Dynamic View of Asymmetric Conflict." *Terrorism and Violence* 22 (2010): 641–657.
   Friction: How Radicalization Happens to Them and Us. Oxford: Oxford University Press, 2011.
McDonnell, Jim. "From Certainty to Diversity. The Evolution of British Religious Broadcasting since 1990." In *Faith and Media: Analysis of Faith and Media: Representation and Communication*, edited by Hans Geybels, Sara Mels and Michel Walrave, 151–174. Brussels: Peter Lang, 2009.
McIver, William J. Jr., William F. Birdsall and Merrilee Rasmussen. "The Internet and the Right to Communicate." *First Monday* 8, no. 12 (2003).
McNair, Brian. *Glasnost, Perestroika and the Soviet Media*. New York: Routledge, 1991.
McQuail, Denis and Siune, Karen, eds. *New Media Politics: Comparative Perspectives in Western Europe*. London: Sage Publications, 1986.
Mejier, Roel and Edwin Bakker, eds., .*The Muslim Brotherhood in Europe*. Oxford: Oxford University Press, 2013.
Menza, Mohamed Fahmy. *Patronage Politics in Egypt: The National Democratic Party and Muslim Brotherhood in Cairo*. London: Routledge, 2012.
Meyer, Anneke. "Moral Panics, Globalization and Islamophobia: The Case of Abu Hamza in *The Sun*." In *Global Islamophobia: Muslims and Moral Panic in the West*, edited by George Morgan and Scott Poynting, 181–196. Farnham, Surrey: Ashgate, 2012.
Meyer, Birgit and Annelies Moors, eds. *Religion, Media, and the Public Sphere*. Bloomington: Indiana University Press, 2005.
Miles, Franklin B. *Asymmetric Warfare: An Historical Perspective*. Carlisle, PA: U.S. Army War College, 1999.
Miller, Spencer Jr. "Radio and Religion." *Annals of the American Academy of Political and Social Science* 177 (1935): 135–140.
Milton, John. "Areopagitica: A speech of Mr. John Milton for the Liberty of Unlicenc'd Printing, to the Parlament of England (1644)." In *Milton's Selected Poetry and Prose*, edited by Jason P. Rosenblatt. New York: W. W. Norton & Company, 2011.
Montgomery, Kathryn C. *Target, Prime Time: Advocacy Groups and the Struggle over Entertainment Television*. New York: Oxford University Press, 1989.
Morgan, William J. "Cosmopolitanism, Olympism, and Nationalism: A Critical Interpretation of Coubertin's Ideal of International Sporting Life." *OLYMPIKA: The International Journal of Olympic Studies* IV (1995): 79–92.
Morozov, Evgeny. *The Net Delusion: The Dark Side of Internet Freedom*. New York: PublicAffairs, 2011.
Nafziger, James A. R. "International Sports Law: A Replay of Characteristics and Trends." *American Journal of International Law* 86, no. 3 (1992): 489–518.
Nelson, Michael. *War of the Black Heavens: The Battles of Western Broadcasting in the Cold War*. Syracuse, NY: Syracuse University Press, 1997.
Nordenstreng, Kaarle and Herbert I. Schiller, eds. *National Sovereignty and International Communication*. Norwood, NJ: Ablex, 1979.
Nye, Joseph S. Jr. "Public Diplomacy and Soft Power." *The Annals of the American Academy of Political and Social Science* 616, no. 1 (2008): 94–109.
Oded, Arye. *Islam and Politics in Kenya*. Boulder, CO: Lynne Reinner Publishers, 2000.
O'Malley, Tom and Janet Jones, eds. *The Peacock Committee and UK Broadcasting Policy*. Basingstoke: Palgrave Macmillan, 2009.

Ottaway, Marina and Thomas Carothers, eds. *Funding Virtue: Civil Society Aid and Democracy Promotion*. Washington, DC: Brookings Institution Press, 2000.

Ownby, David. *Falun Gong and the Future of China*. New York: Oxford University Press, 2008.

Parks, Lisa and James Schwoch. *Down to Earth: Satellite Technologies, Industries, and Cultures*. New Brunswick, NJ: Rutgers University Press, 2012.

Payne, Michael. *Olympic Turnaround: How the Olympic Games Stepped Back from the Brink of Extinction to Become the World's Best Known Brand*. Westport, CT: Praeger Publishers, 2006.

Pelton, Joseph N., Robert J. Oslund and Peter Marshall, eds. *Communications Satellites: Global Change Agents*. Mahwah, NJ: Lawrence Erlbaum Associates, 2004.

Pickard, Victor. *Media Democracy Deferred: The Postwar Settlement for U.S. Communications, 1945–1949*. Dissertation. Urbana: University of Illinois at Urbana-Champaign, 2008.

Post, Robert C. "Equality and Autonomy in First Amendment Jurisprudence." *Michigan Law Review* 95 (1997): 1517–1559.

Powell, Jon T. *International Broadcasting by Satellite – Issues of Regulation, Barriers to Communications*. Westport, CT: Quorum Books, 1985.

Price, Monroe E. "Free Expression and Digital Dreams: The Open and Closed Terrain of Speech." *Critical Inquiry* 22 (1995): 64–89.

Television, the Public Sphere, and National Identity. Oxford: Clarendon Press, 1995.

"What Price Fairness?" *Media Studies Journal* 12, no. 2 (1998): 82.

Media and Sovereignty: The Global Information Revolution and Its Challenge to State Power. Cambridge, MA: The MIT Press, 2002.

"Satellite Broadcasting as Trade Routes in the Sky." In *In Search of Boundaries: Communication, Nation States and Cultural Identities*, edited by Joseph M. Chan and Bryce T. McIntyre, 146–166. Westport, CT: Ablex Publishing, 2002.

Price, Monroe E., Bethany Davis Noll and Daniel De Luce. *Mapping Media Assistance*. World Bank-USAID Paris meeting, Programme in Comparative Media Law and Policy, 2002.

Price, Monroe E. and Daniel Dayan, eds. *Owning the Olympics, Narratives of the New China*. Ann Arbor: University of Michigan Press, 2008.

Price, Monroe E., Douglas Griffin and Ibrahim Al-Marashi. *Toward an Understanding of Media Policy and Media Systems in Iraq: A Foreword and Two Reports*. CGCS Occasional Paper Series, Number 1 (May 2007). Philadelphia: Center for Global Communication Studies, Annenberg School for Communication, University of Pennsylvania.

Price, Monroe E. and Peter Krug. "The Enabling Environment for Free and Independent Media." In *Media Matters: Perspectives on Advancing Governance and Development from the Global Forum for Media Development*, edited by Mark Harvey, 95–102. Paris: Internews Europe, 2006.

Price, Monroe E., Beata Rozumilowicz and Stefaan G. Verhulst, eds. *Media Reform: Democratizing the Media, Democratizing the State*. London: Routledge, 2002.

Price, Monroe E. and Stefaan G. Verhulst, eds. *Broadcasting Reform in India: Media Law from a Global Perspective*. New York: Oxford University Press, 1998.

Price, Monroe E., Stefaan G. Verhulst and Libby Morgan, eds. *Routledge Handbook of Media Law*. Abingdon: Routledge, 2013.

Putnam, Robert D. "Diplomacy and Domestic Politics: The Logic of Two-Level Games." *International Organization* 42, no. 3 (1988): 427–460.

Putzel, James and Joost van der Zwan. *Why Templates for Media Development Do Not Work in Crisis States: Defining and Understanding Media Development Strategies in Post-War and Crisis States.* London: LSE Research Online, 2006.

Queeny, Kathryn M. *Direct Broadcast Satellites and the United Nations.* Alphen aan den Rijn: Sijthoff & Noordhoff, 1978.

Rabasa, Angel, Cheryl Benard, Lowell H. Schwartz and Peter Sickle. *Building Moderate Muslim Networks.* Santa Monica, CA: RAND, 2007.

Raboy, Marc. *Missed Opportunities: The Story of Canada's Broadcasting Policy.* Montreal: McGill Queens University Press, 1990.

Rahimi, Babak. *Censorship and the Islamic Republic: Two Modes of Regulatory Strategies for Media in Post-Revolutionary Iran.* Philadelphia, PA: Iran Media Program.

Rid, Thomas and Thomas Keaney. *Understanding Counterinsurgency: Doctrine, Operations, and Challenges.* Abingdon: Routledge, 2010.

Röling, Niels and Marleen Maarleveld. "Facing Strategic Narratives: An Argument for Interactive Effectiveness." *Agriculture and Human Values* 16, no. 3 (1999): 295–308.

Roselle, Laura. "Strategic Narratives of War: Fear of Entrapment and Abandonment During Protracted Conflict." Paper Presented at APSA 2010 Annual Meeting.

Sabet, Farzan and Roozbeh Safshekan. "Soft War: A New Episode in the Old Conflict Between Iran and the United States." Philadelphia, PA: Iran Media Program, 2011.

Saeed, Abdullah and Hassan Saeed. *Freedom of Religion, Apostasy and Islam.* Aldershot: Ashgate Publishing, 2004.

Sakr, Naomi. "Frontiers of Freedom: Diverse Responses to Satellite Television in the Middle East and North Africa." *Public/Javnost: Journal of the European Institute for Communication and Culture* 6, no.1 (1999): 93–106.

Sandvig, Christian. "The Internet as Infrastructure." In *The Oxford Handbook of Internet Studies*, edited by William H. Dutton, 86–108. Oxford: Oxford University Press, 2013.

Sarat, Austin, ed. *Sovereignty, Emergency, Legality.* New York: Cambridge University Press, 2010.

Sassen, Saskia. *Territory, Authority, Rights: From Medieval to Global Assemblages.* Princeton, NJ: Princeton University Press, 2008.

Schauer, Frederick. "Who Decides?" In *Democracy and the Mass Media: A Collection of Essays*, edited by Judith Lichtenberg. Cambridge: Cambridge University Press, 1990.

Schiller, Herbert. *Communication and Cultural Domination.* New York: International Arts and Sciences Press, 1976.

    Culture Inc: The Corporate Takeover of Public Expression. Oxford: Oxford University Press, 1989.

Schmidt, Vivien A. "Discursive Institutionalism: the Explanatory Power of Ideas and Discourse." *Annual Review of Political Science* 11 (2008): 303–326.

Schmitz, Jason K. "Ambush Marketing: The Off-Field Competition at the Olympic Games." *Northwestern Journal of Technology and Intellectual Property* 3, no. 2 (2005): 203–208.

Shaw, Jonathan Eberhardt. "The Role of Religion in National Security Policy Since September 11, 2001." *Carlisle Paper*, February 2011.

Sidorenko, Alexey. "Russian Digital Dualism: Changing Society, Manipulative State." *Russie.Nei.Visions* 63 (2011).

Simon, Karla W. "Dissolution Dos and Don'ts." *The International Journal of Not-for-Profit Law* 2, no. 2 (1999).

"Recent Developments in Chinese Law Affecting CSOs/NGOs." *International Center for Civil Society Law*, June 2010.

Simpson, Brian. "New Labor, New Censorship? Politics, Religion and Internet Filtering in Australia." *Information and Communications Technology Law* 17, no. 3 (2008): 167–183.

Smith, Rodney K. "Regulating Religious Broadcasting: Some Comparative Reflections." *Brigham Young University Law Review* 4 (1996): 905–943.

Snow, David A. and Richard Malachek. "The Sociology of Conversion." *Annual Review of Sociology* 10 (1984): 167–190.

Soley, Lawrence C. and John Nichols. *Clandestine Radio Broadcasting: A Study of Revolutionary and Counterrevolutionary Electronic Communication*. New York: Prager, 1987.

Spiecker, Ben and Jan Steutel. "Multiculturalism, Pillarization and Liberal Civic Education in the Netherlands." *International Journal of Educational Research* 35 (2001): 293–304.

Sreberny, Annabelle. "Too Soft on 'Soft War,'" *International Journal of Communication* 7 (2013), Feature 801–804, https://www.mysciencework.com/publication/show/1623 473/talking-soft-about-soft-war

Sreberny-Mohammadi, Annabelle and Ali Mohammadi. *Small Media, Big Revolution: Communication, Culture, and the Iranian Revolution*. Minneapolis: University of Minnesota Press, 1994.

Stahnke, Tad. "Proselytism and the Freedom to Change Religion in International Human Rights Law." *Brigham Young University Law Review* 1 (1999): 251–350.

Stone, Geoffrey R. *Perilous Times: Free Speech in Wartime from the Sedition Act of 1798 to the War on Terrorism*. New York: W.W. Norton, 2004.

Straubhaar, Joseph D. *World Television: From Global to Local*. Los Angeles: SAGE, 2007.

Stremlau, Nicole. "Hostages of Peace: The Politics of Radio Liberalization in Somaliland." *Journal of Eastern African Studies* 7, no. 2 (2013): 239–257.

"Towards a Diagnostic Approach to Media in Fragile States: Examples from the Somali Territories." *Media, War and Conflict* 6, no. 3 (2013): 279–293.

Svete, Uroš. "Asymmetrical Warfare and Modern Digital Media: An Old Concept Changed by New Technology?" In *The Moral Dimension of Asymmetrical Warfare: Counter-terrorism, Democratic Values and Military Ethics*, edited by Th. A. van Baarda and D. E. M. Verweij, 381–398. Leiden: Martinus Nijhoff, 2009.

Taishoff, Marika N. *State Responsibility and the Direct Broadcast Satellite*. London: Pinter, 1987.

Tartoussieh, Karim. "Virtual Citizenship: Islam, Culture, and Politics in the Digital Age, *International Journal of Cultural Policy* 17, no. 2 (2011): 198–208.

Taylor, Paul M. *Freedom of Religion: UN and European Human Rights Law and Practice*. Cambridge: Cambridge University Press, 2005.

Thierer, Adam D. and Clyde Wayne Crews, eds. *Who Rules the Net?: Internet Governance and Jurisdiction*. Washington, DC: Cato Institute, 2003.

Turow, Joseph. *Breaking Up America: Advertisers and the New Media World*. Chicago: University of Chicago Press, 1997.
   The Daily You: How the New Advertising Industry is Defining Your Identity and Your Worth. New Haven, CT: Yale University Press, 2012.
U. S. Department of State. "21st Century Statecraft." n.d., http://www.state.gov/state craft/overview/index.htm
   "Human Rights Reports." n.d., http://www.state.gov/j/drl/rls/hrrpt/
   "*2010 Report on International Religious Freedom: Saudi Arabia*." September 13, 2011, http://www.state.gov/j/drl/rls/irf/2010_5/index.htm
Vaidhyanathan, Siva. *The Googlization of Everything: (And Why We Should Worry)*. Berkeley: University of California Press, 2011.
Van Baarda, Th. A. and D. E. M. Verweij, eds. *The Moral Dimension of Asymmetrical Warfare*. Leiden: Martinus Nijhoff, 2009.
Van der Ven, Johannes A. and Hans Georg Ziebertz, eds. *Tensions Within and Between Religions and Human Rights*. Leiden: Brill, 2012.
Waldron, Jeremy. *The Harm in Hate Speech*. Cambridge, MA: Harvard University Press, 2012.
Wanner, Catherine. "Missionaries of Faith and Culture: Evangelical Encounters in Ukraine." *Slavic Review* 63, no. 4 (2004): 732–755.
Weber, Max. "Politics as a Vocation." Munich: Duncker & Humboldt, 1919.
   Economy and Society. Berkeley: University of California Press, 1922.
Weiss, Jonathan. "Privilege, Posture and Protection: 'Religion' in the Law." *Yale Law Journal* 73, no. 4 (1964): 593–623.
Welch, Claude E. *NGOs and Human Rights: Promise and Performance*. Philadelphia: University of Pennsylvania, 2001.
White, Stephen. "Carnegie II: A Look Back and Ahead." *Public Telecommunications Review* 5, no. 2 (July/August 1977).
Wiktorowicz, Quintan. *The Management of Islamic Activism: Salafis, the Muslim Brotherhood, and State Power in Jordan*. Albany: State University of New York Press, 2001.
Williams, Bernard. *Truth and Truthfulness: An Essay in Genealogy*. Princeton, NJ: Princeton University Press, 2010.
Wimmer, Hannes. "The State's Monopoly on Legitimate Violence. Violence in History and in Contemporary World Society as Challenges to the State." Paper presented at Transformations of Statehood from a European Perspective, Austrian Academy of Sciences Vienna (January 23–25, 2003), http://homepage.univie.ac.at/johann.wimmer/Wimmer-AkadWiss.pdf
Witte, John Jr. and Michael Bourdeaux. *Proselytism and Orthodoxy in Russia*. New York: Orbis Books, 1999.
Witte, John Jr. and Richard C. Martin, eds. *Sharing the Book: Religious Perspectives on the Rights and Wrongs of Proselytism*. New York: Orbis Books, 1999.
Yan, Mei Ning. "China and the Prior Consent Requirement: A Decade of Invasion and Counter-Invasion by Transfrontier Satellite Television." *Hastings Communication & Entertainment Law Journal* 25 (2003): 265–305.
Yang, Guobin. "Activists Beyond Virtual Boarders: Internet-Mediated Networks and Informational Politics in China." *First Monday* 7 (2006).

Yemelianova, Galina. "Islam and Power." In *Islam in Post-Soviet Russia*, edited by Hilary Pilkington and Galina Yemelianova, 61–116. London: RoutledgeCurzon, 2003.

Yu, Peter. "The Graduated Response." *Florida Law Review* 62, no. 5 (2010): 1373.

Zittrain, Jonathan. *The Future of the Internet and How to Stop It*. New Haven, CT: Yale University Press, 2008.

Index